The publisher gratefully acknowledges the generous contribution to this book provided by the Jewish Studies Endowment Fund of the University of California Press Foundation, which is supported by a major gift from the S. Mark Taper Foundation.

The Crime of My Very Existence

The Crime of
My Very Existence

NAZISM AND THE MYTH OF JEWISH CRIMINALITY

Michael Berkowitz

UNIVERSITY OF CALIFORNIA PRESS

BERKELEY   LOS ANGELES   LONDON

University of California Press, one of the most distinguished university presses in the United States, enriches lives around the world by advancing scholarship in the humanities, social sciences, and natural sciences. Its activities are supported by the UC Press Foundation and by philanthropic contributions from individuals and institutions. For more information, visit www.ucpress.edu.

Sections of an earlier version of chapter 1 appeared in Michael Berkowitz, "Unmasking Counterhistory: An Introductory Exploration of Criminality and the Jewish Question," in *Criminals and Their Scientists: The History of Criminology in International Perspective* (Washington, DC: German Historical Institute; New York: Cambridge University Press, 2006), 61–84. Photos from the collections of the United States Holocaust Memorial Museum (USHMM) are reproduced by permission. The views or opinions expressed in this book, and the context in which the images are used, do not necessarily reflect the views or policy of, nor imply approval or endorsement by, the United States Holocaust Memorial Museum.

University of California Press
Berkeley and Los Angeles, California

University of California Press, Ltd.
London, England

Library of Congress Cataloging-in-Publication Data

Berkowitz, Michael.
    The crime of my very existence : Nazism and the myth of Jewish criminality / Michael Berkowitz.
        p.   cm.
    Includes bibliographical references and index.
    ISBN: 978-0-520-25112-0 (cloth : alk. paper)
    ISBN: 978-0-520-25114-4 (pbk. : alk. paper)
    1. Antisemitism—Germany—History—20th century.   2. National socialism.   3. Propaganda, German—History—20th century.
4. Holocaust, Jewish (1939–1945)—Causes.   5. Jews—Germany— Public opinion.   6. Public opinion—Germany.   7. Germany—Ethnic relations.   I. Title.

    DS146.G4B484   2007
    305.892'404309043—dc22   2006029807

Manufactured in the United States of America

16   15   14   13   12   11   10   09   08   07

10   9   8   7   6   5   4   3   2   1

This book is printed on New Leaf EcoBook 50, a 100% recycled fiber of which 50% is de-inked post-consumer waste, processed chlorine-free. EcoBook 50 is acid-free and meets the minimum requirements of ANSI/ASTM D5634-01 (*Permanence of Paper*).

To the memory of George L. Mosse
and his family of colleagues, students, and friends
who carry his spark with generosity, grace, and humor

It is I who created the smith
To fan the charcoal fire
And produce the tools for his work;
So it is I who create
The instruments of havoc.

No weapon formed against you
Shall succeed,
And every tongue that contends with you at the law
You shall defeat.
Such is the lot of the servants of the Lord,
Such their triumph through Me
—declares the Lord

ISAIAH 54:16–17
Third Haftarah of the Consolation *(R'eih)*

When the inmates of the house, attracted by Oliver's cries,
hurried to the spot from which they proceeded, they found
him, pale and agitated, pointing in the direction of the
meadows behind the house, and scarcely able to articulate
the words "The Jew, the Jew!"

CHARLES DICKENS
"Book the Second, Chapter the Twelfth," *Oliver Twist* (1841)

Someone must have told lies about Joseph K. because,
without having done anything wrong, one morning he
was arrested.

FRANZ KAFKA
Der Prozess (1925)

CONTENTS

ILLUSTRATIONS

IN 1946 A SURVIVOR OF the Warsaw ghetto uprising asked, "Why did the Jews die such strange and horrific deaths?" and "What were they guilty of in the eyes of the world?"[1] Vital strains of Nazism were based on the idea that Jews deserved their fate under Hitler because they were "criminals." "Judentum," Jewry and Judaism, proclaimed a prominent Nazi billboard, "ist Verbrechertum"—is criminality.[2] This libel, directed at Jews as individuals as well as at a mythically unified, archconspiratorial entity, was a protean weapon in the Nazi arsenal. It was the stuff of Nazi patter, platitudes, and policy. The following study details this dimension of the persecution of the Jews and analyzes its part in stimulating and rationalizing gratuitous violence and murder. The accusation that Jews were criminals shaped how the Nazis and their collaborators, and post–Second World War sympathizers with the Nazi regime, endeavored to justify the Jews' stigmatization and attempted annihilation.[3]

Though stereotyped images of "Jewish criminality" were an important part of the mental landscape of European anti-Semitism and the Holocaust, they have received sparse scholarly attention.[4] Yet the significance of the Nazi association of Jews with criminality is clear in recent historical work that convincingly demonstrates that a major appeal of the Nazi regime was its image as a bastion of "law and order." The Nazi State incessantly declared that it was waging a successful "war on crime" and therefore making all Germans—except for Jews, "Gypsies," homosexuals, "leftists," and other "social outsiders"—much safer. The Nazis' claim that they had instituted a respite from "lawlessness" is an enduring image of the regime that is similar to the myth of National Socialism's "eternal victory" over unemployment. Neither of these claims was greatly discredited in German popular memory, even after the colossal failure of National Socialism.[5]

This book also surveys and interprets the Jewish response to the "Jewish criminality" charge. Numerous survivors have commented on the irony of the Nazis' branding the Jews "criminals" while Hitler's Germany and its helpers conducted an unprecedented campaign of state-sponsored robbery, mayhem, torture, and murder that violated every convention of civility. Though exemplary figures such as Emmanuel Ringelblum, Marcel Reich-Ranicki, Primo Levi, Hugo Gryn, and Victor Klemperer have written explicitly on the "criminality" canard of the Holocaust, there has been little scholarly follow-up on these reflections. I will explore how Jews reacted to the criminality accusation and how it influenced their self-perceptions and regard for themselves—as individuals and as members of a group. I have found a great amount of comment in published and unpublished accounts about the Nazis' equation of Jews and criminals.[6] I will argue that this association had a noticeable impact on Jews in ghettos and concentration camps as well as on survivors in displaced-persons (DP) camps.[7] In many settings where Jews were compelled to violate Nazi law to survive, they saw themselves as appropriating a tradition akin to that of the "social bandit,"[8] as well as possibly devising an "honorable" identity for themselves.[9]

This study, therefore, offers perspectives that I find to be underrepresented in the secondary literature on the Holocaust and anti-Semitism but that are prevalent in a large number of primary sources on the perpetration of the Holocaust as well as in survivors' recollections. By no means do I contend that the accusation of Jewish criminality is the essence of the Holocaust. Although the charge that Jews are criminals played a prominent role in anti-Semitism, it does not represent the key to anti-Semitism in all times and places. But the perception of Jews as criminals occupied a larger role— and was intertwined in other anti-Jewish efforts, political, economic, and "racial"—than has heretofore been acknowledged in the history of the Holocaust and anti-Semitism, both before and after the Third Reich. That the Nazis played upon older stereotypes of Jewish criminality to obfuscate and justify their persecution of the Jews might have had particular resonance for those Germans who were not carried away by the theoretical racism of the regime—but who did buy into its so-called war on crime. The anti-Semitic obsession with Jewish criminality furthermore played a more formidable role in Jews' understanding of the discrimination and oppression they confronted than has previously been noticed.

Nazi Germany has long been viewed and dissected, for the most part sagaciously, as "The Racial State."[10] That National Socialism was fundamentally committed to a pseudoscientific ideal of world domination by "Aryans" and to the "industrial" destruction of the Jews as their antithetical, enemy "race," is beyond doubt.[11] The crackpot notion that Jews are a distinct race and that Germans are a pure Aryan race colored almost every facet of the Nazi State and all it held in its grasp. Once in power, the Nazis expended copious amounts of time and energy subduing and annihilating those they deemed a racial menace. Racism, clearly, was central to the systematic mass murder of Europe's Jews in the Holocaust.

Nazi administrators of numerous departments were awash in a sea of bureaucratic gobbledygook as they attempted to assure themselves that those who peopled their Reich,[12] especially its vaunted SS, were of "pure" racial stock.[13] The concentration camps and extermination camps were "laboratories" of a sort, supposedly to foster the "racial state" and a racialized world order.[14] They were predicated on the idea that Jews and other undesirables should not be free to inhabit the same earth as the Germans, who as Aryans par excellence were uniquely endowed and destined to rule.

As powerful and far-reaching as this racial Weltanschauung was, it did not always provide enough direction and support to Germans and those in their orbit. Nazi policy makers—including Adolf Hitler—found that exposure to purported racial truths did not guarantee that the German public would internalize and consistently uphold such ideals.[15] The Nazis sometimes had to exert considerable pressure "to break the resistance" of Germans, particularly those who regarded themselves as "apolitical."[16] Furthermore, before the outbreak of the war, the Nazis learned that prising Jews from German society was not always easy.[17] For example, Deutsche Arbeitsfront (DAF) officials were perplexed that there was more than a smattering of Jews in supposedly un-Jewish realms—such as the civilian airnational guard, motor-sports clubs, and even police forces.[18] Singling out Jews for their "racial" otherness, they found, did not automatically trigger the Jews' expulsion.[19]

Although National Socialism's incarnation as "The Racial State," was primary, Nazi Germany also earned the title of "The Police State."[20] Despite important distinctions in their respective interpretations, Christopher Browning, Richard Breitman, and Ulrich Herbert have shown that Nazi genocide evolved and was perpetrated because of the coalescence and mutual support of the SS, which pursued its "racial" program, and various police and security services, which acted in the name of domestic law and order and state security.[21] "Police" support for Nazi operations, such as in the Baltic states, Belorussia and Ukraine, France, Belgium, Norway, and the Netherlands, was of paramount importance.[22] Within the Third Reich, the courts and the "criminological" infrastructure buttressed these actions.[23] Criminal law as taught in German universities, particularly by the leading criminologists Edmund Mezger and Franz Exner, also adopted the idea that "race played a role in determining the criminal behavior of the Jews." Interestingly, Mezger and Exner urged caution and tended to offer qualifications to offset gross generalizations, setting themselves apart from the hacks and outright ideologues who pontificated about Jews and crime.[24] As early as 1941 the Allied Powers were aware that the German police and the SS were becoming intricately enmeshed in the mass murder of civilians, especially Jews, but they failed to appreciate the intent or consequences.[25]

In this regard, the careers of men such as Kurt Daluege and Werner Best—who were not known as racist fanatics but became key proponents of the Holocaust—are illustrative.[26] Many Nazis who propelled or assisted the racist system were not, and were not required to be, dyed-in-the-wool racists. A number of Jewish victims noticed the tension, in the early years of the Third Reich, between "regular" policemen and Nazis.[27] One survivor, recalling Vienna in 1938, reported, "Police [had] become nightwatchmen while all administrative matters" were taken over by the Nazis, who were "loud-mouthed and obnoxious." One could see the dismay, if not disgust, on the faces of the "grey-haired policemen" who only a few months earlier would have delivered a swift "kick in the ass" to the punks who were now in charge.[28] Sometimes a kindly policeman was recognized as "a Social Democrat of the old school."[29] But the police, in all its manifestations, proved quite amenable to the Nazis.

Historian Konrad Jarausch, delving into "the conundrum of complicity," has attempted to explain the "ease with which racist zealots succeeded in overturning humanist traditions," especially among those who should have known better, the "educated."[30] Surely "different types of support," specifically "factors other than ideological zeal," must be taken into account to see how fascism actually functioned.[31] Many professionals, including intellectuals, artists, and musicians, needed to believe that they benefited, in some way materially, by the removal of Jews.[32] Yet, between 1933 and 1938, the Nazis discovered and nurtured ways to assure their stalwarts and the general public that National Socialist Jewish policies were desirable, or at least unobjectionable. This strategy has been described as "the quest for a respectable racism."[33] Even after Jews were systematically killed, the Nazis sought ways to explain why they acted as they did, and racism was only one factor—if it was cited at all. Among the most effective and prominent reasons the Nazis put forth for persecuting, torturing, murdering, and having murdered Jews was the stigmatization of the Jew as criminal.[34]

Noted scholar Raul Hilberg argued (as early as 1955) that racial ideology provided a rationalization and a core philosophy for National Socialist policies, but the Nazis and their accomplices did not need to adopt it as their primary, or replacement, secular religion. Although the German population had more than enough racial enthusiasts in its midst, most Germans simply had to comply.[35] One of the chief reasons why the German public greeted Nazi anti-Semitism without great suspicion, Hilberg asserts, is because the ideology derived most of its character from the so-called old, or preracial, anti-Semitism. This type of anti-Semitism had been part of Christian religious discourse since Luther turned his pen against what he saw as a recalcitrant Jewry in the sixteenth century.[36] Ian Kershaw, as well, maintains that identifiably premodern varieties of anti-Semitism remained a vital force in Nazi Germany.[37]

The stigma of criminality helped to inculcate the sense that Jews were "beneath respect and abnormal" as the German State was heralded as the embodiment of the Aryan race.[38] Given that Nazism operated to some extent as a secular religion, the association of Jews with criminality had a "liturgical quality," easily harnessed to older forms of Christian anti-Jewish hatred and polemics critical to the "self-representation" of the Nazis.[39] The imagined struggle against "Jewish criminality" was a means of bridging official Nazi ideology and informal "rituals" of the movement, integrating its more irrational elements with supposedly rational ones.[40] The slogan and stereotype of "Jews as criminals" painted Jews as "racial" and "diseased" outsiders who posed a threat to "respectable" Germans but also as men, women, and even children who had willfully chosen to abrogate the laws of society. Overall, this book is a response to the questions George Mosse posed in *Nazi Culture:* "How did National Socialism impinge upon the consciousness of those who lived under it?"[41] "Why did so many people accept and help to strengthen the Nazi rule?"[42] I have diverged, however, from Mosse's concerns in asking another question: How did the Jews themselves deal with this particular kind of victimization? Jews, to the Nazis, constituted a palimpsest in which any number of meanings could be inscribed, including the taint of criminality, which often proved essential along the way to dehumanization and murder.[43]

The men of the SS, Robert L. Koehl has written, "were permitted to torture and kill, to conquer and destroy, and to take part in a theatrical production of immense proportions."[44] The result was a grotesque pantomime. In the chapters that follow, I explore a distinct dimension of this Nazi "theatrical" endeavor: the attempt to cast all Jews as suspects, culprits, petty criminals, and archvillains—and the condemned. I also, however, illuminate the Jewish victims' responses to what they correctly saw as a bizarre assault that bore only highly selective and scant relationship to any previous notions of crime, punishment, and administration of justice.

Chapter 1 begins with pre-Nazi discourses on Jews and crime to show the interplay between myth, reality, and stereotype in non-Jewish and Jewish perceptions of "Jewish criminality." In the late eighteenth and nineteenth centuries, debates about the so-called *Kriminalstatistik,* including criminal statistics on Jews, were a part of public discussions on many levels. In contrast to many studies of anti-Semitism, the focus here is not on racism per se but on the application of stereotypes of Jews as criminals, in which allegations of duplicity and financial impropriety loomed largest. The notion of endemic Jewish crookedness was particularly intense in the wake of Germany's defeat in the First World War, when a number of Jews were apparently involved in a barrage of highly publicized scandals. In chapter 2, we see that the right wing's essentialized construct of the Jew as criminal in the Weimar period was translated into policy and action in Germany after 1933. Until 1938, when the Nazis unequivocally embraced the guiding principle that "The Jew is outside the law,"[45] they often took pains to charge individual Jews with specific crimes, usually focusing on technical aspects of tax laws and currency-exchange regulations. On the one hand, they sought to exploit the racist agenda and traditional anti-Semitic stereotype; on the other hand, they wanted to give the impression that the Nazi State was simply zealous in applying the letter of the law.

The third chapter explores "crime" in Nazi-created ghettos. The ghettos could not have been anything but incubators of crime, because the Nazis fashioned them in such a way that living beyond the law was the only way to survive. The Nazis claimed that the exhibition of criminality in the ghettos revealed the true character of the Jews and was proof that their ghettoization was an urgent necessity. It is little wonder that "smugglers" often became the Jews' heroes of the ghettos.

Chapter 4 examines the practices and rituals surrounding the Jews' supposed "criminal behavior" in the concentration camps. "Criminals" might have been those who were brought to the camps as conventional lawbreakers, those charged with "criminal" activity specific to the wartime context, as well as those accused of a crime within the camp confines. This chapter also discusses the process of "criminal photography" in Auschwitz, which helped perpetrate the fraud that Auschwitz was a prison. Among themselves, the Nazis fostered the delusion that Auschwitz and other concentration camps were penal institutions for those who had committed crimes and therefore deserved punishment. This fantasy probably made it easier for some Germans to believe that what they were doing to the Jews was more palatable than it otherwise may have felt. Hangings by rope—in camps and ghettos and in the theater of (normative) battle—occupied a far weightier role in Nazi self-perceptions than has been acknowledged. The Jewish American POWs captured at the Battle of the Bulge who found themselves at the obscure Berga camp were profoundly shocked by the routine hangings, whereas most of the inmates seemed numb to the spectacle.[46]

Chapter 5 centers on a specific Nazi propaganda directive, of June 1944, in which the anti-Semitic conspiracy fantasy of "The Protocols of the Elders of Zion," of a general Jewish attempt at world domination, was replaced by a more contemporary version that would suit a post–Second World War order. Zionism, the late nineteenth-century political movement to create a Jewish home in Palestine, was reconfigured as the apex of Jewish evil and organized criminality to rationalize the decimation of six million.[47] Previous scholars have assumed that the crossover from Nazi anti-Semitism to anti-Zionism was an outgrowth of Nazi Middle Eastern Realpolitik and the fact that a number of key Nazis were taken in by postwar Arab governments. Although this factor was important in the rise of anti-Zionism, anti-Zionist sentiment grew into an all-embracing ideology in 1944 when the Nazi press office launched its concerted effort to make it so. Otto Dietrich and Helmut Sündermann, possibly inspired by Hitler himself, spearheaded an effort to reenergize the big lie(s) that "actions" against the Jews were of a "defensive" nature. As a result, the world Jewish conspiracy lived on, more ominously, through Zionism.

The sixth chapter shows that the stigma of Jews as criminals was one of the most resilient and widespread perceptions among Germans as they confronted the remnant of European Jewry in post–World War II Europe—in what came to be known as the DP, or "displaced-persons" problem. Because racial anti-Semitism was a possibly questionable way to express opinions in postwar Germany, especially in the U.S. zone of occupation toward which most Jewish DPs migrated, Germans' view of Jews as criminals was a major factor in the dynamic between Jews, Germans, and the U.S. Army. The presence of a thriving black market, ubiquitous in postwar Europe, certainly abetted the perception of DPs as a "criminal element," and a number of forces combined to ensure that DPs had few other means, outside of the black market, to survive. Many Germans conveniently forgot that the black market had also operated, and had even been out of control, during the Nazi reign.

Chapter 7 looks at criminality among the Jewish remnant through the eyes of the American Jews who advised the U.S. occupation forces as well as from the perspective of the DPs themselves. It also examines how Jewish self-defense (often termed *Haganah,* the same word used for the army of Palestine's Jews) was manifested in the creation of Jewish police forces after Nazi Germany's defeat. The Jews' attempt to instill law and order among themselves is little noticed in the scholarly literature of the postwar period.[48] Unlike the "Jewish police" in Nazi ghettos, which had checkered or unsavory reputations, the Jewish police forces in the DP communities emerged as responsible institutions in which Jews were able to take pride, and the police thereby strengthened the communities' material and spiritual well-being, despite having to function in a sometimes hostile and ghost-ridden atmosphere.

The epilogue revisits the end of a small Jewish community, that of Estonia. Because this tiny Baltic nation had little native tradition of anti-Semitism, the Nazis and their accomplices had to resort to more circuitous methods to convince the local population that massacring their Jews was appropriate. Compiling "criminal dossiers" on more than a majority of the remaining urban Jewish population was part of the Nazis' travesty but was consistent with many other aspects of their Jewish policy. The perpetrators of this sham seemed to see it as having some sort of explanatory, civil-educative, or pedagogic function. The dossiers were also a hypocritical stab at self-exculpation in the midst of genocide.

The association of Jews with criminality was part of the evolving history of a little-acknowledged but widespread Nazi practice. This book probes the view of Jewish victims as criminals, documenting its role as a central mechanism of the prehistory, persecution, and systematic mass murder of European Jewry. It also considers the influence of these practices on the Jews' "surviving remnant" in postwar Germany. While scribbling and shrieking that all Jews were criminals, the Third Reich caught the world—and especially European Jewry—off guard as it robbed and murdered like few other regimes in modern history. Scholars and the world at large are still struggling to unravel the sprawling web of lies, deceit, greed, treachery, barbarism, and willful destruction of humanity and culture that spread over the Nazi empire. The reality of the Nazis' massive plunder and bloodbaths of innocents mirrored their grotesque caricature of a "criminal" Jewish menace.

We do not know to what extent the Nazi equation of Jews with criminals eased the path to genocide. Yet we can be sure that it helped assure the Nazis and their accomplices, who might not have been rabid racists or ardent ideologues, that their path was legitimate. Claims about Jewish criminality, after all, had been in the air since anyone could remember, and it was probably recalled that Jews had publicly and ardently defended themselves. Before 1939, however much Jews were concerned about their respectable image, they were not shy about talking about Jews and crime. They knew that "Jewish criminality" was a relatively small, if curious, phenomenon that had been almost totally overcome wherever Jews had an opportunity to make a decent living. Jews surmised—and were correct—that they had no reason to be more ashamed of the "criminality" of their people than any other national or religious community did. Survivor Hermann Leyes, recalling a conversation as a youth during the Third Reich, writes that when he "unhappily referred to some 'black sheep' among Jews," a friend "turned serious":

> "This only proves that you too have become infected. Why do you assume that the Jews were only noblemen? There are statistics to the effect that there were relatively fewer criminals among Jews than among Christians. But does this really matter? What does it prove? Doesn't everyone have the right to be judged according to his personal guilt or merit?" He then cited something unknown to me, perhaps it was from Heine: "If pride of birth were not something silly and contradictory, one could be proud of being the descendants of those martyred ones who gave to the world One God and a morality on which Western civilization is built."[49]

But to the German community at large, the notion of Jewish criminality was made to seem more reasonable than many other facets of the anti-Jewish onslaught, in part because there were a few kernels of truth—however anachronistic—to some of the anti-Semitic claims, which had been subject to scrutiny and discussion long before the Nazis. "Race" was obviously, fatally significant in the Nazi definition of "who was a Jew." Yet from the inception of the Third Reich to its last gasp, the association of Jews with criminality proceeded apace and did not end with the demise of National Socialism. Identifying Jews with criminals was not invariably genocidal, but it was a key factor in stripping Jews of their rights and respect, and it was often instrumental in their eventual physical decimation.

ACKNOWLEDGMENTS

THE CONCEPTION OF THIS BOOK would have been impossible if not for my teacher George L. Mosse (1918–99). I started thinking about the historical association of Jews and criminality in 1980, when George (Professor Mosse to me then) suggested I read Michael Gold's *Jews without Money* (1930), replete with its tales of Jewish crooks, con men, and prostitutes on New York's Lower East Side. In writing my MA thesis on Max Nordau, I was intrigued by connections between Zionism's founders and the pioneers of criminology, including the much-discussed Cesare Lombroso. Over twenty years later I finally embarked on a study of Jews and perceptions of criminality from the sixteenth through the twentieth centuries. The current book began as a chapter of, and then a detour from, that project (to which I hope soon to return).

A number of individuals and institutions have assisted me, although, of course, this book is solely my responsibility. I first wish to thank the colleagues and friends I have had the pleasure to know through working with George Mosse: Joel Truman, Barry Fulks, Steve Aschheim, Judy Doneson z'l, Judy Cochrane z'l, Tom August, Gloria Levine, Andy Rabinbach, Sterling Fishman z'l, Edward T. Gargan z'l, Irv Saposnik z'l, Allan Sharlin z'l, Seymour Drescher, Alex Orbach, David Weinberg, Paul Breines, Andy Bachman, Bruce Saposnik, Randall Halle, Laurie Baron, David Sorkin, Dan Pekarsky, David Biale, Chris Browning, John Efron, Geoffrey Giles,

David Gross, Nancy Green, Robert Pois z'l, John Tortorice, Jim Steakley, Elaine Marks z'l, Sander Gilman, Shula Volkov, Bob Koehl, Ted Hamerow, David Dennis, Alex Busansky, Dan Sussman, Steve Kale, Andrew Patner, Leslie Adelson, Elizabeth Panzer, Monys Hagen, Maureen Flynn, Domenico Sella, Jeffrey Herf, Steve Brockmann, Mark Ferguson, Bernard Friedman, Mark Bassin, Doug Mackaman, Wendy Lower, Joan Ringelheim, and Joanna Bourke.

It is my honor and pleasure to record my debt to many students for their engagement with my work and their contribution to an unusually convivial atmosphere in the Department of Hebrew and Jewish Studies at University College London. At the risk of leaving out some fine students, I would like to acknowledge Lucy Glennon, Anastasia Hancock, Clara Nieto, Nick Perry, Pek Yih Senn-Tham, Helen Whatmore, Alan Swarc, Amy Shapiro, Jason Smith, Sevgi Hassan, Ciara McManus, Sylvie Tannen, James Renton, Lars Fischer, Julia Cartarius, Alan Traynor, Benjamin Behrman, Hila Baron, Paul Hanson, Jessica Coburn, Angela Debnath, Frieda Kosmin, Matthew Martinson, Samantha Smith, Maki Sugimori, Sheila Chait, John Zamet, Rhoda Atkin, Paul Dyer, Emmeline Burdett, Judith Bauernfreund, Susi Schmidt, Jonathan Lelliott, Vivianna Ravaioli, and Joanna Michlic. I wish to warmly thank my departmental colleagues—John Klier, Ada Rapoport-Albert, Tsila Ratner, Mark Geller, Helen Beer, Willem Smelik, Sacha Stern, Tali Loewenthal, and Neill Lochery—for their support and good humor. Beyond Bloomsbury, scholars who lent advice include Joanna Newman, Nils Roemer, Peter Longerich, Martin Geyer, Ian Kershaw, Nikolaus Wachsmann, and Michael Brenner. While in London, Scott Spector read parts of the manuscript and made several helpful comments.

St. John's College, Oxford, initially sponsored my research on perceptions of Jewish criminality. St. John's award of a summer Visiting Scholarship (1998) allowed me to reside at college and read in the magnificent Bodleian Library. That was followed by a research trip to New York's Public Library and the Yiddish Scientific Research Institute (YIVO), supported by the Central Research Fund of the University of London and a Research Fellowship of the British Academy. The Central Research Fund and the British Academy likewise supported my research in 2003–04, which enabled site visits to Belgium, France, and Lithuania.

Originally I intended to devote only a single chapter of a book on "Jewish criminality" to Nazism, and I assumed that I could largely rely on the body of excellent scholarship on National Socialist anti-Semitism. I learned, however, that the Jews' treatment as criminals was not exhaustively mined. When I mentioned this fact to my colleague Alan Steinweis, he suggested that I look at the Berlin Document Collection of the YIVO archives. Upon perusing the files on "Jewish criminality" from the Institut der NSDAP zur Erforschung der Judenfrage in Frankfurt am Main, I found that the Nazi association of Jews with criminality—which I thought would be straightforward and inseparable from the discourse on race—was extremely complicated and not always directly tied to racism per se. There I started to see that the Nazi application of the "Jewish criminality" canard was more contagious and widespread than most historians assumed. At YIVO I also found the Nazi memorandum on Zionism of June 1944 that became the basis for chapter 5. Dr. Ernest Oliveri, distinguished as both a political scientist (of Latin American political economy) and a photographer (Pygmalion Studios), took photos from the YIVO archives of the Nazi files that were remarkably revealing about how a discourse on "Jewish criminality" was concocted. A first research trip to the archives of the United States Holocaust Memorial Museum (USHMM) in Washington, DC, confirmed that the Nazis made abundant and varied use of the charge of "Jewish criminality" in the Third Reich. In a few days in Washington, however, I was able only to scratch the surface.

In addition to investigating the Nazi deployment of "Jewish criminality," I was interested in exploring how this charge functioned in Europe immediately after the Second World War. In the mid-1980s a seminar paper by an MA student at Ohio State University, Christopher O'Connor, confirmed that the perception of Jewish "displaced persons" as "criminals" was part of the challenge survivors faced in post–1945 Germany. His paper cited observations of Rabbi Philip Bernstein (1901–85), who was the second adviser on Jewish Affairs to the U.S. Military Government in Germany. I found this information particularly interesting, because having grown up in Rochester, New York, I was aware of Rabbi Bernstein's sterling reputation. My father, William Berkowitz (1917–95), although not one of his congregants at Temple B'rith Kodesh, was a great admirer of the Rabbi. As an "island-hopping" GI in the Pacific during the Second World War, my father thought the world of Bernstein's humanitarianism and good sense, as reflected in his advice to chaplains serving Jewish soldiers. As it turned out, Rabbi Bernstein's Nachlass in the archives of the University of Rochester, superbly organized by Walter Nickeson, became an invaluable source for the chapters dealing with DPs. I worked in Rochester in April and August 2003, while holding a fellowship at the Center for Advanced Holocaust Studies (CAHS) of the USHMM.

Upon my presentation of the first phase of research at the annual meeting of the Association for German Studies in 2000, several colleagues offered criticisms, encouragement, and extremely helpful suggestions. The assistance of Bob Waite, of the Office of the Special Prosecutor in Washington, DC, was especially fortuitous. Andy Rabinbach, Geoffrey Giles, Christopher Browning, and Jeffrey Herf (who are among the extended Mosse-*Familie* to whom this book is dedicated) also made constructive remarks, as did Gordon Mork. Geoffrey Giles and John Efron expertly commented on research proposals I prepared for the CAHS, and John later reviewed a draft chapter with his usual razor-sharp insight.

In the summer of 2001 I arranged a tour for graduate students to Zamość and the remnants of the Operation Reinhard death camps (Belzec, Sobibor, and Treblinka), which were purpose-built for the mass murder of Europe's Jews. That venture was partly modeled on a study tour undertaken by Sir Martin Gilbert and a group of MA students of the Department of Hebrew and Jewish Studies of University College London in 1996.[1] Robin O'Neil— a former criminal investigations officer—who was writing on the transition from police practices to genocide in Belzec for his dissertation, animated both tours. Although little of the current book directly concerns the Operation Reinhard camps, throughout that tour I was struck by the prominence of policing and police-type work in the perpetration of genocide. Robin's concern for layers of deception and the distortion of accepted police practices informs this study in numerous ways.

Back in London, my resourceful PhD student Lars Fischer alerted me to several books and pamphlets in the library of the Zentrum für Antisemitismusforschung at the Technische Universität (TU) in Berlin, which led me to make a trip there in the winter of 2001. Johannes Heil went beyond the call of duty in assisting me with my research at the TU and the Berlin Staatsbibliothek. A gracious invitation to address the seminar at the Moses Mendelssohn Zentrum at Universität Potsdam was extended by Joachim Schlör, who also gave me run of his wonderful library-flat in Kreuzberg. Although my subject for the seminar related only marginally to the current project, the students made a number of excellent suggestions, and a few of them provided me with references in the coming months.

At an important juncture, the Lucius Littauer Foundation funded my work in New York and at Princeton University's Mudd Library. Pamela Ween Brumberg (z'l) of the Littauer Foundation had been consistently supportive of my research for decades, and I will miss her. In November 2001 a gracious invitation to the inaugural conference of the Lithuanian Emigration Institute of Vytautas Magnus University in Kaunas opened another vista for research. That experience provided the opportunity for gaining knowledge of Einsatzgruppe 3, whose murderous sweep included the communities from which my own family originates in the Kovno region. The knowledge and assistance of Chaim Bargman (who is immortalized as "Shlomo" in the memoir *Heschel's Kingdom* by Dan Jacobson) permitted me to transcend nostalgia on a cold winter journey through the Lithuanian hinterland. I was able to return to Kovno on two other occasions, in November 2003 and June 2004; support was provided by the Central Research Fund of the University of London and the British Academy, for which I am most grateful. During the June 2004 visit, in addition to pursuing my research, I led a Kovno-based study tour for students in the "history of the Holocaust" MA seminar. That excursion was financed, in part, by donations from the Shapiro family of Houston, Texas; Joseph Maduro of Atlanta, Georgia; David Goldstein of Houston, Texas; and Bernard Friedman of Los Angeles, California, under the auspices of the American Friends of University College London. In the summer of 2004, as part of my British Academy award, I traveled to the Natzweiler-Struthof concentration camp memorial with my colleague and friend Steve Kale. Steve, a historian of modern France, was extremely helpful in gleaning information from the site.

The lion's share of research and writing of this book was facilitated by the Charles H. Revson Fellowship for Archival Research of the USHMM's CAHS. I was in residence at the center in the summer of 2002, and spring, summer, and early fall of 2003. For two weeks in the summer of 2005, I cocoordinated a research seminar on DPs with Dr. Avi Patt at the CAHS and was able to supplement my earlier research. In Woodside Park, Maryland, all kinds of generosity and logistical support were furnished by Leonard and Mary Arzt, and the first leg of my fellowship was enjoyed as a cat-and-house sitter for Ken and Sandi Lee.

I wish to express my gratitude to the CAHS for making my stays in Washington extraordinarily productive. I enjoyed the good fellowship and wise counsel of Wendy Lower, Peter Black, Martin Dean, Severin Hochberg, Patricia Heberer, Geoffrey Megargee, Suzanne Brown-Fleming, Benton Arnowitz, Robert Ehrenreich, Paul Shapiro, Avi Patt, Anne Millin, Joan Ringelheim, Andrew Koss, Steve Kanaley, and Laura Brahm of the staff, and I appreciate the many kindnesses and good work of the supporting team, especially Tracy Brown and Lisa Zaid. My fellow fellows, who were there (or nearby) for varying stays, enriched my experience all the more. Among the many scholars who were stellar in this regard are Christopher Browning,

Howard M. Sachar, George Eisen, Marc Sapperstein, Rob Eisen, Marsha Rozenblit, Richard Wetzell, Steven Zipperstein, Sara Bender, Jennifer Evans, Thomas Sandkühler, Richard Breitman, Götz Aly, Susanne Heim, Robert Moses Shapiro, Carol Zemel, Anton Weiss-Wendt, Michael Bazyler, Steven Bowman, Holly Case, Wolf Gruner, Limor Yagail, Diane Afoumado, Bob Moore, Balacz Szelenyi, Steven Carr, Atina Grossmann, Boaz Cohen, Laura Hilton, Tamar Lewinsky, Laura Jockusch, and David Weinberg. The staffs of the archives and library, including Aaron Kornfeld and Henry Mayer, and Judith Cohen, Sharon Mueller, and Maren Read of the Photographic Archive of the USHMM were tremendously helpful.

While a fellow at the CAHS, I had the opportunity to present work in progress at Nazareth College (Rochester, New York), Georgetown University, the George Washington University, and the University of Maryland–College Park. Scholars and students at these institutions were a great sounding board.

When I arrived at a frustrating but exciting point in my research, my exploration of the practice of "police photography" at Auschwitz, Wendy Lower, then director of Fellowship Programs of the USHMM, suggested that I contact Helen "Zippy" Tichauer. This is not the first book on the Holocaust to record the recollections and insights of Zippy, who worked in the main office at Birkenau and is an unparalleled informant about the inner workings of Auschwitz. The authors of an intriguing biography of Alma Rosé (the niece of Gustav Mahler, a distinguished violinist who led the women's orchestra at Birkenau—in which Zippy played the mandolin)—sing the praises of Zippy for her help.[2] Likewise, for this book, the assistance of Zippy Tichauer was priceless, as she was able to provide information about aspects of Auschwitz that otherwise would have remained obscure or would have been left to loose speculation. I only wish I could do justice to the extent to which Zippy has committed to memory the murderous and paradoxical world of Auschwitz, about which her knowledge and analysis have proven to be sterling.

From the end of my fellowship at the USHMM (summer 2003) through 2004, Severin Hochberg, Derek Penslar, Andy Koss, John Efron, Scott Spector, Alan Steinweis, and Patricia Heberer read and offered comments on drafts of chapters, for which I am grateful. Severin and Patricia suggested sources that turned out to be immensely instructive. I also benefited from the responses to my work at the "War, Culture and Humanity" conference at Manchester University; Wolverhampton University's colloquium on "Beyond Camps and Forced Labour" (held at the Imperial War Museum,

London); the British Association for Jewish Studies meetings at Southampton University and the University of Birmingham; the Centre for German-Jewish Studies of Sussex University conference at Chatham House, London; and the symposium of the Academic Response to Racism and Antisemitism in Europe (ARARE) of the Simon Wiesenthal Centre, Paris, in cooperation with the Italian Historical Studies Center "Olokaustos" under the auspices of the UNESCO Regional Bureau (ROSTE), held in Venice in December 2003.

A fortuitous meeting with Stan Holwitz in Washington, DC, led to the publication of this book with the University of California Press. I wish to thank Stan; his associate editor, Randy Heyman; Jacqueline Volin; David Anderson; and Adrienne Harris for their dedication in seeing this project through to a timely completion. Maren Read of the USHMM Photo Archives was especially helpful in arranging copies and rights for several of the images.

I would like to record my debt of love and gratitude to my wife, Deborah Rozansky, and my children, Rachel and Stephen. I appreciate their putting up with my absences, and with my occasionally schlepping them along to research-related destinations. My children are among few (if any) of their contemporaries who have been photographed on the lap of (the sculpture of) Cesare Lombroso in a small park in Verona.

Perhaps as is appropriate for a book on perceptions of criminality, I should acknowledge some of my heists along the way. I have liberally adopted the scholarship of Anton Weiss-Wendt for the epilogue, and I have appropriated the comments of astute critics of the manuscript in preparing the final version. Should there be anything else that appears to be unaccounted, either it is inadvertent or I wish not to say.

ONE

Above Suspicion?

Facts, Myths, and Lies about Jews and Crime

Being perceived wrongly is no less painful than being treated wrongly.

FRANZ ROSENZWEIG

FOR MANY GERMANS THE LINKING of Jews with criminality might have seemed less speculative than "scientific racism" as a basis for Nazi policies. Although some scholars detect the roots of racial anti-Semitism in pre-Christian antiquity,[1] for the sake of illuminating the Holocaust, it suffices to begin with the broad Christian background. In European Christendom a rationale for discriminating against the Jews, accompanying the apparent incompatibility of the Jewish and Christian belief systems, was that Jews were socialized toward criminality and overrepresented in the realm of criminals. This conviction long predated the rise of racism, although sometimes the persecution of Jews based on heredity, such as during the Spanish Inquisition, is characterized as racist.[2] To be sure, racial theories developed since the eighteenth century buttressed and embellished the connection between Jews and crime. Yet a notion of Jewish criminality could exist—and even thrive—without knowledge of or belief in "racial science" and its various offshoots.

As Raul Hilberg and other scholars have demonstrated, National Socialism often elicited "Christian" and "Reformation" persecution of the Jews as a precedent.[3] The Nazis made an effort to demonstrate the good sense of their anti-Semitism by showing that discrimination against the Jews was part of the normal business of every modern state that wished to defend itself. Simultaneously they sought to prove that their actions were consistent

I

with the development of Christian theology and even with the history of nations such as England and the United States. A huge pseudoscholarly tome, reissued at least three times, expounds on the idea that anti-Semitism has been a major theme of English history, and there were efforts to "prove" that Benjamin Franklin attempted to thwart the acceptance of Jews in the founding of the United States.[4] Although the decision to recast Franklin as an anti-Semite was not quite as absurd as the Nazi campaign to identify the gangster Al Capone as a Jew,[5] it was a poor example. In fact, Franklin is well remembered for his design for the official seal of the United States, which pictured "Moses standing on the Shore, and extending his Hand over the Sea, thereby causing the same to overwhelm Pharaoh who is sitting in an open Chariot, a Crown on his Head and a Sword in his Hand. Rays from a Pillar of Fire in the Clouds reaching to Moses, to express that he acts by Command of the Deity." Even more inappropriate for Nazism was Franklin's "Motto": "Rebellion to Tyrants is Obedience to God."[6] Germans, however, did not fare so well in his estimation. Considering "the German settlers in the hinterland of Pennsylvania" in 1764, Franklin wrote: "Should the Palantine Boors be suffered to swarm into our settlements, and by herding together establish their language and manners, to the exclusion of ours?"[7] A reputed anti-Semitic diatribe of Franklin's cited by the Nazis (still circulating on hate-mongering web sites), was easily revealed as a fake, not least because it assigned the incorrect date to the Continental Congress.

On more conventional grounds the Nazis portrayed the inception of Christianity as the watershed of Jews' supposed revelation of their "criminal" character. Through Judas's betrayal of Jesus in the Christological drama, it is possible to render Judas as the prototypical Jewish criminal— for allegedly undermining the nascent church and threatening Christians as individuals. The assumption that Jews are deceitful, following the example of Judas, is one of the most dogged anti-Semitic tenets.[8] If one assumes that Jewry had been willfully obstinate in its ongoing refusal to accept Christianity, as was pronounced in church authorities' "disputations" in the Middle Ages, it is not a giant leap to suppose that Jews are more inclined toward criminality than Christians. Martin Luther expounded on the "treachery" of Jewry in his "little book" *On the Jews and Their Lies* (1543), after it was clear that the Jews could not be enticed to his movement en masse. For the most part he fulminated against Christians who had permitted the Jews' practice of "usury" to become transformed into acceptable "thievery": "Moreover, they are nothing but thieves and robbers who daily eat no morsel and wear no thread of clothing which they have not stolen and pilfered from us by means of their accursed usury. Thus they live from day to day, together with wife and child, by theft and robbery, as arch-thieves and robbers, in the most impenitent security."[9]

Luther blurred the distinction between "thieves and robbers" in a literal sense and Jews engaged in the legal pursuit of money lending who were nonetheless "guilty" of "robbing" unwitting Christians. "Usury" as a nefarious trade of the Jews was a major theme of *Jud Süss* (1940), a hugely popular Nazi film loosely based on the legend of an eighteenth-century "Court Jew" who served as an adviser and financier to the duke of Württemberg.[10] The professed necessity for "Aryanization," which was little more than institutionalized theft of Jewish property and assets, was that any and all Jewish economic relations with "Aryans" were destructive and duplicitous and therefore had to be eliminated.[11]

One of the initial campaigns against Jews as criminals—which did, unlike the vast majority of anti-Semitic allegations, have some basis in reality—was a reaction to the involvement of Jews in prostitution. Charges that Jews were procurers of prostitutes had been lodged in Venice in the early fifteenth century. This activity was seen as part and parcel of a community that was prone to no good—one that fenced stolen goods and took undue advantage of Gentiles through pawnbroking.[12] Prostitution did not, however, continue to be identified with Italian Jewry, as "white slavery" was primarily seen as spreading from the most impoverished quarters of Eastern Europe to Berlin, London, Paris, New York, and Buenos Aires, especially in the last decades of the nineteenth century. Thus, it came to be associated with the international traffic in both willing and coerced women. Jews overwhelmingly regarded this practice as abhorrent and managed to virtually eliminate it as soon as they developed their own "policing" savvy in the early twentieth century in their own communities and by undermining global networks.[13] Yet the highly sexualized "racial pollution" charge could also have appeared more plausible when mixed with the white slavery canard—which did contain a kernel of historical truth. When the Nazis wrote about the phenomenon in 1939, they failed to attach more than a handful of names, and no pictures, to their accusations.[14] Nevertheless, the charge that white slavery was esteemed and protected by Jewish communities was wildly overstated in the 1930s and 1940s, with anti-Semites conveniently ignoring Jews' protests against the practice and their successful efforts to eradicate it within their community. Other criminal activities of individual Jews were noted beginning in the fifteenth to sixteenth centuries as real and imagined niches of Jewry. At the time, many segments of European Jews faced guild-based discrimination, property-owning restrictions, and chronic poverty that severely undermined their range of livelihoods. Some Jews, it is true, turned to crime. Early modern Italian history includes swashbuckling Jewish outlaws, and Northern and Central Europe were beset by mixed "robber bands" of Jews and non-Jews who treated one another as equals and often accepted Jews as leaders, as noted by the pioneering scholar of Jewish mysticism, Gershom Scholem. The robber bands became a staple of discussions whenever the issue of "Jewish criminality" came up. Smuggling, kidnapping, and arson became common charges against Jews in the mid-sixteenth century.[15] Modern Jews knew of these premodern gangs through academic books but mostly from the popular play *Die Räuber* (Robbers), by the non-Jewish German writer Friedrich Schiller (1759–1805), which included Jews as leading figures. In the late nineteenth century there were at least four Yiddish translations of the play, which was a staple of the Yiddish stage in Eastern Europe, London, and America; many Jews also read it in the original German.

German history in particular had encountered the specter of "Jewish criminality" mainly in four guises. First, it was commonly known that some Jews had been notorious, flamboyant criminals in the time of the robber bands of the seventeenth and eighteenth centuries. Second, beginning in the late eighteenth and early nineteenth centuries, the debates over Jewish emancipation frequently engaged the notion of "Jewish criminality." This idea was revived when anti-Semites sought to curtail Jewish rights in the 1870s. Third, the association of revolutionary socialism, communism, and anarchism with "lawlessness" sometimes evinced anti-Semitic manifestations. The response to social unrest and upheavals, such as in the wake of the attempted revolutions of 1848 and 1918 in Central Europe, often prompted anti-Jewish recriminations and violence. Fourth, a number of Jewish individuals were convicted of small- and large-scale malfeasance during the First World War and early years of the Weimar Republic. Several of these incidents were fodder for long-running, highly publicized, and politicized scandals. Concomitantly, the "cultural war," which the Nazis and other right-wing conservatives believed they were waging against sexual promiscuity and liberal thought, such as in literature, the arts, and public entertainment, was deemed to be a battle against sinister, "criminal" Jewish forces.[16]

Before the Nazi rise to power, therefore, Germany and other European states had had a long history of recognizing the phenomenon of "Jewish crime." But not all the commentary on Jews and crime was of a crude anti-Semitic variety. From the late eighteenth to the early twentieth centuries, Jews themselves had occasionally written of this curious legacy, which by the late 1920s had been reduced to a statistically minute aspect of Jewish existence overall—despite the well-known exploits of "Jewish gangsters" in the United States that reached their peak around 1935.[17] Indeed, the identification of Jews with crime has a long and complex history that is not often recalled, in large part because many scholars would not think to ask. This blind spot is also a result of reticence or censorship on the part of historians who believe it impertinent to even deal with the subject, especially in the wake of the Holocaust.[18]

Theories about Jews and crime were articulated in debates about Jewish emancipation and the extension of Jewish rights in the German states beginning in the late eighteenth century.[19] These expressions departed from earlier polemics because their authors tended to present themselves as largely detached from religious motives. Christian Wilhelm von Dohm's *Über die bürgerliche Verbesserung der Juden* (Berlin, 1781) reveals the widely accepted view that Jews are "guilty of a proportionally greater number of crimes than the Christians; that their character in general inclines more toward usury and fraud in commerce." Still, in what was regarded more as a defense than a reprimand of Jewry, Dohm contended, "Everything the Jews are blamed for is caused by the political conditions under which they now live, and any other group of men, under such conditions, would be guilty of identical errors."[20]

In his attempt to undermine Dohm's plea to enhance the standing of the Jews, Johann David Michaelis responded that "reports of investigations of thieves" had shown that half the members of gangs of thieves were Jews. This finding was alarming, he contended, because Jews comprised no more than "one-twenty-fifth of the total German population." The nation's "riff-raff," he concluded, was overwhelmingly Jewish.[21]

Moses Mendelssohn, the illustrious forerunner and proponent of Jewish emancipation, felt compelled to address the issue. He incisively ascribed the deeds of Jewish criminals to their abominable social position and described the turn to thievery by a small number of Jews as a transitional, rather than a permanent, aspect of their vocation. For the most part, Jews in his time had not, Mendelssohn argued, been involved in crimes such as "grand theft," murder, sedition, arson, prostitution, adultery, and infanticide. He did concede, however, that there was more than a smattering of "thieves and receivers of stolen goods" among the Jews. But

> this number should not be viewed in terms of that people's proportion of the entire population. The comparison should rather be made between traders and pedlars among the Jews on the one hand, and among other peoples on the other. I am sure that such a comparison would yield very different proportions. The same statistics, I do not hesitate to maintain, will also show that there are twenty-five times as many thieves and receivers of stolen goods among German pedlars as among Jewish. This is aside from the fact that the Jew is forced to take up such a calling, while the others could have become field marshals or ministers. They freely choose their profession, be it a trader, pedlar, seller of mouse-traps, performer of shadow plays or vendor of curios.

Mendelssohn acknowledged that "quite a number of Jewish pedlars deal in stolen goods." He believed that only a few among them, however, were "outright thieves." And those who were, unequivocally, "thieves," were shunted into this line because they were "without refuge or sanctuary anywhere on earth." But even these men did not see thievery as a means of sustaining themselves in the long term:

> As soon as they have made some fortune they acquire a patent of protection from their territorial prince and change their profession. This is public knowledge; when I was younger I personally met a number of men [Jews] who were esteemed in their native country after they had elsewhere made enough dubious money to purchase a patent of protection. This injustice is directly created by that fine policy which denies the poor Jews protection and residence, but receives with open arms those very same Jews as soon as they have "thieved their way to wealth."

Mendelssohn charged Michaelis with "blaming the victim"—in this case, impoverished Jews. Mendelssohn refused to accept that Jews were "bad people" or that criminality was an indelible stain on their character. "Among the Jews," Mendelssohn wrote, also taking a swipe at the Jews who had elevated themselves into respectable society, "I have found comparatively more virtue in the quarters of the poor than in the houses of the wealthy."[22]

Mendelssohn was aware that "a number of Jews existed in Central Europe who supported themselves by both stealing and trading," as Jason

Sanders has written. "These thieves benefited from both activities that mutually reinforced each other. Salesmen on the roads seem to have found ample opportunities to steal, and theft augmented some traders' meager income. Such Jews were frequently recent immigrants from Eastern Europe who had not yet secured the right to live in a German city. As a result, they attempted to earn a living on the road by trading, begging, and sometimes stealing. Banditry provided an alternative for the poorest of the poor Jews who had difficulties sustaining themselves in low-income, or irregular occupations."[23] It enabled them to gain a permit to engage in lawful business. To accuse the Jews of immorality, Mendelssohn lamented, was to "confuse cause and effect."[24]

It is not surprising, then, that Gotthold Ephraim Lessing chose the stereotype of the Jewish thief as the instrument for undermining the myth that the Jews lacked virtue in his play *Die Juden* (1749). The dénouement of the play was the revelation that the supposed Christian traveler who bravely fought the supposed Jewish villains was himself a Jew. A similar sentiment motivated the amendment of an eighteen-page article by Gabriel Riesser to *Geschichte der Juden in Lübeck und Moisling* (History of the Jews in Lübeck and Moisling, 1898) to rebut a so-called spiteful attack by Friedrich Christian Benedict Avé-Lallemant (1809–92) alleging that Jews had dominated crime in the region.[25] Such ideas, however, were not exclusive to the German states. In Britain, as Parliament debated the right of Baron Rothschild to sit in its midst in the mid-nineteenth century, a speaker asserted that Jews "have never, in any age or any country, been prevalent in crime." But the subsequent phrase is telling: "Their crimes have mostly been the result of the degraded position to which they have been reduced, the degraded pursuits into which they have been compelled."[26]

With Mendelssohn leading the way, as early as the eighteenth century a number of Jewish authors suggested that crime and criminals exist as something contingent, situational, and transitional—relative to the established order. Did not the Jews' contributions to society, many of them reasoned, far outweigh any damage wrought by Jewish crooks?[27] Some Jewish writers even came close to arguing that crime and criminals are "socially constructed," using the term at least a century before it came into intellectual parlance. This stance could not be more different than the view that criminality is an innate trait, the foundations of which were undermined by the "Positive" or "Positivist" school of criminology led by Cesare Lombroso. (Ironically, Lombroso is best known for propagating the notion of a biologically determined "born criminal," and he later took pains to distance himself from its appropriation by anti-Semites.) Some might argue that the presence of a disproportionate number of Jews at the forefront of criminology's emergence as a "secular" science is not coincidental. Jews did not typically see criminals among themselves as extraordinary or evil individuals, but mainly as "unfortunates."[28] Multidimensional Jewish criminals were known in plays and literature embraced by Jews, such as Isaac Babel's Odessa gangster Benja Krik, Joseph Opatoshu's "Romance of a Horse Thief," 'Ozer Varshavski's *Shmuglars* (Smugglers) and *Unterwelt* (Underworld), and Sholem Asch's "Motke Ganev" ("Mottke, the Thief"). Secular Jewish literature, similar to trends in other "national" naturalist genres, was unabashed in imagining the mind-set of Jewish crooks,[29] as seen below in "Romance of a Horse Thief":

> Zanvl got out of bed and began to pace the room making plans: the Polish church was said to contain a golden Madonna with diamond eyes that was worth a few hundred thousand. He would break in and steal the holy statue. The money would buy him some long-tailed Cossack horses and the weapons he needed. Then he would round up a band of trusty men and hole up in the Radzenov Forest. They would build a hideout among the oaks, near the Zholdevke River, so that in case of danger they could swim across to Prussia; they would do as they pleased. Every week they'd saddle the Cossack horses, take their rifles and loot the neighboring estates, or ambush a group of merchants travelling to Plotsk or Warsaw. . . . Soon the whole region would lie in fear of them. But they wouldn't harm the poor, and in time, every dispute would be brought to them for arbitration. He, Zanvl, would be king; his pale Rachel with the beautiful black eyes and long black hair would be his wife, his queen!

Nevertheless, Zanvl had a sincere desire "to give up the life of a thief, as of tomorrow. He would avoid his old friends and soon the whole town would know that Zanvl had become an honest Jew."[30] Sigmund Freud probably articulated a widely shared view of secularized Jews when he said that "we hate the criminal and deal severely with him because we view in his deed, as in a distorting mirror, our own criminal instincts."[31]

The relationship of radical socialism, communism, and anarchism to conservative and right-wing concepts of crime and punishment also heightened anxieties about so-called Jewish criminality.[32] Karl Marx's ruminations on criminality were likely filtered through the discourse of Jewish emancipation. Marx obtained much of his insight about crime from his teacher,

Eduard Gans, who before his conversion and Professorship in Law at the University of Berlin had been one of the founders of the Wissenschaft des Judentums, the movement for the academic study of Judaism and Jewish history.[33] Gans, like his Wissenschaft des Judentums colleague Heinrich Heine, was well aware of the legendary Jewish robbers[34] and was acerbic when analyzing police and penal institutions. Historian Otto Ulbricht writes, "After 1830, Jewish banditry began to disappear, and after the middle of the century nothing more was heard of it. When full legal emancipation was finally reached in Imperial Germany in 1871, the Jewish crime rate was considerably lower than the Christian one." Herbert Reinke, however, has commented on the unfortunate coincidence of "the institutionalization of modern criminal statistics" in the 1840s with the last decades of significant Jewish criminal activity.[35] In other words, just as professional police and detective forces were emerging, the threat of Jewish criminality seemed more ominous than it actually was.

Although recent scholarship on Marx interprets his exposure to the legal theorist Karl Friedrich von Savigny (1814–75) to be of utmost consequence,[36] Gans may have had more influence on the young Marx. Marx's musings about crime poked fun at both Savigny and Gans but display an ironic detachment closer to the spirit of Gans, as his "Abschweifung über produktive Arbeit"[37] reveals: "A philosopher produces ideas, a poet poems, a clergyman sermons, a professor compendia and so on," Marx wrote. "A criminal produces crimes." After all, is the criminal not also responsible for "producing criminal law," and by extension, "the professor who gives lectures on criminal law and in addition to this the inevitable compendium in which this same professor throws his lectures on to the general market as 'commodities.' "? The criminal is responsible, as well, for providing the vocation of police, the entirety of the criminal justice system, "constables, judges, hangmen, juries, etc.; and all these different lines of business, which form just as many categories of the social division of labour, develop different capacities of the human mind, create new needs and new ways of satisfying them. Torture alone has given rise to the most ingenious mechanical inventions, and employed many honourable craftsmen in the production of its instruments." In terms of cultural "production," how could one conceive of the German classical tradition, Shakespeare, and even the Bible were it not for the phenomenon of criminality? "The criminal produces," Marx expounded, "not only penal codes and along with them legislators in this field, but also art, belles-lettres, novels, and even tragedies, as not only

Müllner's 'Schuld' and Schiller's 'Räuber' show, but 'Oedipus' and 'Richard the Third.' " In a statement that might be the closest Marx would come to saying something praiseworthy about Jews, he may have been paying a backhanded compliment by emphasizing the criminal vocations that were then seen as areas of Jews' special expertise: "The effects of the criminal on the development of productive power can be shown in detail. Would locks ever have reached their present degree of excellence had there been no thieves? Would the making of banknotes have reached its present perfection had there been no forgers?" No matter how marginal Marx might have been as a political organizer, his message to the powers that be was that their own authority could be construed as "criminal" in nature: "And if one leaves the sphere of private crime, would the world market ever have come into being but for national crime? Indeed, would even the nations have arisen?"[38] Last, applying his assertion that " 'religious sentiment' is itself a *social product,*" Marx postulates that organized religion would never have emerged if not for crime: "And has not the Tree of Sin been at the same time the Tree of Knowledge ever since the time of Adam?"[39]

Despite the aforementioned apologetic tendencies of Jewish scholars, at times Jews have been fascinated, and even enthralled, by the real and mythical exploits of Jewish crooks—though this interest is not synonymous with an internalization of the anti-Semitic discourse on Jews and crime.[40] Marx probably was moved by Spiegelberg's boast in Schiller's *Räuber* that he was "restoring the fair distribution of wealth, in a word bringing back the golden age."[41] The tensions over criminality arising from communist and socialist agitation are more complex and murkier than assumed. Leon Trotsky (1879–1940), the founder of the Red Army, born as "Bronstein" and later known as "Yanovsky" and "Antid Oto," was one of the most-hated figures among anti-Semites despite his apparent lack of empathy for Russian Jewry's distinctive plight. "But to posterity," Ivan Kalmar writes, "his best-known pseudonym was appropriated from one of his prison guards in Odessa—Trotsky."[42] We can safely say that those who perceived a threat in anarchism, socialism, and communism regarded such movements as an affront to law and order and frequently identified Jews as the left's most violent extremists.[43] Certainly this view had more than a kernel of truth because Jewish immigrants often were the backbone of diverse anarchist groups around the turn of the century. Among Jews sympathetic to anarchism, however, pacifists such as Saul Yanofsky tended to be more popular than, say, Alexander Berkman, the man who attempted to murder steel magnate Henry Frick.[44]

From the seventeenth to the late nineteenth centuries, European law enforcement officials sometimes categorized Jews, along with specifically "foreign Jews" and Gypsies, as a criminal menace, as was propounded by Friedrich Christian Benedict Avé-Lallemant and others.[45] Police forces and border guards justified their existence by such threats. Many people became fascinated with the so-called language of thieves, *Rotwelsch,* which has been examined by Sander Gilman and others.[46] Ave-Lallemant, about whom little is written, was a prolific German "expert" on crime in the mid- to late nineteenth century who was resurrected by the Nazis—despite the fact that he did not address the nascent "racial science" per se. He delved into the study of "Jewish criminals" and other groups he perceived to be social deviants. Most likely he did not see himself as an anti-Semite but as an upright Lutheran, an officer of the law and scholar who uncovered a branch of Jewry that had strayed from the path of normative Judaism.[47]

From the mid-nineteenth century to the 1920s, a number of Jews were drawn into discussions of criminality because of the historical legacy of "Jewish crime" and the persistence of Jews as a special category in criminological controversies. This phenomenon was especially apparent in Germany, where the euphemistically termed *Kriminalstatistik* debate, over the relationship of Jews to crime, never abated from 1848 to 1945 and beyond.[48] The debate cast *Kriminalstatistik* in at least three roles: first, as a supposedly neutral means of compiling data about crimes—a notion that is almost entirely a myth, as the compilations were rarely if ever separated from cultural predispositions; second, as an expression of societal obsessions with crime, usually an extraneous alien element; and third, as a subspecies of the second, a practice that mainly equated Jews with criminals. Historian Eric Johnson has shown that some of the contributions to this "debate" emerged not from anti-Semitism, or as a defense against anti-Semitism per se, but from an attempt to assert that Catholics constituted an unusually large number of criminals. Similar debates took place throughout Europe.[49] Those who found the Jewish presence in crime notable usually focused on two points: their contention that the Jewish religious tradition encourages or condones crime and the idea that Jews are criminals far out of proportion to their numbers. Favored writers among the anti-Semites included Theodor Fritsch (1852–1934, a.k.a. Thomas Frey), author of the *Antisemiten-Katechismus* (1887) and the *Handbuch der Judenfrage* (1907), both of which were published numerous times and inspired many disciples; August Rohling (1839–1931), best known for *Talmud-Jude* (1871); and Eugen Karl Dühring (1833–1921), author of *Die Judenfrage als Racen-, Sitten- und Culturfrage. Mit einer weltgeschichtlichen*

Antwort (1881). Arguments ran the gamut from abstruse, pseudoacademic articles to brisk, slogan-filled pamphlets geared to the lowest common denominator.[50]

Such controversies were generally directed against a pro-Jewish emancipatory discourse that attempted to rationally explain, and then overcome, the problem of Jewish criminality and hence facilitate the full inclusion of Jewry in civil society. The debates did not, however, delineate a clear trajectory of mounting anti-Semitism. Jews seemed able and adept at defending themselves until 1933. Against Rohling alone, Jewish writers responded with at least a dozen pamphlets. A few famous non-Jewish scholars, like Franz von Liszt, who confirmed that the evidence did not support allegations of disproportionate "Jewish criminality," took up cudgels.[51] Other non-Jews assumed a sort of middle-ground position, such as Heinrich Lux among the Social Democrats. Lux scoffed at the self-styled racists, claiming that their pretension to scholarship was just a dressing-up of their prejudices. But he claimed that there was, nevertheless, a problem of "Jewish crime," given the fact that impoverished Jews from Eastern Europe were entering the country and often faced poor prospects.[52] Sometimes anti-Semites argued with each other over the roots of their movement and statistics and chided each other for "crudeness"—as opposed to taking a calm, "scientific" approach.[53] Interestingly, in the Third Reich academic criminologists were certainly not the most virulent anti-Semites.[54]

Several Jewish writers, lawyers, and scholars joined these debates, which drove them deep into comparative crime rates of religious communities,[55] as well as into the recesses of the Talmud and other rabbinic literature—mainly via German translations. They therefore refuted the allegations that Jewish religious thought and traditions instigated and perpetuated Jewish crime and double-dealing.[56] A common trope on both sides of these debates was the writers' claim that they were, through their work, holding up "a mirror" to their adversary, showing his "actual" constitution and position—as opposed to his public presentation.[57] The Jews, too, sometimes disagreed with each other.[58] Those from different political groups studied the problem from their respective perches. Theodor Herzl and Louis Brandeis asserted that Zionism could be a means of preventing Jews' attraction to unsavory pursuits.[59] A number of Jewish doctors argued that Jews were less prone to criminality because of their low rates of alcoholism.[60] Overall, however, this aspect of the Jewish effort at "self-defense" ran parallel to the endeavors of Jewish doctors and scientists, as illuminated by John Efron, to explain and defend Jewish practices such as *brit milah* (circumcision) and *shekhita* (kosher slaughtering) against accusations that these rituals were barbaric and illegal.[61] With the rise of right-wing regimes in Germany and East Central Europe between the world wars, Jews were increasingly pressed to defend themselves when "the lofty principles of 'social defence' could be effortlessly distorted into cruel patterns of 'social aggression,' " and it seemed that the Nazis intended to push their version of crime and punishment as far as they could.[62]

Derek Penslar, in an authoritative study of German-Jewish economic behavior and its reception, argues that in the minds of many Germans, "Jewish criminality" was indicative of certain "types" and supposed tendencies that derived from a stereotype of the Jew as a beggar, who would use any means to scrape together a few coins.[63] Although there were not many Jewish pickpockets during the Weimar era, it was nevertheless common to speak of a lowlife pickpocket as a Jew, a type who had come to Berlin without official papers and with no "productive" work (*ohne produktive Arbeit)* and that especially inhabited the Scheunenviertel, the quarter of Berlin known for its "swarms" of Jews from Russia and Poland.[64] The notion of Jewish criminality, however, also was fueled by the stereotype of the rich and well-connected Jew as a conniving, relentless manipulator, drawing on the resources of a vast network of coreligionists (and their accomplices) to devise and carry out the exploitation of unwitting non-Jewish masses.[65]

Although no one can say for certain, concern about "Jewish criminality" likely would have lain dormant or subsided but for the Central Powers' defeat in the Great War and their subsequent crises and humiliation. Gerald Feldman writes that by 1916, circumstances were unfolding in war-weary Germany "in which a variety of traditional forms of social solidarity were breaking down and in which relationships and attitudes were taking on an ugliness nurtured by deprivation. The atmosphere was captured by the Police President of Berlin, who wrote:

> The reproaches concerning the present food situation are directed primarily against the producers and against the middlemen, who are without exception identified as speculators and war profiteers and who are assumed to be mainly Jews. The criticism leveled by a portion of the Berlin population against the measures of the communal, state, and Reich authorities, however, is also not very edifying. In any case, there is here at the present time a feeling of irritation that is not to be underestimated, which stems from the conditions described, from the long duration of the war, and

finally also a general nervousness produced by undernourishment and great overwork."[66]

This report was only one among many of growing anti-Semitism. The conspicuous presence of "Jews in the Central Purchasing Corporation (ZEG, or Zentral-Einkaufs-Gesellschaft), which managed the government food-import monopoly," along with traditional anti-Semitic stereotypes of Jews as unscrupulous cattle dealers and merchants with apparently captive markets, "made them obvious objects of suspicion in a society already inhabited by anti-Semitic charges." The allegation "that Jews capable of frontline duty were working at desk jobs and in garrison duty provoked the War Ministry to undertake the compilation of its notorious *'Judenstatistik,'* " a so-called census of Jews at the battlefront, "the interpretation of which became a subject of considerable controversy. One certain result was to intensify anti-Semitic sentiment." This situation was no doubt exacerbated in wartime by the "influx of eastern Jews from Russian Poland and Galicia" and by the fact that the Jews who populated the Eastern Front—largely the former Pale of Settlement—were seen as driving forces behind smuggling and other nefarious wartime pursuits.[67] Feldman is one of few serious scholars to concede that "many Jews, along with large segments of German society, were involved in black marketeering, smuggling, capital flight, and such activities." It was easy, however, to focus on them, as opposed to non-Jewish Germans, through "manipulating the Jewish 'question.' "[68]

Even before the end of the Great War, and throughout the Weimar period, anti-Semites attached accusations of wanton public criminality to specific persons whose "Jewishness"—whether they were Jewish or not—was claimed to be their defining characteristic. The individual who came to be identified with the worst excesses of the "inflationary economy" was Jacob Barmat. After having "worked closely with some leading Social Democrats in the importation of foodstuffs from the Netherlands after the war," he began "speculating with credits from the Prussian State Bank and the Postal Service during the inflation until his operations collapsed in late 1924 under the burden of a ten-million-mark debt. The case was used by the far right to launch accusations and charges of bribery and treason." A number of prominent Social Democrats were implicated, encompassing both wrongdoers and innocents; President Ebert (a non-Jew) was predictably defamed. Feldman states that "the significance of the affair was that it supplied grist for right-wing propaganda against Jewish black marketeers, as well as innocent politicians, especially Socialists and other supporters of the Weimar Republic." This became "an ideal way of whipping up the resentment of middle-class victims of the inflation and all those who felt that milk and other food supplies had been shifted about to the detriment of themselves and their children."[69] To a lesser extent, the case was exploited by the far left, in smears that occasionally evinced anti-Semitic attacks similar to those of the right.[70]

The Barmat case was shaped by anti-Semitism. Enemies of the Social Democrats were behind the creation of a highly partisan committee in the Prussian Landtag charged with investigating the case. The committee's main target was the leader of the Social Democrats, Ernst Heilmann; in fact, he was the chairman of the party's Fraktion in the Landtag. Although Heilmann, "a brilliant if brash politician," was known to associate with Barmat, whether he gained personally from this relationship is unclear.[71]

The term "November Criminals" typically refers to the men whom the right wing in Germany held responsible for the Central Powers' laying down their arms and accepting the Versailles Treaty to end the First World War, from which emerged the Weimar Republic, established on November 9, 1918. The right loathed the Versailles agreements for demanding supposedly colossal and ludicrous reparations, supported by the "war guilt" clause alleging Germany's overwhelming, sole culpability for the worldwide conflict. The claim that Germany did not have to consent to an armistice—that it could and should have fought on to realize the victory that was hers—became a staple of the right. The postimperial leaders' agreement—demanded, in fact, by the German Army—to end the fighting and the ensuing Versailles Treaty thus became known, on the right, as the "stab in the back."[72] The image of the *Dolchstoss* conveyed the notion that the politicians' actions emanated from a mix of left-wing ideology and personal opportunism, that their partisan interests overrode the good of the nation and the sentiments of the majority of its people. The *Dolchstoss,* the cardinal sin of the November Criminals, came to be intertwined in people's minds with a succession of financial scandals that greatly exacerbated anti-Semitism and seemed to bring stereotypes to life.[73]

Corruption and economic crises from different periods and circumstances were knitted together in numerous right-wing narratives and pictorial presentations. A slide show entitled "Jewry, Freemasonry, and Bolshevism" (Judentum, Freimaurerei und Bolschewismus)—purporting to reveal the "Kings of Corruption"—featured an attorney associated with the Social Democratic Party, (Johannes) Werthauer. The presentation alleged

Montage depicting the purported "Kings of Corruption," from the slide show "Judentum, Freimaurerei und Bolschewismus" ("Jewry, Freemasonry, and Bolshevism"). Desig. No. 4.559, W/S no. 04096, Photo Archives, United States Holocaust Memorial Museum, Washington, DC (USHMM). Reproduced by permission of the Bildarchiv Preussischer Kulturbesitz, Nuremberg.

that Werthauer was a confidant and helpmate of the notorious Kutisker. Most likely one of Werthauer's actual roles, in liberalizing abortion legislation, added to his infamy in the eyes of the Nazis. Jakob Goldschmid (Goldschmidt), a widely admired public figure, had been the head of the Darmstädter und Nationalbank (Danat or Danatbank), which collapsed in the wake of "the great banking crisis of 1931" that was obviously precipitated by the worldwide economic depression.[74]

The initial thrust of the right wing's efforts, however, was to destroy the president of the Republic, Ebert. The right made great hay of Ebert's recommendation in 1919 that "Barmat be given a permanent visa for his many trips to Germany." This action was considered to be aboveboard "since Barmat was at that time engaged in supplying Germany with food supplies." Although Barmat was accused of taking the food out of Germans' mouths, none of his "dealings with foodstuffs bore the slightest relation to the offenses of which he had been accused." But the anti-Semites on the commission persisted, "by means of unfounded statements and petti-fogging questions, to create suspicion against the President," which consti-tuted an important part of the campaign against Ebert.[75]

Barmat's jury trial in Berlin, which dragged on for more than a year, re-sulted in a meticulous 545-page unraveling of the complex case. This report was due, in no small measure, to a fair-minded and intelligent judge. "The formal findings," Erich Eyck records, "bore little relationship to the popu-lar indignation with which the proceedings had begun." Barmat was found guilty of two bribery counts "and was sentenced to eleven months impris-onment; half of the sentence had been served while awaiting trial. He was found innocent of all the other charges. This result is not to be regarded as Barmat's moral rehabilitation; on the contrary, the court made quite clear that it disapproved of many of his commercial acts. But all sense of the gross villainy with which the Barmats [the defendant and his brother] had been depicted for years is certainly absent from this judgment."[76] These pro-ceedings, however, were exceptional, as there were a number of "notorious cases in which the judiciary allowed itself to be used as the lackey of a blind nationalism that discredited the parties of the Left and other republican institutions through a campaign of systematic vilification."[77]

The belief became commonplace on the right that superwealthy, publicly known Jewish crooks, often in family groups, found fertile ground in the leftist governments following the demise of the *Kaiserreich* and effortlessly maneuvered the Social Democrats to do their bidding. This notion was concretized through a handful of highly visible Jews, as well as some non-Jews whom anti-Semites identified as Jewish, who were thought to be—and in some cases were—guilty of wrongdoing, and subject to public and judi-cial scrutiny. More often than not, the right-wing gutter press in pre-Nazi times and the state organs that succeeded them invariably cast any Jew under suspicion in the glare of his indubitable high crimes and saw any crime as proof-positive of the duplicity of the Jews in total.

There are a number of names, faces, and incidents in German anti-Semitica from 1918 to 1945 that are not necessarily well known to scholars of German, Jewish, and Holocaust history but triggered specific and strong reactions contemporaneously with regard to Jews and criminality. One Nazi tract from 1939 (from which the Nazis later drew extensively for a con-certed propaganda campaign) claims that "all one had to do was to say the names"—a sort of magical incantation—and the intended anti-Semitic vis-age would come into focus. Merely reciting the list neatly tied together black-market profiteers, speculators, Social Democrats, Jewish finance capitalists, and Bolsheviks, via the schemes and misdeeds of "Sklarz [Sklarek], Barmat, Kutisker, Holzmann, Bosel, and Castiglioni."[78] Along with citing the panoply of this group's misdeeds, including fraud, robbery, illegal arms dealing, and embezzling, the Nazis claimed that all of the players had been involved in narcotics trafficking. These kinds of scandals were said to be distinctively "Jewish domains," as were Weimar's ubiquitous and apolitical illegal gambling clubs.[79] Among these drug barons one could also count "the Chief Rabbi" of New York, Isaac Liefer.[80] (No such entity as a "Chief Rabbinate" has existed either in New York City or in the United States.)

There were, to be sure, "a few instances of Socialist association with political corruption, as in the Barmat and Sklarek scandals," but they were "isolated cases and rare exceptions."[81] Nevertheless, copious entries appear under each of these names in one of the great compendiums of anti-Semitica and other right-wing garbage—namely, the *Semi-Kürschner,* which served as a reference tool for the Nazis and their ilk and remains a source of inspiration for present-day anti-Semites.[82]

Anti-Semites raged that even the Jewish "martyrs," those the Jews claimed had had unfair treatment in the courts—such as Dreyfus—had won their innocent verdicts only through "swindles."[83] Pictures and thumbnail sketches of Barmat, Sklarek, and Kutisker—whom most Jews had wished to see brought to justice and duly punished—were frequently featured amid the gallery of so-called November Criminals.[84] But this very term, "November Criminals," has retrospectively limited the historical field of vision to the most prominent politicians: Friedrich Ebert, Philipp Scheidemann, and Walter Rathenau. However, those the right wingers called "Scheidemänner und Co." were castigated as "Jewish" and recalled from time to time to reignite the supposedly heady days when the *Freikorps* were battling communists on the German street, crushing the "Jewish masters" of vast "criminal endeavors."[85] The illustrated slim volume *Juden sehen Dich an* compiled by Johann von Leers reconfigured various non-Jews as Jewish, including Matthias Erzberger, Konrad Adenauer, Albert Grzesinski, Erwin Piscator, and Charlie Chaplin.[86]

Among Ebert, Scheidemann, and Rathenau, only Rathenau was Jewish. Rathenau's vilification by the right was intense even by grotesque Nazi standards. Some ten years after his assassination by right-wing thugs, Rathenau's photo was prominently displayed—with those of Bernard Baruch, Felix Frankfurter, Lord Leslie Hore-Belisha, Maxim Litvinov, and Kurt Eisner—in a poster declaring that "Those Who Pull the Strings—Are All

Jews!" An article in 1938 referred to Bernard Baruch as "the Rathenau America hates." Like Rathenau, the right wingers claimed, Baruch—through his admitted "speculation"—had plunged the United States into "financial chaos."[87] A similar role was reportedly played by Fritz Mannheimer in France, Germany, and the Netherlands, who increased his fortunes by speculating on, and manipulating a collapse of, the stock exchange and futures market. Among the beneficiaries of his dirty dealings were the old, established Jewish banking houses and the German Social Democrats.[88] The accusation of Friedrich Ebert's involvement in the Barmat scandal was thought to have hastened his death, at the age of fifty-four, in 1925.

In 1933, almost as soon as they came to power, the Nazis devised a minutely choreographed apprehension and incarceration of Ebert's son, Friedrich, known as Fritz. He was to be arrested and taken to the Oranienburg concentration camp along with Heilmann and four men who were charged with corruption in the radio-broadcast service of the former government—Hans Flesch, Alfred Braun, Kurt Magnus, and Heinrich Giesecke, none of whom were household names—and were said to be "corrupt criminals."[89] Heilmann, the editor of the *Chemnitzer Volkstimme* from 1909 to 1917, was a member of the Prussian Diet from 1919 to 1933 and of the Reichstag from 1928 to 1933 and was later killed in Buchenwald. He was singled out for abuse in Oranienburg as a "mob leader." Despite the fact that Ebert, and possibly others, were not Jews, "whenever Nazi visitors came to the camp, the six were presented to them: 'Just have a look at these Marxist criminals, profiteers, rogues, these greedy swine.' "[90]

When the Nazi daily, the *Völkischer Beobachter,* relaunched in February 1926 after it had ceased publishing in the wake of the failed Beer Hall Putsch, Hitler himself said the paper should be glorified because of its leadership in inflaming the Barmat scandal: "The hatred of Jews, of the Marxist criminals, of racketeers like Barmat and Kutisker, was poured out in no other newspaper as much as the organ of the NSDAP, the *Völkischer Beobachter.*"[91] The gutter press also rehashed the misdeeds of the Sklarek brothers, accused of running rigged gambling halls and selling drugs. It was alleged that they encouraged unwitting Germans to borrow increasing amounts of cash for "games of chance." Having no real opportunity to win, the public was cajoled to gamble more and then gouged with outrageous interest. All these allegations, the Nazis asserted, were backed up by the vaunted "criminal statistics."[92] National Socialists lauded their handling of the Sklarek case as one of the best examples of "modern propaganda" in a monthly devoted to professional journalists, *Unser Wille und Weg.*[93] To the extent that the Sklarek family is recognized in the annals of Jewish history, it is noted for the scientific achievements of a family member who died in 1915; the *Great Jewish-National Biography* of 1925 records that he fought for Germany in 1864, 1866, and 1871, before founding a leading scholarly journal.[94]

After Barmat, the figure who seemed to invoke the most scorn was Ivan Kutisker, who colluded with Barmat. Historian Martin Geyer has raised suspicion about whether Kutisker was in fact Jewish. No matter his origins, Kutisker, like Barmat, Holzmann, and others, was said to be an Eastern Jew—in this case, from East Galicia, with ties to his scheming brethren in Lithuania—whose intimates included Social Democrats and Zionists.[95] Despite the fact that these men were "high-finance" archcapitalists, anti-Semitic polemicists had no problem connecting them to communist fronts in Belgium, Holland, and Moscow.[96] The liberal "Jewish press," it was alleged, obscured the network behind Kutisker's crimes in his "defense."[97] One reason that Kutisker and Barmat inspired such scorn is the suggestion that they had used public institutions, not simply unwitting shareholders and associates, in gaining and absconding with their fortunes. The Nazis said that "Judko (Julius) Barmat was the protégé *[Schutzling]*" of Social Democratic leader Gustav Bauer, "who with his brothers Henry and David stole 30 million Marks from the Prussian State." Kutisker, "in league with Ivan Baruch and Michael Holzmann," the Nazis charged, "swindled 14 million Marks from the Prussian State Bank." Likewise, under a picture that seems to be retouched to make them appear as gangsters, it was reported that the "Sklarek brothers swindled the Berliner State Bank out of around 12.5 million, and another six to ten million disappeared without a trace."[98] Camillo Castiglioni, in contrast, was primarily seen as undermining the German automobile industry, despite the fact that he remained active in BMW.[99] In this respect the Barmat and Kutisker scandals reflect the anti-Semitism that flared up in the Panama Scandal in France's Third Republic, with much of the public furor exacerbated because of the notion that the all-knowing government (as opposed to the unwary investing public) had had a hand in propping up shady and dishonest ventures.[100] Yet in addition to causing a decline in the fortunes of Germans generally, Kutisker and Barmat, along with Sklarz, Jakob Michael, and Michael Holzmann, were accused of stoking inflationary fervor to swell their own fortunes.[101]

Intriguingly, the Jewish "capitalist" and suspected swindler who comes closest to the kind of pro-Communist conspirator the Nazis bewailed is not often featured, or even present, in their diatribes.[102] Perhaps the sole once-affluent Jew in Germany who did hobnob with revolutionaries such as Trotsky and Lenin and sent cash to the Bolsheviks was (Alexander) Israel Helphand (1867–1924), also known as "Parvus."[103] Although such a character seems tailor-made for Nazi propaganda, those who were aware of Parvus might have deliberately avoided dealing with him, because Parvus had reputedly participated in the efforts of the *Kaiserreich*, even before the German collapse leading to the armistice, to lend secret (German) support to the Bolsheviks.[104] He was, however, among the few men of his time to try both the capitalist and communist cards, and he died broke and miserable, not respected in any camp. His career, however, remains very much alive in debates about the "international Jewish conspiracy" in Russia.[105]

The demonization of these "openly venal and corrupt" men also coincided with what the Nazis perceived as their *Kulturkampf* with left-liberal forces. Bernhard Weiss, the reviled (Jewish) vice president of the Berlin police, was accused of promoting illegal gambling and pornography. *Rassenschändlich* films, peep shows, and sex clubs were both frequented by and protected by "Isidor" Weiss, the Nazis complained.[106] Ludwig Katznellenbogen, former director of the Schultheiss-Patzenhofer Brewery, came into disrepute for seeking to extend his control over beer brewing and the production of cement and yeast. The Nazis disregarded his conversion to Protestantism and particularly vilified him for his support of the avant-garde workers' theater of Erwin Piscator, which was no doubt due to the interests of his non-Jewish actress wife, Tilla Durieux (1880–1971).[107]

Although the right wing used these scandals for expressly anti-Semitic purposes, the scandals were not necessarily seen at their time as representing an "Aryan versus Jewish" conflict. Indeed, it was possible to attack many of these figures without raising their Jewishness as an issue. Germany's Jews, Donald Niewyk writes, "applauded stern measures against the malefactors" Barmat and Sklarek. Seeking to underscore their social and cultural distance from the more recent immigrants, they emphasized that "no German Jew had been involved in either case"—revealing their disdain for the so-called *Ostjuden*.[108] Levelheaded commentators realized that it was mainly non-Jewish Germans who were the "Kings of the Inflation," sometimes called "Rat-Kings."[109]

Yet it also was possible to use euphemisms to cloak anti-Semitic sentiments. "The Nazi slogans of 'System' and '*Bonzen*,'" Gerald Feldman

Image of a reputed "crafty scoundrel, Hoscheneck," identified as a "Jewish robber of the eighteenth century" in
"Judentum, Freimauerei und Bolschewismus." This picture, imitating the noted artist Johann Böcklin, appeared
in many publications beginning in the early eighteenth
century. For the slide-presentation version, see Desig. no.
4.557, W/S no. 07612, CD no. 0153, USHMM. Reproduc-
tion from a private collection.

argues, "like all their other slogans, were combinations of lies, slander, and
half-truths."[110] ("System" apparently refers to a network of insiders and
"*Bonzen,*" to party bosses.) As early as 1920 "the term *Volksschädling* had become a widely accepted code word for the Jew, a term used to identify those
who injured the people but which also suggested a noxious insect whose
elimination could only serve the public good."[111] It was common to describe the Sklarzes and their *Genossen* as parasites—without explicitly playing the Jewish card.[112]

The specter of the November Criminals certainly must have lost a great deal of its power after the Weimar democracy was obliterated and the despised Treaty of Versailles overturned by Hitler's diplomatic conquests. Nearly everything that was demanded had been secured even before World War II commenced in 1939. Despite the dramatic reversal of the nation's fortunes, the outcry was reinvigorated after 1933 against the "swindlers," the supposed supreme profiteers of the *Nachkriegszeit*, who had been connected to those in power. In this way the Nazis simultaneously hammered away at two main points: that the Social Democrats had never looked after the interest of the working class, instead aggrandizing the riches of the plutocracy, the Jewish Republic, some members of which were only a half-step from their Eastern European origins. Similar to Eduard Drumont's charges against the Jews in France, the Nazis warned that even though the Jews' numbers were small, they were a cancer in the German body politic. Furthermore, the Nazis repeatedly connected the Social Democratic associations and "high finance" criminal dealings of Barmat, Sklarz, and others to the Bolsheviks—who they claimed were the most bloodthirsty threat to humanity of all time.[113] To be sure, the fact that individuals "of Jewish origin" were prominent among the Bolshevik leadership, particularly its security forces, made this charge all the more vivid. Of course, there were no such organic Jewish connections except in the anti-Semitic imagination, and this notion hinged on all the guilty parties' acting first and foremost from a conspiratorial Jewish solidarity. The Nazis conveniently forgot that the Social Democrats, in their desire to cling to power, also had entered into a marriage of convenience with shady characters and literally with armies on the right—which was tragically crucial in giving the right wing a foothold to begin its ascent.

Even after 1933, despite the facts that anti-Semitism was deeply ingrained in German society[114] and increasingly brutal anti-Jewish measures were being justified in the guise of war-related exigencies, the Nazis apparently believed that simply telling Germans, in broad terms, that they should hate Jews was insufficient. From the nineteenth century onward, discourses in support of "Jewish emancipation and rights 'existed side by side' to those extolling anti-Semitic prejudice."[115] It is little wonder that in anti-Jewish polemics Nazis frequently seized on "the criminality of the Jews" and strategically deployed the so-called history of Jewish criminality.[116]

TWO

The Construction of "Jewish Criminality" in Nazi Germany

THE VAST MAJORITY OF JEWS in Germany were neither among the power elite nor suspected criminals before 1933. The philosopher Slavoj Žižek offers a penetrating analysis of the deliberate "paranoid, pathological" construction of Nazi anti-Semitism:

> Let us . . . take a typical individual in Germany in the late 1930s. He is bombarded by anti-Semitic propaganda depicting a Jew as a monstrous incarnation of Evil, the great wire-puller, and so on. But when he returns home he encounters Mr Stern, his neighbour: a good man to chat with in the evenings, whose children play with his. Does not this everyday experience offer an irreducible resistance to the ideological construction?
> The answer is, of course, no.[1]

Like many commentators on National Socialism, Žižek seems unaware that a great deal of improvisation and trial and error were involved in the process of separating Jews from "Aryans," with the criminal canard increasingly recognized as an effective instrument:

> On the level of discourse analysis, it is not difficult to articulate the network of symbolic overdetermination invested in the figure of the Jew. First there is displacement: the basic trick of anti-semitism is to displace social antagonism into antagonism between the sound social texture, social body, and the Jew as

the force corroding it, the force of corruption. . . . This displacement is made possible by the association of Jews with financial dealings: the source of exploitation and of class antagonism is located not in the basic relation between the working and ruling classes but in the relation between the "productive" forces . . . and the merchants who exploit the "productive" classes. . . . This displacement is, of course, supported by condensation: the figure of the Jew condenses opposing features. . . . Jews are supposed to be dirty and intellectual, voluptuous and impotent, and so on. What gives energy, so to speak, to the displacement is therefore the way the figure of the Jew condenses a series of heterogeneous antagonisms: economic (Jew as profiteer), political (Jew as schemer, retainer of a secret power), moral-religious (Jew as corrupt anti-Christian), sexual (Jew as seducer of our innocent girls).[2]

The Nazis gave much thought to how to cultivate hatred of Jews—even after murdering them. At different points during the reign of National Socialism, within the *Altreich,* the Nazis stepped up, refashioned, and relaunched their campaign of associating Jews with criminality.[3]

Numerous Nazi leaders, aping Hitler, went on record identifying Jews with "criminals," deriding them as "thugs and beasts of prey, who commit so many crimes that their elimination would enable the Reichstag to cut the criminal code in half."[4] The Nazis took pride and solace in quoting Martin Luther on Jew hatred generally and "Jewish criminality" in particular.[5] In 1935 a "typical speech" by Julius Streicher to the Hitlerjugend equated "the Jewish people" with an "organized body of world criminals."[6] It was possible for anti-Semites, and even those indifferent to Jews who were not moved by anti-Semitic ideology, to be impressed by the notion of a connection between Jews and crime. The vast majority of Nazis and their accomplices apparently found the proposition that "Jews have more or less criminal tendencies" to be unobjectionable.[7]

Interspersed in countless Nazi statements, reports, and orders were equations of Jews with "criminals" or "gangsters," which automatically jettisoned any ground for humane treatment. A Nazi poster that appeared between 1933 and 1935, and possibly afterward, urged Germans "not to do business with Jews, and to see Jews as enemies of the German people." It quoted the Chief Rabbi of Great Britain, Dr. Joseph H. Hertz: "The portion of Jews who engage in crime against the English war-economy laws [of World War I] have defamed Jewry and the reputation of Jews in England."[8] In this regard the Nazis employed a double standard: Jews were trustworthy as long as they testified to the "truth" of the stereotype. So-called Jewish knowledge was especially revered as sound source material for a wide array of Nazi "scholarship" and anti-Semitica.[9]

Some of the efforts of the Nazi State to demonstrate the criminality of Jews, such as the previously cited case against Benjamin Franklin, are in retrospect particularly ludicrous. Their opinion shapers were, however, desperate to show that the nation's Jews—who were overwhelmingly decent, respectable, and law abiding—were actually criminals, or latent criminals. For months, various ministries and security services devoted a flurry of absurd correspondence to substantiating that gangster kingpin Al Capone was "a Polish Jew" and "Legs" Diamond a "racial Jew."[10] (Both were well known in the United States as non-Jews.) It is surprising that anti-Semites did not make greater use of American Jewish gangsters, some of whom were especially notorious for "contract killings" during the grisly reign of "Murder, Inc."[11] The possibility exists, however, that the Nazis really could not distinguish Jews in the United States from Gentiles, because many of the Jews had normal-sounding "German" names. As Richard Wetzell has argued, although the German criminological discourse on Jews was not monolithic before the rise of the Nazis, all of the potential anti-Semitic strands were exploited, fused, and made prominent beginning in the early years of National Socialism.[12] Yet the most respected non-Jewish criminologists, however much they accommodated themselves to Nazism, did not lead the pack.[13]

It is little wonder that Victor Klemperer, with his keen gift of observation, noted the topsy-turvy world in which criminality would later indicate respectability, as he was arrested and imprisoned on the pretext of violating a blackout order:

> A very old Third Reich joke . . . gave me real consolation. Questionnaire of the fourth Reich: "When were you imprisoned under the previous government? If not, why?" It is honourable to be imprisoned now, it will be advantageous to any future character reference. I am not guilty of anything, I am not imprisoned because of my blackout misdemeanour, but I am in prison as a Jew. Nothing can truly humiliate me, every humiliation only raised me up and secures my future. I preach it to myself again and again, and it did help a little.[14]

Likewise, in the police photograph of one Moritz Reich, of Kitzingen—condemned to one year and three months in prison for "abusing the German greeting"—the accused appears somewhat bemused. His gaze at the camera expresses a calm feeling of "Can you be serious?" as opposed to shock or

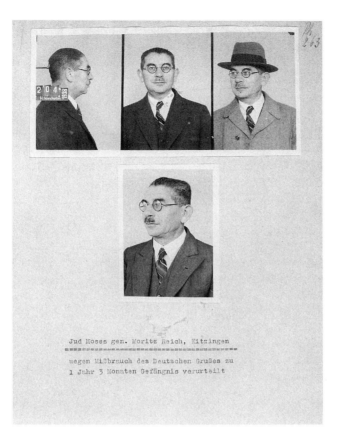

Jud Moses gen. Moritz Reich, Kitzingen
wegen Mißbrauch des Deutschen Grußes zu
1 Jahr 3 Monaten Gefängnis verurteilt

Moritz Reich, photo from files on "Jewish criminality" of
the Institut der NSDAP zur Erforschung der Judenfrage
(Nazi Party Institute for Research on the Jewish Question),
Frankfurt am Main, included in correspondence between
the Nazi press and various police and security services.
Folder 63, Berlin Document Collection, YIVO Institute for
Jewish Research, New York.

dread.[15] To exist as a Jew one had to, in the words of Harry Richard Loewenberg, "apply reverse standards," because Germany was now "ruled by criminals with criminal means."[16] At least one "Aryan" public official "was dismissed without notice and sent to a concentration camp for 'reeducation.' He had committed the crime of having on the street congratulated a Jewish neighbor on his 60th birthday!"[17]

Other Jews, sometimes surprising themselves, drummed up the courage to defy their persecutors openly. Shortly after her flight to England in 1939, Anna Bluethe wrote of her family's *Kristallnacht* (Night of the Broken Glass, November 9–10, 1938) experience in Kaiserslautern. She reported that upon leaving an interrogation at the local police station with her grandmother, "On our way home I overheard one woman saying: 'how high and unintimidated she holds her head.' At that moment she could not have said anything more encouraging and uplifting to me. Arrogance was not normally in my character—but perhaps some deep-seated martyr's pride of our ancestors manifested itself. I wanted to show these people that they could not bring us down."[18]

Klemperer even gives the impression that during his imprisonment his jailers knew that he was not a criminal, in any ordinary sense:

> My cell was opened: "You, go over there!" . . . in the circumstances the two ununiformed officials displayed an almost comical kindness. One lent me his glasses so that I could sign the statement, which did not help me much, and consoled me, saying that I would be getting my own back soon. The other, while taking the statement, asked "Religion, Mosaic?" The word Jew, stamped as a word of abuse, was avoided. It was as if here they did not want to accept the distinction between Aryan and non-Aryan, as if they wanted to have nothing in common with the Jewish persecution by the Gestapo and were a little ashamed of it. To the question as to religion I replied: "Protestant." Surprised look. "But your identity card?"—"By law, by descent." Silence, even greater politeness than before. I returned to my cell in better heart—but it was the cell.[19]

Anna Bluethe, as well, found that ordinary policemen were more civil to her and her elderly grandfather than were the Gestapo and the Nazi thugs who looted and vandalized her family's home: "The officer at the police station to whom we reported and gave our personal particulars was very correct and polite and asked us to return home after completing his task." She believed that "the regular police did not sanction the destruction and action initiated by the Nazis," resulting in their placing "a more civilized-looking man," wearing a railroad employee's uniform, at the entrance to their home—to dissuade further looting and violence.[20]

The experience of innocent Jews who were imprisoned has received little scholarly attention, which is understandable given that ghettos and concentration camps became gothic antechambers to death. In the wake of *Kristallnacht* some thousands of Jews "were viciously assaulted and tortured, often for several weeks, before they were released, physically and mentally broken. Several hundred men were murdered or killed themselves, in the days and weeks after their arrest."[21] The prison experience was for countless Jews absolutely devastating.[22] A woman imprisoned in Lutsk ghetto felt that all of her strength was drained from her, leading to hopelessness and "paralysis."[23] Although many realized their incarceration was "shameful," the shame was "not for us, but for those who had put us into this position. Nevertheless, to be put on display as a prisoner in the place where you were born and raised was a most painful sensation—especially if you were not guilty of wrongdoing—and I must confess that most onlookers were simply appalled."[24] One may contrast Bluethe's and Klemperer's treatment in custody with the assessment of historian Hsi-Huey Liang, who noted "how effectively and with what professional detachment the German uniformed police provided security to 'Aryan' property adjoining Jewish shops" when the SA destroyed and looted Jewish businesses, and that regular police behaved in similar ways in France, Belgium, Norway, and elsewhere.[25]

A major part of the Nazi effort to cultivate anti-Semitism among Germans, especially between 1934 and 1938, was the attempt to portray, and then to prosecute, Jews as criminals, for transgressing any number of rules, but especially as violators of laws requiring them to report their property and assets, rules for transferring funds, the "flight tax" and "atonement tax" (imposed after *Kristallnacht*),[26] and currency-exchange regulations. Although the systematic nature of this imposition of rules seems very clear in hindsight, Jews caught in its midst did not always see "a logical sequence of events," however much they were in "shock."[27] In Germany, and later in Nazi-occupied territories, Jews found that soldiers and officials made "higher and higher ransom demands as if conducting perfectly legitimate business transactions." The authorities made it known that once a Jew "stopped fulfilling those demands they will murder us all, in the same matter-of-fact manner" as they had earlier demonstrated.[28] Any attempt to emigrate opened Jews to charges of violating a number of laws. Before leaving Germany for the Netherlands in 1939, a "racial" Jew recalled that before getting permission to leave he had to have his luggage approved by the customs office; he had to secure

the permission of the foreign currency office of each and every single item I intended to take with me and I was not allowed to take out valuable items, for instance, items made of gold and silver (with the exception of a wedding ring and the gold that the dentist had mounted permanently in the mouth) nor a camera or a typewriter and so on. These rules had been tightened from time to time. For instance, now after the beginning of the War, no Jew may take with him more than he carries on his person. As far as money goes, I was allowed to take only the equivalent of 10 Marks in foreign currency. But even that caused problems: the bank where I had been a customer for almost twenty years, for this small amount demanded a special permit from the foreign currency department. When I applied for one there, it was refused . . . the reason given [was] that such a permit was not necessary. Finally I got the money at the Exchange Office of the Friedrichstrasse Station, but even there only after having submitted proof as to why I needed 10 Shillings and 3 Dutch Guilders.

When, after many visits with much trouble and long waiting, the list of my few belongings had finally been approved by the foreign currency office, I took my suitcase containing all my earthly possessions, the final result of 26 years of work in my profession, to the customs hall of the Central Berlin Freight Yard. In the overcrowded basement of one of the huge warehouses at the Lehrter Station I had to wait from half-past eight in the morning till seven o'clock at night till my few belongings had finally been cleared.

In the meantime, I had again to rush to Klein Machnow to the town hall and to the internal revenue office at Teltow on Kurfürstendamm to obtain missing receipts about paid taxes.[29]

Staying ahead of rapidly changing laws was impossible, because some of the crucial statutes were not released publicly, supplied only to ministry offices.[30] On June 14, 1938, any form of "Jewish business" was deemed illegal. On November 30, 1938, Jews no longer had recourse to courts of law in Germany, and Austria followed suit on December 31. Jewish doctors, dentists, veterinarians, and pharmacists could no longer practice by December 1938, accused of "crimes against the people." All of this activity played a crucial role in their denaturalization.[31]

Thousands of Jews faced a fate similar to that of the family of Victor Gans in Vienna after the *Anschluss:* numerous Nazis demanded bribery money for Jewish businesses to remain open. But all were targeted, and demolition typically occurred in stages. For three weeks, Gans writes, his father was imprisoned; then he had to sign a pledge "to leave the Third Reich within eight weeks. Our currency was changed from the Austrian shilling to the German Mark. AS 1.50 was 1 RM." The firm's accountant, "Mr. Lughofer [a non-Jew], who had been keeping our books for many years, was interested in our house." The Nazis gave Lughofer the house for less than a third of its value, and the Gans family never received the money from its sale. The Gans's leather-goods business that had thrived for decades was driven into the ground, its remaining wares pilfered. All these steps occurred between March and August 1938.[32]

The bureaucratic manifestation of systematic defamation and theft turned Jews into criminals for refusing to relinquish their property and assets. On February 21, 1939, Jews in Germany were forced "to surrender their gold, platinum, silver, precious stone, and objects of art to purchasing offices of the Ministry for Economy, [the] compensation to be fixed by the Ministry." Everything the Jews owned, Foreign Minister Ribbentrop claimed, was "stolen German property."[33] In Germany, as well as in Poland, the Netherlands, and elsewhere in Nazi-controlled Europe, Jews' refusal to give up money, furniture, works of art, houses, and even the clothes off their backs became a criminal offense.[34] One of the best-known cases on the corporate level is the fate of the Petschek mining enterprises. In Göring's effort to "Aryanize" the firm in 1938, the Justice Ministry informed him that he had no legal basis for its appropriation. The government wished to avoid any abrupt measure, because it feared disruption of the mines. The Finance Ministry came to Göring's rescue: it would provide a pretext by claiming that the company had cheated on its taxes. That charge "proved to be the lever which toppled the Petschek empire." In October 1938, as the Germans stormed through the Czechoslovak Sudetenland, "they took possession of the I. Petschek headquarters in Aussig, with a view to discovering further tax delinquencies." Nazis hailed this episode as a reversal of the earlier order in which Jews had controlled the legal system.[35]

Furthermore, the publicity about individual and corporate resistance to "Aryanization" in the 1930s made Jews seem responsible for the economic travails Germans were facing and fueled fears that the illicit actions of Jews would cause another round of hyperinflation.[36] The Nazis, to justify their measures, raged that Jews in European states that had not imposed rigid restrictions were playing havoc with national economies. In Yugoslavia, for instance, they alleged that Jews had used "grain speculation" to provoke a depression; later, they said this economic feat was perpetrated through an "artful dodge" masterminded in Chicago, New York, Winnipeg, Liverpool, Buenos Aires, Paris, Bucharest, Czernowitz, Constance, Istanbul, Rotterdam, and Amsterdam.[37] In Hungary "Jewish sabotage" was said to have prompted a government crackdown against Jewish "big business," especially publishing, which was alleged to be overwhelmingly in Jewish hands.[38] The Netherlands was compelled, the Nazis charged, with having to defend itself against sedition and terror instigated by Jews who had fled there from Germany between 1933 and 1938 and who were literally snatching bread from the mouths of the native Dutch.[39]

A statistic from the nearly extinguished Jewish community in Germany in 1942 is telling: that year sixty-one Jews were accused of *Rassenschande,* fifty-seven convicted for passport fraud, and fifty-six convicted of currency violations. Information is not available on how many of the "accused" of the first category were convicted. The main reason for the high proportion of *Rassenschande* cases was the existence of numerous German-Jewish couples (possibly with a non-Jewish partner contemplating conversion), intending to marry, who were living together when the Nuremberg Laws were enacted. Such "mixed" couples were prevalent in the minuscule community extant until 1942. Another reason for the high rate of accusations of *Rassenschande* was what Nathan Stoltzfuss has termed "the resistance of the heart," "the unwillingness of mixed couples to separate in the face of a blanket marriage prohibition" and aggressive prosecution.[40] Before 1942, however, non-*Rassenschande* "offenses" probably constituted much more than two-thirds of "Jewish crime" in the Third Reich.

To complement these policies, the Nazis sought to make ordinary Jews akin to convicted felons and stereotypical gangsters. For example, an article was accompanied by portraits of three men described as "Jewish thieves" (*jüdische Gauner),* who were said to have duped Englishmen and Italians in Berlin with their heinous schemes. Accuracy, of course, was never a Nazi priority. If a portrait did not reflect any particularly menacing quality, a caption would be affixed to give the proper impression, such as "This is him! The Smuggler-King, the Jew Leuchttag."[41] Mild-mannered and unthreatening-appearing Jews were condemned in the strongest possible terms for "crimes" such as attempting to circumvent the "Aryanization" of their businesses. Of greatest concern was reinforcing the notion that Jews are crooks who are motivated only by greed.[42] The main objective in local newspapers was to depict Jews as endemically corrupt and prone to lawbreaking, thereby complicit in undermining the social order and fiscal strength of the regime. The point was to demonstrate the reasonableness—by conventional legal and moral standards, relatively devoid of racial considerations—of anti-Semitism, and in particular, to break down the barrier of respect for real-life Jewish men and women.

When the Nazis discussed Jewish crime in the abstract, they were sure to mention "receivers of stolen goods, fraudsters, crimes against respectability,

From a newsletter article accompanied by portraits of three men described as "Jewish thieves" *(jüdische Gauner)*. The caption proclaims, "Characters of the Talmud look you in the eye." Interestingly, the men portrayed may not be Jews. "Talmudgesichter blicken Dich an," record group 222, folder 64, Berlin Document Collection, YIVO Institute for Jewish Research, New York.

and racial pollution." By 1938, even after five years of Nazi crackdowns, they bemoaned that Jews were still dominant in receiving stolen goods and claimed that many had managed to retain their businesses by falsely "Aryanizing" them. "Jewish doctors," the Nazis vaguely claimed, had violated codes of morality. But when they had to locate cases of Jewish impropriety against Aryan womanhood, the examples were bizarre and infrequent—even though the cases resulted in hangings.[43] Hermann Leyes recalls that in 1933 he was summoned to court twice. In "normal times" the charges would have been laughable, but it was clear that these were attempts at entrapment: "In the first lawsuit a young woman brought an action that I was the father of her child. Confronting me in the court, however, she stated, 'Why, I've never in my life seen this man.' " He left the court amid "general laughter." The second suit seemed to lead to my being found guilty of "miscegenation." I could not deny that I had traveled in my car to Cologne in the company of a young woman and had returned with her the following day. Would they believe me and her that I had taken her along at her own request when she heard that I was going to Cologne on business? If they did not believe me, I feared being dragged off to a concentration camp or something even worse. Her fiancé's courage saved me. The young man stated under oath that the young woman had spent the night with him.[44]

Indeed, the failure of these attempts to entrap Leyes, and certainly others like him in the early months of Nazi rule, probably helped focus the efforts at Jewish criminalization on the realm of the financial and legalistic. In these areas the authorities were less dependent on the inevitably perjured testimony of non-Jews that might blemish the record of an "Aryan" woman. In the concoction of cases against individuals,[45] in order to rob them, humiliate them, and force them to leave Germany—if leaving was still a possibility—the notion that Jews were untrustworthy and duplicitous is much more important than the idea that they were a pathological threat.

On a pseudoacademic level the Nazis argued that Jews had striven assiduously to nurture sociopolitical and legal edifices to allow for the free rein of Jewish criminality. Some of the best legal minds in the nation, who had not before been known as anti-Semites, indulged in this campaign.[46] Progressive concepts such as "social reform" and "humane treatment" of the accused were alleged to be smokescreens for Jewish interests, including leniency toward the accused. The Nazis and their collaborators suggested that Jewish lawyers, and Jews who had been central in the development of "criminal psychology and psychiatry," had cleverly designed bureaucratic havens for crooks and devised means for Jews to avoid prosecution. Jews had supposedly pioneered the notion that criminals were led to their acts by environmental forces or circumstances over which they had no control *(Schicksalsverstrickung)*. Formerly high-positioned and influential Jewish academics and officials had engaged in a "cult" of criminality, using their respectable professions as a cloak.[47] Through protecting pawn-broking, bail bonds, and other inherently dishonest practices, the goal had always been the impoverishment, swindling, and sundering of Germany.[48] In the business world, the Nazi claim was that Jews were able to use the laws of "bankruptcy" and "receivership" *(Konkurs)* and "partial satisfaction of creditors" *(Ausgleichsverfahren)* to their devious advantage.[49]

A vast number of survivors' recollections attest to the centrality of "criminalization" within the Nazi program and to Jews' diverse reactions to it. These people's diaries and memoirs show that the Nazis' efforts to criminalize Jewry succeeded in damaging or breaking the spirit and bodies of some Jewish victims. But in a number of instances the victims—who correctly identified their Nazi persecutors as thugs, robbers, and murderers—inverted Nazi allegations of Jewish criminality, as did Victor Klemperer.[50] Surely the activities that the Nazis identified as horrid crimes, Jews' efforts to find ways to flee the country and to help fellow Jews, along with their many varieties of resistance, were (and are) seen quite differently by Jews.[51] A survivor from Vienna recorded that between the *Anschluss* and *Kristallnacht* her grandfather,

> a wealthy man, [who] was a respected member of the stock exchange, and a pillar of the Jewish community . . . kept busy, together with my mother, by contacting his clients—notifying them that he would buy back all the securities at the same price at which they had bought them. He saved many people from total disaster because, as you know, Jews had to sell their securities at Juden Preise which had plummeted to near nothing. To my grandmother he explained, "Darling if Hitler gets me I want to be naked, I want to have NOTHING and if Hitler doesn't get me . . . then G'd will help."[52]

Few records remain of this type of effort to obstruct the fleeing of German Jewry, because if caught, such Jews would have been subject to the severest of penalties.

In the wake of *Kristallnacht* the Nazis feared that Jews might appeal to the courts to recover their losses, which was likely because the Nazi State did not admit to perpetrating the violence. As Hilberg relates, the Justice Ministry responded with a decree forbidding German Jews from registering "legal claims in any case arising from the 'occurrences' of November 8–10. The 'foreign Jews,' " those who held citizenship in countries other than Germany, "who had suffered injury or damage, naturally had recourse to diplomatic intervention and claims against the State." This decree frustrated Hermann Göring, who was told by the Foreign Office that he would have to answer to the United States: "[The United States] was in a position to retaliate. Göring replied that the United States was a 'gangster state' and that German investments there should have been liquidated long ago." But Göring grudgingly admitted that the matter did have to be considered.[53]

There was no such qualification, however, by the SS newspaper, *Das Schwarze Korps,* which stated that the "extermination" *(Vernichtung)* of the Jews was necessitated by their "criminality." Their actions warranted their treatment as "ordinary criminals" who had to be "annihilated" *(auszurotten).*[54] A poster that was plastered around Germany, with a picture of Herschel Grynzspan (whose murder of a Nazi official in Paris provided the pretext for *Kristallnacht*), proclaimed, "Enough of this pack of criminals!" and "Germans are not fair game for Jewish criminals!"[55]

The Nazis did not simply "report" instances of Jewish "crimes": they meticulously shaped and wildly exaggerated the instances that came to light, and totally manufactured specific crusades against these alleged criminal actions.[56] Perhaps this strategy is most transparent in the requests from the Nazi Central Party Archives in 1936 for members to supply material showing unequivocal "proof of Jewish traitorous plans and activities."[57] In the short term this material was to be used to "defend" city and NSDAP officials in Danzig against charges by local Jews of character defamation. Undoubtedly, had anything been unearthed, it would have become fodder for numerous articles. But the replies did not yield what their seekers had hoped.[58] Among the responses by various bodies were statements that no such evidence could be found. Nevertheless, the Party persisted in its claims.[59] At the behest of Kurt Daluege in particular, repeated attempts were made to give the utmost publicity to "Jewish criminality."[60] These requests were often accompanied by the names of companies believed to be Jewish owned, against which action needed to be taken.[61] Publicity about Jews and criminality aimed to inspire Germans to bring charges against Jews who were seen as violating their interests, and to unmistakably "criminalize" them in total. In the wake of *Kristallnacht* Göring could not have been more explicit: in order to rationalize their "fine" *(Kontribution)* of one billion marks, his very "definition" of Jews pointed to those who had committed "abominable crimes."[62]

In addition, the Gestapo and other security services made available anti-Jewish material, such as that used in criminal cases, to *Der Stürmer* and to ostensibly less inflammatory local newspapers for their ironically termed "work of 'enlightenment' " *(Aufklärungsarbeit).*[63] Giving official sanction to a policy that had long been in place, a "Strictly Confidential" memorandum from the Nazi Zeitschriftendienst (Periodical Service) of January 9, 1942, stated that "in view of the task" of further exacerbating anti-Semitism, "it is expected that German periodicals will make comprehensive use of the material appearing in the *Deutsche Wochendienst* to conduct the orientation on Jewish guilt with a tenacity that leaves no doubt in the mind of anyone that every single Jew, wherever he is and whatever he does, is an accessory to crime."[64]

Nearly every article that appeared accusing a specific Jew of a "crime" states that the "criminal" received a prison sentence that did not appear to be grossly inhumane. For instance, "the currency smuggler" Emilie Kahn, who was said to have "concealed her vast wealth," reportedly had received a prison term of one year along with confiscation of her assets.[65] Although this effort at defaming an entire people consisted largely of reporting Jewish "crimes" and punishments, as much as possible *Der Stürmer* and other papers tried to accompany articles by photographs, as evidenced in a request for "a picture of the Jewess Jenny Sarah [sic] Freundlich, born August 1, 1904."[66]

Amid these calls for grist for propaganda, as well as encouragement to spread the word far and wide, internal memoranda reveal the depths of Nazi hypocrisy.[67] Notably, a report was circulated—in confidence—in the spring of 1944 containing detailed statistics on crime in Germany. Jewish crime is indeed mentioned, but it clearly made up a small proportion of the total. What is distinctive, instead, are two categories: crimes perpetrated by youth and those of "foreigners," who one may assume are forced laborers from Eastern Europe. Most strikingly, the document reveals that contrary to the Nazis' claim to have restored order and security, there was little difference between the level and types of criminality during the First and Second World Wars.[68] Goebbels himself, apparently having read this report or something similar, wrote in his diary on June 4, 1944, that criminality in wartime Berlin developed "normally," untroubled by the notion that its main causes were supposed to have been rooted out.[69] Leading Nazis knew well, however, that murdering all of their Jews had not fostered a total, organic unity of upright Germans. By the fall of 1944 National Socialism was engaged in "a struggle against youth cliques," which the Party saw as a fundamental threat to its authority. The most disturbing trend was the prevalence of youths who evinced "a criminal-asocial outlook" *(Cliquen mit kriminell-asozialer Einstellung);* next were those with "a political-oppositional outlook," and third were those with "a liberal-individualistic outlook." There could scarcely have been a more striking admission that the endeavor to stamp out these tendencies, by murdering their Jews, was a total fraud.[70]

Material accumulated for a planned anti-Semitic newspaper in the files of the Institute for Research on the Jewish Question in Berlin makes several points of strategy apparent. The Nazis tried to show that anti-Semitism existed everywhere—and thereby that the Nazi program was in no sense unique or harsh and that everywhere Jews existed there was a recognized menace of "Jewish criminality." Reflecting on the attempt to prove that Al Capone and "Legs" Diamond were Jews, they also wished to convince Americans that their crime problem was actually a Jewish problem.[71] But as the Nazis developed their case, no corner of the world was untouched. Egypt, they reported, was plagued by the gold smugglers Ralph and Albert Stern; Argentina was investigating the corruption of the Jewish beer brewer Bemberg; the Bolivian government had been threatened by Jewish financial duplicity; in Bulgaria the police were compelled to take sharp measures "against Jews and bandits"; in Denmark "the big Jewish swindler" Max Rothenberg, who had embezzled around six hundred thousand kronen, received a sentence of four years' imprisonment and was forced to pay court costs. Rothenberg was furthermore prohibited, for the rest of his life, from resuming his profession as an upper-level judge. In France the police apprehended the brother of the former French prime minister Leon Blum, Marcel Blum, and his wife for carrying false papers. And even the Nazis' enemies sometimes showed their good sense by denouncing Jewish crimes. The story was reported during the war, supposedly based on information from a captured British officer, that Jews were peddling tainted blood for transfusions at the front and that "many English and American soldiers died" as a result. As an added insult to the British, Jews were entering Palestine illegally, compelling the colonial administration to intern them on the island of Mauritius. Jews, the Nazis claimed, were the ones primarily responsible for unrest in Vichy France: "three Polish Jews" were arrested in connection with the murder of a village mayor. Here and in other reports Jewish partisans were termed "terrorists" and "bandits."[72] Jews, the Nazis claimed—in one of the most grossly hypocritical statements of all time— had stolen art treasures in Normandy, and the U.S. "finance minister," Henry Morgenthau, was in possession of the famed Bayeux tapestry. In Italy one hundred Jews were killed as a reprisal for an anti-Fascist murder. Even the Poles had their own Jewish problem, as the Nazis related a story of massive Jewish desertion from the Polish army. The Jews of Palestine themselves were forced to deal with criminal terrorists who were thwarting their own designs, the Stern gang. Although the newspaper for which these stories were collected never materialized, the Nazis found multiple forums for them in their publications, especially in the *Mitteilungen über die Judenfrage.*[73] The failure of any party in the Evian Conference in the summer of 1938 to open its doors to Jews was smugly interpreted as proof that all the world's nations shared such views. England in particular, Nazis liked to claim, had an acute distaste for Jewish emigrants.[74]

In all of these stories is a mix of reporting, from relatively reliable sources and from their own dubious organs, and pure fantasy. The point, however, is that this "reporting" presents criminality as the predominant, consistent trait among Jews. Concomitantly the Nazis used a number of discernible visual strategies: Jews were consistently photographed in the "anthropometrical" style of "mug shots," originated by the nineteenth-century French criminologist Alphonse Bertillon, who was himself a believer in inherent Jewish criminality. This style was achieved in part by forcing those photographed to place their head into a metal brace, which is visible in side views.[75] The Bertillon method employed here, and in some of the concentration camps, was different from that used for the compulsory photo-identification card for Jews beginning in 1938, in which the photo was supplied by the subject.[76] Although existing portrait photographs were often placed in police files, they were hardly ever used in the press. The caption accompanying pictures of "Currency Smugglers!" Max Schul and Simon Friedmann, claiming they had been sentenced to six- and ten-month prison terms, plus fines, respectively, were typical, as were the shots of Leopold Rosenzweig and Haim Weinberger.[77] Survivors' memoirs reveal exactly how the photographers made Jews look like thugs. One survivor recalled, of his time in a Viennese prison, "It was not difficult to tell who was a Jew during our daily walks [in prison]; while the others were permitted to get a shave twice a week, we did not enjoy such a privilege. So we had to march[ed] unshaved and unkempt so we would look more like criminals."[78]

When Jews were shown "appearing" like Germans, especially in folk costumes—as was typical before National Socialism—the reporting charged that they were deviously trying to "camouflage" themselves. "Isidor has himself photographed," is the caption of two typically German portraits: "As a native of the Tyrolean region and as a fraternity man. Two pictures, two costumes, one Jew!"[79] A picture labeled "Is this a fisherman's family on the Ostsee?" follows with the rejoinder: "No, it is a photograph from the Löwenstein Studio that sticks the shitty Jew Achselweiss there with his family." Similarly, the caption of a Jew dressed in Bavarian folk costume mockingly proclaims: "Saul turns himself into a super-Bavarian."[80]

"Jews in prison," a survivor writes, "were photographed and their pictures were published with idiotic captions and lies. After weeks of imprisonment, those pictures, to be sure, were not exactly flattering."[81] The proliferation of these ridiculous images continued throughout the Third Reich,

Jüdische Devisenschieber!

Max S c h u l, geb. 11.9.1910 in Hannover,

erhielt wegen versuchten Devisenvergehens
6 Monate, 1 Woche Gefängnis und RM. 6000.- Geldstrafe.

Simon F r i e d m a n n , geb. 9.7.1914 in Antwerpen,

erhielt 10 Monate Gefängnis und RM. 12000.- Geldstrafe.

Despite being arrested for what is generally considered white-collar crime—evading currency-exchange regulations *(Devisenschieber)*—the accused, Max Schul and Simon Friedmann, were made to seem like ruffians. Folder 63, Berlin Document Collection, YIVO Institute for Jewish Research, New York.

Der Stürmer photograph called "The Talmud Triptych." From *Der Stürmer* Archive [SAr], Stadtarchiv Nürnberg, E39 No.393/6, neg. 10472, Desig. no. 485.15, W/S no. 58812, CD no. 0375, USHMM.

including years after most of their subjects had certainly been murdered. In the German press dozens, if not hundreds, of documentary-style pictures appeared that were supposed scenes of Jews involved in criminal activity or "looking" like crooks. One photograph of two men with Jewish-star armbands sitting on a bench reads, "Two old crooks."[82] Judaism and Jewry are equated with criminality in a picture labeled "The Talmud Triptych," which supposedly identifies "the 'lookout' next to the thief, and in between is their 'receiver.' "[83] A group photo of nine older Jewish men with yellow stars is labeled "Criminals from the very beginning. Can these crooks, all of whom are common criminals, be convicted, so that none of them will be released from prison in their lifetimes?"[84] "One is just like the other!" proclaims another caption. "Five wearing Jewish stars, five of the circumcised, five talmudists, five crooks from the Generalgouvernement."[85]

Although the Nazis employed malicious humor to try to make Jews seem pathetic, Jews did not have the prerogative, even as "prisoners," of using any type of humor. This probably helped fuel the rich trade in jokes in the ghettos, as Emmanuel Ringelblum and others attest in the case of Warsaw. "Jewish humor," or "Jewish jokes" (*jüdische Witze*), the Nazis charged, were part of an insidious criminal plot by Jews to make Gentiles believe that Jews are lighthearted and weak willed, which would serve to lull Christians into submission while Jews bilked them in innumerable ways.[86]

Women as well as men were described and pictured as criminals, perhaps to prevent any sympathy that might be more evident for women than for men. Even a white-haired seventy-two-year-old woman, Anna "Sara" Rosenheimer, was such a threat that she had to be confined to the big prison in Ulm.[87] A newspaper photograph, labeled "A Jewish Screen," in which a "Jewish" store was renamed to mask its ownership, was reported to be the property of the "Jewess Seligmann."[88] One should not assume, articles inferred, that women simply followed the dictates of their devious husbands, as reports emphasized that "a married couple" engaged in currency fraud.[89] To drive home the point that Jews who had been regarded in pre-Nazi times as respected members of the community must be shunned, the press ironically used the headline "Again, an 'Upstanding' Jew," to detail the crimes of Reinhardt Brock, who allegedly "gave 'counsel' to fill his own pockets."[90] A subtext was that Brock was a man whom the greater community had held in esteem.

Such patterns of texts and photographs likely evolved and persisted because conventional photography—straightforward pictures of Germany's Jews—did not indicate significant Jewish difference from "Aryans." As has been explained by George Mosse, Saul Friedlander, and others, the Nazis were obsessed with images and image making.[91] As I will show in a later chapter, this obsession even extended to Auschwitz, where the official photographic regimen helped nurture the myth that Auschwitz was a prison.[92] Indeed, some "news" articles seem to have intentionally avoided using photos because of the pleasant appearance of the alleged perpetrator.[93] The Nazi press never showed blond Jews; dozens of pictures of fair-haired Jews remained in files or within envelopes. Contrary to the teachings of racial anti-Semitism, few police photos showed "Jewish criminals" with disproportionately large, hooked noses, or big ears; most people in the photos were "normal" looking.[94] Ironically, the very style of the Bertillon anthropometric photos, with straight-on and side views, often made for stark contrasts to anti-Semitic caricature. In one extensive archival collection, the only photo of a Jew with a big nose was part of a series of pictures that sought to prove that Jews resort to rhinoplasty to "camouflage" themselves.[95]

In most cases, therefore, pictures of so-called Jewish criminals were by necessity joined to carefully worded captions and articles so that the intended message would be clear. Moreover, this program complemented portrayals

Such pictures, which apparently did not fit the stereotype, were ignored. From the files on "Jewish criminality" of the Institut der NSDAP zur Erforschung der Judenfrage. The files do not state for what crime Rella Eltes and Benno Hofstätter were arrested. Folder 64, Berlin Document Collection, YIVO Institute for Jewish Research, New York.

of "criminal" Jews across time, professions, and national boundaries and included a revival of eighteenth- and nineteenth-century literature about Jewish robbers.[96] Bolshevism, according to the Nazis, was criminality and "mass murder" at a national level,[97] as leading communists and socialists could only be understood in a continuum of crooks, sexual perverts, and murderers. To the inextricable mesh of anti-Semitism with anti-Bolshevism, exacerbating both, the Nazis often added the specter of criminality as an exclusively Jewish preserve.[98] Perhaps the greatest irony in the Nazis' criminalization of Jewry is that the Jew who seemed to most embody the stereotype was none other than Dr. Bernhard Weiss, formerly the Deputy Chief Constable of Berlin. He was one of the city's highest-ranking and most venerated policemen. Even more to the Nazis' dismay, Weiss was said to be physically and mentally tough and always challenged Nazi attacks. Goebbels wrote and assembled a volume of over 150 pages to ridicule him.[99] As Nazi propagandists grasped for ways to teach their children anti-Semitic stereotypes after having annihilated German Jewry, they waxed nostalgic about the days when they had "Isidor" Weiss as a presence in Berlin to malign.[100]

As scholars such as Peter Longerich, Christian Gerlach, Götz Aly, and Susanne Heim have shown, the task of anti-Semites and perpetrators of genocide in the Holocaust was made easier when they couched their efforts in terms of allocation of scarce resources, especially limits of food supplies—thus giving a more logical reasoning for inhumane and murderous policies.[101] The Nazi discourse on criminality, as well, was in part cultivated to appeal to Germans and their supporters without having to rely on the more mysterious racial doctrines. One of the more terse statements, mentioning "heredity" and "disposition" but curiously omitting a reference to race, was a directive to the German press on April 2, 1943, that accompanied a special issue of its weekly guide:

> Jews are criminals. Continuing its series of contributions on the criminal elements in the ranks of the enemies of Germany and her allies, the *Deutsche Wochendienst* again deals with Jewry. As the actual reason for their treatment, the mention of Jewry in the last speech of the Führer may be taken, further, [that is] the crimes of Bolshevism and the Jewish orgies of hatred against Germany in Great Britain and the USA. . . . It must be emphasized that with Jewry it is not the same as with other peoples, that there are individual criminals but that Jewry as a whole springs from criminal roots and is criminal by disposition. The Jews are not a nation like other nations, but bearers of a hereditary criminality.

As a final point, reverting back to Luther and the robber bands—with the German Jewish community nearly exterminated—the Nazis proclaimed, "The criminal class of all lands speaks a specialized language, of which the most important elements are hebraic."[102]

This statement was followed by "specific instructions on what to emphasize and what to avoid in the editorial treatment of the Jewish problem." Among the "subjects and suggestions" from which editors were to draw were the blood libel, white slavery, the robber bands in early modern times, swindlers, frauds, sex criminals, murderers, and "financial" criminals.[103]

A handful of Nazi authors—including Herwig Hartner-Hnizdo, Johann von Leers, Hanns Andersen, and Josef Keller—who authored books with footnotes and published in pseudoacademic journals and newspapers, sought most explicitly to tie the myth of a Jewish race with what they described as the proof of "Jewish criminality." The entire history of Jewry, they claimed in their nearly interchangeable works, was punctuated by manifestations of the "true" character of Jews as criminals, reaching its dénouement in the establishment of Bolshevik rule in Russia. Jews, they claimed, were not only the main perpetrators of crime; they invented and reinvented it. Synagogues, even after their desecration and destruction, were identified as "criminal caves."[104] In this mix there is almost no criminal of note without Jewish ancestry or connections; numerous non-Jews are scooped up as fodder in these supposedly fact-based accounts. One of the reports' most interesting assertions, which might be among the few bits of historical insight, is that the American Jewish gangster Max Eastman was the first criminal to escape from a bank robbery in an automobile, pioneering the concept of the getaway car.[105]

None of these books seemed to be well known or frequently cited before 1943, but one of the authors, Johann von Leers, was a moving force in numerous dimensions of the Nazi project, especially in the realm of education.[106] All of the pseudoscholarly claptrap spewed out by these men was propelled from obscure journals and the back pages of Nazi newspapers into the screaming headlines and mock exposés of the Nazi press in March 1943, as the transports from the ghettos in Kovno, Bialystok, and Warsaw were speeded up. Moreover, at this moment some Nazis who were not totally blind sensed that the Third Reich might not emerge victorious. The men in charge of publicity were groping for alibis as early as the final surrender of German forces at Stalingrad on February 2, 1943. Eventually, simply being a Jew was beyond the pale of the German Reich; as one survivor wrote in a memoir, "Human beings were being sent to the gas chambers just because it was a crime to be a Jew."[107]

THREE

The Self-Fulfilling Prophecy
of the Ghettos

The only way Jews can live these days is to break the law. . . .

In a refugee center an eight-year-old child went mad. Screamed, "I want to steal, I want to rob, I want to eat, I want to be a German."

FROM *The Journal of Emmanuel Ringelblum: Notes from
the Warsaw Ghetto*

SETTING THE SCENE IN HIS 1936 novella, *Beichte eines Mörders: Erzählt in einer Nacht* (*Confession of a Murderer, Told in One Night*), Joseph Roth describes a clock hanging in a dingy café.[1] Frozen at the moment it broke, the clock does not just fail to tell the time; it "ridicules" the very notion of time. Throughout the Third Reich, Victor Klemperer and other sensitive observers perceived that hundreds of terms no longer held the same significance they had before 1933. The words often demeaned or ridiculed what Nazism's opponents saw as the original, unequivocal intent or gist.[2] Of these, "resettlement," which became a euphemism for deportation, ending in certain death, is one of the most notorious formulations, exposed as a fraud well before the end of 1942.[3] An analogous notion in the literature of "totalitarianism" received its best-known expression in George Orwell's *1984,* in which Big Brother deems that "War is Peace." Although the Nazis used a number of euphemisms to malign Jews and to cloak atrocities and mass murder, the National Socialist conflation of Jew and "prisoner" into an essentialist construct perhaps deserves more scholarly attention than it has elicited. Martin Broszat, analyzing "the phase of revolutionary take-over 1933–4," specifies that *Schutzhaft* (protective custody), a leading concept in the Third Reich that derived from the emergency decree of February 28,

1933, was not devised "as an instrument for dealing with punishable offences but as a 'preventive' police measure aimed at eliminating 'threats from subversive elements.'" A privy councilor (*Regierungsrat*) in the Gestapo, Hans Tesmer, wrote in 1936, "Whereas hitherto," that is, before February 28, 1933, "the police, under Para. 112 *et seq.* of the Code of Criminal Procedure, could only make arrests as auxiliaries of the Public Prosecutor when he was instituting criminal proceedings, or could under certain conditions . . . take people briefly into police custody, they were now entitled, when combating subversive activities, to use the most effective means against the enemies of the State—deprivation of freedom in the form of protective custody." At Nuremberg Tesmer based his defense on the claim that the Gestapo "was a State police organization similar to police systems to be found in other countries," that "it acted within the German penal code to prevent political crimes and to maintain the security of the State," and that it had "suppressed illegal concentration camps and other abuses."[4]

Rather than take at face value the idea that Jews, whether in their places of prewar residence or as "deportees," were "prisoners" of the Nazis, we need to understand the edifice behind this assumption.[5] Interestingly, in German the term *Häftling* translates in English both to "prisoner" and "detainee." Although Jews were routinely called "prisoners," the vast majority of Jews under National Socialist control were neither prisoners of war, as defined by the Geneva Convention, nor prisoners as envisaged in modern criminological discourse—that is, inmates of a penal system who are suspected, or have been convicted, of a specific infraction of the law. As captives of the "preventive" or "preemptive" concept of National Socialism,[6] Jews were in effect suspended in a state between that of a detainee, as persons held for some wrongdoing that (usually) remained to be established, convicted felons, and those awaiting execution for a capital offense. Another rationale for treating Jews as prisoners was the idea that Jews were "born (and habitual) criminals," according to official Nazi racism. Most significantly, this reasoning was equivalent to classifying all Jews as criminals who deserved no "rights" under the law.[7] The creation of ghettos and camps, shaped by local conditions and actors as well as by the vicissitudes of wartime, was a chief means by which National Socialism sought to attain a pure Aryan state, in order to institute and perpetuate its dominance. In this respect, Jews were clearly subjects and victims of a massive racial experiment and a program of (supposedly) biologically based social engineering enacted on a previously unimagined scale. Yet the idea that Jews comprised a social threat, by virtue of their alleged criminality, also played

This photograph from *Der Stürmer* bore the following description: "Criminals from the very beginning. A snapshot from the Generalgouvernement." The men were from Nazi-occupied Poland. From SAr, E39 no.394/11, neg. 10473, Desig. no. 485.15, W/S no. 58826, CD no. 0375, USHMM.

a sizable role in the massacres of the Einsatzgruppen and in the evolution of ghettos and concentration camps in the Third Reich.

Overwhelmingly, Nazis could be counted on to presume that Jews deserved to be treated as prisoners. Yet National Socialism actively cultivated the association of Jews with criminality, legitimating its treatment of Jews as prisoners *(Häftlinge)* in enclaves where Jews mixed with non-Jews and in facilities fashioned exclusively for Jews. Jews needed to be contained and closely watched, the Nazis contended, because of their propensity to criminality, and they had to be dealt with aggressively, because Jewish communal existence was an incubator for vice.[8] A great amount of thought, energy, and effort was directed, then, to substantiating the stereotype that Jews in occupied Poland were always and preeminently a community of crooks and that the key to managing and controlling Jews en masse was to deal with the phenomenon of Jewish criminality. This strategy spanned both normal "policing" and "national security," which the Nazis repeatedly sought to justify by means of photojournalism.[9]

In his pioneering study of the Lodz ghetto, Isaiah Trunk asserted that "the entire legal-administrative system that the Germans introduced into the ghettos was a mockery of the most elementary principles of legality, even in times of war. Therefore, the concepts of 'crime' and 'punishment' were very elastic in the ghetto," if not meaningless, given the "absence of rights" and "arbitrary" nature of the penalties imposed—including count-less deaths by shooting, hanging, and beating.[10]

In the process of ghettoization and the murderous sweeps of the Ein-satzgruppen, the charge of "Jewish criminality" played at least as significant a role as the purported threat of Jews as a biological menace. This fact is im-plicit in one of the more transparent Nazi reports on the annihilation of Eastern European Jewry, the *Jaeger Report*. The "Jewish criminality" canard was ubiquitous and provided ideological support for Jaeger and other Ein-satzgruppe operatives.

Sizing up the decimation of Lithuanian Jewry from the summer through winter of 1941, the commander of Einsatzkommando 3, SS-Standartenführer Karl Jaeger, reported that a few weeks before his unit "took over" in early July, around four thousand Jews had been "liquidated by pogroms and exe-cutions." These murders were carried out by the Nazis' accomplices, the so-called Lithuanian partisans, who are not to be confused with partisans who fought the Germans with guerilla tactics. The "Lithuanian partisans," Jaeger inferred, had incited and carried out "pogroms" like those that had flared intermittently for centuries in Central Europe and, most intensely, after 1881 in Russia and Poland. These "partisans" on the Nazi side also enacted individual, small-group, and mass executions.[11]

According to Jaeger's discriminating, detailed account, the troops under his command engaged in "security police duties" *(Aufgaben sicherheitspol).*[12] His men believed they had conducted a formidable campaign of public service. Its culmination was the moment Jaeger's men released a group of (non-Jewish) Lithuanian prisoners and encouraged them to go about their normal lives. Jaeger's detachment, members of the Security Police (Sicherheitspolizei, SP or Sipo) and the Reich Security Service (Sicherheitsdienst, or SD), found the locals' obsequiousness and displays of gratitude embarrassing, as "women, children and men with tear-filled eyes tried to kiss our hands and feet."[13]

One might almost think that by performing their "police" duties, the men of Einsatzkommando 3 were attempting to suppress or prevent the kinds of wanton destruction perpetrated by the "Lithuanians." Jaeger omits the fact that a great deal of the dirty work was carried out by the in-digenous Lithuanian police and other officials such as "forest rangers," who had been under Nazi orders since late June 1941.[14] The *Jaeger Report,* how-ever, exposes the scope of Nazi murder as wider ranging than that of the na-tive Lithuanians; Jaeger's victims included not only Jews and supposed po-litical opponents but also the infirm and mentally ill. Their work, Jaeger simultaneously boasted and complained, was conducted "systematically," requiring "painstaking preparation."[15]

What was left unstated—one of the reasons the campaign took such meticulous planning—was that the nearly one hundred locales listed in the *Jaeger Report,* which records the numbers of Jews killed—divided into men, women, and children—were not simply the cities, towns, and villages where Jews lived. In many cases the victim numbers indicate a town's or city's residents—but in addition, the place names subsume Jews who were gathered from neighboring towns and villages, some of which had only one or two Jewish families. For example, the town Krakes (*Krok* in Yiddish), which appears under the entry for August 28 to September 9, 1941, tallies the number killed at 448 Jewish men, 476 Jewish women, and 201 children, for a total of 1,125.[16] But the reported breakdown of victims masks what was behind these numbers.

The Jews murdered in Krakes were not only those of that town but also the residents of *shtetlakh* like Pašušvys, Grinkisis, and Saukotas *(Shakot),* places that do not merit mention in the most arcane Nazi document. In these tiny settlements a single armed Lithuanian policeman, a public official serving the Nazi Security Police, loaded Jews onto horse-drawn wagons—parents and children—knowing that they were to be shot in Krakes. A witness to the sight of the families being taken away in Saukotas recalls the scene, reliving the horror, as "a black day." The children were gently placed in the wagon, on top of bedding to ease their rough journey; these were the witness's playmates, whom she knew were going to be slaughtered. Her father had worked for and with their father, who owned a small lumber mill. No more than five or six Jewish families lived in Saukotas. The woman recalled that there had not been bad relations between Jews and non-Jews in the town; all the children played together, they were friends.[17] The space that was once occupied by the wooden *shul* remains empty.

Indeed, Jews in similar towns in the Kovno Guberniya thought that they "got along fairly well with their Lithuanian neighbors until the war broke out." The pretext for the Lithuanian aggression, and cooperation with the Nazis, was that the Jews had dealt "with the Soviet regime and with the families of those who were able to escape to the Soviet Union."[18] Jews, too, openly lamented the fact that a few "Jewish communists" among them had openly sided with the Soviet Union in its vicious yearlong occupation.[19] Anguished by her memories, the woman in Saukotas exclaimed, "But what could we do? This was the policeman, who claimed to be doing his job, with the might and authority of the Nazis behind him."[20] Although historians have undertaken the essential groundwork,[21] they have barely begun to discern the matrix of killing that the Nazis perpetrated in those bloody months.

It is intriguing that in the *Jaeger Report*, which was not intended for the press or otherwise for public consumption—"a secret Reich matter" (*Geheime Reichssache*)—an SS man describes his unit's work as a "police task." Why did Jaeger, the equivalent of a colonel in the SS, not describe these deeds as a project of racial cleansing or as a state service in the name of eugenics? After all, he and his men expended great effort to annihilate all of those who were "undeserving of life" according to Nazi racial ideology. Were the Nazis and SS not, above all, concerned with "race"? Interestingly, Jaeger's only recourse to the term "hygiene" was in bemoaning the sanitary conditions in an overcrowded Lithuanian jail. Listing a woman, originally from Germany, who was killed on January 9 in Mariampole because she had married a Jewish man, Jaeger calls her a "German citizen"—not an "Aryan."[22] For those who were not slaughtered by the Einsatzgruppen, the Nazi occupation usually entailed confinement to a ghetto.

Ironically, at several stages throughout the Second World War Jews perceived being incarcerated in a "prison" as preferable to confinement in a ghetto. On May 11, 1941, Chaim Hasenfus noted in his diary that he "had a conversation" in the Warsaw ghetto,

> typical of the times—with three ladies who had recently been released from prison. They had been sent there for several months for not wearing armbands or for living outside the ghetto. All three were wealthy and well educated; all three were Catholics—one was even born into that faith. The Germans turned them back into Jews. One of the ladies explained that most of the women in prison were Jews who had been christened—the wives of Polish officers. Twenty-five people are kept in one cell. The daughter of the second lady is still in prison, and the husband of the third was sent to a prison in Siedlce. All three talked about passing secret messages, and the whole experience of prison made such an impression on the youngest that she's collecting literary accounts of prison experiences. They claimed that in general they were much better off there than in the ghetto.[23]

Other Jews, however, found the experience of imprisonment in Warsaw literally unbearable. A friend's mother, Samuel Puterman writes, "died in the Central Jail" of Warsaw. "The old lady had gone out to buy bread and forgotten to put on her armband. She ran into some gendarmes on patrol who sent her to prison. After two weeks she died of a heart attack."[24] By the middle of 1942 conditions in both the Pawiak and Gesia Street prisons in Warsaw were horrific. Yet the Gesia Street jail was visited at least once by an international humanitarian organization—which recognized "oddities" but failed to grasp the nature and scope of Jewish and Gypsy (Roma and Sinti) persecution within its walls. Emmanuel Ringelblum recorded that the

> delegation from abroad that visited the jail was unable to comprehend how people could receive death sentences merely for crossing over to the Aryan side of Warsaw. This, they declared, is inconceivable. These people must have committed some crime on the Other Side. The jail was ideally clean (for the delegation!). [They were shown] a special bathroom where the prisoners were bathed and disinfected twice weekly. Most of those arrested were beggar children who had sneaked out to the Other Side; a number were smugglers. These were the chief criminals. The plaza that used to be covered with tile has been transformed into a flourishing garden whose fruits will bring in more than 200,000 zlotys. The garden is tended by prison gardeners.[25]

The SS administrators of Theresienstadt, despite the effort to make the camp appear to be a civilized enclave to the outside world generally and the International Red Cross in particular, also were obsessed with the phenomenon of "Jewish crime" in their cynical theatrical exercise. "Legality" was bound to be a problem within this system, a sham from its inception. Yet distinct from the ghettos, the Jews of Theresienstadt could claim that they had a "right" to exist, which the (debarred) lawyers especially attempted to press.[26] The Nazi prodding of the Jewish council to set up a ghetto patrol, economic control agency, and detective division served the Nazi myth that Jews were to a great extent autonomous and that a main function of the camp was to ensure "law and order" among the inherently unruly Jews. "Criminality," as in the rest of Nazi-controlled Europe, was largely a factor of the deliberate malnourishment of the population. Certainly some "brutes" and "opportunists" took advantage of the situation, but most "crime" consisted of hoarding and "smuggling." A huge amount of energy went into playacting and histrionics, trying to show that the specific and general punishments exacted by the Nazis, even in the confines of Theresienstadt, fit the Jews' "crimes." Though the official statistics on "Jewish criminality" were exaggerated, this fact did not mean that there was a total absence of crime. Some "real" crimes went unreported because the Jewish administrators knew that their reports would result in certain "transport." Hence, the Jews manipulated their own "criminal statistics."[27]

According to an anonymous "former lawyer" who was in Warsaw's Jewish police until escaping to the Aryan side in January 1943, for "the Jewish inmates imprisoned at Pawiak, Mikotów, or Danitowiczowska . . . misdemeanors were punishable by death; they fell under the jurisdiction of the Special Court and were prosecuted by the German authorities." In the summer of 1942, the Jewish Council of Warsaw itself was moved into a building at Zamenhofa 19, which had been home to both Russian and Polish military prisons.[28] Likewise, the selection of the site of the Lodz ghetto was most likely influenced by the stereotype of Jewish criminality.[29] "The ghetto in Lodz," Lucille Eichengreen recalls, "was closed off from the world with barbed wire, and we lived in isolation, surrounded by armed guards, in the former Batut section of the city. This area, which had been the poorest, most run-down district of this large industrial city, now 'accommodated' Jews who were essentially captives. Before the war, thieves, black marketeers, and other unsavory characters lived among hard-working, honest Jews and Christians, but once the war began, the Christians were made to leave."[30] The historian Isaiah Trunk, however, is unabashed, admitting that Batut had been home to the prewar "Lodz Jewish underworld." It was especially known as a haven for pickpockets, with the so-called chief of the pickpockets—a thief with a good heart—one of the chief gangsters.[31] Furthermore, it is no coincidence that two of the most notorious, unconcealed killing grounds of the Holocaust, Auschwitz and the Ninth Fort (Kaunas, Lithuania), had been, respectively, a "prison camp" and a prison—in a more conventional sense—which no doubt eased their transition to installations of "extermination."[32]

The classification of Jews as prisoners in ghettos raised the possibility—in the minds of a few Nazis—that National Socialism and the war effort would be better served by having the prisoners perform hard labor and otherwise be made "productive." Historian Christopher Browning has discussed this phenomenon in the Starachowice labor camp (in central Poland), and a humane approach to incarcerated Jews was exemplified by their treatment at the hands of Major Karl Plagge at the HKP (Heereskraftfahrzeug-Park 562), the repair depot for motorized vehicles in Vilnius.[33]

Just as other aspects of the Nazi treatment of Jews became self-fulfilling prophecies, National Socialism contrived and nurtured bizarre situations to accentuate the stereotype that Jews were prone to criminality, and that criminality, especially smuggling, "black marketeering and theft"[34] were endemic in any Jewish milieu. Natan Zelichower, a dental technician in prewar Warsaw, who "lost both his wife and daughter . . . despite his tremendous efforts to free them from the *Umschlagplatz* [deportation area]," described the Warsaw ghetto as "one huge mass of castaways doomed to extinction, subsisting on a daily diet of anguished news and heart-wrenching notices. . . . Shadowy figures emerged from the depths of the blackened city to feed off the street like leeches, and these in turn feed others, even to the point of nourishing delusions of a bright future built on easy living and abundant earnings."[35] Criminality, in this sense, is analogous to the Nazi interweaving of myths and realities about contagious diseases, especially typhus, to bolster the anti-Jewish policy. "In a bitter twist of fate," a historian writes of the Warsaw ghetto, "German policy thus unleashed the very epidemic that had been invoked as the rationale for sealing off the Jewish district in the first place. Famine led to typhus, typhus was followed by tuberculosis, and after that came the deportations."[36]

In a diary entry of April 2, 1941, Chaim Hasenfus wrote, "Tens of thousands of Jews have been relocated from the provinces and crammed into a closed district inside Warsaw, which was already packed with half a million. The move has meant the ruin of many families. Add to that the range of economic prohibitions and it's no wonder that people are turning to begging and thieving."[37] The Nazis cited the supposed criminality of Jews as a reason for their confinement in ghettos, as well as for harassing them with a barrage of legislation that further circumscribed their ability to move about and to provide basic sustenance. Stanislaw Sznapman, who escaped the Warsaw ghetto in July 1943, recalled that in the first weeks and months after the Nazi invasion, "a huge propaganda campaign designed to vilify Jews in the eyes of Poles" was launched "to drive a wedge between Poles and Jews and to thwart possible joint action against their common enemy. . . . Walls were covered with posters depicting Jews as repulsive and dangerous criminals or as vampires sucking Polish blood."[38] A series of photographs were staged to show that Jews presented a threat to security by having buried caches of weapons. As a special affront to non-Jewish Poles the Nazi Sicherheitsdienst in Warsaw "discovered" that the graves of Polish soldiers had been used for the Jews' potential arsenal.[39] As the Criminal Police and the Gestapo competed over who was to get greater control of the Lodz ghetto, Kriminalinspektor Bracken supported the extension of his jurisdiction by saying that "in the ghetto live, at any rate, about 250,000 Jews, all of whom have more or less criminal tendencies." This statement was considered convincing, and his "detachment moved in." In February 1941 the three factors necessitating the creation of the Warsaw ghetto were cited

A staged photograph of the Nazi Sicherheitsdienst (SD), Security Service, forcing traditionally dressed Jewish men to unearth weapons supposedly hidden by Jews in the grave of a Polish soldier in Warsaw, taken between October and December 1939. The photographer was Arthur Grimm, an SS photographer documenting the so-called investigative work of the SD in occupied Warsaw for the *Berliner Illustrierte Zeitung*. Reproduced by permission of the Bildarchiv Preussischer Kulturbesitz, Nuremberg (WWII 23); Desig. no. 481.053, W/S no. 26613, CD no. 0243, USHMM.

as "first, epidemics; second, Jewish black market activity and price gouging; and third, 'political and moral reasons.' "[40]

The Nazis were always eager to demonstrate that the ghettos were awash in crime. Jews were accused of hiding valuables that they were supposed to have turned over to Nazi authorities, thereby making possession of these goods a crime. They were required to give almost anything useful or movable to the Nazis. "All ghetto inmates," SA Captain Jordan ordered in Kovno on August 30, 1941, "must hand over their electrical appliances such as kitchen stoves, ovens, etc."[41] After extensive regulations were promulgated requiring registration of remaining possessions, on September 3, 1941, the Kovno Jews were informed:

All Ghetto inmates must deliver immediately, by 6 P.M. September 4, 1941, at the latest, the following articles to the Council for their transfer to the respective authorities:

1. Any money in Russian or German currency exceeding 100 (one hundred) rubles per family.
2. All valuables, including gold, silver, precious stones, and other precious metals, or items made from such metals.
3. Securities, receipts of deposits (if there are any).
4. Valuable paintings, valuable fur products, and furs (except for sheepskin and very worn furs), good carpets, and pianos.
5. Typewriters.
6. All electrical appliances, including those which can be used for medical or professional purposes.
7. Good materials for suits and coats.
8. Cows and poultry.
9. Horses with harness; carts.
10. Stamp collections.

Emphasizing the severity of the crime of withholding these items, the statute specified, "If this duty is not followed scrupulously and completely, it is not only the offenders who run the risk of the death penalty, but all other Ghetto inmates." Furthermore, the Nazis attempted to prod Jews to inform on violators, stating that they were "aware that some items are buried or otherwise concealed. In view of the risk to which individuals as well as the total population are exposed, it is absolutely necessary to find and deliver these items." Not surprisingly, "many denunciations written by Ghetto inmates" reached the Gestapo.[42]

Synthesizing reports from numerous locales and levels of administration, Raul Hilberg writes:

> Already in 1940, several agencies busied themselves with the task of "discovering" hidden ghetto treasures. Such activities led to accusations of "sabotage" and "corruption." In Lodz, a Criminal Police detachment had established itself inside the ghetto. From this vantage point, the detachment hauled out so many goods, gold and valuables that the Ghettoverwaltung complained of "sabotage." On October 23, 1940, the Criminal Police and the Ghettoverwaltung made an agreement to the effect that all goods confiscated by the detachment in the ghetto be delivered to the Ghettoverwaltung. On its part, the Ghettoverwaltung declared that it

would have no objection, if Criminal Police personnel "reflected" upon certain items and wished to buy these at appraised prices.

The open sale of Jewish property was deemed legal, while the Jews' possession of goods was illegal hoarding. The Nazis themselves, including the upper echelons, were aware that corruption, feeding off of stolen Jewish goods, was rampant.[43]

One of the most striking and effective means by which the Nazis endowed their Jewish policy with the appearance of autonomy and the pretension of law and order was through the establishment of "Jewish" police forces. This term, although true to the time and useful for historians, is a misnomer. With rare exceptions, the "Jewish police" was a purely Nazi concoction, and it often included men who did not consider themselves Jews but were deemed Jewish through Nazi racial doctrine.[44] In Warsaw "converts" or so-called baptized Jews occupied "the most important posts in the Jewish Council, the police, and similar institutions," Emmanuel Ringelblum wrote, perhaps with some exaggeration, in September 1941. "They look after each other. They push their way into every situation, and are very successful. Some of the rabbis and nationalist Jewish elements have begun to put up a fight, have called meetings, but so far without results." Driving home the notion that the Nazis would always call the tune, the Jewish police force of the Warsaw ghetto, on the day of its inception (November 16, 1940), "was ordered to dance on one foot around a group of Jews performing calisthenics in the street."[45] In most ghettos the Jewish police "became an institutional accessory to murder"; in Warsaw in particular, "the gradual co-opting of many of its members" was said to be "one of the ghetto's greatest tragedies."[46] Ringelblum expressed his fiercest revulsion in the face of evidence that

very often, the cruelty of the Jewish police exceeded that of the Germans, Ukrainians, and the Letts. They uncovered more than one hiding place, aiming to be *plus catholique que la pope* and so curry favor with the Occupying Power. Victims who succeeded in escaping the German eye were picked up by the Jewish police. I watched the procession to the wagons on the Umschlagplatz for several hours and noted that many of the Jews who were fortunate enough to work their way toward the spot where the exempted people were standing were forcibly dragged back to the wagons by the Jewish police. Scores, and perhaps hundreds, of Jews were doomed by the Jewish police during those two hours. The same thing happened during

Jewish police in the Kolbuszowa ghetto allegedly demonstrating "how Jews beat each other." Part of the Norman Salsitz collection, Desig. no. 444.2, W/S no. 67242, CD no. 0076, USHMM.

the blockades. Those who didn't have the money to pay the police were dragged to the wagons, or put on the lines going to the Umschlagplatz.[47]

It is little wonder that the Jews of Warsaw lambasted the Jewish police as " 'gangsters,' derision that was flung at them hundreds of times" during meetings to condemn "the melancholy practice of kidnapping" for "press gangs." "The Jewish gangster police," Ringelblum fumed, "exploit every situation to make money."[48] Jan Mawult, a Jewish policeman in the Warsaw ghetto, understates the fact that "inherent in the setup was the potential for corruption."[49] In the Lodz ghetto were a "summary judgment court" (Schnellgericht), a prison, a "reformatory" (oysbeserung-hoyz) for juveniles, and a "Moral Hygiene Department" supposedly dedicated to stamping out prostitution, all of which were under direct orders of the Nazi Kriminalpolizei (Kripo) and later the Ordnungsdienst (the Jewish police, or Jewish Order Service).[50] On May 8, 1942, Ringelblum confirmed that "the [Pawiak] Street prison has become the point of departure for Oświęcim [Auschwitz]." In its own right, though, the facility was "a center of persecution" where "the prisoners are tortured ceaselessly," and large numbers of inmates were "taken from the prison and shot outside, right in the street." By the summer of 1941, the prisons for Jews in Warsaw were running out of space for both the living and an increasing number of corpses, the disposal of which "became a very pressing problem."[51]

The man chosen to be the prison commandant in Lodz was a notorious thug, Sh. Hercberg, who was known for cruelty and sadism; the "reformatory," at least for some time, was run by "a woman from Frankfurt" who had experience "in Germany in similar penal institutions for adolescent criminals, and a specially assigned Order Service functionary."[52] Symcha Spira, head of "the so-called Ordnungsdienst" in Kraków, had a uniform specifically tailored for him "with all kinds of distinguishing insignia." Immediately he "became a 'big shot' " who exploited his position in every possible manner. The "Civil Division" of the Kraków Jewish police wore "blue jackets with lapels and neckties," whereas the rest of the force, the "Odemans," had "coats buttoned to [the] neck," and all of them had patches on their right sleeves identifying them, in Hebrew characters, as Ordnungsdienst. According to the perceptive memoir by non-Jewish pharmacist Tadeusz Pankiewicz, the Gestapo preferred to have the "Civil Division" do its dirty work. One of Spira's chief henchmen was Szymon Szpic, whom Pankiewicz described as "a man of about fifty-five years, drawn, slender, tall, swarthy faced, slightly stooped, with a fixed sneering smile on his face." He was infamous in prewar Kraków because of a well-publicized "trial for fraud." He was found guilty of "swindling people out of their money" by promising to find them jobs. "He was sentenced to several years in prison." In Warsaw he was described as "the terror of the ghetto—pity the man who started a quarrel with him."[53] The Nazis attempted to show that the plight of the Jews was exacerbated by their cruelty toward each other, despite having been given the means to police their own enclaves.

In Warsaw the Jews in "law enforcement" positions had varied reputations. Adam Fels supervised the so-called *Arrestanstalt* (the Pawiak Jewish prison). Jan Mawult recalls,

Unasked and under no one's orders, he performed acts of kindness, such as delivering letters or packages to family members, and helped in any way he could whenever there was an explosive situation involving the [Jewish police]: a roundup, individual detentions, or finally at the terrible *Umschlagplatz*. He wanted to do something and he accomplished a good deal; probably everyone he encountered has only the best recollections.

He was one of the few—the very few—who shunned all honor or advantage, who shrank from positions of authority, who was always eager to serve, kindhearted, decent, and gentle. And this good, sensitive and honest man met with a vile and sorry end: In April 1943, on the first day of the uprising, he was accused of being a German flunky and felled by a Jewish bullet. The ghetto had its share of such paradoxes.[54]

The commandant of Warsaw's Jewish prison on the corner of Gesia and Zamenhofa streets was Yussele Ehrlich. Emmanuel Ringelblum recorded that prior to the Second World War "he was a confidence man and a strong-arm guy," who had "worked at counterfeiting until 1936," then possibly had something to do with the stock market:

> When the Germans took Warsaw and the police began to liquidate the criminal elements, particularly among the Jews, Yussele Ehrlich was arrested and sent to Oświęcim [Auschwitz]. Apparently, he assumed certain duties of a despicable character, because he was released rather quickly. He then went off to the provinces, where he organized three or four factories (one of them near Warsaw) for counterfeiting money, which he later issued.
>   Since June (or July) of this year [1941], he has been the commandant of the Jewish prison, where people in the know say that he is the complete opposite of men of this type—actually, really, a man with an explicitly evil character, with despotic tendencies. His underlings tremble in fear of him.[55]

Interestingly, even though Ehrlich was clearly a criminal (by pre-Nazi standards), Ringelblum remarks that it was somewhat unusual for such a man to be known for harshness and cruelty. Like the greatly varying reminiscences and historical judgments of the Judenrät, the evaluations of individual Jewish policemen and different ghetto forces vary, ranging from seeing authorities as brutal Nazi accomplices to seeing them as men driven to alleviate the distress of their fellow Jews as much as possible, and to side-step Nazi decrees.[56]

Although there were, no doubt, exceptions, in general the Jewish police force of the Kovno ghetto is remarkable for the degree to which its members attempted to distance themselves from corruption and aid those involved in resistance.[57] Historian Solon Beinfeld writes that although recruitment was difficult, the force made a determined effort to attract men from "all classes and shades of political opinion." In the ghetto's "early days at least, there was a good deal of idealism and sense of responsibility to the welfare of the community as a whole among the members of the police."[58] Yet over time, the Kovno police force's "privileged position, protection from deportation," and corruption of some of its men was "understandably resented." Survivor Harry Gordon recalled, "We didn't want anything to do with members of the police. . . . To meet up with them could only mean trouble. We suffered from the blows and the kicks of the police and being dragged out of our homes into one working brigade or another, not knowing if we would return. This is why we felt so bitter as we watched the Jewish police living well while we did the backbreaking labor. . . . We saw them working hand in hand with the Germans." Beinfeld notes that Kovno's Jewish police "were well aware of the attitude of the population, but insisted that without force it would be impossible to maintain order"[59]—a self-justification for all such units. In November 1942, an extraordinary event occurred: the Kovno police assembled, publicly, "to swear loyalty to the Ältestenrat [Council of Elders]—itself a significant gesture since in other ghettos the Jewish police often acted independently of 'civilian' control and at times, as in Vilna, overthrew it." In part, this public display may have been a demonstration of support for the council's leader, Dr. Elkhanan Elkes, who was widely praised for maintaining his humanity in the most precarious of positions. Even crude Soviet-era polemics, which denounced the entire "bourgeoisie" as "exploiters," showed respect for Elkes, or at least muted their typically harsh invective. (Indeed, the first chief of the Kovno ghetto police was Michael Koppelman, "the representative of Lloyd's of London in Lithuania.")[60] In the November demonstration the police force, which included former soldiers of the Lithuanian Army and several "sportsmen . . . marched and sang Jewish national songs from their days in Jewish schools and youth groups, while the audience, tears in its eyes, joined in. As the anonymous authors of the 'History of the Vilijampole Jewish Ghetto Police' pointed out, the ceremony might look like 'playing at soldiers' under ghetto conditions, but in reality it was intended as a 'moment of national demonstration, solidarity, pride, and hope.'"[61] There is little chance that the Jewish police of, say, Warsaw—consisting as it did of a number of men who had little or no attachment to Jewish communal life—would ever have conceived or taken part in such an exercise.

Within the German Jewish community organized as the *Reichsvereinigung*, one of the main duties of the Jewish police, known (like elsewhere) as the Ordnungsdienst, was to round up victims.[62] Delivering members of their communities for transports to other ghettos and concentration camps became one of the most notorious functions of Jewish policemen throughout Europe. As a matter of routine, the SS in the ghettos was "accompanied by members of the SP," in these cases the Jewish police.[63] Calel Perechodnik asserts that a great deal of the quasi-official function of Jewish police, in his town of Otwock and elsewhere, was to supervise and facilitate "transactions" of money, food, and goods between Jews, for which the policemen received a sizable percentage.[64] In Warsaw, it was said, "Every German policeman ran his own business, letting things be smuggled into or out of the ghetto, and naturally the terms had to be discussed. Of course the Polish policemen received their take as well."[65] Obviously the placement of Jewish policemen—along with Polish and Nazi police—at "sentry posts" in ghettos gave them ample opportunity to engage in such practices. In addition, although German, Polish, and Jewish policeman were supposed to maintain separate positions, the fact that Jews—many of whom knew Polish, German, and Yiddish—served as translators in matters arising between the Polish and German forces, and in the forces' dealings with Jews, made the Jewish police uniquely situated to extract demands.[66] Similar situations ensued in Lithuania, revealed in songs from the Kovno and Vilna ghettos, mainly in Yiddish but incorporating Lithuanian, Polish, and German.[67] Such dealings were more or less unsavory depending on the individuals involved.[68] In the Warsaw ghetto Jewish police were responsible for disposing of the bodies of Jews murdered by Germans.[69] Jewish policemen also used their authority to place Jews in hiding among non-Jews and traded in identity documents, which typically included a substantial payment. As opposed to operating as a disciplined force, individual policemen tended to look out for their own interests, and, Perechodnik wryly observed, "In general, each policeman was constantly robbed by another."[70] There never was any doubt, though, that the Jewish police force in Warsaw was subordinate to the Nazis and to the Polish police. Jan Mawult recalls that "Perhaps the most important result" of the Jewish police's subordinate status to the Polish police "was that all personnel files were transferred to the PP [Polish police]. This meant that the PP headquarters had the final say in appointments or dismissals, as well as in determining punishment in disciplinary actions."[71] At worst, the Nazis, through the establishment of the Jewish police forces, created an officially sanctioned caste of henchmen and corrupt officials who were free to unleash physical force; at best, they added another layer of economic middlemen who may have smoothed difficult exchanges and attendant wrangles, and provided opportunities for safety and flight. But the complex and contradictory parts played by Jewish policemen were overshadowed by their complicity in Nazi "actions." This sentiment is at the heart of Perechodnik's question, "Am I a Murderer?"

In the city of Kalushin (east of Warsaw, west of Siedlce), the Polish mayor created a twelve-member Judenrat under Nazi orders. "The closing of the ghetto," Mojsze Kisielnicki wrote, caused great distress and worry among Jews over how they would provide for themselves. "Even though they were in great fear, some went to the village risking their lives. The Judenrat was forced to position Jewish police to prevent Jews from leaving the town because people ignored them. Every day, gendarmes imprisoned Jews they encountered outside of the town and confiscated their possessions." Some fifty persons "were shot on the road." Kisielnicki, who made himself into an interlocutor between the Nazis and the Jews, "began to obtain from the Gestapo office in Minsk permits allowing Jews to go to work in the village." Given that he was unable to obtain permits for everyone, some smuggled themselves out, fearing they would fall into the hands of the "bandits." Interestingly, here "bandits" refers to those who were turning in Jews to the Nazis, as well as to the Nazis themselves who demanded ransom for "hostages" and engaged in general extortion. "The Jewish police," this recollection asserts, "also suffered at the hand of the [anti-Semitic mayor]. . . . At first, the Jewish police worked in the interests of the people of Kalushin. Though the police had to obey the commands of the Germans, they did whatever they could to lighten the burden of the Jews. When the deportations began, the police did not cooperate with the Germans. They could move freely and sought ways to escape, and indeed this is what they did." At the conclusion of the memoir the author states that Kalushin, which numbered eight thousand Jews before the Nazi onslaught, was entirely decimated except for eleven survivors.[72] The tiny remnant recalls a vibrant community, utterly destroyed and almost totally annihilated.[73]

In his extensive discussion of criminality in the Lodz ghetto, Isaiah Trunk asserts that above all "hunger," and the incessant quest for food and warmth, "weakened concepts of morality and ethics among a portion of the population" and led to widespread activity he defines as "criminal": "Since people could not survive for long on the meager food and heating fuel allotments and wages, people sought out all sorts of ways to bring home in an illegal fashion a little food, heating fuel or money, so as to be able to buy something additional on the black market."[74] Among the ways they did so, none of which were unique to this situation, were "using pull or connections with employees of the cooperatives and kitchens to collect double or even multiple food allotments and meals on the same ration card or coupon; stealing or counterfeiting food cards, shoplifting food from the food shops and warehouses, making off with accessories and goods from the workshops, money embezzling by officials, etc." Acts that Trunk defines as the most common "thefts"—often termed "organizing" by ghetto and camp inhabitants—included taking wood from a workshop to prepare a meal, stuffing potatoes into one's clothes, grabbing food "from a wagon, which was mainly done by children and adolescents," stealing a loaf of bread from a bakery, and taking "major quantities of flour from a food warehouse." None of these acts were for the sake of making money or gaining power; they were "a form of struggle for physical survival" that was "specific to the ghetto." Occasionally bloodshed and killing "motivated by hunger" occurred, but such cases were few and far between, especially compared to the countless "crimes" of the "organizing" variety. Although extremely difficult to quantify, a great deal of theft and destruction of property also took place that were forms of "sabotage and a quiet form of revenge," such as an outbreak of sorts that occurred after one of the large *Aktionen* in Lodz in September 1942.[75]

Encapsulating the system in which Jews were compelled to break the law to exist, Calel Perechodnik in 1944 cast himself (as a Jewish policeman) as the lesser evil to the German and Polish police: "Let us not forget that all of Jewish life during the war was illegal. A policeman could pick on anything. What do you live on? Where do the potatoes in the ghetto come from? Where did you get the bread? Where are the fields planted with rye? And if there are, where did you get the seed for sowing? Where did you get the meat? Through the war the Polish policemen, who officially did not have the right to be in the [Otwock] ghetto, lived off that ghetto and lived well."[76]

Nazi leaders continuously and assiduously manipulated the environments where Jews were compelled to live in order to promote the idea that criminality was rife. In the Kovno ghetto, on July 28, 1941, Jews were "forbidden to walk on sidewalks." It furthermore was proclaimed that "Jews must walk on the right side of the road and go one behind the other"; as of August 10, 1941, it was a criminal offense for Jews to "walk on the shores of the Vilija River" and "to walk in the streets with their hands in their pockets."[77] Along with such stipulations for perambulations of any kind, convoluted regulations and prohibitions about acquiring food and other necessities made it virtually impossible to exist within the bounds of Nazi law. A German Jew deported to Lodz received a prison sentence of six weeks for writing a letter to an "Aryan" friend. Another person, attempting to be more circumspect, sent a friend a "fictive receipt for a sum of money that he had never received," apparently an appeal for money, but also possibly to indicate that things were not as they were said to be in the ghetto. "For this he was sentenced by the Gestapo to six days of arrest and additionally to get fifteen lashes every third day from the Jewish Order Service [Ordnungsdienst]."[78]

Meticulous Nazi stage managing to achieve the effect of wanton lawlessness was clear to many who recorded their experiences in the ghettos and camps, as is evident in the writings of Emmanuel Ringelblum, Chaim Kaplan, Avraham Tory, and Tadeusz Mankiewicz.[79] "This was a real theater of marionettes," Perechodnik lamented, "but what a tragic theater! Nevertheless, the manner in which the Germans implied to all the Jews, without exception, that they were doing all this for themselves, for their own good, for securing their material well-being for the future, this will remain forever Satan's secret."[80] The first entry in Emmanuel Ringelblum's journal, of January 1, 1940, states that a photograph he saw published in the *Berliner Illustrierte Zeitung* (Berlin Illustrated Daily) was staged: "They imported five Jews who had been picked up elsewhere and photographed them being caught in a raid. . . . *The intent is clear.*"[81] In the middle of May 1941, Ringelblum revealed "the kind of trickery [the Nazis] resort to" in shooting a film that was supposed to detail Jewish life in the ghettos: "A German guard stands in the middle of Zgierza Street in the Lodz ghetto; he is flanked on either side by Jewish guards. The German guard detains a German police officer for jaywalking; he orders the Jewish guards to hold the German police officer. And they film that."[82]

At the beginning of December 1941, rumors circulated in the Warsaw ghetto that "a gang of Jewish scoundrels" had been removing gold teeth from murdered Jews under the cover of night. Those found guilty were imprisoned. Word got out, however, that the Nazis had staged these "scenes of Jews pulling teeth from corpses," again, for the making of a propaganda film.[83] In early May 1942, a German film crew in the Warsaw ghetto "drove a crowd of Jews together on Smocza Street, then ordered the Jewish policemen to disperse them. At another place they shot a scene showing a Jewish policeman about to beat a Jew when a German comes along and saves the fallen Jew."[84] To further drive home the message in another scenario, "they ordered a child to run outside the Ghetto wall at the corner of Leszno and Zelana Streets, and to buy potatoes there. A Polish policeman catches the boy and raises his arm to beat him. At that moment who should come along but a German policeman. He grabs the Pole's arm—children are not to be beaten!"[85] The staging of similar scenes for "the propaganda swindle" also was a major characteristic of Nazi activity in Kraków. Thadeus Pankiewicz recalls that professional still photography as well as film were used to provide "documentary evidence," especially to substantiate "The

German Help with the Humanitarian Resettlement of the Jews." One particularly elaborate charade, "photographed in the minutest detail by the Germans," aimed to prove that Jews were being hanged in the Kraków ghetto for the crime of "murdering Poles."[86]

However, certain instances of "Jewish crime"—most of which were in fact acts of sabotage to hinder the German war effort—were indeed threatening to the Nazis.[87] Throughout Kovno, for instance, telephone, telegraph, and electrical wires were cut on a regular basis. "In June 1942," Dmitri Gelpernus writes, "Leib Moshkovich cut the wiring of the Kovno airdrome sirens," preventing warnings of a Soviet bomber attack. Gelpernus reveals that such acts were well organized and "systematic." Other means the Jews devised to frustrate the Nazis included adding snow to grain sacks, draining gasoline from military vehicles, breaking boxes containing medicine in glass bottles, removing filters from gas masks, and producing boots with very thin soles. The greatest amount of damage, however, was to the railways. "It was reported on the radio," Gelpernus asserts, "that German transport suffered badly because of mix-ups in labeling and documentation. People trained for performing special tasks were sent to railway depots and workshops for forced labor. They caused havoc in the work of the railway. Carriages were delayed or sent in the opposite direction." On the initiative of Jewish resistance fighters,

> parts of locomotives were removed and hidden, railway points switched without orders. At the beginning of 1942 a train full of goods passed at full speed near the factory "Maistas," collided with a stationary group of carriages and completely destroyed them. Resistance fighter Lucia Zimmerman initiated this act. Leib Gempl, Itzik Weiner and others working in the depot systematically removed and changed carriage labels which had information about necessary repairs. This resulted in not only chaos, constant arguments and quarrels in the railway workshops, but also one frequently heard of accidents with carriages which had only recently left the workshops due to remaining faults.[88]

Obviously the Nazis considered these acts not just crimes but major outrages.

Of course, in addition to carrying out direct Nazi punitive measures, Jews themselves, beyond the police per se, were called on to ensure the obedience of their cohort. The compulsory hierarchy, within Nazism, of Jews serving Jewish masters—whether as Judenrat officials, "Jewish police," or "Kapos" in concentration camps—was a way for the Nazis to administer their plans while expending as little of their own manpower as possible and sowing the fiction of Jewish autonomy. The Nazis sought to exacerbate corruption and discord among the Jews in Warsaw by creating, and giving prominence to, the "Office for Combating Usury and Speculation" (known as "The Thirteen" because of its location at 13 Leszno Street) as a rival to Jewish Council. Although "The Thirteen" was known as a front for the Gestapo,[89] Emmanuel Ringelblum says that there were "some honest people among 'the Thirteen' gang"—which also was termed "the Law and Order Service." Nevertheless, on May 11, 1941, Ringelblum wrote, "The battle against black-market speculation supposedly waged by 'the Thirteen' takes the form of demanding a rake-off from each shop. Besides, individuals from 'the Thirteen' accept bribes, as well as bread and produce, at every step." A month later he referred to some of them as "well-known thieves."[90] "They conceal their ugly work behind a veil of decency, reminiscent of the [brothel keeper] Yankel Shapshovich in Sholem Asch's [play] 'God of Vengeance,' who builds a synagogue to cover up his ugly profession."[91] On May 25, 1942, "the biggest wheels" of The Thirteen were murdered, which was ironically said to be a punishment for their criminal behavior: "There is a theory that the reason why [some of] 'the Thirteen' were shot was because they smuggled products worth large sums of money into the Ghetto."[92] This system also helped buttress the illusion that Jews were in the main autonomous, responsible for social welfare and control, especially crime and punishment, in their own community.

With benefit of hindsight, we can see that the imposition of the "Jewish star," to be sewn onto clothing and worn on an armband, was one of the most tangible way stations toward the stigmatization and annihilation of Jewry.[93] That Germans devised such an instrument was largely possible because few Nazis faced honestly—and certainly did not express openly—that most Jews could not be distinguished simply by their face or body type. Jews and Poles had frequent discussions about Jews with "Aryan looks" and the possibility of "passing" because of one's appearance. In his study of Jews hiding in Warsaw, Gunnar Paulsson shows that "non-Jewish looks" were often crucial for a Jew's survival in "Aryan" Warsaw.[94] At the core of Nazi racism was the idea that an Aryan could intuitively tell who was an Aryan or not, but the Nazis knew that this supposed radar did not work. Hermann Göring had proposed that Jews be outfitted in an entire uniform, whereas Reinhard Heydrich preferred "an insignia." Despite the fact that Hitler himself was not in favor of marking Jews—given his supreme faith in racial ideology—several government departments made "recurrent suggestions for introducing the measure in Greater Germany." Hitler's reversal on this matter was one of few cases in which he admitted to changing his mind.[95] Along with the supposed danger of not recognizing a Jew was the concomitant danger of mistaking an Aryan for a Jew, beating him (or her) up, sending him to a concentration camp, or instigating any such random, brutal turns that might befall a Jew in Germany and throughout Nazi-occupied Europe. Perhaps the most graphic "mistake" occurred on November 23, 1939, when "a number of trucks filled with SS-men drove through Posen, whipping passers-by on the head with horsewhips. Of course the SS were confident that they were punishing Jews and Poles. They soon learned that a number of ethnic Germans had been among the victims." Hence, the need to distinguish Jews from the non-Jewish population was felt more urgently.[96]

In countless instances the marking of Jewry served as "a powerful weapon in the hands of the police" and was akin to equipping Jews with a costume in which they were to play the role of criminals, convicts, and fugitives from justice. Raul Hilberg writes that "it was as though the whole non-Jewish population had become a police force, watching and guarding the Jews' actions." Germans and non-Germans in the Nazi domain accustomed themselves to participating in, or at least accommodating, "police" orders. "As the destruction process proceeded into its more drastic phases, it began to take on more and more the characteristics of a Police operation. Movement control, round-ups, concentration camps—all these are Police functions."[97]

Outright massacres that disrupted established routines (in the midst of more orderly genocide) were condoned as a response to "Jewish criminality." Survivors even repeated Nazi rumors in their accounts. "Early on the morning of 17 March 1942," Marek Stok wrote,

> we learned that a small pogrom had taken place in the [Warsaw] ghetto. The Germans dragged fifty-seven people from their homes and shot them on the nearby streets. The police cleaned up the corpses just before morning, and the bodies were hauled off to the cemetery. Among those shot were Blajman, a well-known baker, and his wife, as well as a printer, a teacher, a smuggler, and so on. The mood in ghetto was very grim. Everyone wanted to know why those people in particular had been dragged out and killed during the night. Some said it was all part of a campaign against smuggling and profiteering (Blajman and the smuggler); others said the reasons were political (the printer and the teacher). The Jewish Council circulated a reassuring memorandum that said, "According to information

obtained from the German authorities, the execution was a singular event and would not be repeated."[98]

A particular macabre choreography applied to "Jews caught on the Aryan side" of Warsaw, who were then "brought to the ghetto and shot. This occurred in broad daylight. In several cases the person was returned right to his doorstep; a Gestapo officer would politely extend his hand in farewell and say, 'So now you've made it back safe and sound,' but the minute the man turned around to go inside the same officer would dispatch a bullet to the back of his head. The officer would then calmly order the nearest Jewish policeman to take care of the corpse and casually drive away."[99] Here we see the apparent maintenance of law and order, as a cardinal symbol of civility. Yet merely by being on the "Aryan" side of Warsaw, a Jew was marked as a criminal, deserving a death sentence—but disguised up to the end. "Later," Stok wrote, "things got even worse, in a bizarre way," as pedestrians were randomly shot by Germans in official vehicles and private cars, including "a small sports car. . . . It was a game . . . they shot people for attempts at smuggling or for no visible reason at all."[100]

It is not surprising that "embezzling and swindling," particularly in the Provisioning Department, was characteristic of Chaim Rumkowski's administration in the Lodz ghetto. Varying levels of corruption existed in most Judenräte, contrived and stoked by the Nazis. As opposed to the thefts of property and food, several high-profile cases in Lodz were born of a desire to exploit the desperate circumstances and to "procure an illegal income" for well-placed functionaries.[101] Like innumerable political figures across time and space, Rumkowski prided himself on his dedication to law and order while presiding over a deeply corrupt regime. Albeit "in his own fashion," Isaiah Trunk writes, "Rumkowski conducted an intense fight against crime in the ghetto with the help of serious penalties (not only for the relevant person alone, but also for the family by confiscating from them the right to relief grants), even up to deportation to death. In almost all of his numerous speeches," the question of criminality "occupies the most prominent place." Supporting the observation that "crime" was tied directly to hunger and cold weather, the greatest wave of theft occurred during "the severe winter of 1941."[102]

We now know that Rumkowski exploited the circumstances of the ghetto in other ways that added to the horror of his pseudoreign. When the Nazis picked him to head the ghetto—a "random" choice among a group of twenty to thirty men—they apparently had no knowledge of his reputation for molesting children.[103] Rumkowski, however, used his position to assault, terrorize, and blackmail a number of Jewish girls and boys, despite a number of testimonies asserting that Rumkowski was impotent. Rumkowski's rule, although the point is still a matter of heated controversy, is considered among the most corrupt and divisive. "On one occasion," Lucille Eichengreen writes,

> we saw Chaim Rumkowski in his droshky as it came rushing past us. He was well-dressed, well fed, and seemingly without a care in the world. Most of us feared and detested him, although sometimes we thought of him with envy. He seemed to suffer none of the deprivations we did. He didn't know the pain of hunger and cold. Even his horse and driver were well fed. He was responsible to the Germans for the entire ghetto, and it often seemed to us that he was more on their side than ours.
>
> All orders issued by the Germans appeared in ghetto posters over his name and signature, and his temper and power were said to be awesome.[104]

Eichengreen was to be one of Rumkowski's victims. She had been expressly warned that he was "a pig, a child molester, and a lecher,"[105] but because of his absolute control over the Jews of Lodz, she was trapped. Eichengreen furthermore recalls,

> During the early deportations, Rumkowski ordered the Jewish ghetto police or the Jewish ghetto *Sonder,* "special force," to be in charge; at times, however, he deployed both of them. These men were not as brutal as the Germans—they "simply" followed orders, and rounded up everyone whose name appeared on their list. *Did they have a choice? Were they as helpless as the rest of us?*
>
> Questions such as these ran through my mind.[106]

Jews devoted a great amount of mental energy to such dilemmas. They often anguished over what constituted "criminality." During a horrible ghetto winter, "because my feet felt as heavy as stones and I barely had the strength to drag them along, I decided to embark upon a dangerous course," Eichengreen writes.

> I would risk imprisonment or deportation in order to steal the leather I needed to resole my boots, and I did not hesitate in implementing my plan. Once or twice a week, and never on the same days, I stole two strips

of leather. I made sure that I was not observed, and then I stuffed them hurriedly into my boot. On the evenings when I stole strips, I walked past the inspection personnel and out into the street, relieved that my treasure had remained hidden and secure. My heart pounded wildly with each step of the way, but, although it seemed to me everyone could see through my scheme, I persevered. This was not simple—and taken altogether, the thefts were a long, tediously slow process. Each boot had six strips—but in order to bribe the cobbler not to denounce me, I had to steal an additional twelve strips for him. Using my technique, it therefore took me weeks to complete the theft.

One night as Luba and I were parting, I told her what I had done. She stopped in her tracks, turned white, and cried: "Are you crazy? What if you had been caught?" I shrugged my shoulders. I knew that what I had done was wrong, but ghetto life had made me a thief, and I felt no remorse. All my life I had been taught that decent people do not steal, but I was no longer a decent person. The ghetto had changed me, and it was not a decent place either.

Agony and fear were behind me. The cobbler readily agreed to resole my boots, and greedily looked forward to the twelve strips of leather I would get for him. I was sure that he would not betray me, and that he would probably "buy" a loaf of bread with his prize, but I had learned my lesson. On reflection, I knew that I did not want to be a thief; not here, not anywhere, and I never stole again. My feet were dry once the boots were repaired, but my toes were dark blue and infected.[107]

As later chapters will show, concentration camp inmates also contemplated and struggled over the protean meanings of terms such as "stealing" and "thief." From the Nazi perspective, however, the main function of associating Jews with criminality was to justify their actions and to cajole or compel local populations to follow their lead. Although the process was by no means instantaneous or consistent, the mass murders of the Einsatzgruppen, the erection and destruction of ghettos, and deportation of Jews to concentration and extermination camps was fueled and rationalized by the mythical need to conquer the problem of Jewish criminality. "As they set about liquidating the ghetto," Stanislaw Sznapman wrote, "they launched a vicious campaign against Jews, which they blew up to monstrous proportions. Every crime anywhere in the city—every murder, fire, and robbery—was blamed on Jews, to convince Poles who their worst enemy was and to persuade anyone who was hiding a Jew to hand him over to the Germans. In the papers, over the radio, on wall posters—everywhere they warned of the Jewish fiend. The streets became a genuine hunting ground, with Jews as the quarry." In this topsy-turvy moment, which had been well prepared, "shady characters," knowing accomplices to murder, "were rewarded by the Gestapo with money and valuables taken from Jewish homes, so the rabble ran riot." Jewish and Polish police also approached this task with great zeal.[108] In contrast, some Jews known previously as criminals earned the veneration of ghetto inhabitants for their smuggling operations, known as "working the wall," which brought in desperately needed food and supplies.[109] Michael Temchin writes with warmth about one such "small operator," the man who became his "best friend," Ele Baumsecer:

> Before the war, the Jews of Warsaw had their famous synagogues, a fine Judaic institute, elegant restaurants, their own theatres and—Krochmalna Street. On one end of this thoroughfare was the headquarters of the Kehilla, the official Jewish community, but starting from the corner of Ciepla, toward Zelazna and outward, Krochmalna turned into the capital of the Jewish underworld, swarming with Jewish prostitutes, pimps, thieves and pickpockets. The Jewish underworld was not known for murderers, but safecracking, pickpocketing and prostitution flourished there. (There was, however, one typically "Jewish" attitude that was not found among Gentile criminals. In certain cases one could negotiate for the return of stolen goods if one could convince the thieves that their victim was poor and that the theft had therefore been an act of real injustice.) My friend Ele was the king of Krochmalna Street, even as his father and grandfather had been before him.

Conceding that Baumsecer's family was less than "illustrious," as "his mother, his sisters and his fiancée had all been prostitutes," Temchin argues that Ele preserved his dignity by refusing to give up his family, which would have allowed him to escape. Temchin even suggests that Baumsecer became a valiant fighter in the Warsaw ghetto uprising.[110]

Meanwhile, the German police styled itself as the very paragon of professionalism. One incident in the Kraków ghetto seemed, in the eyes of Tadeusz Pankiewicz, to capture the Nazi concept of law and order more sharply than any other:

> One morning, a long column of German cars passed through Plac Zgody toward Limanowska Street—a long parade of cars rolling east. One of the cars hit a young Jewish boy running across the street. The car stopped and

behind it so did the whole line of German cars. Someone lifted the boy and carried him to the hospital. The German police arrived. At their headquarters on Fransiszkanska Street, they had been informed of the accident by telephone by the local OD [Ordnungsdienst]. Investigations began, the policemen measured the distances, asked about the speed of the offending car, and finally wrote their report. After a delay of almost an hour, the cars starting moving again. I could not understand it, with the memory still vivid of so many killed, what a senseless adherence to regulation, what an extraordinary example of bureaucracy! The boy, only slightly bruised, recovered very quickly; he regained his health only to lose his life in the first Aktion where mass murders were already beyond the control of law.[111]

Yet this action can been seen as something greater than an obsession with bureaucracy. The Germans had to erect a veneer of legality not only for the sake of appearance to the Jews and the subject Polish population, but also to assure themselves that they were the supreme guardians of law and order.

FOUR

Inverting the Innocent and the Criminal in Concentration Camps

"I dare say, Dad," I said, "that these new people are common thieves."

"I wouldn't say they were thieves," replied Dad, "they are just very hungry. In fact one of our bed-comrades gave me a pretty thorough search and he wouldn't lay off until I kicked him in the chin." He stopped for a few seconds and concluded, "You must be very careful. Food is very precious here, but I hope you will not have to steal."

"I shall never steal!" I exclaimed.

"Let's hope you won't have to," was all Dad would say.

HUGO GRYN

recollecting his arrival at Auschwitz, in Chasing Shadows

A FUNDAMENTAL PROCLIVITY CONNECTING GHETTOS with concentration camps and labor camps in the Third Reich was the Nazi effort to cast all Jews as convicted criminals. This chapter focuses on three aspects of Nazi control of the camps that sought to concretize the preconception that all Jews were outlaws deserving of incarceration (without possibility of parole or release), harsh treatment, slave labor, and ultimately, execution.[1] The first category may be termed the criminal-bureaucratic. Administrative procedures in the camps were devised to exaggerate the idea that "Jews" and "criminals" were synonymous and to propagate the myth that concentration camps were, in essence, penal institutions. If authorities maintain that inmates in security installations are criminals, they generally have little difficulty justifying the use of the inmates for slave labor. From the Nazi perspective, this approach had the added advantage of being "good" for Jews, no matter how lethal the conditions.[2] During the Second World War, and in other civil and international conflicts before and after the war, groups identified as dangerous elements were forced into something akin to "protective custody" or "administrative detention." Often, political refugees, "resident aliens," or "asylum seekers" fall into this category. Two of the better-known examples among the Allies during World War II are the internment of "foreign" Jews in Britain and of Japanese Americans in the United States. No doubt the unfortunates in these facilities found their detainment dehumanizing. Certainly many women and men were treated like criminals, and both countries presumed potential wrongdoing by the vast majority of innocent internees. Although British Jews and American Japanese were not subject to mass murder and systematic torture, their detainment facilities and other settings are commonly described as "like" concentration camps. Nevertheless, a distinguishing feature of the Nazi camps, which affected how the Jews were compelled to live and die, was the dramatic, multifaceted, intensive, and relentless effort to see and treat Jews as criminals—an onslaught that may be differentiated from callous and inhumane treatment in a general sense.

The second area of control was the use of forensic photography, which played a distinct role in Nazi administration and self-perceptions in the camps. Despite the fact that many publications about the Holocaust, and Auschwitz in particular, contain prisoners' "mug shots," few scholarly discussions look at the photographic process itself.[3] Janina Struk's account, while contributing to the history of photography in a more formal manner, does little to illuminate the criminological discourses that shaped Nazi efforts during the Holocaust.[4] Another guide to photographs from Auschwitz states that the Nazis took some 405,000 "mug shots"—of which 40,000 negatives remain—but we have no idea how many of them are of Jews.[5] Some writers suggest that all of those photographed during the "criminal-prisoner" induction procedure were non-Jews, with only rare "exceptions" to the rule.[6] This claim, however, is contradicted by hundreds, if not thousands, of photographs of "Jewish prisoners" and by testimonies about the photographic work of the Erkennungsdienst, the "Information Service" at Auschwitz.[7]

In addition to analyzing the "mug shots," this chapter looks at a specific incident, the 1942 massacre at Budy, an Auschwitz women's subcamp. Nazi officials apparently intended to use photographs from Budy for a "criminal-photographic" project. Although no evidence exists that the photos were used for this purpose, the episode is nevertheless instructive in assessing the significance of forensic photography in Auschwitz.[8] The attempt to make use of the Budy massacre was tied to the work of the Erkennungsdienst at Auschwitz, which was dedicated to documenting the deaths of those reportedly killed "while trying to escape" or "revolt." In addition to reacting to these horrific incidents with pseudoprofessional police procedure, the Nazis exploited them to create compulsory rites to which all prisoners were subject. This phenomenon has been recounted in scores of memoirs, yet few scholars have noted its importance.

The third aspect of the camps to be examined may be deemed the "ceremonial." Repeated, staged scenes took place in most if not all camps containing Jews, intended to be witnessed by staff and inmates, that the Nazis invested with quasi-religious or liturgical significance supposedly to inculcate the value system of the camp. While these spectacles were meant to dramatize the purported racial "otherness" of the Jew, they also sought to magnify and reinforce the identification of Jews with criminality. The two ritualized phenomena that were especially tied to the Jewish criminality canard were public hangings, proclaimed to be responses to "Jewish crimes," and assemblies in response to prisoners killed "while trying to escape."

To gain information about these features of Auschwitz in which the Jewish criminality myth was operative, particularly the photographic records of Auschwitz, I was guided by the insights of my friend and informant Helen (née Spitzer) Tichauer, whom I refer to here by the name by which she was known in Auschwitz and afterward, "Zippy."[9] (Zippy is a short form of her Hebrew name, Zipporah.) Zippy was among the 20,000 young Jews from Slovakia transported to Auschwitz in late March 1942, and she had a distinctive role in the camp that enabled her to save her own life and that of many others.[10] Zippy, born in Bratislava and now living in New York City, is a commercial artist by training, the first and only board-certified woman to hold such a position in her native Czechoslovakia (later the puppet state of Slovakia). Zippy's expertise as a "sign painter"—the colloquial term for her highly skilled profession—led to her employment in the registration and induction of prisoners, particularly of women inmates of Auschwitz and later Birkenau, which she described in interviews to scholars such as David Boder, Robert Lifton, Joan Ringelheim, Deborah Dwork and Robert Jan van Pelt, and Wendy Lower. Because of her training as a graphic artist, Zippy was entrusted with producing a scale model of Auschwitz—routinely consulted by staff and visitors to the camp in order to orient themselves, as buildings were largely unmarked—as well as a monthly statistical survey of the camp's operation, in the form of a large, unified set of graphs and charts, that was sent to RSHA (Reichssicherheitshauptamt, the Nazi Department of Security) headquarters in Berlin. The comprehensive nature of this duty meant that she was privy to an overview of Auschwitz that was shared by no other prisoner-workers, whose perspective was severely blinkered. Zippy's role in the Auschwitz administration, which afforded her a small but private office in Birkenau and extraordinary breadth of knowledge of the camp's workings, as well as unusual mobility within its confines, provides us with critical knowledge about countless aspects of Auschwitz.[11] Zippy enlightened me about a paradox central to this chapter: that if an inmate—regardless of being a Jew—was classified as a "criminal" upon entering Auschwitz, the Nazis took pains to ensure that he or she was not sent to the gas chambers. In other words, Jews died en masse for the crime of having been born a Jew. But in the bizarre universe the Nazis constructed at Auschwitz, if one was considered a "criminal" in a more conventional sense, the camp authorities made some effort to document that the accused had had recourse to "justice." In addition to Zippy's testimony, the "mug shots" and three other independent sources allowed me to document this institutionalized contradiction at Auschwitz.

EQUATING JEWS WITH CRIMINALS ADMINISTRATIVELY IN LABOR AND CONCENTRATION CAMPS

The regulations and spatial arrangement of concentration and labor camps accentuated the equation of the inmates, especially Jews, with criminality.[12] Prominently placed gallows in the camps constituted a laboratory, of sorts, for crime and punishment that had a function similar to that of gas chambers and medical-experiment rooms in the Nazi racial Weltanschauung. The gibbets and prisons within the camps are perhaps more significant than has been suggested, because they represented, in microcosm, the supposed greater purpose of the institution and exemplified the ostensible "penal" rationale of the entire system.[13]

The relative significance and juxtaposition of gallows, prison, gas chamber, and medical-experiment rooms are particularly evident in the concentration camp Natzweiler-Struthof (in present-day France, near Strasbourg), which one survivor-poet described as an "amphitheater of torture."[14] The main camp, set on a timber-concealed mountaintop, is in an elevated position, with the parade ground and gallows occupying the highest plateau. The gas chamber, converted from an existing hotel building, is a few hundred meters down the road from the camp entrance—present but not nearly as conspicuous as the formidable gibbet and the prison building, occupying opposite ends of the camp. The internal administration of Struthof claimed to enforce strict rules for determining which prisoners were to be incarcerated in its prison block and detailed the treatment the inmates would receive once imprisoned. Though punishment was in fact largely

Gallows at the Natzweiler-Struthof concentration camp, near Strasbourg. Photo by Michael Berkowitz.

random, superficially the procedures sought to show that the Nazi rulers were pursuing their grand schemes in the realms of both law and order—Struthof was notorious as a final destination for apprehended members of the French resistance—and "racial hygiene."[15] The site was apparently selected because of a combination of factors: for the camp to act as a warning to a possibly recalcitrant Alsatian population, and more practically, for it to provide a labor force to mine granite, "a primary material for public buildings" in Nazi Germany and "as important in [Albert] Speer's plans as brick." "Breaking rocks," which also was central to the large Mauthausen camp, had long been considered a classic prison work detail.[16]

Legislation governing camp personnel was simultaneously adjusted to accommodate their brutal character.[17] As early as September 1933 the behavior of guards and soldiers in concentration camps was ruled outside the normal purview of German law. This precedent was established when the police arrested several SS members for "mistreatment of Jews." SS officials in Aschaffenburg then directed that no SS man "could be arrested by a policeman." This decree was so unusual, and clearly unprecedented, that the Bavarian Minister of Justice, Hans Frank—a leading Nazi figure—"questioned the claim and asked the Bavarian Minister President (Siebert) to discuss the matter with the SS Chief Himmler and with Himmler's superior, the SA Chief Röhm. Shortly after that incident, a few killings took place in the Bavarian concentration camp Dachau. The victims were two Germans and a Jew (Dr. Delwin Katz)." Himmler and Röhm requested that proceedings against the responsible SS men be quashed for " 'state-political' reasons." Bavaria's Minister of the Interior, Adolf Wagner, consented, but said he did not want to be bothered with similar requests in the future. In a letter to Frank, Wagner asked the Minister of Justice to simply dismiss the concentration camp case, because the institution "houses, as is well-known, almost exclusively criminal characters."[18]

The notion was continually reinforced, among the Nazis, that Auschwitz was a penal institution, which is not surprising, given the origins of the camp as a center for "protective custody" (*Schutzhaft*, established by the decree of February 28, 1933). It provided what the Nazis regarded as a safe haven for themselves from any legal prosecution or oversight. Though they justified their actions in the guise of state security, the Nazis took additional steps to give their activities in Auschwitz a cover of legality.[19] The camp owed its origins partly to an attempt to relieve the pressure of bloated prisons—due mainly, of course, to Nazi oppression.[20] But Auschwitz evolved into a hybrid entity—forced-labor camp and death factory—while maintaining a self-image as a "prison." From Auschwitz's beginnings, the minds behind the camp embarked on something entirely new, by making its original thirty "prisoners," brought from Sachsenhausen, serve as "prisoner-functionaries."[21] Apparently the Nazi upper echelon needed to put forth the idea that the camp was the site of sessions, held roughly every four or six weeks, of the "police summary court" (*Polizeistandgericht*) of the State Police Office in Kattowitz.[22] Rudolf Höss depicted this "tribunal" as one of the cardinal purposes of Auschwitz, where "all the prisoners whom I saw tried admitted to their actions quite freely, openly, and firmly" and notably, "some of the women answered bravely for what they had done." Here he seems to be referring mainly to Polish partisans. In this way Auschwitz was a place of noble, normal—even dignified—death, as happens in conflicts between nations: "They all met their death with calm and resignation, convinced that they were sacrificing themselves for their country." But the focus of Auschwitz, according to Höss, was its "criminals": "men who had taken part in robberies with violence, gang crimes and so on." These men, according to Höss, died ugly deaths: "They whined and cried out for mercy."[23] All Jews, however, were invariably grouped with the "robbers" and members of "gangs."

Even prior to their deportation, many Jews felt that they had entered a world in which those who had earlier been "criminals" were now their overlords. A survivor from Miechow, William Eisen, writes that "with the assistance of local Polish police and many paid informers, the Germans had full control of our town in days." Men he described as "local stooges" could simply "identify" a Jew—inferring that they could not be spotted by traditional clothing—which was a signal for the accused to be "beaten by a Nazi soldier." The main motivation for Poles, he understood, was that if Jews were pressed into forced labor, Polish non-Jews would not be subject to such treatment. But in addition to the "stooges," in his eyes the scum of the earlier social order shot up the ladder:

> Poles of low character suddenly became important personalities with Jewish lives dependent on the judgment of former criminals, petty thieves, and common hooligans. They collected rewards from the Germans for turning in a Jew, and bribes from Jews for protecting them. I knew most of them personally; in a town as small as ours it would be difficult not to. Some claimed German ancestry, but many were just collaborators, opportunists, or the lowest breed of human life before the occupation. Few, if any loyal Polish people would stoop to cooperate with their conqueror for any reason.[24]

But the camps to which they were transported were not simply worlds turned upside down, where the former hooligans now reigned. They were the sites of a radically reconceived order that saw the alliance between the police and guards, and those who had formerly been branded as criminals—usually, as long as they were not Jews—as the privileged caste.

Upon their arrival at concentration camps many Jews were struck by the fact that they were thrown into "a real mix of good people with professional killers." Jewish inmates, then, "had the opportunity to meet the criminals"—that is, criminals by pre-Nazi, conventional standards. From the perspective of Jews, such people were to be avoided, "just like you do in civilian life. But here the criminals were put in charge of good, decent people. And that was the danger and we had to be very careful to stay out of their way, to not be noticed. They were killing, hitting, kicking. They were the worst, the Germans with those green triangles, they were our enemy, men and women alike."[25]

The processes of induction varied from camp to camp and changed over time in the same locale; even at Auschwitz the procedure depended on the incoming numbers and available manpower. There was no absolutely unified model. Because Reinhard Heydrich reorganized the concentration camps along roughly "uniform lines," procedures were replicated from camp to camp.[26] A number of accounts are similar to that of Lucille Eichengreen, who described her arrival at Auschwitz after her transport from the Lodz ghetto:

> About five in the morning, the train came to a jolting halt. . . . From within the car I could hear the shout of the Germans' orders and the barking of dogs. Once the doors were thrown open, I saw a brightly lit platform and the menacing sight of Germans in uniform, holding onto the leashes of restless dogs. *"Raus! Macht schnell! Alles antreten!"* We had to hurry; we had arrived, and we were in Auschwitz. Things. They had referred to us as "things," not people—and from this we could infer that our ordeals were not to end, but rather to intensify. . . . Within minutes men were separated from women. Men were marched off, and disappeared into the distance—But women were broken down into two groups: the young and the old. Those who had somehow managed to hide their children from the Germans during the *Sperre* [forced separations], or those who had children younger than ten, were pulled out and pushed over into the lineup of old women and made to walk along with them. We, who were younger and supposedly fit, were marched off to barracks, ordered to undress, fold our clothes, and remove all jewelry. Our heads and bodies were shaved, and not a strand of hair remained.

Eichengreen relates, "This was done to immediately identify us as prisoners, as by this time [August 1944] the incoming were arriving in such numbers that the camp personnel could not manage to tattoo each of us with a now-famous Auschwitz identification number."[27] There may, however, have been practical considerations interwoven as well, such as delousing and the use of human hair. Nevertheless, Eichengreen recalls that "Elli, the friend I had encountered in the cattle car, was so mortified" at the prospect of having all her hair cut off "that she timidly asked a nearby Kapo if we could be tattooed with a number like hers instead of being shaved, but the Kapo laughed coarsely and said: 'Here, you take what you get.' Amazingly, the Kapo were also Jews, camp police chosen from among the prisoners to guard the others. It was a rare prisoner guard who did not treat us as horribly as did the Nazis themselves."[28]

Among the numerous descriptions of the experience of inmates in concentration camps, several describe their identification by "badges" of varying shapes and colors.[29] Those taken into Auschwitz who were not on transports that went immediately to the gas chambers were given a loose-fitting blue-striped uniform with a registration number and a special mark of identification: a triangle made of cloth to be worn on the left side of the chest as well as on the right pants leg. It is well known that Auschwitz prisoners in the early days were tattooed, an experience that many survivors recall as dehumanizing and literally painful.[30]

Each category of inmate had a color by which it was known.[31] "Political" prisoners were labeled, probably intentionally, with red; "criminals," green; "homosexuals," pink; "emigrants" (conscientious resisters), blue; "aso-cials," black; Jehovah's witnesses, purple; and "Gypsies," brown.[32] These markings, however, were not always consistent from camp to camp, or even in a given camp for the duration of its existence. For Jews the two triangles making a "Jewish star" were yellow, unless the prisoner happened to be in one of the other categories as well, in which case he or she would wear a two-colored star. It is likewise well known that in Nazi Germany and throughout Nazi-occupied Europe the compulsory law to wear a yellow star was a stage in the stigmatization of Jewry, toward the path of loss of human rights, and for most, the loss of their lives. Of course, prisoners also were differentiated for practical purposes, such as being identified as a foreman or Kapo through a distinctive armband.[33]

As is evident from a plethora of images from Auschwitz, Dachau, and else-where, concentration camp prisoners wore uniforms that resembled prison garb. But this policy was not consistent, even in Auschwitz. Some prisoners in 1942 were given Russian uniforms from dead POWs. Others were supplied with "civilian clothing from the Jewish arrivals." Higher-quality apparel of the inmates' was shipped to Germany. Civilian clothes were turned into prison wear with the addition of a red stripe that made them easily visible. Zippy Tichauer, because she knew how to mix paint from her training as a graphic artist, was assigned to paint the stripes. The camp administration demanded this stripe so inmates "could not run away. We had no hair, but that did not mean that one was automatically recognizable as a camp inmate. In those days, shaven hair was not an uncommon sight, with the illnesses, lice, skin rashes. The next day I received in abundance painting supplies, all that I had asked for including the necessary brushes. I started painting those red stripes and did this for weeks and weeks. After the new inmates had those red stripes they were allowed to go out to their work detail, whatever was necessary."[34]

Konrad Kwiet and Helmut Eschwege have written that the marking of concentration camp prisoners had two distinct functions: first, to create a hierarchy and obvious divisions among prisoners, to make their authoritarian self-administration more expedient; and second, to irritate existing social, political, and religious conflicts. This view is consistent with Karin Orth's statement that Nazi "power struggles" had a decided influence on the shape of Auschwitz.[35] Rudolf Höss, the infamous commandant, was known for regarding the "greens," the "real" criminals, as the "mainstay" of the camp, while his successor, Arthur Liebehenschel, was said to favor "reds," political prisoners, in the Auschwitz regime.[36] Höss himself said that "almost without exception," the "Germans" held sway over other prisoners.[37] According to former prisoner Wladyslaw Fejkiel, from the camp's beginning until 1942, "the common German criminal H. Bock performed the functions of camp senior.[38] He was not a bad person, though without any ideology, but in regard to the SS he was rather loyal. His successors were also Germans. In addition to this Bock had certain 'weaknesses,' which brought about a very bad atmosphere in the [camp] hospital. He used morphine and adored young boys, whom he kept around, demoralized and what was even [worse]—whom he entrusted with the most responsible posts in the hospital."[39]

Another former inmate, writing of the hospital at Birkenau, testified that he "sometimes watched some [of] the capos 'at work'" murdering groups of prisoners. A certain "Capo Bernard," armed with a club

> arranged the heads of the selected prisoners at the edge of the bunk and struck once with his club. Then he gave the order to drag out the corpse. And the same fate befell the other prisoners. When I arrived there were close to 100 corpses lying on the porch. The capo did not interrupt his killing procedure and was not at all put out of countenance noticing that I was watching how skillfully he was killing. He was by no means an athlete; quite obviously murdering was a pleasure for him. Besides, he was a genuine bandit, wearing the green *"Winkel"* [triangle].[40]

Such demonstrations apparently proved to the Nazis that prisoners were capable of—and even enthusiastic about—decimating each other. Jerzy Rawicz stated that "the Jewish prisoners . . . were killed off by SS-men and, with their approval and encouragement, by the German criminal offenders in the camp."[41] Although the numbers are moderate compared to the masses murdered by gassing, the phenomenon of prisoner-bosses killing their charges was a significant aspect of Auschwitz. A survivor testified that "Each capo did the killing in his own block. I remember one of them," apparently a non-Jewish Pole, "very well. . . . He not only killed for the fun of it, but for profit."

> That was the athlete Isaak. Already in the *"Stammlager,"* in the punitive company he was ill-famed for his powerful blow. Here in Birkenau he carried neither a stick nor a mace. He arranged the prisoners as he wanted them to stand and then hit them with the edge of his hand in the neck. One blow sufficed and the prisoner had to be delivered to the morgue. Isaak would have been ashamed if he had to hit twice. He made no differentiation as regards nationalities. He boasted that he had already finished off close to two thousand Jews.[42]

Stanislawa Leszczynska, who "spent two years as a midwife-prisoner in the women's concentration camp Auschwitz-Birkenau,"[43] reported that known murderers were put in charge of genocidal operations: "Until May 1943 all the new-born babies in the Auschwitz camp were murdered in a cruel manner: they were drowned in a small barrel. This job was performed by Schwester [nurse] Klara and Schwester Pfani. The former was a midwife by profession and had been sent to the camp for child murder." When Leszcynska was directed to be a midwife, Klara was "forbidden to assist at childbirth, because as a *'Berufsverbrecherin'* [professional criminal] she had been deprived of the right to perform the functions of her profession. She was ordered to do the jobs which were more along her line. She had also been entrusted with the function of the so-called block leader. Her assistant was Schwester Pfani, red-haired, freckled and a streetwalker." Following each delivery one could hear "a loud gurgle and the splashing of water, which lasted quite a long time. . . . The mother who had just given birth would often be forced to witness her baby's body thrown out of the block and torn to pieces by the rats."[44] This division of labor was one of the most grotesque examples of the Nazis, on the one hand, cynically adhering to "legal" standards—not having the disbarred nurse assist childbirths—but on the other hand, assigning her to murder newborn Jewish babies.

The favoring of criminals, as Nazi accomplices, was common in camps besides Auschwitz. Many Jews believed that people who were "just and incorruptible" would never accept positions such as "Kapo." In the women's camps, perhaps, there was more of a sense that one could remain a decent person in such a role. "I must state," a survivor of the Posen camp wrote, "that in the men's camps unscrupulous subjects had pushed themselves forward who had acquired SS manners and who were hated by their mates as much as by the SS itself."[45] The consistent policy of having "real criminals" lord over Jews, particularly in Auschwitz, caused all internees to be subsumed into the category of convicted criminals—no matter the cause of their internment.[46]

Ironically all Jewish "prisoners" were thrown into an explicitly criminal regime, but one in which there were, apparently, rigidly enforced rules. "In the concentration camp," a survivor writes, "there was a very strict code." He was not speaking about "the rules and regulations" imposed by "the German guards," of which "there were some strict ones," or the formal "orders" of Kapos, but a "code" of prescribed behavior "among prisoners" upon which their survival depended. The description that follows, however, blurs the boundaries between punishments imposed by prisoners and those administered by the Germans:

> If you tried to steal clothing from another prisoner, or you tried to steal bread from him and you were caught, you had severe penalties. Also while at work which was done under the supervision of German guards, if they thought you tried to do the least work you could do, maybe let the other guy work harder, the German guards would let you know who's boss. They had a whip with several endings made out of leather for any things you did wrong against the code. Let's say you did steal from your fellow prisoners and you were caught, they would put you over a block and pull your pants down and you would get ten, fifteen, twenty-five lashes.[47]

A sort of order was imposed, at least in the minds of some survivors:

> I have to say at no time did I even try to steal anything from anybody, but I did see it happen. I did not squeal because it was not in my nature, but there were prisoners who [one would call] stool pigeons, and they would tell on anybody. If it comes to stealing from another prisoner I have to say it should be reported, but if you were working, if you could get away with it you do as [little] work as possible. I think that under the circumstances that was right because you worked for nothing, you worked only for the German war machine, and there was no reason for us to help them get the results of success and victory against the rest of the world.[48]

The choice of references in this testimony—using terms such as "squeal" and "stool pigeon" that one would find in detective comics and gangster movies—reveals the extent to which even the inmates internalized the idea that they were in a prison. Although inmates had limited scope to manipulate the system, such that it was, some Jews clearly tried to gain the upper hand over others.

In addition to the case of (non-Jew) H. Bock in the Auschwitz hospital, in an atmosphere where sexual abuse was rampant, some survivors testify that homosexual prisoners exploited their status in the camp hierarchy. Because homosexuals were commonly stereotyped as "degenerates," placing Jews under their servitude was a deliberate attempt at degradation and humiliation. Overwhelmingly, however, homosexuals were more the victims of this system than willing perpetrators. A survivor of the Buna camp at Auschwitz writes of consistent sexual mistreatment of prisoners by long-serving Kapos who "had quite a bit of authority." Without specifying whether or not these prisoners had been interned as homosexuals, wearing pink triangles, he writes that "advantage was taken of younger prisoners," which was not "by consent of both parties," but coerced by "bullying and force. . . . This was done under the threat of death." All the tormentor had to do was report the prisoner for unspecified misbehavior, and the victim could face beatings, torture, and even execution. Apparently, this reminiscence was prompted by a postwar discussion of homosexuality in prisons. The writer emphasizes that the vast majority of Jews in the concentration camp were there simply because they were born Jewish, not because they had records of past criminal activity. They were unlikely to have immediately internalized or accepted the forced transition to "prisoner" status—as occurs in a "normal" prison.[49] In other words, they were unprepared for a homosexual assault, which perhaps would have been less of a shock for a "normal" incarcerated criminal. A survivor from Kosice tells a similar story about his experiences at Birkenau, of Kapos soliciting "favors" from Jewish boys; he recalled that the Kapos had been imprisoned as homosexuals.[50] A memoirist states that the Janoshu concentration camp outside the city of Lemberg (Lvov) was ruled by "bloodthirsty homosexual degenerates," "murderers" who "had pleasure killing and mutilating Jewish men, women, and children."[51] Although we can assume that the overwhelming majority of non-Jewish homosexuals interned by the Nazis did not act this way, mistreatment by homosexuals was a form of brutality experienced by at least some Jewish prisoners at Auschwitz and other camps. In contrast, a survivor of Flossenbürg recalled, "The leader of our camp [where he did skilled forced labor] was a criminal who killed his mother. In our shop supervising about 200 people, one of the Capos was a pickpocket, the other one a safecracker, two were socialists, and one a homosexual. In general, they were not bad fellows. They did not punish the inmates because they felt that they were also prisoners here." Breaking precedent with other camps, the Kapos "wore normal clothes, not stripes as we did, did not work, their food rations were better. Many a time they also participated in our discussions about war, liberation, and freedom, because they also had the same longings."[52]

Few if any records exist documenting cruelty and abuse of Jewish inmates by "political" prisoners. We see little comment about contact with "Gypsies" and Jehovah's Witnesses. But extraordinary conduct—good or bad—was often remembered. "The behavior of the other [Pawiak prison] inmates," a Warsaw survivor recalled, "all political prisoners—towards us, Jewish prisoners, deserves high praise. They showed good comradeship and solidarity with us. When passing the street of the prison, they threw us their bread rations through the prison windows. On Sunday, when we were brought to the prison for [delousing], the kitchen personnel, with the inmates' agreement, had kept for us the entire rations of soup and bread for distribution among us: What that meant to us, only people who have suffered acute hunger as we had under the Nazis can know." Such acts brought "comfort and encouragement[, both] physically and morally."[53] This account reports one of the rare occasions when distinctions between prisoners had a fortuitous effect on Jews.

As in "normal" prisons, Auschwitz and other camps had higher-security and even more grossly inhumane jails for "criminals" who already were incarcerated or were transferred from other prisons. This division at Auschwitz made the overall character of the camp seem less severe to its Nazi rulers. "The air in these underground corridors" of Auschwitz's Block 11, according to SS man Pery Broad, "was so stifling that breathing seemed almost impossible." When the door was opened

> a choking stench issued from the crowded, narrow cell. One prisoner shouted, *"Achtung!"* and, their faces apathetic, the emaciated men clad in dirty, white and blue rags, stood up in a line. One could see that some of them were barely able to stand erect. . . . [Hans] Aumeier held against the door the list of men who would be tried that day. The first prisoner gave his name and stated how long he had been in prison. The camp leader briefly questioned the reporting officer as to the cause of the arrest. Should the prisoner have been arrested by Section II (the Politische Abteilung), which was usually the case with recaptured fugitives, then the matter was within Grabner's competence. Both camp dignitaries [Grabner and Höss?] then took their decision—either penal report 1 or penal report 2. Prisoners of either group left the cell and formed ranks in two groups in the corridor. The rest remained "in prison pending the investigation." The "criminal activities" of

prisoners from group 1 amounted to having somewhere stolen a few potatoes, having one undergarment too [many] or having smoked a cigarette
during work, not to mention other trifles of this sort. They were lucky if
they escaped with flogging or a term in a penal company, which meant ex-
cessively hard work. But the unlucky ones, whose further fate was decided by
the code word "penal report 2" would fare much worse. Aumeier drew with
his blue pencil a thick cross at every name, putting small lines round the cor-
ners of the cross, and everybody could see it. It was no secret what "penal
report 2" meant.[54]

Although Broad was contrite in the dock at Frankfurt and in his memoirs,
he still reverts to the Auschwitz pretense: that "prisoners" had done something wrong, even if their punishments were horrifically exaggerated relative to the "crime."

The extant photographic records we have of the Erkennungsdienst indicate that Jews were much more likely than others to be subject to "penal report 2," meaning that they were shot or beaten to death, although the fact
that they "were sentenced to death" was not necessarily written into the
record. Surely a significant number were killed by phenol injections as well.
Usually, though, they were shot in the back, or in the back of the head at
close range.[55] "The clerks of Section II," wrote Broad, were then busy "writing the records of the executions. Cause of death—several shots through the
chest, among them one through the heart and two through the lungs . . .
thus the records." In an especially telling conclusion, he recalls, "It is better
to be cautious and even in those confidential papers it would never do to put
down in writing that shots in the back of the head *(Genickschuss)* were prac-
tised in Nazi Germany . . . which the Nazis exploited very successfully in
their propaganda." When the condemned did not die immediately, "nobody
cared that the victim suffered unbearably during the protracted execution."[56] Just as the Jewish handicapped had their tragic role as the vanguard
of genocide,[57] the Jewish "prisoners" of Auschwitz, prior to the transports,
were forerunners to the fate of the annihilated Jewish masses.

Of course, the numbers murdered through assembly-line methods over-
whelmed the number of those who met their deaths by beating, hanging,
shooting, and injection. But the very existence of these "Jewish prisoners,"
who seemed closer to the ostensibly "penal" origins and Nazi self-
perception of Auschwitz, perpetuated the charade that Auschwitz served a
"law-and-order" function. The majority of Jews who went through an identification process were most likely classified as *Schutzhäftlinge* (prisoners in

protective custody), while a number of Jews were among those (or otherwise treated like those) known as *Polizeihäftlinge* (police prisoners), who started arriving in Auschwitz as a result of overcrowding in the prison at Myslowice in February 1943.[58] There were, after all, Jews among the "common criminals" in Eastern Europe who sometimes maintained a sense of fraternity even during the Holocaust, and Jews who conducted criminal activity continued to be arrested by the Nazis during the deportations and mass slaughter.[59]

"Initially," one historian states, speaking primarily of Poles' Auschwitz "prison" experience, "they were held on the ground floor of Block Nr 2 [and] subsequently transferred to the ground floor of Block Nr 11, where they were not allowed to leave their assigned quarters. For them, the concentration camp served as a substitute for a criminal prison. The [Polish] police prisoners kept their civilian clothes and were not tattooed with camp numbers." Written accounts report that such "criminal" prisoners "received paper cards with numbers, which they kept in their pockets, but did not attach them to their uniforms in any way." Zippy Tichauer regards this description of prisoners "keeping cards on their person" as highly doubtful.[60] The account is worthy of mention, however, because it seems to misconstrue a policy I describe below, which makes the treatment of Jewish "prisoners" all the more contradictory and bizarre. The usual fate of anyone who entered this system was an "investigation" and "trial" before a *Polizeistandgericht* (police summary court), which might have taken but a few minutes; then "a death sentence," apparently by shooting, "was carried out on the spot."[61]

"From time to time," recalled Pery Broad, "the Police Office, which had forwarded a prisoner, would fix the date for his interrogation, but as little attention was paid to such dates as to the possibly decreed treatment according to camp status 1, 2, or 3"—which was ostensibly a guide to how severely a prisoner was to be treated. "This differentiated division of prisoners existed on paper only. In reality the guiltless got the worst treatment and had to work hardest, while prisoners with functions in the camp, usually called capos, were convicts, known for their brutality."[62] The inversion of innocent and criminal could barely be more stark.

There is one aspect of the categorization of inmates that neither Broad nor any of the scholars who have written on "criminal prisoner" identification in Auschwitz have discussed in detail. Using a term that does not appear in the extant literature—*karteimässig*—Zippy Tichauer states that Jews (and non-Jews) went through a procedure in which they were assigned a place in a card file. Perhaps the existence of the card was supposed to show that they were to be treated "fairly." In other words, it indicated that they had entered more like "criminal prisoners" than most of the Jews had and thus were not to be gassed. They were spared from the invariably lethal "selections."[63]

The most graphic corroboration of this arch-hypocritical policy is in the testimony of Sophia Litwinska, given before the "Belsen trial." In these proceedings held in the British zone, the British tried to combine crimes committed at Belsen and at Auschwitz, because most of the staff in the dock served at both places. The charge sheet cited two counts: Count One was for crimes committed at Bergen-Belsen, and Count Two, for crimes committed while the guards were previously working at Auschwitz.[64] Litwinska spoke about her experience in Auschwitz, because she had been called to give evidence about a doctor there who was later transferred to Bergen-Belsen. In the course of her testimony, she stated that while she was in the prison hospital after having broken her leg, she was "selected" for the gas. The court heard the following tale:

Q: When you reached the crematorium what happened there?

A: We left the trucks and were led into a room which gave me the impression of a shower bath. There were towels hanging round and sprays, and even mirrors.

Q: How did you leave the truck?

A: The whole truck was tipped over in the way as they do it sometimes with potatoes or coal loads.

Q: How many of you were there in the room altogether?

A: I cannot say really because I was so terrified about all these happenings that I have no idea about the numbers which were there.

Q: Were the doors closed?

A: I cannot say; I have never thought when I was there I shall leave and be here present in the court to speak about it.

Q: What happened next?

A: There were tears; people were shouting at each other; people were hitting each other. There were healthy people; strong people; weak people; and sick people, and suddenly I saw fumes coming in through a window.

Q: What do you mean when you say a window?

A: On top, very small sort of window.

Q: What effect did this have on you?

A: I had to cough very violently; tears were streaming out of my eyes, and I had a sort of feeling in my throat as if I would be asphyxiated.

Q: What happened to the other people around you?

A: I could not look even at the others because each of us was only concentrated on what happened to himself.

Q: What was the next thing that you remember?

A: In that moment I heard my name called. I had not the strength to answer it, but I raised my arm. Then I felt somebody take me and throw me out from that room.

Q: When you got out did you see anyone there?

A: Then Hossler took me on a motor-cycle—he put a blanket around me—and took me again into the hospital.

Q: How long did you stay in the hospital?

A: Six weeks.

Q: What effect did the gas have on you?

A: I have still quite frequently headaches; I have heart trouble, and whenever I went into the fresh air my eyes were filled with tears.

Q: Were you subsequently taken to the political department?

A: Yes.

Q: Did you receive any explanation as to why you had been taken out of the gas chamber?

A: Because I came with a transport from a prison which apparently makes a difference, and, apart from that, my husband was a Polish officer.[65]

Most likely, the prisoners' numbers had been noted but were not checked in time to prevent the selection. Zippy states that one of the jobs of the secretaries in the Politische Abteilung, where Litwinksa was taken after being pulled out of the gas chamber,[66] was to look up the numbers of those selected for transport to the gas. This episode illustrates the possibility, however remote, that a prisoner might have been "saved" because she or he was considered a "criminal." In her deposition, Litwinska said that "I was arrested because I was a Jewess; my husband, who was an Aryan and a Polish officer," was arrested and "taken to Auschwitz, where he died. The reason why my husband was arrested was because he married a Jewess. On my arrest I was taken to Lublin prison, where I remained for one year before being taken to Auschwitz. I was taken to Auschwitz in company with other Jews who were said to be partisans."[67] Strange as Litwinska's experience sounds, her testimony fits the convoluted Nazi policies. Apparently the mistake of sending Litwinska to the gas was discovered late, but in time to save her life.

Holocaust deniers have ridiculed Litwinska's testimony, but scholars have not scrutinized it. However strange, it is worthy of attention. It also may be supported by the recollections of two women who worked as "secretaries" for the Politische Abteilung. They reported that they

> had saved a number of prisoners from being gassed. They related that after every selection and before the actual admission to the gas chambers, the numbers of the condemned were checked in the Politische Abteilung. Only those prisoners who had been sent to the camp with RSHA transports could be gassed.[68] The ones who had come through Gestapo or Kripo offices (and therefore had political or criminal records) were, paradoxically, released and returned to their blocks. The women claimed that by erroneously reporting some of the candidates as Gestapo cases they had saved the lives of quite a few inmates.[69]

Although the possibility that this ruse was successful on more than a few occasions is unlikely,[70] recognition of this kind of glitch in the supposed total solution to the Jewish problem is instructive. Lore Shelley, one of the "secretaries" who collected the group's reminiscences, writes that these two women "promised to write about such incidents, but, regretfully, omitted doing so." Too often it is forgotten that even Auschwitz, in the words of Zippy Tichauer, "was full of paradoxes."[71]

This policy provides a possible key to what seemed, to some survivors, to be extraordinarily puzzling experiences. Although why he escaped the gas chamber remained a mystery to Rabbi Hugo Gryn (1930–96) throughout his life, his father understood that being classified as political prisoners might exempt his son and himself from the gas. When asked at their induction why they were sent to Auschwitz from a labor camp in Hungary, his father's reply seemed shocking: " 'I was charged with being involved in politics,' he said. It was ridiculous. Dad had nothing to do with politics. Why, then, did he say he had? The man filling in the forms was not surprised in the least. He wrote something down, and asked finally: 'Have you any relatives in the camp?' 'Yes,' Dad replied, 'my cousin. We were arrested on the same charge.' He pointed to me." Later his father told him that a Polish Kapo had "informed me that unless you are here for politics or sabotage, you might stay for months on end. On the other hand, political prisoners are sent away to work as soon as possible. So the choice was obvious. 'And anyway,' he concluded, 'I am not as innocent as you may think. Perhaps some time I will tell you more about it.' "[72]

He spared his son the knowledge that without the crucial information passed to him they might not have evaded the gas chamber.

In Auschwitz and elsewhere the practices of identification—and execution—of a segment of Jews as "criminal" held a larger and more important role in the destruction of European Jewry than has been recognized.[73] One of the main functions of the SS Erkennungsdienst was to process incoming "criminal prisoners" who were brought to Auschwitz by the Gestapo, Kripo (Kriminalpolizei, criminal police), and other security units.[74] As discussed earlier, the literature seldom mentions that some of the Jews who were transported to Auschwitz and other concentration camps were, in fact, "criminals" by pre-Nazi standards. One survivor recalls that in the Pawiak prison (where Jews were later shipped to Auschwitz) "the block-elder was a German [Aryan]; he wore the green insignia of the professional criminal. The room-serviceman was a Jew from Lodz, Poland, whose criminal career had also not begun in the camp, but already in his homestead."[75] But the vast majority of the Jews who were caught in the sprawling Nazi security apparatus had been thrown into ghetto jails for any number of flimsy or absurd reasons, such as belonging to an outlawed organization, which might have been simply a communal, charitable organization, or a more expressly political grouping, like Zionism or the Bund, the preeminent Jewish socialist party in Eastern Europe. Certainly many Jews in Polish prisons, later transferred to concentration camps, were there because of their communist sympathies or activities. Their presence also could simply have been a matter of bad luck—being in a place where others were being rounded up.[76]

Memoirs and diaries also help to reconstruct how Jews came to be processed as "criminal prisoners." Dr. Elise Kramer, a doctor for concentration camps in the Posen region, informed a somewhat sympathetic supervisor, Dr. Sieburg—who considered himself a "nationalist" but not a "Nazi"—of the abominable conditions of prisoners, and "he tried to bring about some improvement." Sieburg suggested that Kramer prepare a report on the existing state of affairs, the hygienic defects, and the low allotment of calories. He promised to support the petition with his own comments and further advised Kramer to state "malnutrition" as cause of death in the death certificates. He believed that such dreadful conditions could not have been fostered intentionally by the Nazis. To Kramer's surprise, her report was submitted and "an improvement became noticeable. Food was more plentiful and the work better organized. The prisoners of the Antoniek Camp thanked me for my help."[77]

Unfortunately, though, like so many instances in which victims had some kind of relief, this improvement was not to last. Some weeks later Kramer was arrested and taken to a Gestapo prison in Poznan. There she was accused of "sabotage of German work" and physically threatened. She remained in that jail "for about three weeks under wretched conditions. "One of my co-prisoners," Kramer recalled, "had helped English prisoners of war to escape." After being transferred to the prison at Alexanderplatz, she was sent to a prison on Bessemer Street for three weeks. The inmates there "were women of all nations, some of them Jewesses who waited for their transport to the nearest concentration camp."[78]

Although Eugen Kogon provides an excellent synthesis of concentration camp procedures based on his experience at Buchenwald—offering it as a template for Jews' experiences, including those at Auschwitz—his description does not explain Auschwitz's "mug shots" of Jews. Kogon reports that prisoners were photographed relatively soon after their arrival, before their clothing was confiscated and they were given prison garb. The Auschwitz photos of prisoners, Jewish and non-Jewish, overwhelmingly show their subjects in zebra stripes.[79] "Besides being tattooed," Tadeusz Iwaszko writes of Auschwitz, "another element in the registration process for new [criminal-prisoner] arrivals was being photographed in three poses. In the first photograph, a profile, the camp number was visible as well as the letter symbols for the category and nationality of the prisoner."[80] As mentioned earlier, camp photographers used a specific style of photography associated with identifying criminals, the Bertillon system.[81] Jews who arrived in RSHA "mass transports" beginning in 1942, around the time of the Wannsee Conference and afterward, were not photographed because their execution was a foregone conclusion.

Although Bernhard Walter and Ernst Hoffmann of the Erkennungsdienst had not been trained professionally as photographers, both of them acquired the necessary skills sometime after joining the party. Walter reportedly took part "in selections on the ramp." He may have done similar photographic work while at the Sachsenhausen concentration camp,[82] which, like its predecessor, Oranienburg, was noted for its exhaustive "publicity work" *(Öffentlichkeitsarbeit)* to defend itself against charges of maltreatment of its inmates. In the early years of the Third Reich Nazis referred to the depictions of their concentration camps by internal adversaries and the foreign press as "atrocity propaganda" *(Greuelpropaganda)*. Oranienburg supplied the material for the Nazis' *Anti-Brown Book (Das Antibraunbuch über das erste deutsche Konzentrationslager)*, which attempted to show that concentration camps were normal prisons, engaged in sensible punishment and rehabilitation of inmates.[83]

Among those Jews processed by the Auschwitz Erkennungsdienst, we can sketch the origins, and gain some sense of the fate, of many Jews who were received as "criminal prisoners." Wolf Birnbaum was prisoner number 20133, occupation "unknown." Forty-four years old, he arrived in Auschwitz on February 6, 1942, and died February 17, 1942. He was one of "eight prisoners sent in a group transport." Who sent him, from where, is unknown. The Auschwitz "occupancy register" does not, however, bother to mention that there was at least a single Jew in this transport.[84] Stanisław Borski, prisoner number 24508, an "electrician" who arrived in Auschwitz on December 15, 1941, was killed three days later. Born April 13, 1887, in Warsaw, Borski was in a group of a hundred prisoners sent by the Sipo (Sicherheitspolizei, Security Police, which combined the Kripo [Criminal Police] and the Gestapo) and Sicherheitsdienst (Security Service within the SS) from Montelupich Prison in Kraków. Again, the group of which he was a part is not designated as containing any Jews.[85] Jakob Weisbart, a tanner, who arrived in Auschwitz on November 12, 1941, was assigned number 22575; he died December 11, 1941, at age sixty. Weisbart was among nineteen prisoners sent by the Prague Stapo (Staatspolizei), in which group there were nine Jews, one German, and nine Czech non-Jews.[86] Reuben Winter, a baker, born June 22, 1900, in Ranizow, Poland, arrived in Auschwitz on October 22, 1941; given number 21887, he died November 1, 1941. He manages to look back into the camera with quiet dignity, as if to say, "Do what you want with me." He was among forty-eight prisoners sent by the Sipo and SD from the Kraków district prison in Reichshof (Rzeszow). There is no distinction made between Jews and non-Jews in the record of Winter's group.[87]

The portraiture does not vary from the Bertillon method. As opposed to photos of non-Jews, few if any nonpolice photos were placed in Jews' files. The small signs in the far-left, side-view images label all of them as "Pole," but the subjects' double-cloth star, making a six-pointed star of one yellow and one indeterminable color, marks them as Jews. If we accept as fact that most of these Auschwitz photos were intentionally destroyed with the bulk of documentation pertaining to the camp,[88] the recurrence of such pictures represents something greater than an aberration. Prior to the mass transports

Auschwitz prisoner Jakob Weisbart. Such photographs—again in the Bertillon anthropometric style—helped the Nazis maintain the illusion that Auschwitz served a "penal" function. Desig. no. 132.0, W/S no. 12936, CD no. 0327, USHMM. Reproduced by permission of the State Museum of Auschwitz-Birkenau, Oświęcim-Brzezinka.

Auschwitz mug shot of Reuben Winter. Desig. no. 132.0, W/S no. 08471, CD no. 0327, USHMM. Reproduced by permission of the State Museum of Auschwitz-Birkenau, Oświęcim-Brzezinka.

of Jews the early Auschwitz logs refer repeatedly to "prisoner transports," often without specifying the national or religious origin of the groups. However, these groups seem to have included a substantial number of Jews. Just as Henry Friedlander suggests that Jews with disabilities were the initial victims of genocide, tone can make a similar statement about Jewish "prisoners." For example, on June 23, 1941, of the sixty prisoners sent by the Gestapo from Oppeln, thirteen were Jews, and on July 11, 1941, out of 182 "prisoners" from Montelupich Prison in Kraków, 171 were Jews.[89] Already we have 184 "exceptions."

Few if any of the known Jewish subjects of the Erkennungsdienst photographic unit in Auschwitz survived. Hermann Langbein, a survivor who became a significant historian of Auschwitz, is remarkable for having recovered his own "mug shot."[90] His case is, in fact, instructive: Langbein entered Auschwitz as a "German"—not a Jew. Arrested as a communist and ex-fighter in the International Brigade (of the Spanish Civil War), and registered initially in Dachau, Langbein claimed "that his father was partly Jewish, a so-called Mischling but that he did not know exactly to what degree, except that it [this designation] would not usually classify him as a Jew. Surprisingly, no one ever followed up, and therefore he was also registered in Auschwitz as not being Jewish."[91] Hence, the fact that Langbein wore one triangle, not two overlapping ones (to designate him as a Jew), meant that he was in a privileged caste in Auschwitz. The SS's description of the camp suggests that most of the Jewish "criminals" sent to Auschwitz ended up in Block 11, where they met their deaths.

One of the chief rationales for the documentation of "criminals" sent to Auschwitz was its potential use for "circulars distributed to local police stations as part of the manhunt" in the unlikely event of an outbreak.[92] Aleksander Lasik writes that the Erkennungsdienst also had to supply the "photographic documentation of cases in which prisoners died violently (for instance by suicide or during an escape attempt). Such photographs were added to the [photographs and fingerprints] and sent to SS-WVHA Office Group D along with the prisoner's file. The Erkennungsdienst also provided photographs of internal camp events—documentation, at the request of Department V" of the RSHA (Reichssicherheitshauptamt), the Kripo, dealing mainly with nonpolitical crimes, the handicapped, and "Gypsies." These photos included images of "medical experiments performed on prisoners, or of camp staff and visiting dignitaries at the behest of the commandant."[93] Most commentators have overlooked the fact that the very photographing of the prisoners used for "medical experiments" was part of their hideous treatment.

PHOTOGRAPHING THE BUDY TRAGEDY

One particularly horrific episode at Auschwitz, in which Nazi officials tried to use "criminal photography" to justify their acts as a response to Jews' "criminal" behavior, occurred during the "Budy" tragedy. Survivor Hermann Langbein has written about Budy, although he did not witness the events there. Historian Deborah Dwork has also written about the tragedy, particularly its illumination of the significance of gender in the Holocaust, and her work has attracted the attention of sociologist Nechama Tec. It is helpful, however, to revisit the background of the massacre, as it has largely escaped the notice of scholars.[94]

In October 1942 the gas chambers and crematoria of Auschwitz-Birkenau were fully operational. One morning a handful of SS men of the Politische Abteilung were summoned to investigate a disturbance at Budy, a village a few miles west of the camp, just south of the Vistula River.[95] Budy, with three to four hundred women and a small contingent of SS guards, was one of some forty Nazi subcamps created in the region around Auschwitz, within the camp's designated "area of interest" (Interessengebiet).[96] The main function of the Budy camp, which also was home to a women's penal company (Strafkompanie), was to supply slave labor for farming and drainage projects, "dredging and cleaning fishponds, cutting reeds and wild shrubs, and demolishing buildings of the former Polish inhabitants."[97]

On the morning in question the SS officers were instructed to take their typewriters along. Apparently something extraordinary had occurred that necessitated an immediate, on-the-spot evaluation, and the tension of their superior, SS-Untersturmführer Maximilian Grabner, was palpable. As they approached the camp their vehicle was "stopped by a sentinel." "But recognizing Grabner, head of the Politische Abteilung, the guard quickly apologized." The nervous guard explained that according to the camp commandant, Rudolf Höss, he was "not to let any unauthorized persons pass through."[98]

Included in the party dispatched to Budy was SS-Unterscharführer Pery Broad, who later wrote a detailed account of the incident. Although he was not high ranking, the equivalent of a corporal, Broad was distinctive, possibly even a bit suspect among his SS colleagues, because he was from South America.[99] He was the son of a Brazilian merchant and German mother, whose mother brought him to Germany in the early 1930s. One survivor remembers that Broad liked to speak English if he had the chance; he described himself as a "student of chemistry" before joining the Nazi party, possibly to elevate himself above the riff-raff. Broad's particular brief in Auschwitz's Politische Abteilung was later described as "Gypsy and bordello affairs,"[100] although he in fact had a number of roles at Auschwitz.

During the short drive, Broad recalled, Grabner insinuated "that a revolt had broken out at Budy." Broad and his colleagues found this suggestion "curious." Nothing seemed out of the ordinary as they neared the village, and the camp (now synonymous with the village, from which its original Polish population had been driven out) was known for its relaxed security. The surroundings—"lovely" meadows, fields, woods, and lakes—appeared tranquil, although the men were certainly aware that "starvation, brutality, and despair" reigned in the camp.[101]

When the SS detachment approached the gate, the men got out of the car, and "the guard saluted." Once outside, the SS men began to notice a distinct "buzzing and humming in the air. Then they saw a sight so horrible that some minutes were gone before they could take it in properly." A square to the side and back of a former school building used to house the inmates "was covered with dozens of female corpses, mutilated and blood-encrusted. . . . All were covered only with threadbare prisoners' undergarments. . . . The groaning of those barely alive was mixed with the buzzing of immense swarms of flies that circled round the sticky blood puddles and the smashed skulls." The SS men now saw the cause of "the singular humming sound they had found so peculiar when they entered." They also noticed, above ground level, that "some corpses hung in a twisted position on the barbed wire fence." Other bodies were in a heap, "evidently thrown out from one still-open attic window."[102]

Without a thought to rendering assistance to possible survivors, Grabner, Broad writes, "gave the order to find some women among those lying on the ground who could be interrogated, and obtain their testimony as to what had happened." Grabner's assistant, a Pole considered *volksdeutsche,* SS-Untersturmführer, Georg Wosnitzka, "stepped around the corpses and tried to find among the victims somebody who could speak. Failing in that, he approached a group of women a short distance away from most of the bodies who were washing themselves at the well." They proceeded, in any event, to regale Wosnitzka with the background to the gruesome scene.[103]

We may assume that the women who spoke to SS-Untersturmführer Wosnitzka were mainly Poles, but perhaps also Russians, Czechs, Yugoslavs, and Ukrainians who lived amid a number of German (non-Jewish) women, including at least a few known prostitutes, and "a considerable number of Jewish women" prisoners at Budy.[104] Wosnitzka, from Chorzow near Kattowitz (Upper Silesia), spoke Polish but attempted to "conceal his knowledge of the language from prisoners," possibly to avoid the appearance of fraternization with Poles.[105] The German women were a mix of "green" (criminal) and "black" (asocial) inmates from Auschwitz. (One scholar asserts that the German women prisoners were sent to Budy for having "committed crimes" in the main camp of Auschwitz.)[106] The non-German women eagerly told Wosnitzka that the SS camp guards "used to prod the German prisoners to annoy and molest the Jewish women." If they did not comply, the Polish women said, "the Germans were threatened with being 'shot while trying to escape.' These men took great enjoyment," the informants explained, "in abusing the Jewesses in this way." This led the German women "to fear that the Jewish women whom they tormented" might someday try to "take vengeance on them." The women briefing Wosnitzka maintained, though, that these fears were groundless, because in their view, "the Jewish women, who mostly belonged to intellectual circles, e.g. some had been formerly students of the Sorbonne or artists, never even thought of getting down to the level of the vulgar German prostitutes and of planning revenge, though it would have been understandable if they did so."[107] Though this assessment might have been partly true, the Jewish women had a deeper motive for not wishing to bring notice to themselves. They knew that they were in a relatively privileged situation, especially in the fall of 1942, when thousands of Jews were being murdered daily.[108]

The uninjured women telling Wosnitzka the story then proceeded to relate the immediate background to the massacre. "The evening before," they reported, a Jewish woman "was returning from the lavatory and was going upstairs to the sleeping quarters." The ground floor of the building housed the "block- and camp-seniors," those who did the SS's bidding, two women who were "citizens of the Reich and former prostitutes." Several Jewish women slept in the attic, while most of the other Jews, along with the majority of the remaining prisoners, lived in the barrack nearby.[109] One of the German "elders" claimed that "the Jewess had a stone in her hand"— presumably to attack her—"but that, of course, was her hysterical imagination only. . . . At the gate below was a guard, who was known to be the German woman's lover. . . . Leaning out from the window, she cried for help," screaming that she had been "attacked by the Jewess." At least three SS guards ran upstairs, joined by the German women prisoners, and all of them "began to beat the Jewish women indiscriminately." They threw some of the Jews "down the winding stairs," and the women landed "in a heap, one upon the other. Some were thrown out of the window. . . . The guards also drove the Jewish women from the barrack into the yard."[110]

The witnesses told Wosnitzka that the German elder "who had instigated the butchering," later identified as the " 'Axe Queen,' Elfriede Schmidt," stayed behind in her bedroom with her lover. They alleged that she planned the incident to redouble his devotion. With the couple upstairs, the so-called rebellion continued outside, "with bludgeons, gun butts, and shots. Even an axe had been used as a weapon by one of the female capos. In their mortal fear a few Jewish women tried to creep under the wire fence in order to escape the butchering. They got stuck and were soon killed. Even when all women lay on the ground, the fiends, drunk with blood, kept hitting the helpless victims again and again. They wanted, above all, to kill everybody, so as to destroy all witnesses of their atrocities."[111]

This event happened in the late evening or early morning hours. Sometime around 5 A.M. the women said that Commandant Höss had been called to Budy about "the so-called rebellion, which had been successfully overcome." Already a rumor was launched that the German women and guards had quelled a "rebellion" by the Jewish women. Höss recounts his version of the event, with "French Jewesses" as the main victims of the massacre, in his well-known memoir.[112] An aide quickly drove him there, probably between 5 and 7 A.M., and the commandant "inspected the traces of the bloody orgy. A few wounded women, who had hidden among the corpses, then rose, [believing that] they were saved. . . . But Höss quickly left the camp. As soon as he departed, the surviving, wounded Jewish women were shot."[113]

Broad's version of the incident, which has been closely followed thus far, apparently begins later in the morning after the massacre, some three to six hours after Höss's cursory inspection. Grabner and his party, including Broad and Wosnitzka, "SS investigators" of the Auschwitz Erkennungs-dienst, Walter and Hoffmann,[114] and "medical orderlies" were summoned, allegedly to survey the scene and render "medical help to the injured." Broad writes that "some less seriously wounded women had managed to hide at the beginning of the tragic incident and did not leave their hiding places. That is, they had survived the (supposedly final) shootings imme-diately after Höss' visit. The women were interrogated and then 'looked after' by the orderlies." Later, though, Broad writes, they were killed by phe-nol injections.[115] The Erkennungsdienst men, who Broad respectfully calls "criminal investigators," took a great number of photographs of the scene "from all possible angles." About their activities in the field that day in Budy, Pery Broad writes, "Only one copy of each photograph was later de-veloped in the dark room, under strict supervision. The plates had to be de-stroyed in the presence of the commandant and the photos were put at his disposal."[116]

According to Broad's telling of the tale, despite the brutality of the episode, some semblance of justice was rendered. He states that among the guilty women murderers, who we may assume included some non-German women, six German women prisoners were administered phenol injections that day in Auschwitz's notorious Block 11. Their camp records, however, were doctored to reveal no mention of their crime, and the reports to their families gravely cited deaths due to "natural causes." As an added touch, families were assured that "an urn with the ashes would be sent on request."[117] Although Broad's narrative is for the most part accurate, if incomplete, his statement about the fate of the German women prostitutes is open to question. Hermann Langbein, an Auschwitz survivor and scholar, does not dispute the contention that the Nazis immediately put the female murderers to death, because that act would have "spared the SS-guards the painful consequences of having to answer to dereliction of their duties."[118] Broad concludes his history of the "Revolt at Budy" by claiming that with the execution of the six German women, "the crimes at Budy were sufficiently expiated, in the opinion of the camp authorities. The guard in question [Schmidt's lover] got an admonishment, and in the future guards were not allowed to enter that camp. The number of prisoners rose again to normal, why, Jews were arriving daily!"[119]

Another motivation for Broad to underscore the "justice" meted out to the German women prisoners was his awareness of the sexual undertones to the massacre, and suggestions that the women's killing not only robbed them of their lives but violated their womanhood. Reflecting on the first few months of the Nazi invasion of Poland, a detailed survivor's memoir records that large numbers of "Jewish daughters in the big cities and small towns [in Poland] were forced into military bordellos. There they found a fatal end, bodily and mentally violated, desecrated. Rapes were frequent, indeed encouraged by the Gestapo. Guided by Polish riff-raff soldiers broke into Jewish homes, raping and stealing. . . . The news of these crimes reached other countries. . . . Goebbels denied such rumors vigorously."[120] The reasons for these vehement denials were numerous and offer insight into Broad's narrative of the Budy story. The Nazis were squeamish about admitting to sadism and sexual crimes within their ranks, because they did not want to expose their own men as failing to heed the prescribed racial ideology and subverting middle-class family values.[121] There is evidence, in scores of published and unpublished survivor memoirs, that (at least) hundreds of German soldiers, SS included, had no reservations about raping Jewish women.[122] These men apparently did not fear the repercussion of a racial "taint." But crimes of a sexual nature undermined the edifice of respectability the Nazis sought to exhibit.[123] Even in the killing fields of the

Eastern Front SS men were sometimes reprimanded or punished for their "harsh" treatment of Jewish women.[124] These "punishments" for misconduct, however, like Broad's narration of the execution of the German women, should be seen as a hypocritical gesture to cover up or exculpate state-sponsored crimes of the most horrific dimensions.[125]

Let us revisit the suggestion made by Grabner, apparently at the behest of Höss, that Budy had been the scene of a "revolt." It is doubtful that a revolt, or even an attempted escape, as suggested by Robert Jan van Pelt and Deborah Dwork, had occurred.[126] The event at Budy was a massacre. Why would the Nazi authorities call it a revolt? After examining the scene in the early hours, albeit briefly, Höss most likely thought that it would be a good subject for pictorial propaganda illustrating "Jewish criminality." A memo about the situation of the native populations and the economic conditions the Nazis faced at the end of 1941 in the "eastern region" *(Ostgebiet)* noted that "the population takes great interest in the propaganda notice-boards *(Propagandatafeln)* in public squares and municipal buildings, especially photo-montages *(Fotomontagen).*"[127] Extant photos indicate that similar use of photo propaganda was avidly pursued.

Höss surely noticed those who had been killed on or near the wire fence. They had certainly been shot or beaten to death—not electrocuted—because the fence was not then electrified.[128] We can assume that Höss believed that pictures of the women on or near the fence would be useful to show off to other Nazi authorities, or possibly to keep for the sake of the camp's records, to illustrate how to handle a "revolt" by Jewish prisoners. No other explanation exists for calling the Erkennungsdienst to the scene to snap rolls of photographs.[129]

Furthermore, we have ample evidence of how Höss and his underlings treated "prisoners shot while trying to escape." "Escape" was a euphemism for a prisoner suicide, because the Nazis hated to grant prisoners the freedom to take their own lives in Auschwitz and other camps.[130] Broad recalls, "When working in the outside squads they ran through the chain of sentries to be shot by them or they 'ran into the wires,' as it was called in camp jargon. The high voltage electricity current or the shots of machine guns saved them from further misery."[131] On such occasions, Walter and Hoffmann sprang to action, it seems, with enthusiasm: "The officers of the Erkennungsdienst hurried to the place and photographed the body from all angles," and witnesses were interviewed in drawn-out sessions supposedly "to make sure that the victim had not been killed by other prisoners." Broad states, "This was truly a farce full of unsurpassed cynicism! As if the SS

Photograph taken by the Erkennungsdienst, the "Identification Service," at Auschwitz, apparently of a prisoner who had committed suicide at the electrified fence. In Auschwitz and other camps the Nazis devised ceremonies for such occasions, often making prisoners stand for hours or march around those who were killed for "the crime of trying to escape." From the Instytut Pamięci Narodewej, Desig. no. 130.120, W/S no. 37175, CD no. 0015, USHMM.

authorities in the camp, where daily thousands were systematically tortured to death, cared what happened to the unhappy man!"[132]

At least one official photograph survives of a "suicide of a prisoner on the electrified barbed-wire fence" at Auschwitz, and another shows "a prisoner who attempted to climb the barbed-wire fence . . . killed by machine gun fire and subsequently left hanging as a warning to others."[133] Such photographic exercises were a cynical farce in another way: they attempted to mimic the vocation of professional police photographers whose main purpose is to establish the facts of a case. A survivor who worked in the Politische Abteilung recalled that for non-Jewish prisoners who were killed, camp authorities would file "death notices," but no such procedure existed for Jews.[134] What made the roles of Walter and Hoffmann even more perverse is the fact that SS men were rewarded with at least three days' leave for killing a prisoner "who had approached the wire fences. It was officially termed a prize for 'preventing a prisoner's escape.' "[135]

What Höss hoped to accomplish through the pseudopolice photography at Budy was to supply a striking illustration of what happens to Jews who "revolt" or "try to escape."[136] He sought to capture "transgressions," but the resulting photographs "only framed cruelty."[137] At some point, he realized that the photography project was not a worthwhile exercise, and was possibly even a risky endeavor. Indeed, it could have been used to verify the "*Greuelpropaganda*" that so irked the Nazis. The photographs have been lost. The Budy episode obviously was a "bloodbath," but it was not necessarily an event from which his audience would ever be able to draw a lesson. Even with contrived captions, the photographs probably would not bear out the story that the massacre was the result of prisoners trying to escape; it would not serve the lesson. Höss later claimed to have immediately recoiled when faced by the massacre: "It is still before my eyes," he wrote in 1946. "I find it incredible that human beings should ever turn into such beasts." The way the "greens," meaning the German women criminals, "knocked the French Jewesses about, tearing them to pieces, killing them with axes, and throttling them—it was simply gruesome." Höss concluded that the killings were the work of "criminals" and "asocials" who happened to be "utter brutes."[138] In the fall of 1942, however, his first impulse was to use the Budy tragedy as fodder to show that the bad end for Jews was a result of their propensity to "revolt," and more generally, that it was a just punishment for their "criminality."[139]

To reconstruct this tragic event we need to delve further into the background of the camp. The Auschwitz subcamps, varying greatly in size and function, were known by a number of names, such as *Arbeitslager* (work camp), *Nebenlager* (secondary camp), *Zweiglager* (branch camp), *Arbeitskommando* (work detachment), and *Aussenkommando* (external detachment), which in themselves are not revealing. A leading scholar of Auschwitz minimizes their differences, stating that they all "had the same organizational structure."[140] Yet from the perspective of the camp's Jewish victims, Zippy states, a fundamental distinction existed between the myriad subcamps as well as between selected components of the Auschwitz domain. These units were known as *Abschnittslager* or *Zweiglager;* again, the terms themselves, "sector camp" and "branch camp," are superficially meaningless. But placement in a *Zweiglager* was, in the universe of Auschwitz, a possibility of life, because no selections for the gas chambers occurred there. Budy was one such *Zweiglager* entity, along with the Harmense and Rajsko camps, and the work detachment at the barracks known as "Canada," where clothing and possessions of incoming inmates were sorted.[141] The inmates assigned to the women's orchestra in Birkenau, as well as its supporting functions—such as copying music—also were protected from "selections."[142] Zippy's testimony furthermore helps us understand why Budy was so lightly guarded. It had "a single barbed-wire fence that was neither lit nor electrified"; its prisoners "were not considered dangerous."[143] Jews had virtually nothing to gain from an escape attempt, because they would most likely land back in either the Auschwitz main camp or Birkenau, and therefore be subject to "selections." (At the village of Rajsko the greenhouses from its Auschwitz days exist to this day. As of the late 1990s there was no indication of Rajsko's history as part of Auschwitz.)[144] Although we know in retrospect that the Nazis intended to eventually murder all of the Jews in their grasp, at least a few specific work details—including, ironically, those Jews involved in the Nazi efforts to counterfeit foreign currency in Sachsenhausen—were indefinitely relieved of the specter of selections for mass murder.[145]

Given that she was involved in the induction of newcomers, Zippy occasionally was in a position to influence the placement of individuals at subcamps and work details.[146] Sometimes other Jewish women workers also had the opportunity to divert or transfer Jews to specific assignments. If given the opportunity, Zippy had Jewish women, including friends and relatives, assigned to Budy, as well as to other enclaves that were immune from selections.[147] Normally the assignment of Jews to Budy would have been unlikely, because the Nazis tended to send prisoners there whom they considered to have experience in agriculture—mostly non-Jewish Poles. The Nazis' racial stereotyping would usually have precluded them from dispensing Jews, especially Jewish women, to such a camp.[148]

The women whom Höss termed "French Jewesses" were, most likely, women deported from Poland, Slovakia, Russia, and Latvia who became "stateless" and were interned, initially, at the camps of Drancy, Beaune-la-Rolande, and Pithiviers. The Jews who were later dispatched to Budy did not necessarily have any memory of the earlier makeup or fate of the subcamp's Jewish inhabitants.[149] When the camp was expanded in 1944, the Nazis again shipped a relatively small number of Jews there to work, men as well as women. Although the Jews who were sent to Budy realized they had been saved, at least temporarily, they were, occasionally, subject to "transports to the gas chambers."[150]

Official photographs that purported to document the unnatural death of prisoners, such as those of Budy, added to the juridical fantasy. As such, they helped give the impression that Auschwitz was an institution in which justice was dispensed, according to universal criteria of crime and punishment, although it was nothing of the kind.[151]

RITUALS OF "RETRIBUTION" AND "WARNING"

In *After Auschwitz,* theologian Richard Rubenstein expounds on the idea that the Nazis' delivering Jews into furnaces is a central symbol of the primordial aspect of the Holocaust.[152] However much these killings took place with the knowledge of the entire camp—certainly the smells and smoke were ever present—for numerous reasons they were not done in full public view. In the case of the Operation Reinhard extermination camps, Yitzhak Arad convincingly argues that tremendous effort was expended to disguise the purpose of the killing centers.[153] Conversely, death by hanging in Auschwitz and other concentration camps was a recurrent public spectacle. The fact is often recalled that only days before the liberation of Auschwitz, "four Jewish women"—Regina Sapirsztein, Alla Gartner, Ester Weissblum, and Rosa Robota—"were hanged in front of a roll call" for their part in attempting "to blow up the crematoria during the prisoner revolt."[154] Elie Wiesel has famously memorialized the gallows "ceremony" at Auschwitz.[155] For the Nazis this ritual was legitimated by historical precedent, because hanging was often described and depicted as the appropriate fate for Jewish villains.[156]

A survivor of the Lida and Vilna ghettos wrote that the "perfect performance" of Nazi henchmen and their accomplices before deportations depended partly on "several hangings in the village market," staged to be as visible as possible. The victims "were innocent people who were supposedly caught because of 'economic offenses,' disobedience at work, etc. It was not difficult to catch a 'criminal' of this kind because everything depended on the interpretation of the governor, the soldier, or just a Polish informer."[157] A survivor of the Shavli ghetto in Lithuania wrote, "In spring 1943, the German SS hanged Mazuvesky, a Jewish family man in our ghetto. He was caught with two loaves of bread and a few packs of cigarettes, trying to bring them into the ghetto after working on the outside. The Germans forced us to witness the hanging so we would know not to make any such attempts."[158] Jews, often police—and sometimes relatives and friends of the condemned—were pressed into the role of hangman. Isaiah Trunk noted that a Jew convicted of murder and sentenced to death in the Lodz ghetto was killed "by a Jewish hangman and his Jewish assistants." In

March 1943 the inmates of the Lvov ghetto were forced to witness the hanging of twelve Jewish policemen "from balconies in Loketka Street," which the Nazis justified as a fitting response to the killing of a notorious SS man earlier that day. Such actions served to intensify what one survivor has referred to as "the drama at the gallows."[159]

In the camps around Posen, people identified as a Jew's friends would be forced to hang a Jew (said to be) caught "attempting to escape." The hanging was accompanied by punishment for the entire camp, which entailed withholding of meals, work on Sunday, the beating of every tenth prisoner, and "parading in the yard for hours in any weather."[160] At the "men's camp" in Posen, hangings "took place in the 'Stadion' [arena, presumably the central assembly square] and in the presence of 'delegations' from the other camps. This was standard punishment for the 'crimes' of smuggling letters, stealing, and attempting to escape." "After the execution the women were ordered to dance around the hanged bodies. The condemned persons mostly died bravely."[161] One woman from a labor camp some twenty miles from Kraków, which she called "Julag I," wrote that one of her searing memories involved

> a twelve year old boy who had committed the "crime" of leaving the camp in an attempt to obtain food from some Aryan friends for his sickly and starving father. Both the boy and his father were to be executed for their crime, and as an example for the rest of us. Before each execution, the victims were forced to undress; the Nazi murderers were methodically efficient; clothes with bullet holes or blood on them required unnecessary expenditure of labor to repair for the next prisoner to wear. The father, without resisting, undressed, kneeled, and was shot, but the boy refused to undress. He pleaded vainly for mercy and forgiveness, but his plea fell on deaf ears. Finally, the boy attacked the guards with his bare hands. He was shot, but he never gave his killers the satisfaction of seeing him cringe in submission.[162]

When the Nazis' carefully stage-managed demonstrations were disrupted, such exceptions sometimes had the greatest impact on the assembled victims.

In a Dachau subcamp a survivor recalls that six boys in the camp acquired an army blanket and cut it up to keep their feet from freezing. They were

> taken to the *Appellplatz* [the assembly area, particularly for roll call]. The Germans were running around and screaming and cursing and telling us of the horrible crime that these young boys committed. Unheard of to cut up an army blanket, to destroy government property! They will think of a

proper punishment to fit the crime so the stupid inmates will under-stand *[sic]* in the future that it is not permitted to do such a thing. All the inmates stood in complete silence waiting for the verdict. First they kept the unfortunate boys in the kitchen cellar without any food or water. The verdict finally came. Death by hanging. One of the boys had a mother and sister in our camp. The mother fainted. . . . The gallows were built in the middle of the *Appellplatz*. All the inmates were ordered to stand and witness the execution. The camp orchestra had to play while six young boys were hanged for cutting up a blanket. They remained hanging the whole day. I was beside myself. It reminded me of the execution of Bezalel Mazavetzki in the [Traku] ghetto. I couldn't sleep the whole night. I can still see them in front of my eyes. The German sadists needed music for their beastly work. Nobody ever talked to each other when we returned to the barracks. Everyone was just stunned.[163]

Also at Dachau, Yudel Beiles writes of "a pole with corpses hanging for their 'crimes' against the Germans" and of being threatened that he would share that fate if he did not behave as told by his block elder. In addition there was a family Beiles knew from his youth in Kovno, "a father and two sons. . . . The older son fell in the cement hall, and bags of cement spilled all over him. By the time they dug him out, he had suffocated. Soon after, the other son fell into disfavour with the camp head, who ordered his father to hang him. We were in shock, but could do nothing. The Nazis were merciless: they threw a noose around the young man's neck, and ordered the father to pull away the chair he was standing on. It was terribly sad to watch the father hang his own son." Some among the Jews sought to glean a sense of justice in this grotesque display. "Religious Jews who had lived with him earlier said that the Lord was punishing the man for his bad deeds: back in the ghetto he collaborated with the Nazis, and had betrayed more than one Jew."[164]

The frequent occurrence of "those shot trying to escape" was transformed into a ceremonial aspect of Auschwitz. In his memoirs Rudolf Höss scoffs that "all that was needed" for a "successful escape" from Auschwitz was "a little courage and a bit of luck." This pronouncement was a way of denying his own responsibility for creating and enforcing the terror regime that made "attempting to escape" a means of suicide for Jews. "Once beyond the ring of sentry posts, the local civilian population would help them on their way," Höss later wrote. Certainly receiving such help was a possibility for Polish non-Jews, but for Jews, the statement was a bold-faced lie. "One way or another," Höss reasoned, attempting to escape "was the solution of their problems." But he wanted to inform his readers, as well, that the experience served a disciplinary, almost pedagogic function: "The other prisoners had to parade past the corpses of those who had been shot while trying to escape, so that they would all see how such an attempt might end. Many were frightened by this spectacle, and abandoned their plans as a result."[165] This policy was recounted by a survivor (seconded by many others), who writes that this ritual was indeed "considered by the SS to be a deterrent to others." But it did not achieve the desired result. "After such experiences our senses became more and more dulled; our facial expressions became different from those of people on the outside."[166]

"In the concentration camps," Richard Rubenstein writes, "Jews were murdered, not for what they did, but for what they were. No possible alteration of Jewish behavior could have prevented this fatality; the crime was simply to be a Jew."[167] The Nazis were aware, however, of the dissonance between this axiom and the reality that Jews were not, in essence, "criminals." A significant measure of the Nazi project in the concentration camps, then, was to construct and nurture this fallacy. During and after the Holocaust Jews recognized that their treatment as criminals within the confines of ghettos and concentration camps was one of the cruelest hoaxes and most outrageous attempts at mass deception in all of history.[168] "Under the present circumstances we are—and will be for some time to come," Géza Gryn told his son,

"compelled to alter our moral attitude towards lots of things. I have never lied—deliberately that is—in my life before. I have always tried to do the right thing and my own conscience has governed me. But now this attitude towards 'right' and 'wrong' will have to change. We are here for no reason at all. You, Hugo, at any rate, had *no time* to commit crimes of any sort. In other words, we are innocent people herded together and persecuted in order to satisfy a mad dreamer's whims. If we stopped doing anything at all about it, this would be a sign of acknowledgement," here Dad raised his voice, "and I shall never acknowledge any sort of action for which I deserve treatment such as this."

Then he pointed at the building facing us. "You know what this building is? It is a gas chamber. And about twenty-four hours ago, your brothers, and my children, were exterminated in that chamber. Like rats! You, yourself, have been nearer to death a few minutes ago than most men ever get."[169]

After a ten-hour train journey westward from Auschwitz, Hugo was inducted into Lieberose, a subcamp of Sachsenhausen, south of Berlin. He was assigned number 80,494, and identified with a red triangle, which overlay the yellow triangle. "I was thus officially inaugurated as a political prisoner of the German Reich," Gryn recalled. "The title appealed to me greatly. I was only sorry that I had not blown up at least a bridge, to justify the Nazi hospitality."[170]

FIVE

Re-presenting Zionism
as the Apex of Global Conspiracy

THE RELATIONSHIPS BETWEEN NAZIS AND ZIONISTS, which were often complex and shifted dramatically in the twelve years of National Socialism, have been subject to heated debate.[1] As soon as the Nazis came to power, Zionists, as individuals and representatives of different streams in the movement, disagreed vehemently about how to deal with Hitlerism.[2] As we know with the benefit of hindsight, in the course of the anti-Jewish "race war" the Nazis and their accomplices persecuted and annihilated Jews regardless of their political creed. If a Jew's voluntary affiliation mattered at all, it usually did so in a negative way: merely being on the membership list of a Jewish organization could subject a person to treatment as a criminal.[3] We will see, however, that an imaginary linkage between the criminality of Jewry and the Zionist movement was a major undertaking of Nazi propaganda in the late spring of 1944. Zionism was virtually substituted for the "Elders of Zion" as the governing and defining body of the alleged world Jewish conspiracy.[4] Nazi writings replaced a vague, mystical, and abstract concept of the Jewish enemy by a concrete political entity that seemed to be the most palpable force within Jewry. Moreover, Nazi leaders surmised that refashioning anti-Semitism as anti-Zionism suited the postwar Realpolitik portending to be increasingly critical of the "empires" of the United States, Britain, and the Soviet Union that would arise from the ruins of war.[5] Zionism, therefore, was transformed in Nazi propaganda from a mildly helpful curiosity, whose leaders merited sparse and even jocular comment, to the ostensible root cause of German aggression against the Jews. This view took shape as an explicit policy directive that coalesced with orders to seize on the notion of the criminality of the Jew. This shift in tactics has rarely been considered in the history of the Third Reich.

Building on the work of Max Weinreich, Joseph Wulf, and others,[6] this chapter shows that the characterization of Zionism as the zenith of "Jewish conspiracy" was conceived and disseminated at a specific moment and through a concerted effort in the late Nazi period. The demonization of Zionism became the primary rationale for the genocide that was already nearly complete and provided a preemptive argument against the expected voices of outrage among the Jewish communities that persisted in the United States and Britain.[7]

Here I develop two main arguments that may seem contradictory but were both apparently suited to Nazism's shifting fortunes after 1943. First, Nazi propagandists focused on Zionism to justify the genocide of Jewry, especially because they feared losing the war and having to face international public opprobrium; and second, the new focus on Zionism in the wake of the largely accomplished annihilation of European Jews reflected a search for new enemies in the permanent revolution of Nazi destruction. The change in tactics was motivated not only by Nazism's needs of the moment but also by genuine panic. Both dimensions contributed to the evil brew of post-1948 Arab anti-Semitism, which stems in good measure from the political needs of the moment and rank opportunism.

This shift reflects, then, the evolution of modern anti-Semitic thinking. However, the Nazi effort is significant not so much because it helped transmit a new line of anti-Semitism (as interpreted by Weinreich) but because it represented the invention of a new form of anti-Jewish discourse. It was not so much a vector of transmission as a common stimulus and reaction. The Nazi realization in 1944 of a possible *Götterdämmerung,* and the *Naqba* that did befall the Palestinian Arabs (and, by extension, the Arab world), are, conceptually speaking, closely related. Both were seen as cosmic catastrophes that could be explained only by the demonic and criminal machinations of preternaturally powerful Jews.

The decimation of Europe's Jews has understandably led to intense scrutiny of those who did escape death while in the Nazis' clutches. A great deal of debate has focused on the relationship between Zionism and the attempted flight or rescue of some—but not other—groups of Jews. Sometimes there seemed to be a correspondence between one's survival and one's political identification. One survivor of the Lodz ghetto wrote that those who appeared on lists for "deportation" were "generally defenseless unless a Zionist, Bundist, Communist, or other comrade with connections looked out for his interests in an act of solidarity."[8] In a few instances being a Zionist helped one's chance of escape. A significant share of the post-Holocaust discussion of Nazism and Zionism, therefore, has focused on "negotiations" and "agreements" between Zionists and Nazis to facilitate highly circumscribed Zionist-directed emigration.[9] Two of the best-known instances of such deals were the so-called *Ha'avarah* (Transfer) Agreement, an instrument by which some fifty thousand German Jews were permitted to emigrate to Palestine between 1933 and 1939, and the effort of Rudolph (Rezső) Kasztner to thwart the destruction of Zionists during the complex closing chapter of the Holocaust in the spring of 1944.[10] The Nazis also permitted the operation of the "Youth *Aliyah*," the Zionist-sponsored emigration of unaccompanied youth, from Germany to Palestine.[11]

National Socialism evinced greater ambivalence about Zionism than about perhaps any other facet of Jewish life.[12] On several occasions the Nazis professed to favor a "territorial solution" to the Jewish problem, as their aborted plans for a "Lublin reservation" and Jewish settlement in Madagascar demonstrate.[13] On the one hand, several key Nazis appreciated the fact that the Zionist movement aspired and acted to remove Jews from German soil to Palestine. Nazi propaganda often portrayed Zionism as the most logical alternative for Germany's unwanted Jews. An anti-Semitic road sign in Fürth, from 1936, bears a caricature of a refugee family beneath a directional pointer that reads "Toward Palestine." A photo that appeared in Nazi publications in Ahlbeck in 1935 and 1936 portrayed (supposedly) affluent Jews in a flashy sports car; the caption reads: "Jews, Halt! The way to Palestine does not lead through Ahlbeck!"[14] On the other hand, National Socialism had no tolerance for Zionism's principle that Jews should have control over their own fate and work to establish a normal and honorable place for Jews, albeit centered in their "ancestral home," which was removed from pressing Nazi concerns. The Nuremberg Laws, however, expressly allowed Jews "to display the Zionist blue-and-white flag."[15] Zionism, until the spring of 1944, does not seem to have figured prominently in the evolution of Nazi Jewish policy, although it was watched with growing interest after the outbreak of the Second World War.

Nevertheless, the pointed references to Zionism in Hitler's *Mein Kampf* and *Tischgespräche* are not surprising, considering that Hitler had lived in Vienna, a crucible of Zionism,[16] in the formative years of his warped ideological development. "Wherever I went," Hitler wrote in *Mein Kampf* about his wanderings in Vienna,

> I began to see Jews, and the more I saw, the more sharply they became distinguished in my eyes from the rest of humanity. Particularly the Inner City and the districts north of the Danube Canal swarmed with a people which even outwardly lost all resemblance to the Germans.
>
> And whatever doubts I may still have nourished were finally dispelled by the attitude of a portion of the Jews themselves.
>
> Among them there was a great movement, quite extensive in Vienna, which came out sharply in confirmation of the national character of the Jews: this was the *Zionists.*
>
> It looked, to be sure, as though only a part of the Jews approved of this viewpoint, while the great majority condemned and inwardly rejected such a formulation. But when examined more closely, this appearance dissolved itself into an unsavory vapor of pretexts advanced for mere reasons of expedience, not to say lies. For the so-called liberal Jews did not reject the Zionists as non-Jews, but only as Jews with an impractical, perhaps even dangerous, way of publicly avowing their Jewishness.
>
> Intrinsically they remained unalterably of one piece. In a short time this apparent struggle between Zionistic and liberal Jews disgusted me; it was false through and through, founded on lies scarcely in keeping with the moral elevation and purity always claimed by this people.[17]

Hitler could not fathom the idea that Jews did not constitute an absolutely unified, resolute entity. That they did not all accept the Zionist movement as a manifestation of their racial essence was repugnant to him, a sign of weakness and degeneracy. Most likely, he was confused and could not accept that the Jews themselves could not find a simple answer to or consensus about the *Judenfrage.*

In another comment on Zionism, Hitler proclaimed that the movement represented the unmasking of the Jews' ultimate goal of control over Gentiles:

> The Jews' domination in [Germany] seems so assured that now not only can he call himself a Jew again, but he ruthlessly admits his ultimate national and political designs. A section of his race openly owns itself to be a foreign people, yet even here they lie. For while the Zionists try to make the rest of the world believe that the national consciousness of the Jew finds its satisfaction in the creation of a Palestinian state, the Jews again slyly dupe the dumb *Goyim. It doesn't even enter their heads to build up a Jewish state in Palestine for the purpose of living there; all they want is a central organization*

for their international world swindle, endowed with its own sovereign rights
and removed from the intervention of other states: a haven for convicted
scoundrels and a university for budding crooks.[18]

In Hitler's view, or at least, the way he wished to present his Weltanschauung, Zionism was significant—but not an obsession. In his depiction, by
the 1920s the central address of the Jewish conspiracy was transferring gradually to the Zionist organization and Palestine. Jewish criminals, after all,
needed a hideout and safe house; the movement, therefore, sought a
"haven" and incubator for its denizens. Interestingly, though, Hitler does
not mention any Zionist by name as particularly menacing, and he was not
sensitive to a distinctively Anglo-American dimension to Zionist designs.
Of course, he depicted the Jews-cum-Zionists' abstract "swindle" as "international," so no country could be precluded. But unlike the portrayal of
the Zionist movement after June 1944, which cast it as a threat to Germany
and made it the casus belli for preemptive actions against German and East
European Jewry, Hitler's prewar formulations were somewhat restrained.
After all, as he correctly noted, Zionism was a minority affair among the
Jews and a great bone of contention.

We do not know for certain what happened to Hitler's concern with
Zionism after the outbreak of the war, but one policy provides some important clues.[19] No evidence exists that Hitler took cognizance of David
Ben-Gurion's famous challenge, in the wake of the British White Paper of
1939 that sought to stem the flow of Jews to Palestine, that "we will fight
the war as if there is no White Paper and we will fight the White Paper as
if there is no war." The Jewish settlement in Palestine (the yishuv) was not
much of a force to be reckoned with. Zionism and Palestine did not even
have much influence on Hitler's perception of the British, despite Germany's status as the power exercising the Mandate over Palestine. "If the
English are clever," he reportedly said in late October 1941, "they will seize
the psychological moment to make an about-turn—and they will march on
our side." We have no hint that the British backing of Zionism, as signaled
by the Balfour Declaration of 1917, compelled England to be committed
against Germany. Hitler continued, "By getting out of the war now, the
English would succeed in putting their principal competitor—the United
States—out of the game for thirty years. Roosevelt would be shown up as
an impostor, the country would be enormously in debt—by reason of its
manufacture of war-materials, which would become pointless—and

unemployment would rise to gigantic proportions. For me, the object is to exploit the advantages of Continental hegemony."[20]

Indeed, Hitler never saw reason to spare abuse for Roosevelt, "an errant Freemason" with "a sick brain."[21] The latter comment might have been a reference to FDR's polio, a reflection of Hitler's desire for the "destruction of life unworthy of life," the so-called euthanasia of the incurably ill and infirm.[22] By virtue of birthright, Roosevelt was "Hebraic"—a Jew, or secret Jew, long a canard of anti-Semites on both sides of the Atlantic.[23] FDR, according to Hitler, "who both in his handling of political issues and in his general attitude, behaves like a tortuous, pettifogging Jew, himself boasted recently that he had 'noble' Jewish blood in his veins. The completely negroid appearance of his wife is also a clear indication that she, too, is a half-breed."[24] Before 1944, the main thread connecting the democratic nations and the world's Jews was not Zionism but imagined "political profiteers" and other commercial opportunists.[25] Roosevelt was in Hitler's eyes both a Jew and a "criminal," but there was no inkling of his identity as "a Zionist criminal." In a terse statement about the content and goals of propaganda, Hitler said, "Good propaganda must be stimulating. Our [radio] stations must therefore go on talking about the drunkard Churchill and the criminal Roosevelt on every possible occasion."[26] In England, British policy did not seem to focus on Zionism as a movement in its own right, but in Hitler's view the apparent British subservience to Zionism was proof of the fact that "the country is ruled not by men of intelligence but by Jews, as one must realise when one sees how the intrigues of the Jews in Palestine are accepted in Britain without comment or demur."[27] Ample proof exists that Hitler admired the Zionists' principal adversary, the Grand Mufti of Jerusalem, describing him "as a realist rather than a dreamer, where politics are concerned"—praising him almost in the same terms he had applied to himself. Hitler made a point of emphasizing that as an Arab the Mufti was not representative of an inferior race:

> With his blond hair and blue eyes, he gives one the impression that he is, in spite of his sharp and mouse-like countenance, a man with more than one Aryan among his ancestors and one who may well be descended from the best Roman stock. In conversation he shows himself to be a preeminently sly old fox. To gain time in which to think, he not infrequently has things translated to him first into French and then into Arabic; and sometimes he carries his caution so far that he asks that certain points be committed straightaway to writing. When he does speak, he weighs each

word very carefully. His quite exceptional wisdom puts him almost on equal terms with the Japanese.[28]

This passage is especially indicative of Hitler's capacity for lying and self-delusion, because the Mufti was as remote, in his physical appearance, from the Aryan ideal as one could imagine. His countenance was closer to *Der Stürmer* Jewish caricatures than to almost any Jew the Nazis could find. Hitler, as is well known, set the tone for the exceptionalism of Arabs among racist anti-Semites, despite the common myth that Arabs were "Semites" and thereby incapable of being anti-Semites.

Like almost every aspect of Hitler's musings, Nazi thought about Zionism found expression in numerous forums. The infamous organ of Julius Streicher, *Der Stürmer*, best known for its viciously stereotyped caricatures of Jews, reported on Zionist endeavors in Palestine. Initially, Streicher went so far as to "congratulate the Jews' efforts." But Zionism was for *Der Stürmer* mainly an alternate setting to exhibit stock Jewish stereotypes, such as the Jews' supposed inability to live off the land.[29] Zionism was derided, but Streicher's famed hate sheet contained few hints that Zionism represented a dire threat to Germany,[30] beyond that of any other organized contingent of Jews acting in their supposed interest.

One of the Nazi ideologues who spoke out most frequently, and apparently shaped policy toward Zionism—but not as much as he wished to—was Alfred Rosenberg. Best known as the author of *Der Mythus des 20. Jahrhunderts* (The Myth of the 20th Century, 1930), which became a central text of the party faithful and much of the general public, Rosenberg held key propaganda posts on the far right, including editor of the *Völkische Beobachter* beginning in 1921. He was named the "Führer's delegate for the supervision of intellectual and philosophical education and training of the National Socialist party" in 1934.

Rosenberg specifically addressed Zionism in *Die Spur des Juden im Wandel der Zeiten* (The Trace of Jewry throughout the Ages, 1920).[31] Under the rubric "Jewry and Politics" Zionism was identified as one of the camps that Jews had developed or infiltrated. But Zionism merited no more than seven pages in his study (in both the 1930 and 1937 editions, whereas "Jews and Freemasonry" was allotted over twenty pages. The significance of Zionism, according to Rosenberg, within "the entire complex of the international Jewish problem" was its novelty: it had not been important before the First World War. Chaim Weizmann is specifically cited for articulating the notion, with which Rosenberg tacitly concurred, that "the existence of the

Jewish nation is a fact and not a question of debate." Rosenberg took this statement, along with those of Theodor Herzl, Kurt Blumenfeld, Felix Theilhaber, and others, to affirm that a Jew could never be a legitimate citizen of an existing state.[32] Although the Zionists had tried to advance their goals through German interests in the Near East during the Great War, now they were firmly allied with England, and this alliance prompted their disloyalty to Germany in the wake of the Balfour Declaration (November 1917). The embrace of Zionism by the British administration had the character, Rosenberg wrote, of a tragicomedy, as the rulers of a nation of seventy million people pledged itself to its tiny minority of "citizens of the Mosaic confession."[33] But when Rosenberg attempts to make his strongest point—that German national interests have been sold out in the service of Zionism—his evidence has no basis in fact.[34] He cannot even dredge up support from Germany's gutter press. Rosenberg claims that at the Versailles conference, a "Zionist leader," one "Herr Melchior," was crucial in subverting the German cause.[35]

Most likely Rosenberg was referring to Carl Melchior, who was best known as banker and counsel to the bank of M. M. Warburg and Co. Melchior had fought in the German Army during the First World War and was seriously injured, and he "worked for the German government's Zentraleinkaufsgesellschaft (ZEG), which was charged with importing foodstuffs."[36] He later was a member of the German delegation at Versailles. However, no record has been found of Melchior's having a position in any Zionist organization or even of sympathizing with the movement. Rosenberg nevertheless calls him "a leader of Zionism" because assigning him this label is the only way to establish a connection between the German Zionists, who were marginal in German-Jewish society and especially in politics, and the so-called November criminals.[37] Other Nazis, however, would take their fantastic indictments of Zionism, as a propagator of "hatred and enmity toward Germany,"[38] to far greater degrees, making them the focus of their efforts to shape German and world opinion. Rosenberg reportedly belittled the Zionist movement in 1922 by saying that "at its best Zionism is the impotent effort of an unfit people to achieve something constructive."[39]

Rosenberg's warnings that Zionism was detrimental to Nazi interests were reiterated in his hefty tome *Novemberköpfe* (November Leaders), in which he raged against Tomáš Masaryk of Czechoslovakia for publicly supporting Zionism.[40] As a result of Rosenberg's feeling that his advice was not being heeded, and as a response to the proposal to partition Palestine into Jewish and Arab states in 1937, Rosenberg dedicated a pamphlet (of eighty-eight pages) to *Der staatsfeindliche Zionismus* (Subversive Zionism) in 1938. In Rosenberg's view, the partition plan was a triumph for the Zionist movement—not that it "earned" this success but because it was able to use diplomatic machinations to attain concessions from Britain. "The educational efforts of the entire National Socialist movement" had, then, to dedicate itself to Zionism as one of its greatest potential threats. Zionism, he argued, had succeeded in uniting Jewry under its banner, and the anti-Germanness of Bolshevism and Zionism made the ideologies one and the same.[41] By stressing, in a less than subtle manner, that Zionism was a danger not only to the German Reich but to "other states" as well, Rosenberg might have been attempting to drive a wedge between Britain and the United States and to prod the nations of East Central Europe to take a harder line against Zionism. He no longer doubted, however, that the United States favored Zionism, "the new-born Cherub Israel."[42] In his conclusion, Rosenberg declares that Germans had been misled because "German Zionists" self-consciously identified themselves as "German," while they were innately hostile to German national interests. The Nazis' abhorrence of "Zionism must be expressed publicly, and all must follow suit." In a veiled reference to Nazi officials whom Rosenberg felt had been too flexible on Zionism, he wrote, "all of our party bosses know the truth only too well, which must be said." Nazism and Zionism were an "either-or" proposition but had not been treated as such.[43] Clearly, to Rosenberg, the threat posed by Zionism had not been systematically assimilated into Nazism writ large.

In no small measure Rosenberg himself was responsible for the lack of consideration for his views. In his best-selling work, *Der Mythos des 20. Jahrhunderts,* the comments about Zionism were rambling, if not incoherent, and he predicted that the movement was "condemned to collapse from the very start." The individuals he highlighted as spokesmen for Zionist ideology, "Arthur Holitscher (1869–1941)," "[Eugen] Höflich [later Moshe Ya'akov Ben-Gavriel (1891–1965)]," "F. Kohn" (most likely Felix), and Martin Buber, were not household names or particularly diabolical ones, despite Buber's growing renown as a philosopher. Rosenberg completely misunderstood the significance of the founder of the movement, Theodor Herzl; he wrote that "Herzl created orthodox Zionism as a protest against the universal European Zionist congress in August 1929 in Zurich." Rosenberg was either making things up or knew next to nothing about the organization. Herzl had died in 1904, and Rosenberg had no sense of the movement as an embattled minority party within world Jewry.[44]

In mid-June 1944, however, the Nazis decided to disown and reformulate their complicated relationship with Zionism. In particular, they would never mention the "transfer agreement." By this time, as was well known to the Nazi upper echelons, the majority of Eastern European Jews had been annihilated. Unlike the insidious strategy that developed after the demise of the Third Reich to deny the systematic mass murder of Europe's Jews, the initial Nazi impulse was to rationalize it.[45] At this point, the demented charge emerged that the Zionists "provoked" the mass slaughter by the Nazis; it later reappeared in Adolf Eichmann's self-defense at his trial in July 1961 and was repeated in other attempts by Nazis to evade or deny responsibility.[46] The canard of "Zionism as the reasonable cause of genocide," trotted out in the *Historikerstreit* in the 1980s, also is rooted in this 1944 policy directive.[47]

Alexander Hardy, one of the U.S. prosecutors at the Nuremberg War Crimes Trials, astutely remarked that it was Otto Dietrich, "more than anyone else, who was responsible for presenting to the German people the justification for liquidating the Jews" —who was more responsible than either Julius Streicher or Joseph Goebbels in this regard.[48] Dietrich was the party Press Chief and Under-Secretary of State in the Propaganda Ministry. His duties, as enumerated in a wartime study, were to "control press policy" and the activities of all "press wardens" who determined press content, to judge if a newspaper or journal was worthy of publication, and to "explain, represent, and formulate the party standpoint to the non-party press in Germany and the world-at-large."[49]

The "direction of the party press machine" was largely shared with Dietrich's "first lieutenant, Helmut Sündermann. At the age of thirty-one, Sündermann was said to be "one of the very few representatives" of the post–World War I generation" who had, by 1942, "already attained high office in the Party." He was, therefore, a product of an intensely Nazi education.[50] In the wake of the *Anschluss,* the annexation of Austria to Nazi Germany in March 1938, he was given "the key job of reorganizing the Austrian press," and his account of the fusion of Germany and Austria was immediately published as *Die Grenzen fallen: von der Ostmark zum Sudetenland* (The Borders Fall: From Austria to the Sudetenland).[51] It was a dramatic narrative of both nations' journey in achieving their inherent destiny. This effort was said to "reveal remarkable journalistic talent," on the level of that of Dietrich and Goebbels.[52] Earlier he had written a step-by-step manual for Nazis who wished to make a career in journalism in the leading newspapers and journals.[53] We need not be surprised, then, that Sündermann was entrusted with running the party Press Office (Reichs-pressestelle), which directed "the whole army of Party pressmen about the treatment of national affairs and issues and ministerial projects and decisions." In this capacity he also was chief editor of the party "official news service, the N.S. Korrespondenz (NSK), providing both the Party and non-Party press with news of the movement and with the official views of the Party."[54]

Although we probably will never know if the new party line in June 1944—Zionism as the greatest incarnation of Jewish conspiracy—was part of a set plan, it had precedents, such as this secret press directive of January 13, 1940:

SECRET!

It is to be observed that, with few exceptions, the Press has not yet understood how to stress, in their daily journalistic work, the propagandistic theme of the New Year's message of the Führer wherein he discussed the battle against Jewish and reactionary war-mongers in the capitalist democracies. Anti-Semitic themes are a part of the daily press material as clear expositions of the social backwardness of the money-bag democracies, who wish to salvage their exploitation methods through this war. In this connection many well known circumstances (London slums, etc.) may be treated in text and illustration.

The anti-Semitic theme, which has become timely in the case of Hore-Belisha [the Jewish, British War Minister], should not be permitted to remain in the background. The NSK will provide current material for both groups of thematic material.

The stressing of these clear propaganda lines must however include appropriate copy, headlines, and commentaries with respect to current news material. Only by closest attention on the part of the editors in directing the Jewish-capitalist theme will the necessary long-term propagandistic effect be achieved.[55]

A file was cultivated specifically to provide fodder for this campaign, which we will see was drawn largely from one source: the weekly published by the Institut zum Studium der Judenfrage (Institute for Studies of the Jewish Question), the *Mitteilungen über die Judenfrage* (Contributions on the Jewish Question).[56]

Other directives also paved the way for the policy turn in June 1944. On August 21, 1941, Dietrich disseminated this message:

SECRET!

It is to our interests that all Jewish statements against Germany or the authoritarian states should be well noted. The reason for this wish is that measures of an inner political nature may be expected.[57]

In early February 1943, as the Nazi drive in the east was failing, journalists were instructed to emphasize that Germany and Europe had been "victimized" by the Jews and that "Europe protects herself against the Jews." The next line became one of the most persistent slogans of Nazi self-exculpation: "The declaration of war by the Jews against the European nations resulted in energetic measures being taken against the Jews, not only in Germany but also in many other European states." But the key configuration of Jews in this directive is not Zionism—it is "their racial composition." Given the Wehrmacht struggle on the Eastern Front, the next section declared that "Bolshevism in all its atrocities is the only Executive of Judaism."[58]

Germany's subsequent humiliation by the Soviet Army rendered problematic the identification of "International Jewry" with Bolshevism.[59] If Germans were to follow Nazi logic, then they would have to conclude that the Jews had delivered the Wehrmacht a staggering setback. The earlier propaganda line had to be reformulated. As early as April 2, 1943, a change in course had begun: "Of equal value with our anti-Bolshevist propaganda is that against Jewry."[60] Now the two evils were being split apart and were no longer seen to be inextricably intertwined. Explicit orders followed to treat Jews as "criminals."[61] "We must see to it," a "Special Anti-Jewish Edition" of the Periodical Service (Deutscher Wochendienst, a supplement of the Zeitschriftendienst) asserted, "that during the coming months not a single page appears in a periodical which does not comment in one way or another on the Jewish problem."[62]

The explicit casting of Zionism as the most treacherous guise of the Jews did not surface until February 11, 1944. The *Tagesparole des Reichspressechefs* (Daily Watchword of the Reich Press Chief) brought journalists' attention to "Churchill's call for support of the Palestine Jews," which was considered "an opportunity" to reopen the Jewish question." The press was instructed to point out that "British soldiers go hungry while the Jews roll in money, and are enjoying themselves in the rear lines." The Daily Watchword of the Reich Press Chief on March 14, 1944, is a reflection of the campaign in which Dietrich and Sündermann had already begun to participate; Nazi editors were "strongly advised to avail themselves of research material prepared by the Institute for Research on the Jewish Question."[63]

This dossier-building exercise apparently led party propagandists to the work of Wolf Meyer-Christian, who had been a regular contributor to the *Mitteilungen über die Judenfrage* (often referred to as *Die Judenfrage*) as well as the author of an academic-sounding tome on the subject of England's relationship to the Jews (*Die englisch-jüdische Allianz. Werden und Wirken der kapitalistischen Weltherrschaft,* The Origin and Impact of the English-Jewish Alliance on Capitalist World Dominion).[64] One of Meyer-Christian's specialties was battling "anti-German propaganda."[65] After the Peel Commission report of 1937, however, he turned almost exclusively to Zionism.[66] *Die Judenfrage,* which has received little close analysis, was "devoted entirely to Jewish affairs" and kept a closer eye on Zionism than did any other Nazi organ.[67] Interestingly, despite a nod or two to the significance of race in most lengthy pieces, it did not have much to say about biologically based racism.[68] Apparently intended for party insiders, it contained a confidential appendix *(Vertrauliche Beilage)* that enumerated anti-Jewish actions and policies.[69] Importantly, it was closer to Otto Dietrich than to Joseph Goebbels.[70] Dietrich and Sündermann had been seeking a means to revive anti-Semitism, which they believed was moribund. "In the course of the past months, an unfortunate retrogression in the treatment of the Jewish Question has been experienced."[71] Perhaps some of their colleagues were getting queasy at the possibility of being held accountable for Jewry's mass murder. In light of Dietrich's proximity to Hitler, we can see why he demanded that his cohort be relentless. "According to its importance," the Jewish question "is again to be placed more to the foreground."[72]

A revised, carefully thought-out strategy nurtured in the Dietrich-Sündermann camp can be reconstructed from a document recovered from the destroyed Propaganda Ministry in Berlin.[73] The document comprises a cover letter by Sündermann and four papers authored by Wolf Meyer-Christian: an eleven-page statement entitled "The Treatment of the Jewish Question in the German Press" ("Die Behandlung der Judenfrage in der deutschen Presse"); a six-page statement, "Details of the Rules for the Treatment of Zionism in the German Press" ("Einzelheiten für die Sprachregelung bei der Behandlung des Zionismus durch die Presse"); a three-and-a-half–page timeline, "Major Dates in Zionist Politics" ("Hauptdaten der zionistischen Politik"); and a fifteen-page lexicon entitled "A Hundred Zionist Words: The Most Important Persons, Organizations, and Facts on Zionism" ("Hundert Worte Zionistisch: Die wichtigsten Personen Organisationen und Tatsachen des Zionismus"). (The original document is in the YIVO Archives in New York.) The letter is dated June 13, 1944, signed by Walter Koerber, and addressed to Sündermann. One of the chief sponsors of this change in course was apparently Sündermann.

Max Weinreich reported in his early classic *Hitler's Professors* that "two respected members of the Reich Propaganda Ministry, Karl August Stuckenburg and Dr. L. Franz Gengler, confirmed the reliability of the material supplied by Meyer-Christian, and Koerber concluded, in his letter launching the memoranda as policy, that: 'Although at present other matters are in the foreground of press policies, I believe that consistent with these proposals a long-range plan of action should be prepared.' " Meyer-Christian's agenda for "the intensification of anti-Jewish propaganda and its change in focus," Weinreich proves, "were well received, as shown by Goebbels' *Deutscher Wochendienst*," which provided grist for Nazi journalists. After June 1944, "this news service carried at least four unsigned articles under the general title "Hinweise für die antijüdische Pressearbeit" ("Guidance for Anti-Jewish Journalism") that so carefully followed Meyer-Christian's memorandum that they might have been written by him. The "chronological table" of Meyer-Christian's version of "the history of Zionism" was appropriated, slightly expanded, "under the compiler's name, in *Weltkampf* IV (1944), 149–152, under the title: '*Hauptdaten der zionistischen Politik.*'"[74]

Although neither Sündermann, Stuckenburg, Koerber, nor Meyer-Christian have attracted much scholarly attention since the Second World War, they were crucial in shaping an anti-Semitic policy that would have a shockingly warm and enduring reception in the wider world, well into the twenty-first century.[75] A direct connection between Hitler and Dietrich, who was Sündermann's close confidant and immediate superior, has been well established.[76] Dietrich actually "lived in Hitler's headquarters," and until "at least the middle of 1944" he seemed to possess "more authority over the headlines of the German papers than did Goebbels. . . . Dietrich's pronouncements were so closely aligned with what was assumed to be the wishes of the Führer that Goebbels had to be cautious about contradicting the 'daily slogan' that Dietrich's man, Helmut Sündermann, supplied the German press."[77] In the summer of 1942, Goebbels vented his anger in his diary: "Without my knowledge Sündermann had been named Deputy Press Chief."[78]

In adopting such a blunt line against Zionism via his promotion of Meyer-Christian's proposal, which probably had been on his desk since March 1944,[79] Sündermann again distanced himself from, and possibly provoked the wrath of, Goebbels, who had never expressed much interest in Zionism. Hence, radicalization of anti-Semitism resulted, at least in part, from a "power struggle" within a particular sphere.[80] The form in which this policy was delivered, the *Tagesparolen des Reichspressechefs* came, then, "from the Führer's headquarters, initiated by Sündermann himself," not only as an efficient way of getting the message across "but as a way to checkmate Goebbels' efforts to undercut Dietrich's authority."[81] Although Goebbels fulminated against what he saw as the forces of Jewry that had amalgamated and raised funds in order to "protest" German atrocities against European Jewry, claiming that England and America had been totally "taken in" by them, there is no indication that Goebbels perceived Zionism as the main threat.[82] He referred to Weizmann rather neutrally as "the Zionists' leader" *(Der Zionistenführer)*, who had "apparently made a big impression on the English administration" by capitalizing on the "great stupidity" *(grosse Dummheit)* of the English. For the Nazis, Zionism's propaganda value was greatest when they trained their messages on the Arabs in order to turn up the heat on the British.[83]

Sündermann and Meyer-Christian were leaving Rosenberg's methods behind, probably because these were not tightly focused on their own message. Most likely, Franz Gengler, who countersigned the directive, also worked with Sündermann and Meyer-Christian, as he had attempted to show in 1939 that the "November Criminals" story had contained a "known Zionist" dimension. Rosenberg's *Der staatsfeindliche Zionismus* (Subversive Zionism) is not mentioned in Meyer-Christian's suggested reading and further instructions for information gathering. Though Sündermann and Dietrich had frequently quarreled with Goebbels, they most likely shared his view that Rosenberg was a "crackpot."[84]

Dietrich and Sündermann propelled these combined documents into the center of Nazi discourse.[85] Except for Weinreich's *Hitler's Professors* and an anthology by the prolific Joseph Wulf, there has been little if any scholarly comment on this highly effective policy. Wulf correctly pointed out perhaps the most significant facet of the document: that it unequivocally proclaimed that the vast majority of European Jewry had been annihilated.[86] This admission may have been responsible for reigniting the archdemonization of Jewry as a deliberate and sustained Nazi policy to rationalize this fact. Weinreich correctly asserted that the memorandum, in total, "intended to show that Zionism was the most menacing of all Jewish movements and the Jewish Agency for Palestine in effect was a world Jewish government striving for world domination."[87] Revealing his own lack of interest in the Zionist movement, Weinreich added, "But whereas the ideology of the document may appear boring, the strategy indicated in it commands attention."[88] Weinreich did not think that the policy itself was of any great consequence, compared to his interest in the dissemination of the message.

I believe that both the strategy and ideology are not only important but also inextricably connected. Taken together, the documents, which were mainly from Meyer-Christian and supplemented by pieces that had appeared in *Die Judenfrage,*[89] were not intended simply to exacerbate and further popularize anti-Semitism, which Weinreich took to be their main function. They were specifically assembled and pitched to connect the charge of collective Jewish criminality with Zionism. That a dyed-in-the-wool ideologue like Sündermann would be keen to champion Meyer-Christian's scheme is not surprising, because the strategy brought the Führer's ideas about Zionism to the forefront of anti-Semitism. The notion that Zionism was a smokescreen for international Jewish treachery, that "the national consciousness of the Jew" could "not be satisfied with Palestine, that what they want is the protection and respect of a nation to enact their schemes and serve as an impregnable fortress for their crooks, for all time to come" surely was well known to Dietrich and Sündermann as compatible with the Führer's thoughts.[90] Hence, they made sure that Zionism was now bound up, and catapulted into headlines, as the zenith of Jewish criminality and conspiracy. However, Weinreich failed to notice the subdued element of race.[91] The strategy documents made no specific mention of the explicitly racial threat that the Jews, as Zionists, supposedly posed.[92] Perhaps this element might have been presupposed. But the possibility also exists that Sündermann, Meyer-Christian, and the others were already attempting to accommodate themselves to a new order that would not indulge much of the older Nazi ideology and that they were trying to devise a strategy that would play well in the wider world—to use "Jewish imperialism" as a means of undermining "the three known 'Imperialisms' of England, Russia, and the USA."[93]

Meyer-Christian furthermore claimed to be motivated by the "aversion to the Jewish question on the part of the German press" evident to him in mid-1944. On the surface this statement seems ludicrous given the number of articles that continued to spew forth about the danger posed by Jews. Making sure not to appear critical of a particular individual, especially no one in the press office, he emphasizes: "The guilt here is not on the administration of the press as such, but on two facts that are outside its domain": first, efforts directed toward "Research on the Jewish Question" that have failed to achieve the kind of popular fascination, as, say, academic treatments of "foreign policy," and second,

Through the new Reich's measures to defend against and remove *(Ausscheidung)* Jewry, wider circles no longer have the feeling that Jews are an immediate threat. For example, through the disappearance of Isidor *[sic]* Weiss, we seem to have forfeited the focus of the struggle, its apparent relevance *(Aktualität)*. The public at large considers the Jewish question settled. This shows the danger, already, that the anti-Jewish enlightenment as well as the old methods, without its former objects, will not arouse interest and will become boring to the common person.

This would be of no consequence at all, had the Jewish problem really become history through German measures. In fact, however, only the domestic German side of the Jewish problem has been settled by the Reich's policy toward the Jews. In its entirety the problem not only continues to exist, but since 1933 it has acquired a most tremendous urgency and poignancy, and must therefore be brought to view more than ever and with greater force than ever.[94]

But much more was at stake here than developing a new line of propaganda simply for the sake of perpetuating the Reich's work to promote anti-Semitism—now that it was no longer a matter of urgency within the country. We must remember the date: mid-June 1944. Certainly the possibility loomed that Germany would lose the war, and the pressmen were searching for alibis. Thus they devised a propaganda strategy for domestic and international consumption, a defensive argument making the case for doing what they did to the Jews.

Rather than attributing the destruction of European Jewry to the drive to create a perfect racial state, the Nazis sought to anchor the instigation of their war against the Jews in the events of 1929,

> when for the first time in the history of the Jewish people the unity of the entirety of Jewry was attained, namely under the banner of Zionism. It was in that year that the leader of Zionism, Dr. Chaim Weizmann, struck a deal with the non-Zionist powerful Jews, above all those from England (Melchett) and the USA (Brandeis), bringing them into the Jewish Agency,[95] joining the awesome financial power of the assimilated Jews to the political activism of the Zionist minority among the Jews. They chose, then, through this solution, to side with the Western powers. The executive of the expanded Jewish Agency was established with a unified purpose, as the administration of Jewish world power. In the years following 1933 this Jewish world leadership showed itself as an anti-German power (such as through the boycott agitation). By the beginning of the war in 1939, far too little observed *[viel zu wenig beachtet]*, they accordingly identified

themselves with the goal of the Western Powers: the destruction of Germany [*Zerstörung Deutschlands*].[96]

The so-called imminent Jewish aggression was so little "observed"[97] that it took Nazi apologists a number of years to fabricate their case. In a substantial article pointing out all the dangers posed by American Jewry's supposed influence in 1937, Zionism was not even suggested. Nor was the movement worthy of mention in an article decrying "New York as the Jewish center of power" in 1938. Likewise, a supposed exposé of the leading Jewish families making up the *Weltkahal* did not identify Zionism as the organizing principle.[98] If the Nazis noticed Zionism at all, they seemed almost amused by Zionist pretensions of influence, Jewish solidarity, and power. Although the extended Jewish Agency did, in fact, take in segments of diaspora Jewry that had earlier been opposed, or indifferent, to Zionism, the argument that it presented a distinct threat to Germany was outrageous for a number of reasons. The Nazis were aware of this fact, and their own publications could easily have been used to underscore the ridiculousness of Meyer-Christian's argument.

In 1929 Jews, even Zionists, were far from unified, split as they were into numerous political, social, and religious groups. Throughout the 1920s Weizmann and the long-time head of Zionism in the United States, Louis Lipsky, quarreled bitterly with Supreme Court Justice Louis Brandeis, who had been identified with Zionism since 1917. A substantial article in *Die Judenfrage* had asserted that deep intra-Jewish divisions fomented by right-wing, Revisionist Zionist "terror" was a "bitter irony."[99] A Zionist newspaper, on September 5, 1939, probably spoke from the heart of its membership when it asserted "The National Socialists, in their demonstrations, designate the Jews as 'enemies of the state.' That designation is incorrect. The Jews are not enemies of the state. The German Jews desire and wish for the rise of Germany, for which they have always invested, to the best of their knowledge, all their resources, and that is what they continue to wish to continue to do."[100] Of course, Zionists and all other Jews were counting on Hitler's government being overtaken by more reasonable people, a hope that proved to be in vain.

Divisiveness among Zionists persisted even as the Nazis continued to see them as a unit. Furthermore, the financial resources of the movement were not even sufficient to carry out and protect their relatively modest program in Palestine, let alone mount a military threat to Europe. Although Theodor Herzl had claimed in 1896 that "we are a people, one people,"[101] and this statement became a popular refrain of the movement, it always remained an ideal, not an actual description of Zionism. Jewry worldwide, as opposed to Nazi characterizations of it, and even as opposed to the views of less-hostile parties, was defined more by intense factionalism than by consensus. Many Zionists were, in fact, "enraged" that the American Jewish Joint Distribution Committee (commonly known as "the Joint"), the closest entity to a central fund of American Jewry, "invested heavily" between 1924 and 1938 in "a Jewish colonization venture in the Crimea and Ukraine" known as the "Agro-Joint."[102] Although there had, indeed, been a significant "rapprochement between the ZO [Zionist Organization] and the Croesuses of American Jewry," the groups were not suddenly of one mind, nor were they dedicated to the Zionists' goals above all else. Although Zionist leaders "demanded exclusivity and total commitment," this level of unity never happened.[103] Certainly many Jews, including the men brought into the expanded Jewish Agency, gave generously to the movement. But their personal affluence did not, and could not, transform Zionism into a world power comparable to the great powers. Ironically, the extension of the Jewish Agency to former non-Zionists was long resisted by a formidable contingent of Zionists, who feared that such a step would dilute Zionist endeavors, making the movement more like a broad, middling philanthropic venture. Reading the reconstituted Jewish Agency in 1929 as a radicalization and protomilitarization of the movement would probably have been seen as a joke had it been articulated before 1933. However, given that the idea was uttered in 1944, it compounded the tragedy of European Jewry. A notion of "taking over" or "fighting" Germany in any way—in 1929!—is simply not to be found, as it would have made absolutely no sense. To the extent that the leaders of "the enlarged Jewish Agency were part of a greater whole," they agreed mainly on one idea: that there had to be "a vast solution to the east European 'Jewish problem.'"[104] How that goal was to be achieved, however, would remain in dispute even after the majority of Eastern European Jewry had been slaughtered.

Around the time of the announcement of the Peel partition plan, August 5, 1937, a leading Nazi paper adopted a tone of mocking, ironic distance from the events in Palestine that did not seem to augur well for the Zionists' future. The politicking was dubbed "Lord contra Lord. The Behind-the-Scenes Play over Palestine" ("Das Kulissenspiel um Palästina").[105] A few weeks later Goebbels wrote in his diary, "The Jews have published an indolent [unverschämtes] memorandum about Palestine. An interview between Chaim Weizmann [spelled incorrectly as 'Waitzmann'] with

Ormsby-Gore [spelled incorrectly as 'Ormbsby Gory'], the English Colonial Minister (*sic*). The English were really treated like shit. Did they deserve something different? The Jews are so stupid. Now they have turned the entire English public against them. That's what they get for being so arrogant." Goebbels gleefully wrote the next day that rather than posing a threat, Weizmann had inadvertently stimulated the "national self-respect as well as the anti-Semitism of the English."[106] On one of the few (if not the only) occasions that *Der Stürmer* showed a picture of Weizmann in 1937, the scene was anything but fearful; the scene of Weizmann, seated at an outdoor table with other Zionists in Egypt, is labeled "They're having a good time. Dr Weizmann, the leader of the Zionist Commission, among his racial comrades."[107] The idea was not so much that they were up to no good but that they weren't up to anything. Earlier references to Weizmann stressed that he was totally committed to the British, but the idea that he was at the center of anti-German conspiracy never came into play.[108] In casting "Professor Selig Brodetsky" and Vladimir Jabotinsky as "leaders of world Zionism," *Die Judenfrage,* the main Nazi paper covering Zionism, accorded the men nearly as much importance as it gave Weizmann.[109] A fairly straightforward article about the spectrum of political parties in Palestine showed that the Nazis were fully aware that even the Zionists in Palestine were far from unified,[110] let alone part of world Jewry acting as one.

Nevertheless, the myth of "a Jewish declaration of war" or "Weizmann's declaration of war" would become a staple of right-wing anti-Semites, especially Holocaust deniers in the last decades of the twentieth century.[111] Eventually, anti-Semites would locate a number of statements by Weizmann and other Jews that they claimed provoked an intensification of anti-Jewish measures, most notably the so-called Declaration of War of Weizmann in 1939, which has been discussed and debunked by Richard Evans. In straining to give their pressmen explicit examples, the best the Nazis could come up with in 1944 was "The telegram of Weizmann to a Zionist group *[eine Zionistengruppe]* in America of 19.1.1942: 'The Jews desire their place in the ranks, among those who have as their goal the annihilation of Germany' [*die Vernichtung Deutschlands zum Ziel*] which says everything about this. In 1943, the inner-council of the North American Jewry, through Weizmann, committed itself to the Zionist aims."[112]

If such a telegram does exist, then the translation in the memorandum is highly dubious. Neither Weizmann nor the Zionist movement was even mentioned in Goebbels's diary in the first three months of 1942.[113] In the annals of anti-Semitism, this obscure telegram of Weizmann to "a Zionist group" came to be replaced by an actual—but intentionally misinterpreted—document of August 29, 1939. At the moment when Britain was pressed to declare war against Nazi Germany, Weizmann wrote to Prime Minister Neville Chamberlain:

> In this hour of supreme crisis, the consciousness that the Jews have a contribution to make to the defence of sacred values impels me to write this letter. I wish to confirm, in the most explicit manner, the declaration which I and my colleagues have made during the last months, and especially in the last week: that the Jews "stand by Great Britain and will fight on the side of the democracies."
> Our urgent desire is to give effect to these declarations. We wish to do so in a way entirely consonant with the general scheme of British action, and therefore would place ourselves, in matters big and small, under the co-ordinating direction of His Majesty's Government. The Jewish Agency is ready to enter into immediate arrangements for utilising Jewish man-power, technical ability, resources, etc.
> The Jewish Agency has recently had differences in the political field with the Mandatory Power. We would like these differences to give way before the greater and more pressing necessities of the time.
> We ask you to accept this declaration in the spirit in which it is made.[114]

Nothing was made of this telegram at the time—because it probably went unnoticed. Any intelligence expert who had been following the Zionist movement would have realized that this type of message was to be expected of Weizmann and probably would result in little if any action. It was also, in large part, an effort to mend fences, because the relationship between Zionism and the mandatory government, which had long been tumultuous, was in fact in deep crisis. Some months earlier, on March 24, 1939, Weizmann had written Chamberlain, "A cloud hangs over the relations between the Jewish Agency and British Ministers." The Zionists in Palestine "have been sorely tried," and he said the further restrictions on immigration would "only add to the turmoil." Weizmann then promised that "every effort will be made and every contact used, to explore the possibility of Jewish-Arab agreement[/]rapprochement."[115] He was, after all, the leader of a desperate movement, playing the role of supplicant. Later the Nazis would paint him as a belligerent, armed to the teeth. By no means, when he made an offer of support to the "western democracies," could he have been referring "to Jews in Germany or anywhere outside Palestine."[116]

Most likely the report of a January 19, 1942, communication was based on statements by Weizmann about the United States' entry into the Second World War as a result of Pearl Harbor, and about the fact that American Jews were both volunteering and being conscripted into the U.S. armed forces. The timing of the document, however, is intriguing: perhaps the date was intended to coincide with the official sanction of the "Final Solution" at the Wannsee Conference. For certain, the date also corresponds to a deportation of Jews from Berlin to Riga, Latvia.[117]

Meyer-Christian's next paragraph shows why this connection is plausible; he assumed that his readers understood that most of Central and Eastern European Jewry had been decimated:

> Leaving out the six million European Jews *[wenn man die sechs Millionen europäische Juden ausser Betracht lässt]*, there are now ten to twelve million Jews politically committed against the Reich. Their disproportionately strong intelligentsia with its exponents stands directly behind the political management of the enemy and, despite all its internal differentiations, constitutes the connecting link with and among England, the USA, and the Soviet Union. These hints suffice at least to outline the fighting front of world Jewry against Germany, which today is actually no longer a phrase. The front remains, but it has been displaced. A question of [German] domestic politics has become one of foreign politics.
>
> These drastic shifts in the situation must be met with a commensurate change in our methods of battle.[118]

Though this document is remarkably transparent, we need to probe beneath the surface. Meyer-Christian assumes that because of Germany's impending defeat, American and English Jews inevitably would bring the world's attention to the systematic mass murder of their brethren and that in some way the Nazis would have to respond.

But the main concern was: what would this defeat mean for Germans? As the war was winding down, the architects of this document were thinking about how to explain themselves to the next generation, the young people in their midst and even their children:

> For what this means objectively, take this example: When asked, young twenty-year-old officers say that they have never yet knowingly seen a Jew. Therefore they find no interest, or only slight interest, in the Jewish problem as it has been presented to them up to now. The term "typically Jewish" is sufficient for us older people. It has no more meaning for them than

the term "typically Chinese." Therefore the danger arises that the speeches of the Führer, who always begins his political messages with a detailed summary of the Jewish problem, lose so much in penetrative power for the younger generation, and in their view assume the character of a historical lecture. This shows the possibility that the consciousness of the Jewish problem might be buried with us of the older generation. In other words: it appears to the younger generation that the calming of the struggle, in which the Jewish question has been solved within Germany through the measures of the leadership of the Reich,[119] the end of the struggle has reached its conclusion and its potential for growth has been forfeited.

The point, Meyer-Christian asserts, is to "renew" the effort, to show that "the enemy which is believed to be dead [totgeglaubte Feind] still lives and struggles and can not be defeated for quite a long time."[120] As early as 1940 the SS brought attention to a growing divide between the "older men" and the newer officers, especially among those who had been recruited among the *Volksdeutsche*. Of particular concern was the need to intensify their "feelings of belonging" to the SS.[121] Certainly by 1944 this problem was ever more urgent for the Nazis and their accomplices.

"But on the other hand," Meyer-Christian argued, "luck" was on their side and would win out over "indifference," because even "the leaders of the Zionist party were aware" that "anti-Semitism is not only one of the foundations of National Socialism but simultaneously one of its most important propaganda weapons among the established nations. Frequently, one finds that anti-Semitism is neatly and appropriately called the Führer's secret weapon. Consequently, the attitude of personalities and organizations, even governments, toward the Jewish problem is considered—above all in America—a measure of political reliability."[122] In other words, the way that Nazis would forever know their friends was through their stand on the Jewish question and the extent to which individuals and states would condone the event that would come to be known as the Holocaust:

> This attitude also holds true among those neutrals whom we are interested in influencing.
> How do we make use of our secret weapon? What does a Swede of good will find in the German press of fundamentals and material on the Jewish question as he sees it, material that concerns him and interests him, and that he can use? What does our radio, our foreign news system, both of which reach listeners in the very camp of the enemy, offer the dissatisfied

and opposition circles in England, say, in the way of powerful material appropriate to and important for England, which could exert its divisive effect there and continue in its oral propaganda? How, and by what means do we, the heartland of anti-Semitism, steer and strengthen the available defense forces against Jewry in England and North America?

Meyer-Christian's immediate, rhetorical response was that "there is, unfortunately, no answer to these questions. We hold the weapon in our hands, without steadily controlling or maintaining its sharpness and without a convincing plan for applying it."[123] This moment, then, is the time for "a new weapon to be introduced. . . . Above all," this response is to be accomplished by "the press." Its delineation is nothing less than a "plan of attack" (Angriffsplan), which is "by no means too late."[124] Implementation of this plan to save the Reich has six stages: "1. Steadfast leadership; 2. A concrete task; 3. A center of gravity, or focal point (Schwerpunkt); 4. Examination of all means of battle; 5. Coordination of all weapons; 6. Exacting preparation."[125]

The most distinctive aspects of this program were its targets—seeking out the younger generation in Germany and worldwide—and its emphasis—against Zionism:

The focal point of this struggle is to be set against Zionism. Battle will be waged against the objectives of its leadership and its motives, its plan of a Jewish State, its ideology and its political praxis.

The creation of a point of emphasis means, at the same time, the abandonment of the countless other at this time unimportant means of attack, such as the essential personal character of the Jewish race, corruption, deceit, greed, laziness, cowardice etc.

Rather than continue the earlier strategy of issuing a wide range of articles, the propagandists' goal now was to concentrate on "world-Jewry in its entirety."[126] How were they to convey this idea when they could see that there were vast differences between Jews of different political groups, religious bodies, and national communities that did not always see eye to eye? The point was to move from the abstract to the concrete. The theoretical, diffuse, and abstract character of Jewish depictions is part of what had led to the current state of indifference, Meyer-Christian argued. Using the knowledge he had accumulated about the Zionist movement, he suggested that it could be overcome in this way:

Between Baruch and Frankfurter, Wise[127] and Silver, Weizmann and Ben Gurion, Brodetzky and Laski exist a series of discrepancies in their motives and goals and tactics. Without knowledge of their points of view, concurrently, their enmity among themselves cannot be unmasked. Therefore address this explicitly! Fix their position! Play one off against the other! Divide and conquer! *(Divide et impera!)* Baruch, for example, is not a Zionist, but a USA-Imperialist and war-monger. Frankfurter is among those who are drunk with power as the most powerful person in the USA. Wise wants to bring Zionism and world Jewry under the administration of the American Jews. All American Jews together agitate for Palestine to be a Jewish state out of fear of American anti-Semitism as a consequence of further Jewish immigration into the USA. Weizmann is the instigator of the English orientation of Zionism. In this way he is, with the City [of London] anti-American. He wants the Jewish state as the experienced leader of its people. Due to his anti-Marxist religious orientation he is opposed by his closest co-worker, Ben Gurion, who works for a solution against England with the Soviets. . . . All of these things must be brought into line *(Einklang).*[128]

The "coordination of weapons" comprises "the newly organized fight against world Jewry as Germany and Europe's enemy [which] must ostensibly—but without its organization being ostensible—be carried by the whole German people and its European friends. It will not do in any case if well-informed, but unknown, specialists dominate the field as editorial writers. The services of journalists who are known as experts on foreign politics, who are not of outspokenly National Socialist derivation or ilk, should be enlisted in this effort, and not at random—but according to their capacity and situation."

This propaganda campaign could not appear to be an official Nazi party project. Indeed, some of the men involved in this project changed their names after entering Arab societies, sometimes by way of South America, as the Third Reich collapsed.[129] The Nazis wanted Germans in all walks of life to be able to forcefully articulate these views—including "representatives of intellectual life, famous writers and scholars, actors and film stars, painters and musicians, generals, recipients of the Knight's Cross, engineers, officials, retailers, housewives—and former functionaries of the Social Democratic Party and other anti–National Socialist Parties." The center and political "left" had to be engaged in this effort. The priorities were to supply the domestic front with a real-life enemy, but even more important, to influence public opinion abroad, to spoon-feed the press with "live ammunition" to fight "the fifth column of the twentieth century." Meyer-Christian asserts that "the enmity toward the Jews" would be the sole means by which those who sympathized with the Nazis would be able to identify each other. Here he again points to a post-Nazi order, in which the ways of National Socialism, at least publicly, will not be practicable. Anti-Semitism, he asserts, "is now the secret password through which all who have understood the signs of the time understand each other. How could we choose not to lead them?" The means to accomplish this unified understanding—the only and best means—was to adopt his reformulation, in the following sections, of "the problems of Zionist politics" and "the Jewish State."[130] In short, he preaches that Zionism has always meant the quest for "a Jewish state *alongside* an all-powerful world Jewry. . . . When Zionists talk about 'solving' the Jewish problem," he urged, "replace that with 'perpetuating' and 'intensifying' the efforts they commenced." One can do so by comparing Herzl "positively (within limits) with Weizmann the troublemaker." A practical result of Weizmann's efforts was that all Jews, wherever they were, would have to be treated as American or British nationals—which the Nazis thought would be repugnant to the neutral powers of the world.[131]

Meyer-Christian specified that this effort be undergirded by his works and those of two others, Giselher Wirsing and Heinz Riecke.[132] He probably assumed that Rosenberg's warning against Zionism, however pointed, would be dismissed as the gobbledygook it was. Wirsing's *Engländer, Juden, Araber in Palästina* (English, Jews, Arabs in Palestine) of 1938 is a relatively detached analysis of the emerging order in the Middle East, despite the fact that Wirsing prefaces his work by asserting that he will deal with a clash between three "races" and pays homage to Rosenberg for calling attention to the rising specter of Zionism.[133] Most significant for Meyer-Christian is Wirsing's contention that Zionism has become "a central question in international Jewish world-politics." The small physical size of the land, he writes, is in inverse proportion to its significance on the world stage. Some sections of Wirsing's account have an immediacy, because they draw on his travels to the region. Following the style of an academic monograph, Wirsing grounds his study in "the schools of British Oriental politics." The Jews do not "come into play" until the Great War.[134] Although Wirsing does not get all of his facts straight,[135] for the most part he utilizes documentary sources that are easy to corroborate. However, he departs from the supporting material in his claim that Zionism represents a formerly divided, but now solidly unified, Jewry, rendered visible with the "expanded Jewish Agency." He reported that Palestine, in effect, had become the "Vatican" of the Jews. Besides being a center for Jewish political interests, Wirsing contended that Jewry's turn to

Zionism, through the British, was also instigated and nurtured because of the vast oil reserves in the region over which Jews would gain control.[136] He was correct about the oil becoming a principal instrument of world politics, uppermost in the affairs of Britain and France, but his estimation of Jews as beneficiaries was wildly exaggerated. Over the next decades Arab oil became one of the sharpest weapons the opponents of Zionism wielded.

In a number of respects, however, Wirsing offers a more sophisticated analysis, including a dispassionate treatment of "pan-Arabism" and "pan-Islamism" that explains why he believes they will not become a dominant force anytime soon.[137] He concludes that the Arabs will require Nazi help to thwart Zionist designs. Wirsing's main focus, writing as he was in the wake of Britain's entry into the war against Nazi Germany, is clear—that British interests and those of world Jewry via Zionism were one and the same: "Great Britain is Israel, and its sovereignty over the Land of Israel is unified and indivisible. The British throne is the modern avant-garde of the throne of David."[138] Lending this idea even greater force was the fact that such metaphors were taken from polemical literature, in English, that supported British backing for Zionism. Of course, awareness that the enmity between the Zionists and the mandatory power was increasing dramatically—in large part because of refugees' seeking to escape the Nazis and the crush of anti-Semitic persecution in Eastern Europe—had no part in his treatise. He predictably overlooked the fact that his own country was exacerbating tensions.

The selection of Wirsing's book as a source for Meyer-Christian, and its specific endorsement by Sündermann, most likely was neither a random choice nor an indication of the perceived merits of the work. In Wirsing's personnel file is a curious item: recognition for a ceremonial honor presented to him by the King of Bulgaria. This honor is not simply noted; it is followed up by a declaration on November 19, 1943, signed by Hitler, lauding Wirsing for this achievement.[139] The possibility exists, therefore, that Hitler knew of Wirsing's treatment of Zionism, and this recognition may well have played a role in Zionism's altered status in 1944. Given Hitler's personal background, he was likely to have taken a more than passing interest in Wirsing, an SS and SD man, who in 1934 became the chief editor of the *Münchner Neueste Nachrichten*. After 1945 Wirsing enjoyed a long career as one of the pioneers of both the "New Right" and anti-Americanism as a Weltanschauung, particularly in the Third World.[140]

The critical difference between Wirsing's book of 1938 and Meyer-Christian's 1944 adaptation for the press is that the latter minimized the culpability of England. England was effectively Jewish and Zionist to Wirsing, whereas the official line in 1944 painted the Jews as the archculprits and Britain and America as unwitting accomplices or dupes. On April 4, 1945, Goebbels reported receiving a six-point directive from Sündermann that sought to overcome the old observation that "the German press no longer shows its thoroughly war-like character." The first order, "to use all direct and indirect means to reach the listening and reading public,"[141] helped energize the directive on Zionism of nine months earlier.

Similar to Wirsing's book, Heinz Riecke's 1939 pamphlet on Zionism is based in large part on the writings of Zionists themselves. It was reviewed in Nazi organs when published,[142] but it failed to make a big splash. To a great extent Riecke simply describes the development of the movement. His argument makes a turn toward fundamental antipathy to Zionism when he attempts to show continuity from Moses Hess, one of the forerunners of both communism and Zionism—who was unknown to Herzl when he started the movement—to Leon Trotsky and Béla Kun. Riecke warns that as in the French and Russian revolutions, the Jews will try to spread their influence internationally through Zionism.[143] Ironically, he identifies what has come to be known as "cultural" Zionism—the notion that the Jewish settlement in Palestine should serve as a source of intellectual and spiritual invigoration and sustenance to Jewry worldwide—as the origin of this plan. Riecke interprets this form of Zionism, however, as a naked power play aimed at world domination, with Zionism's ostensible quest for a "spiritual center" serving as a front for communist insurgency.[144] Drawing on a handful of articles from Martin Buber's journal *Der Jude,* Riecke attempts to demonstrate Zionism's affinity with anarchism, pacifism, and revolutionary socialism, as manifested in the thought of Gustav Landauer and Erich Mühsam and in the short-lived Bavarian republic of Kurt Eisner.[145] He also suggests that the Zionists revealed their deviousness in their support for Kun in Hungary and for "Bolshevism" in the Spanish Civil War.[146] Therefore he again accentuated the tie between the "November Criminals" and Zionism, as the communists were but organized "arsonists."[147]

Especially because the Zionists sided with the Entente in the Great War, there was now no question that Jews of any land could be "patriots" of any nation except their own. If they claimed to be "neutral," the statement was surely a ruse. The culmination of Zionist efforts at nationalizing Jewry and lodging itself in the center of world politics was the "expanded Jewish Agency," also identified by others as the primary instrument of "a unified world-Jewry." Overall, Riecke seems to distrust the fact that anti-Semitism has given way too easily to tacit support for Zionism. In 1939 annihilation is not discussed. He sees, however, the necessity of placing "Jewish emigrants" in a "closed-off " settlement detached from their European host nations. But if Zionism is given the chance to exploit these understandable impulses, the result could be dire—because Zionism contains the seed of a much larger, potential threat.[148]

As one might expect, the Meyer-Christian memorandum and supporting documentation drew most heavily on his own book published in 1940, *Die englisch-jüdische Allianz.*[149] The book's subtitle *(Werden und Wirken der kapitalistischen Weltherrschaft)* points to a subsequent adjustment. The older and savvier Meyer-Christian no longer emphasizes "capitalism" as a system that binds Jewish means and motives with the English national-religious character. In 1940 he had written, "The capitalism and imperialism of England draws power from its religious substructure. This, however, is Jewish."[150] The line that he explicated from Judaism to Puritanism, and back to Judaism, at the core of the conspiracy has been abandoned. Another important change in the 1944 version is his omission of the point that England was beholden to Jewish interests through "financial and family alliances, resulting in the merger of English and Jewish upper classes" beginning in the mid-seventeenth century.[151] The defeat of the English and the solution to the Jewish question were portrayed as one and the same, goals to be pursued with equal vigor: "The Jewish question for Germany and the European continent will not be solved until that of England is solved, that is, when the alliance of the present English upper class with that of the leadership of world Jewry is destroyed for all time. This alliance is the mortal enemy *[Todfeind]* of Europe."[152]

Knowing in 1944 that Nazi Germany was not destined to prevail, the Nazis could not consider England on its own to be a prime enemy, so all of the scorn and sense that it was a repository of evil was foisted on "world Jewry." There is no suggestion in the "Treatment of the Jewish Question" and its supporting material that the "English upper class" was a key co-conspirator, despite the fact that these connections were supposedly made transparent in *Die englisch-jüdische Allianz.*[153] Within the tales Meyer-Christian weaves in 1940 are a number of well-worn tropes of Jewish duplicity and criminality, such as Jews profiting through the trade in illicit narcotics and the labeling of leading personalities as "gangsters." Likewise, a photograph of Lilian Montagu, "daughter of the First Lord Swaithling [Swaything] from the House of Samuel, leader of the Jewish women's movement," has been doctored to make her look like a convict. Zionist settlement is reduced to "Jewish bank-robbery in Palestine."[154] Meyer-Christian devoted significant attention to the "Wedgwood Letter," a statement by a well-known sympathizer with the Jews,[155] imploring them to adopt methods of passive resistance as opposed to what the author characterized as "terror bombing" and "lynch-justice."[156] Meyer-Christian considered this letter to be convincing proof of the Jews' duplicity, because Wedgwood had been among the first British officials to speak out against Hitler, and he had worked for the right of refugees from Nazism to settle in Britain.

But even more important for Meyer-Christian's argument was what he termed "the Goddard Case," which he claimed had unmasked "even the English themselves in the role of murderers, in the Jewish interest": "In July the British police sergeant Collinge in Tel Aviv was shot in the back. The official report maintained that he was killed in a battle with Arab guerrillas. In fact it was known that Collinge was murdered by a Jew but the police did not want this to be followed-up and the case made public." This murder was not simply for the sake of facilitating illegal Jewish immigration. "Under oath," the British police chief Gilpin claimed that "Goddard told him that two British ministers, among them [the Jewish] War Minister Hore-Belisha, said that it was their explicit understanding that the smuggling of Jews into Palestine would occur." This event proved, Meyer-Christian declared, that the "arming of the Jews was effectively legalized under the cover of British police assistance" in order to terrorize and disenfranchise the Arabs.[157]

The "human rights of the Arabs" are mentioned as a reason for opposing the creation of a Jewish state, and Meyer-Christian charges the "London mob," along with bringing "misery and proletarianization," with assaulting the Arabs by means of "bloody terror," disguised in soldiers' uniforms. The Jews, Meyer-Christian asserts, are trying to provoke an "English-Arab war" as a pretext for, "above all, the attempted extermination *[Ausrottung]* of an entire people through British military force." Yet the main reason for opposing such a state is because it will not constitute a state like any that has been previously known. Following Hitler, Meyer-Christian says it will be a pretext and camouflage for a "completely different," monstrous entity. "Such a state would in no way solve the Jewish question. It would bring about its very opposite." Above all, "the Jewish Agency as the Government of World Jewry" was the most blatant manifestation of the changes wrought since the Great War. It was "the most remarkable of the creations of the mandate statutes for Palestine—or to put it more precisely: of the Jewish adroitness *[Geschicklichkeit],* to be construed and used as the Mandate for the Jewish interest."[158]

The element that Meyer-Christian now cited as the trigger and preeminent pretext for action against the Jews appeared only in a vague formulation in 1940, not set off as an especially ominous signal. The closest Meyer-Christian came, in 1940, to locating a "declaration of war" by Chaim Weizmann is his almost bland report that

> Scarcely a week after the English declaration of war, Weizmann submitted a message to the British government, with the appearance of utter altruism [*Uneigennützigkeit*]. He placed his 20,000 man strong Jewish "Army" at their disposal, which was the first time this opportunity presented itself. Furthermore, he boastfully offered to raise an army of 100,000 trained men whose full arming and equipment would be undertaken by Britain. This force would make it possible to relieve England of the defense of the Suez Canal, and after a bit of rest this same force could be pulled out of the Near East and deployed to Europe. One can see the intention, but a War Minister like Hore-Belisha was hardly annoyed.

The Jewish army, even as Meyer-Christian saw it, would not challenge Arab interests as support for Zionists' illegal immigration.[159] There was no inkling, either here or in other Nazi publications, that "a Jewish army" loomed as a threat to Germany as was later claimed.[160]

In the full-fledged program articulated by Meyer-Christian in mid-1944 there is scant concern for a party one would expect to figure in the Nazis' calculations: the Arabs of Palestine. Obviously there were, and remain, understandable reasons for Palestine's Arabs to oppose the Zionist movement. But the national aspirations and overall well-being of Arabs for their own sake was not a motive for the men behind this plan. The notion was, nevertheless, ardently appropriated in many of its aspects by Arab governments and self-styled anti-Zionist—and anti-Semitic—organizations toward the end of, and after, World War II. In much of the hate that spews forward supposedly in Arab interest, the Zionist is once again part world-Jewish powermonger and part archcriminal. We should remember that this thinking was first fleshed out before the massive dispossession of Palestine's Arabs in the Jewish State's War for Independence of 1947–48. Zionists were deemed "criminal," as a reworking of the *Protocols of the Elders of Zion*—and the moniker has stood—before the Arabs' self-described national catastrophe *(Naqba)* of 1947–48.

In an additional, creative—but horribly sickening—twist, some of the offshoots of the Nazi propaganda strategy of June 1944 alleged that the

Zionists propagated the myth of the murder of six million Jews in order to realize their aims. There could scarcely be a more ludicrous turn to a written directive by the Nazis, their plan for the "Treatment of the Jewish Question," which chillingly included the phrase "leaving aside the six million" and elsewhere inferred that the Jewish question, outside of England and the United States, had been "solved."[161]

That Sündermann played a role in the propagation of this idea is all the more understandable, because he himself had written at the end of 1940 that "the end of the bastardized, poisonous Jewish race" was drawing near. Soon the Jews would be but an "ugly memory."[162] He also was careful, however, to tie visceral hatred to political tactics: in his book on the *Anschluss* (1939), rather than portraying Jewry as a menace in and of itself, he muses about ways to use anti-Semitism to further connect the Austrian people to the Nazi party and, especially, to integrate other national groups that would remain.[163] "In the Nazi state," Geoffrey Giles has written, "some men became very powerful by translating Hitler's passing thoughts into policy."[164] Sündermann, perhaps because of his "expertise" on Vienna and Austria, likely became more aware than most Nazis of Zionism, and of Hitler's early reference to it. An earlier press directive, of May 1943, had stated: "line to be taken: emphasize: Every single Jew, wherever he is and whatever he is doing, shares the guilt. There is no such thing as a 'good Jew,' but only degrees of skill and camouflage. The Jew is a notorious criminal."[165] The directive's authors conveniently forgot that less than six years earlier the Nazis had proclaimed that the "world government" of the Jews was centered in Poland, manipulated by the anti-Zionist, socialist *Bund.* Immediately after *Kristallnacht,* the most nefarious incarnation of Jewish evil was said to be the LICA, the International League against Anti-Semitism, headed by "the Minister King of Israel," Bernard Lecache—an organization and its head that virtually disappeared without a trace. On the eve of Germany's launch of the World War II by invading Poland, the Nazis had dismissed the Zionist goal of a Jewish state as an "absurdity."[166] How it was transformed from an "absurdity" to a menace that demanded no less than genocide is a twisted path indeed. In light of this initiative, we cannot be surprised that at a late stage in the war, some Nazis "blamed the conflict on the American and English Jews," which helped them to feel that their part in the anti-Jewish assault was justified.[167]

Yet another tragic confluence of events was to come for European Jewry. The remnant that survived the Holocaust increasingly found that few alternatives existed for their future lives outside of Palestine and Zionism.

The German society in which most of the Jewish "displaced persons" found themselves had been indoctrinated, for at least a year, to see Zionism as the most cunning and insidious treachery the Jews had produced. This and many other scavenger ideologies coalesced to raise the possibility that the fraction of Jewry that survived, and increasingly gravitated to the American zone of occupation in Germany, would be perceived as criminals just for being who they were.

SIX

Lingering Stereotypes and Jewish Displaced Persons

However they do live together for the most part in an unbroken though uneasy peace.

PHILIP S. BERNSTEIN (1946)

IN THE AFTERMATH OF THE AXIS DEFEAT, Jews in Central and Western Europe comprised a fraction of the millions of DPs, or displaced persons, anxious to resume a normal life.[1] Along with the conundrum of memory and accountability vis-à-vis the Nazis' Jewish victims, there were real, live Jews to deal with in Germany, and their ranks swelled considerably after 1945.[2] The comparatively small fragment of Jews may have seemed almost negligible in the vast sea of dislocated peoples in the eyes of the Germans as well as in those of the Allied powers.[3] Yet the Jews posed a set of distinct problems. Originally the Jewish DPs were survivors of the camps, those who came out of hiding, and men, women, and children who had successfully concealed their identities. After mid-1946, many thousands of Jews who had repatriated from the Soviet Union to Poland joined them. With Polish and Hungarian Jews in the majority, Jewish DPs numbered around 250,000 in 1947 and by that point were centered in Germany. Although motivations varied for leaving Poland, the Kielce pogrom in 1946 was clearly a signal event that prompted many Jews to do what earlier had seemed unthinkable: to seek refuge on German soil. Thousands of survivors, whether they eventually landed in Israel (before 1948, Palestine), the United States, or elsewhere, spent anywhere from several days to several years in DP camps or else lived on their own as DPs in German cities and towns.[4]

In the wake of the Nazi defeat many Germans understood that it was impolitic, at least outside their confidants, to refer to the Jewish "surviving remnant" by the racial terms ubiquitous in the Third Reich.[5] Informal and later compulsory restraints did not, however, vanquish well-entrenched stereotypes, as a number of scholars, most recently Eva Kolinsky, Suzanne Brown-Fleming, and Zeev Mankowitz, have demonstrated.[6] One of the means by which many Germans dealt with the postwar Jewish remnant was to perceive and treat Jewish survivors as criminals, or as having an inordinate propensity toward criminality. Like the charges against the *Ostjuden* from the 1880s onward, the suggestion was that after 1945 Jews swarmed over from Poland to exploit the Germans, and that reports of the lethal threats facing Jews there were merely "hearsay." Rather than admitting that temporary residence in Germany was their only alternative, Jews supposedly chose Germany because of the opportunity to fleece Germans—who became the "victims" of the DPs.[7]

This chapter focuses on five aspects of the history of Jewish DPs in Germany that pertain to the "Jewish criminality" stereotype. First, the very attempts by Jews to flee Europe were often seen as part of a criminal and conspiratorial undertaking on behalf of "world Jewry" and, often, the Zionist movement was viewed as the leading embodiment of Jewish national aspirations. To be sure, enabling individuals to emigrate to the United States, and groups to Palestine, often entailed subtle to flagrant violation of the law. Second, the perception of "Jewish criminality" intensified because of the sense that some Jews were behaving outrageously and taking advantage of their previous status as victims. Third, and perhaps most significant in propping up the stereotype of Jewish criminality, were the real and imagined roles of Jews in the ubiquitous black market. (I will discuss Jews' impressions of the relationship between crime and the black market in chapter 7.) Jewish DPs were caught up in occasional violent conflicts about the unregulated flow of goods and services that came to public attention; an analysis of these episodes makes up the fourth section.[8] Last, I shall revisit two specific endeavors by American Jews in the occupation forces—by Abraham Klausner and Philip Bernstein, who were deeply sympathetic to the plight of the Jewish DPs—to understand and alleviate problems growing out of the "crime" question. Although the canard of Jewish criminality remained vital, the general atmosphere between Jews and Germans was one of civility, and as Atina Grossmann has demonstrated, regular and intensive contact was for the most part taken for granted.[9] Nevertheless, the predisposition to regard Jews as criminals was close enough to the surface for it to be easily mobilized when someone needed a way to explain Germans' (past or current) injustices toward Jews.

An important pretext for Germans to see Jewish survivors as a criminal threat is that the Nazis did, in many respects, succeed in turning Jews into their enemies—and the animosity did not always subside with the Nazi defeat. Certainly many Jews believed they were "hated," especially where there had been forced resettlement of "locals," and that "most Germans lived in a state of denial," maintaining that the persecutions and the annihilation of the Jews had never occurred.[10]

The fact that Jewish survivors, by all rights, should have hated the Germans passionately is rarely admitted. Such attitudes were especially evident among children: "nearly all" of those resident at Kloster-Indersdorf were said to have "had one attitude in common—that of intense hatred of the Germans and all that was German. It was extremely difficult to help the children with these feelings, when everything in their daily lives was surrounded by the German atmosphere and when they had to continue living in Germany after the liberation. The staff of the Center often wondered what damage was being caused and how the rehabilitation process was being slowed by these factors."[11]

In the first months after the war, one observer of the DP camps wrote that "the most shattering thing" she witnessed was the need for Jews to live among "former SS men, Gestapo, Nazi party members, Polish voluntary labor (not slave labor but Poles who offered their services voluntarily to the Reich for a wage), Russian voluntary labor, Yugoslavian fascist soldiers all of whom have disguised themselves as displaced persons and gone into the camps to escape detection." Certainly, and predictably, victimized Jews thought that Germans should, as much as possible, "be working for them."[12] A constant problem for the occupation authorities was that many Jews did not want to work "for" Germans or for any enterprise that appeared to serve the general benefit of the locality or the reconstruction of the country. Not surprisingly, this attitude sometimes led to riots and other forms of violent protest.[13]

By applying the stereotype of Jewish criminality, Germans could assure themselves that Jews had rightly been, and should remain, objects of contempt, and that they had possibly been the cause of their defeat and distress. Though this notion was a self-serving delusion, the view of Jews as crooks had a symbiotic relationship with the desperate and ambiguous circumstances in which Jewish survivors found themselves, as well as with the preconceptions of the UNRRA (United Nations Relief and Rehabilitation

Agency) and occupying forces.[14] General Sir Frederick Morgan, the first head of the UNRRA, described the Jewish DPs in Munich as "well dressed, well fed, rosy cheeked, and having plenty of money."[15] The interview in which he articulated this view, it should be noted, became the basis for his removal. Similar feelings, however, were shared by many GIs on the ground. In August 1945, a Jewish chaplain in the U.S. Army wrote, "One of the most disheartening attitudes that I have to combat [among American soldiers] is the disgust and repugnance towards displaced persons that the vast majority of people who deal with them develop." This attitude was "the logical result of pity without understanding. . . . Our men . . . came to believe that the Germans were right—[the Jews] are an inferior people. They could in no way be compared to the Germans, who were clean, well-dressed, and accustomed to higher standards." Another Jewish chaplain recorded his dismay at the fact that "the Germans are better clothed, fed and housed, and the Jew is still on the lowest rung of the ladder."[16] As has been discussed by Leonard Dinnerstein and Joseph Bendersky, the renowned but bigoted General George S. Patton helped set the tone of derision and insensitivity in dealing with Jewish DPs, which would have to be undone by a succession of special advisers to the American occupation forces and the implementation of the Harrison Report (August 1945), which acknowledged U.S. Army maltreatment of Jewish survivors and set guidelines for rectifying the situation.[17] To Patton and other authorities, fighting communism and "anarchism" and "restoring normal communications and law and order" was paramount, even if it meant "having some Nazis work for us."[18] Nevertheless, some individual Jews whom he believed rose above the general character of the DPs impressed Patton.[19]

Many of the soldiers and officials who dealt with the Jewish DPs, however, were not swayed by the "Jewish criminality" stereotype. Their reflections nevertheless offer insight into such attitudes. Among the recollections of survivors that shed light on the notion of Jewish criminality are stories about individual Anglo-Jewish and Russian-Jewish soldiers who lent them sympathy and aid. A woman originally from Kraków relates a particularly instructive memory: the Soviet officer who befriended her and a group of girls

> took us to a large house and knocked on the door and a fat German
> woman opened it. He ordered her to feed us and allow us to sleep as long
> as we wanted to. He told her that he would come by from time to time to
> see if the woman was carrying out his orders. The German woman gave us
> the entire second floor. We slept in separate beds with down comforters.

Every morning she called us for break-fast which was already laid out on the table with bread, coffee etc. Her children took one look at us and from fear, burst into tears. The Germans had, evidently, told their children that we were thieves, murderers, bandits and had ordered the children not to come anywhere near us.[20]

To Rabbi Philip S. Bernstein, who served as the second Adviser on Jewish Affairs for the U.S. forces from May 1946 to August 1947, there was no question that a "new" current of anti-Semitism was afoot in postwar Germany, which derived from various sources: "Most of the Germans suggested that [the] economic plight of the German people is the principal cause. Jews serve as a convenient scapegoat that can be held responsible for the plight of the average German. In addition, there is the popular belief that American Jewry is shaping the occupation policy in Germany, and that to avenge the deaths of the millions of their co-religionists, the Jews are deliberately standing in the way of Germany's recovery."[21] Indeed, the specific anti-Semitic campaign from June 1944 linking American and British Jewry as particularly nefarious anti-German entities through Zionism may have propped up this perception.[22] Not least, "occupied with the personal struggle for survival, the Germans have a nostalgia for the regime under which they enjoyed gainful employment and the prospect of a dominant position in the world."[23] Less severe but nonetheless damaging was "another group of Germans"—including some former German Jews—who considered

Jewish DPs as a provocative element in the German scene. The reaction to the Jewish DP is rationalized on numerous grounds: Stemming as they do from east European Jewry, they are the type with whom the German is either not familiar or whom he has traditionally resented. The Jewish DPs are believed to be the hub of the black market that is flourishing in Germany; some German workers, normally inclined to be liberal and racially tolerant, have swelled the ranks of anti-Semites because they were dispossessed to make room for the Jewish DPs; the Germans are uneasy by the presence in their midst of people to whom they owe a colossal debt, and relieve themselves of their guilt by proving to the world that the Jews deserved their fate under the Nazi regime.

From Bernstein's perspective, the leaders among the Jewish DPs were

unanimous in their belief that the resurgence of anti-Semitism in Germany is, to a considerable extent, conditioned by the interaction between the

American troops and the German civilian population. The Jewish DPs recall the sympathetic attitude of the American troops that liberated them, and invariably contrast them with the type of men they now encounter among occupation troops. This difference they ascribe to the immediate influence of the German with whom the soldiers associate. The Germans in turn discard their veneer as soon as they feel secure that the American troops are either indifferent to or are in accord with their anti-Semitic views. . . . Finally, there is a group that offers the simple explanation that anti-Semitism is now deeply rooted in the German culture as a result of the unchallenged indoctrination of the Hitler regime.[24]

Jews in postwar Central Europe were engaged in quite a bit of activity that could be considered illegal. The perception was that they were indulging in two main forms of "criminality": first, in using "illegal" means to try to leave Europe, especially to emigrate to Palestine; and second, in being denizens of the "black" and "gray" markets that were, technically, illegal. In sum, Jews faced a Catch-22: like everyone else in postwar Germany, they depended on black and gray markets to survive. If they wished to leave, they had little recourse other than to stretch, or abrogate, the limits of the law. There was virtually no absolutely "legal" way either to live in the country or to leave it.

Hundreds of survivors' testimonies, and accounts of sympathetic American Jews, confirm this dilemma. It seems that part of the reason why Germans seized as they did on "criminal Jews" as a preeminent problem, especially as black marketeers, was that Germans were prone to idealize Nazi times as supremely orderly. In reality, during the war years there had been a significant amount of crime—much of it perpetrated by the men of the Wehrmacht[25]—including the same type of large-scale smuggling and black marketeering that some later claimed was a postwar Jewish introduction. One historian notes that "hoarding, organized theft of foodstuffs, and illicit trade became increasingly open" as early as 1942 and was rampant during wartime.[26]

Although this and the following chapter deal mainly with Jewish survivors in the American zone of occupation, because it was a primary destination for those seeking to immigrate to the United States or to Palestine, I occasionally refer to the British, French, and Soviet areas. Primo Levi's classic *La Tregua* is an excellent treatment of the Soviet zone, where similar anti-Semitic prejudices reigned, and the vague "gray zone" of necessary "criminal" behavior is well mined. The historian Hagit Lavsky provides a superb study of the British zone, in particular the Bergen-Belsen camp.[27]

In addition to Jewish DPs' seemingly obsessive quest for food and posses- sions, some among the Allied occupation authorities found a sinister taint in the feverishness with which Jews sought to find relatives and friends, and in their need to remain close to the comrades and relatives with whom they had shared their trauma.[28] Most likely, conflicts that ensued over "the spirit" versus "the letter" of the "Truman Project" (December 22, 1945), which intended to ease the plight of refugees, gave rise to perceptions of Jewish impropriety by government officials. "The general attitude of the U.S. Consuls," Irwin Rosen of "the Joint" (or JDC, the American Jewish Joint Distribution Committee; see chapter 5) wrote, "is to follow the letter rather than the spirit of the President's directive."[29] "Further unjustified re- duction" in the number of Jews admitted to the United States "was created by the narrow interpretation of the definition of a displaced person by some of the Consuls." These factors constrained

the execution of the program in extent and thwarted the purpose which was to aid the victims of Nazism. . . . The Consuls have shown an increas- ing stringency in requiring documents such as birth and marriage certifi- cates. The Consul at Frankfurt has recently stated: "It has been learned that these documents can be procured from Poland, Polish-occupied Ger- many, and in many instances from the Russian Zone of Germany and from Czechoslovakia, to name a few areas only. Accordingly, it will be nec- essary for visa applicants to present them at this Consulate General, or at least to present evidence that an unsuccessful effort has been made to procure them."

For many, if not the vast majority, of Jews who found themselves in need of such documents this was an impossible standard.[30] Along with frustrat- ing the emigration of Jews who might have had grave difficulty securing such documentation even under normal circumstances, this requirement undoubtedly gave rise to the fabrication of documents—which, although inauthentic, most likely reflected the realities of the applicant's personal sit- uation. Forgery became a highly prized, even romanticized, skill.[31] Rosen asserted that Jews faced a dilemma:

Even though the President's directive stresses the principle of reuniting families, the interpretation of the policy with regard to members of fami- lies who are eligible leads to separation of families. Parents and children under 18 years who do not fulfill residence requirements are allowed to accompany members of their family who are eligible. This rule was set up by the Consuls themselves who further decided that only unmarried brothers and sisters or children may be included. This causes hardship in many cases, such as widowed daughters and young sisters and brothers over 18 who are left alone here. Thus, contrary to the spirit of the President's directive, the practice of the Consuls leads to separation of families and has caused great distress and anxiety for those who are forced to leave families behind for an unknown period.

A similar attitude was taken by some of the Consuls in several instances with regard to persons who came voluntarily into the U.S. zone after liberation in order to seek relatives or who were fleeing persecution in Poland. One Pole, together with his son, was refused because Mr. Hoffman, the Consul in Frankfurt, believed "he was not persecuted enough." The father and son were evacuated to Russia. When the Germans invaded Russia, they deported the wife, parents and the two daughters to Germany. The father and son hid in the woods for several months until the Germans retreated. After liberation they proceeded to Germany only to find that the rest of the family had perished. Although this practice does not affect the number of immigrants, it undoubtedly conflicts with the spirit of the directive.[32]

The latter case underscores the dilemma of those "evacuees" who had been interned in the Soviet Union. Rosen also brought the following to Bernstein's attention: "Further hardship for many orthodox immigrants is caused by the disregard of the religious observances in technical arrangements. Several transports from assembly centers to Bremen have been sent on Saturdays. U.S. Lines almost invariably have ships sailing on the Sabbath regardless of the protests by the orthodox groups. Neither are any provisions for kosher food made on the ships leaving from Bremen." Thus a significant portion of survivors would have to choose which laws they were to violate if they were to succeed in immigrating. Rosen's suggestions underscore the obstacles that Jews had to navigate or circumvent to emigrate to the United States: "to extend the program to the British and French Zones of Austria for applicants under German, Austrian and Russian quotas by a Presidential directive"; to completely eliminate "the residence requirement for applicants"; to make use of "the quota numbers" that went unused "during the war"; to change the regulations to allow for Jews to be included as "Germans"; to change the restrictive immigration quotas imposed in 1924, according to the circumstances of the postwar period; to "instruct the Consuls to be more flexible in requiring documentation"; to "establish a uniform rule for the consideration of persecutees which should be followed by all Consuls"; to "establish uniform rules for consideration of nonquota cases which should not include requirements impossible to fulfill"; to privilege the uniting of families; and to "instruct all organizations involved to give special attention to the religious observances in technical arrangements." Jews who were determined to leave Europe had to find creative ways to compensate for the "reluctance on the part of the Consuls in general" to implement the president's program.[33] From the perspective of the American and British occupying armies, the desperate attempts by Jews to flee to Palestine, and to emigrate to the United States and other Western countries, were forms of unlawful behavior. By its very nature, then, the American Jewish Joint Distribution Committee qualified as an "illegal" organization, because it fabricated backgrounds of refugees to facilitate their emigration.[34]

It is possible that Allied authorities, especially the British, perceived the movements of Jews to be illegal partly because of unwritten agreements between Jewish organizations and the occupation forces, and individual leaders and generals.[35] For example, the correspondence of Philip Bernstein indicates that he expended a great deal of energy to ensure that large numbers of Jews, especially from Poland, would be able to reach and settle in the American zone and possibly to join groups destined for Palestine.[36] Bernstein vacillates, however, between wanting to take credit for facilitating such movements of Jews, who were increasingly threatened by anti-Semitic violence in Poland, and keeping such arrangements—such as he apparently struck with the American Generals McNarney, Clay, and Clark, as well as the prime minister of Poland and President Harry S. Truman—under wraps to make sure that these deals, ensuring "a temporary haven and assistance to these persecutees awaiting the ultimate solution of their problem," remained in place.[37] In an address celebrating the service of General McNarney, Bernstein may have been partially speaking for himself when he asserted that McNarney "was the savior of one hundred thousand Jews. . . . In all Europe, it was the United States Army alone which granted them haven" in the wake of the Kielce pogrom and terror in Warsaw and Lodz.[38] On one occasion (among few, if any, others) Bernstein became irate upon disclosure that he had made a "confidential arrangement" with General Clay—which probably dealt with the so-called infiltration.[39] There also were concerted efforts to speed Jewish immigration to the United States on the basis of existing "unused" immigration quotas from 1942 through 1945.[40] Describing his experience in Poland, Bernstein wrote that "the Kielce pogrom" and other horrors "deprived the Jews of Poland of whatever sense of security they had formerly possessed." He found the sight of Polish Jewry "on the move," who were compelled to flee Poland, particularly distressing:

> On the way to the points in Lower Silesia from which the movement started which eventually brought them to [the] United States Zone, Germany, they were again beaten, robbed and some of them were killed. They were gathered in shelters near the border where they lay on the floors; no beds, no pillows to rest their heads on, in some cases, no food . . . for everything was taken from them. Like criminals, they had to steal out at night. As one of them said to me, "Apparently we are criminals. Our crime is that we are Jews."[41]

Bernstein personally thanked President Truman for "the policy which kept the borders open for the victims of persecution, particularly in Poland."[42] To fight the fires of anticommunist hysteria, he also had to dispel the myth that "all of the Jews of the Soviet Union" aspired to migrate to the American zone.[43] The influx from the USSR probably caused no end of confusion because there were sure to be at least some communists among the masses of Jews.

In 1947, if not earlier, Jewish DPs were frequently forced to relocate—no matter their legal status—because of the concerted efforts by the occupation forces to nurture a "self-sustaining economy," such as in Austria. Jews could be regarded as criminals, then, for staying put. "The question is," Philip Bernstein wrote,

> not whether this policy is correct. It is U.S. policy and, therefore, must be accepted as a fact. The question is what is to happen when this policy in a given situation runs counter to the welfare of the Jewish DPs. For example, what should our position be when General Keyes plans to move Jews out of good hotels in Bad Gastein in order to increase tourist income for Austrians, or when he decides to move them out of a certain housing area near a factory in order to provide accommodation for Austrian workers? In both instances the DPs and I regard the quarters to which they are to be moved as inferior to those which they are to leave. Is there anything in State Department policy which requires [the U.S. military] to upbuild the Austrian economy at the expense of the DPs, or am I sound in my position that there is nothing in the State Department's policy which requires the Army, when a conflict of interest arises, to sacrifice the DPs to the Austrians?[44]

The DPs never doubted that their interests were systematically "sacrificed" to the betterment of Germans and Austrians, and that this practice, too, often compelled their being moved.

"Zionist groups" were routinely queried about their supposed, "organized criminality." Certainly the clandestine work of the Jewish Brigade, to convey Jews to Palestine—by any means at their disposal—contributed to this practice, but it was not exclusively responsible for the perception. Zionist work was conducted on a number of levels, from the completely aboveboard to cloak-and-dagger. Under the heading "The Modern Wandering Jew," a "Weekly Intelligence Report" from the headquarters of the Third U.S. Army in the winter of 1946 stated that "large scale investigations into the mass movement of Polish Jews into the territory of the Third US Army reveals" that the Jews' "movements are financed and fostered by Zionist groups." Although there appears to have been nothing illegal about giving refugees money (in approved currency), the practice is rendered here in sinister overtones, mixed with the charge that Jews who have evaded "transient camps" made their way because of "false papers" supplied to them from "kibutzes." "Jewish infiltrees in the thousands," who "have been indoctrinated in Poland," were being sent "without authority" and "without the knowledge of the UNRRA." Suspicion was aroused by a report of "an organized crossing of the border (150–200 a day) for the purpose of joining the Polish Army in Munich"; on other occasions there were, naturally, illegal border crossings. All of these movements were deemed anti-American "espionage." Incredibly, the same report also expressed the fear that "if Palestine is inaccessible to them, a Jewish state will be set up in Bavaria." The source given for this information is the "camp police" at Feldafing. The report states authoritatively that "each infiltree is well-groomed in the stories told American authorities," supposedly because of receiving specific instructions in Poland. The American author has no sense of the irony in his characterization of the movement of the Jews—whose "main desire is to get to Palestine whether it be through legal or illegal means"—as an "underground railroad."[45] This was the term used for the routes that black American slaves took to gain freedom in the North.

The British, to a greater degree than the American, forces took umbrage at the illegal movement of the Jews, as the DPs' "ultimate aim" appeared to be "death to the British" in their "garrison situated in Palestine." Yet as much as Jews were scorned for their lawlessness in pursuit of Zionist aims, they also were accorded the status of worthy adversaries: "not only did one admire the skill of the Zionist propaganda campaign, but even more so the whole organisation of the ceaseless movement of these poor people across war-torn Germany, wherein legitimate movement was a highly practical business, down into Austria into Italy and Yugoslavia for shipment often in circumstances of terrifying danger, to Palestine." General Morgan's ire was furthermore aroused because, in his estimation, he believed that the Zionists were selfishly using their non-Zionist coreligionists to serve their cause. He determined that in accepting the directorship of the UNRRA he had, in innocence, "landed myself in the midst of such a political maze as never was."[46]

In contrast to the British and Americans, the French and Italians did not treat the movement of Jews as an urgent concern, although their countries were important bases of operation for the Jewish illegal immigration to Palestine. Dan Segre, in his capacity as a press attaché for the British in Italy, recalls that he routinely surveyed reports "on a low operational level" that concerned the work of "Zionist agents" whom the British accused of "running illegal bases . . . with the full cooperation of the Italians. . . . Since the activities of the Zionist agents presented no danger to Italy, the officers in counter-espionage operated a moving system of silent complicity with me. . . . They usually added a note [to the reports] saying that the information presented was of 'little interest to the top echelons,' which was their way of telling me that I could make whatever use I wanted of their reports, including throwing them in the waste-paper basket." Personally, though, Segre found these reports "of enormous interest."[47]

The Italian nonchalance in such matters was probably not appreciated by the Americans and the British. The "method of operation of the Jewish displaced persons camps," a top secret U.S. report alleged, purposely exploited the black market:

> Up to now, the black market sales of rations drawn from the UNRRA are, in the opinion of this writer, the largest source of income for both the Jewish underground and the legitimate Jewish relief organizations operating in Italy. The amount or value of clothing and food drawn from the UNRRA legitimately, which has been disposed of in the black market, will never be known. The sale value of the articles and foodstuffs which find their way into the black market through this channel is so vast that it can be reasonably assumed that it yields sufficient cash funds to finance the entire Jewish underground organization operating in Italy.

Although the UNRRA and the Joint are not "to blame" for the exploitation of the black market in this way, these bodies unwittingly allowed themselves to be used by "unscrupulous individuals and agencies" that have "maliciously used the names of both organizations to their personal or collective advantage. For example, vehicles bearing the name of either agency travel through Italy without fear of being molested by the Italian authorities, yet it is a known fact that vehicles bearing the names of either of these organizations have and are still transporting contraband and illegal refugees, but the vehicles so used have absolutely no official connection with either of these two organizations."[48]

One of the Joint's own internal memoranda makes clear that committee members saw "population movements" among the Jewish DPs as generally beyond their control and that the decision of individuals to take to the road, whether legal or not, was usually determined by "hardship."[49] In the La Vista report, motivation is taken into account only in the case of the Vatican, which is by far "the largest single organization involved in the illegal movement of immigrants"—in this case, former Nazis. In contrast to Jewish organizations, the Catholic Church is portrayed as driven by its "propagation of the faith," which further is made respectable because of its staunch anticommunist stance.[50] Despite the fact that the Jews' urge to reach Palestine was palpable, there was little cognizance of what prompted their desperation. "Illegal" Jewish population movements were seen as no less pernicious than the attempt by former Nazis, including some of its most vicious mass murderers, to escape to South America.[51]

It is not surprising that there also were charges of Jewish coconspiracy with communists. Certainly a number of Jews remained committed communists, but by definition they acted primarily according to their political, as opposed to ethnic-national, concerns. At the DP camp outside of Rome, a Mrs. Germandorff, "a Romanian Jewess and a rabid communist, who directs the office . . . is believed to aid the illegal activities of the Jews and the Communist agents." The main nefarious activity of Mrs. Germandorff's operation, the memo suggests, is that she runs "a Jewish kitchen," and that "persons can come and go without passing through the control point at the main gate."[52] As one would expect from people looking for carefully constructed conspiracies, there was little or no appreciation of the fact that the remnant of Jews that survived the Nazis were far from unified and were still divided between Bundist and Zionist, orthodox and secular, and numerous other loyalties. Nonetheless, the view was that there were "very few Jews left in the world . . . who did not approve of Palestine as a refugee haven, a spiritual center, a psychological, therapeutic, and normalizing instrument for Jews."[53]

A particularly fascinating phenomenon, which conspiracymongers believed revealed the link between DPs, the movement of refugees, and organized criminal activity, was the theft of hard currency as well as counterfeiting on a grand scale. It was charged that organized Jewish collusion with the Nazis, during wartime, continued into the postwar period: "On the Brenner Pass route from Austria the first stop on the underground railroad in Italy is at a castle in Merano where German is the language of the directors. The castle is believed to be 'SCHLOSS RAMETZ' belonging to CRASTAN, Albert, a Jew, who poses as a Swiss Consul and as a member of the International Red Cross." Supposedly, during the war Crastan had been

an agent of the SS task force "SCHLOSSLABERS" sometimes called "GROUP WENDIG" under the command of SCHWENDT, Col. Frederick, who was responsible only to KALTENBRUNNER and HIMMLER. Four other Jewish agents of this group are known to be at large. One, VAN HARTEN, Jaac, is at present at 184 Hayarkonstr., Tel Aviv, Palestine, from where he claimed 5,000,000 Dollars from the U.S. Government for property confiscated at Merano after the war's end. All this property was the loot of the SS group that had been stored in SCHLOSS RAMETZ, SCHLOSS LABERS, SCHWENDT's HQ, and other buildings in Merano. Included in this loot were large quantities of counterfeit British Pound notes. One of the plants producing these bills, is reported still in operation in the Milan area under a Slav director (see Case No. 4596). Another of SCHWENDT's agents, LOVIOZ, Carlo, another Jew and ex-head of the "Banca Commerciale" in London, is now director of the "Banca Commerciale" in Como. He has a brother who is director of the "Basle Bank" in Switzerland. The remaining two are the MANSER brothers, one of whom used to come to Rome to the German Embassy in an IRC [International Red Cross]-tagged vehicle during the Nazi occupation. One of the MANSER's was in Milan the summer of 1944; both were in Venice the winter of 1944–45. It is interesting to note that CRASTAN, VAN HARTEN, and the MANSER's all used the IRC as a front. VAN HARTEN claims Dutch citizenship falsely, it is believed. The exact connection between the remains of the "SCHLOSSLABERS" and the Jewish underground is unknown at the present time, but the link seems to exist.[54]

In this account, Jewish criminals—in the immediate postwar epoch—are central to a nexus of not only archcapitalists (counterfeiters) and communists, namely, "Russian-Yugoslav intelligence,"[55] but also ex-Nazis, at least one of whom, Jaac van Harten, was said to reside on the beach at Tel Aviv. Especially given the Nazis' radical turn in demonizing the Zionist movement, the suggestion that all this activity is intertwined with "arms-running by the Jewish underground"[56]—supposedly to advance the cause of Zionism—makes the former stories of capitalist and communist conspiracies even more convoluted.

Strangely enough, this allegation would prove, over fifty years later, to be partially founded on accounts of actual persons and events. Interestingly, in his memoir Hugo Gryn writes that he was "astonished"—upon arriving at Sachsenhausen in early 1945—to be given the duty of "loading forged British bank notes on to lorries."[57] Later, "a series of exposés published in 2000 in Israel and elsewhere" revealed that Harten—who lived in Tel Aviv from 1947 to 1973—had been an agent of the

> Abwehr, the Nazi intelligence service, and played a significant role in the Nazis' wartime scheme to undermine the British economy through the production and wholesale distribution of counterfeit British currency. He was shown to have been more than just a successful wholesale peddler of counterfeit banknotes. In possession of a Gestapo-supplied passport, van Harten also played a questionable role as a bogus "Plenipotentiary of the International Red Cross." A Budapest resident between September 1940 and late December 1944, van Harten apparently played the role with such conviction that he acquired the absolute confidence of the top leadership of the Hungarian pro-Nazi Arrow Cross (Nyilas) party and government. By 1944, the Nyilas leaders were most probably also aware of van Harten's dealings with SS-Obersturmbannführer (later SS-Standartenführer) Kurt A. Becher, Heinrich Himmler's personal economic representative in Hungary.[58]

The U.S. intelligence report failed to understand, however, that van Harten's and others' involvement in saving Jews came only after the fate of the Nazis was sealed, and such activities began as a means of providing an alibi for wartime activities in the service of the Nazis and themselves. As noted by historian Randolph Braham, the Nazis' massive counterfeiting operation, which began as Operation Andreas and came to be known as Operation Bernhard, was extraordinary within the history of the Third Reich. Workshops were established in the Sachsenhausen concentration camp, Blocks 18 and 19,

> which were completely isolated from the other areas. They were staffed with mostly Jewish "professionals," including forgers, chemists, photographers, typographers, printers, and graphic artists, recruited from among inmates of various concentration camps. In contrast to the other inmates

of concentration camps, the members of this *Fälscherkommando* (Forgers' Commando) were treated fairly well, wore civilian clothes, and enjoyed many privileges, including access to the canteens. The counterfeiting of British currency grew steadily with the Nazis focusing on the production of 5, 10, 20, and 50 pound notes. The SS were reportedly so satisfied with the results that they decorated not only some of their own but also twelve members of the *Fälscherkommando,* including three Jews.[59]

A survivor's memoir reveals how the operation worked from the inside. Already having a reputation for engraving and turning silver spoons into rings, Sam Stammer saw his life in Birkenau undergo a dramatic change from the moment he responded to an announcement that "engravers and printers should register at the office." Stammer recalls,

> I was the only engraver, and ten others registered as printers. They asked us in detail what kind of work we did, they entered everything and we at once were separated from the other prisoners. After one week we were sent to another camp under SS watch. It turned out that this camp was Sachsenhausen near Berlin. We were quarantined for fourteen days, until we were let to get together with the other prisoners. We had no idea what went on [in] the barracks. Only after we got together with the other prisoners after the fourteen days, we found out what our work would be. There were already a few other engravers and printers and they told us that we were going to make money, namely English pounds and U.S. dollars. The work was quite interesting.[60]

Incredibly, this counterfeiting operation was one of the few arenas where Jews were invited to perform intellectually rigorous and challenging labor. It also was one of the rare instances in which Jews were "rewarded" for their efforts:

> The plates for printing were made in Berlin. Those plates were made from lead and then galvanized and sent to us. However the letters of the plates were much too thick, and that's where the engravers came in. We had to recut the letters the way they should be, and then it went to the printers. After the printing, some selected prisoners had to check if the money was done correctly. The printers were using about eight printing machines and there were 140 Jewish prisoners who were working in this counterfeit department. Because of this we were treated good and also received good food. We were very successful with the English pounds. They were exactly like the ones printed by the English mint. I found out later that after the war Britain had to withdraw a whole series, because the[y] could not ascertain which ones were the real and which the counterfeits. Regarding the U.S. dollars,

the print was good, but we could not make the same paper, whenever our dollars were folded up and crumpled the paper broke. One day the U.S. Air Force tried to bombard the printing barracks, but they did not succeed, as the bombs fell into another barrack. We also made a number of falsified passports. . . . Everything done in these barracks was strictly criminal work. . . . When the Russians started bombing closer to Berlin [and] we had to evacuate Sachsenhausen, we packed up all the machines and were transported to the concentration camp Mattausen [Mauthausen] in Austria. . . . The machines were put in a barrack until the S.S. found the right place to open the counterfeit department again.[61]

The SS reestablished the operation in Redelsipp, Austria, but this activity did not last very long, with the Allied forces closing in on Germany:

The man in charge of our outfit was a stormtrouper [sic] by the name of Kruger . . . he called us all together and said the war is coming to an end and that the strong ones will win. He bade us "good bye." He was one of the very few decent people I met in all the camps, and as I heard he is supposed to live in Switzerland. Two hours after that we were transported or actually we walked to concentration camp Ebensee Austria. There we were kept apart from the other prisoners. They did not want it to be known that we made counterfeit money. The commander of this camp decided that the people who had a secret that should not be known, were to be put in a special barrack which should have been exploded with us in it. But thanks to the American Army which advanced very quickly and were only 3 miles from our camp, our lives were saved.[62]

The irony that he was saved because he was able to participate in a vast criminal enterprise of the Nazis was not lost on Stammer. He went on to work as a jeweler in postwar Austria, and eventually in Charleston, West Virginia, finally settling in Cincinnati, Ohio.[63]

BEHAVING BADLY

In September 1945, a U.S. official, Albert Hutler, noted that "too many" members of the military government "are beginning to take the attitude," imbibed from their surroundings, "that these people [Jewish DPs] are all criminals and are the cause of all the trouble communities are having." Hutler believed that the Harrison Report, which he had seen but which had not yet been released to the public, was both an accurate reflection of the plight of the Jewish DPs as well as a constructive approach to alleviating their situation. Privately, he was not surprised that Harrison chose to omit mention of "those DPs who may be pillaging and looting in organized bands." But in his opinion, the problem was not any closer to being rectified because "the tendency in the lower echelons [of the U.S. military] seems to be to punish 5000 for the acts of banditry committed by 100 people. They can't seem to think of any other way to solve the problem."[64]

In many respects the stigmatization of Jews is not surprising, given the fears of further economic collapse and social disorder, and especially the anxiety that the victorious Allies would implicitly or explicitly encourage starvation and deprivation.[65] Captain Malcolm Vendig, military governor of the Landkreis Dachau, wrote on May 6, 1945, "The Public Safety and Displaced Persons problems are the most critical now faced by this detachment, and they complicate each other." Here Vendig seems to be conflating the "general" and "Jewish" DP problems:

> The majority of complaints and disturbances which occur result from looting, pillaging, and general hell-raising by Displaced Persons who behave as they do for two main reasons.
>
> 1. The enjoyment of their renewed freedom is almost totally unrestricted because a satisfactory quota of military police has not been provided as yet to this detachment which is far too small to handle the problem without aid in addition to that of civilian police who fear the Displaced Persons and the ex-prisoners.
>
> 2. The Displaced Persons are inadequately fed, clothed, and housed, but as yet it has not been possible without Military Police to enforce orders, to induce these people to go and stay in a large lager where these services can and will be furnished them systematically and in sufficient measure. Hungry, ragged people know only the laws of their own needs and of their long-fed resentment.[66]

Germans not only feared that they would become victims of crime in a conventional sense, but many also undoubtedly were terrified at the prospect of punishment at the hands of the U.S. authorities, prompted by an accusation by a Jew. According to Vendig, "Some of the cleverer Displaced Persons have apparently learned a sly trick to gain the backing of American soldiers and their weapons for their looting forays. Let an Auslander level an accusing finger and say 'SS' and the soldier is likely to back up any treatment the accuser chooses to give the German."[67]

Most Germans tended to deny responsibility for the situation of the so-called Jewish plunderers and for producing the atmosphere of brutality. Certainly a number of forces made Germans nervous—such as the specter of communism, the large number of disgruntled foreigners (formerly forced laborers and prisoners of war in their midst), and occupation forces that included an unsettling number of "American colored troops"—who often were imagined as colluding with Jews. Frederick Morgan of the UNRRA believed that Jewish DPs engaged in "all kinds of mischief" to wield their "advantage." Fears were exacerbated by sexual tension and anxiety, especially because many German women learned that American GIs could be a ready source of food and income.[68] Echoing earlier charges of so-called Jewish white slavery, Germans were afraid that women from the DP camps would initiate a massive outbreak of venereal disease. The village of Rischenau, for example, had a complete absence of "police, doctors, and electricity." It is little wonder, then, that crime was rampant and violence not unusual.[69]

More detached observers saw that the crime problem had little to do with Jews and that the vast majority of felonious perpetrators were German youths and "foreigners," former foreign workers.[70] A survivor of Bergen-Belsen, which was liberated April 15, 1945, by the British army, said that although the camp victims were "technically free" they were "ironically unable to rejoice. We were still prisoners, and we were still interned, as the British were afraid of typhoid—which was rampant—and our anger at the Germans. As a result, they left us with two distinct impressions: that our care was not of paramount importance, and that we could not be trusted."[71] Even after the war, the perceived threat of "Jewish disease" and "Jewish crime" shaped German and Allied attitudes and actions.[72]

Certainly the view of Jews as criminals was encouraged by the understandable desire of many former inmates to regard "raising hell" as a virtue. Jonas Landau, a survivor from Stolpce who had fought with partisan bands, recalled that while attending an agricultural training course at Zetlitz, near Bayreuth, the DPs "had a good time riding heavy motorcycles with side wagons, and generally raising hell in the region. We were all very young, ex-partisans, very wild. The Germans usually cleared the streets when we were riding. Occasionally we managed to drive the motorcycles into horse-driven hay wagons." In a number of respects the lines between the illegal and legal were skewed, if not meaningless, to the DPs. Landau admitted that "some of our behavior was perhaps difficult to understand. However, after living in the woods for a couple of years—the ghetto and then the woods—our manners and general behavior were not the best." Enjoying his newfound freedom to travel, Landau met up with some other former partisans in Prague; after getting drunk and loud, which prompted a visit by a hotel manager, "it seems I threatened to throw him down the staircase and showed him a small pocket knife." Later, "while in the agricultural school I visited Biberach and was arrested on the border of the French-American occupation zone (Germany) since I never carried any papers. The French authorities put me in jail for a whole week, and I spent the week mostly with some Polish and Russian bank robbers whose local molls provided them with luxuries. We mostly played poker and chess and had a fine time. I was bailed out again by my future mother-in-law."[73]

The situations in which Jews found themselves, or sometimes voluntarily placed themselves because they lacked better alternatives, contributed to the perception of their "criminality." A study of children at the Kloster-Indersdorf center by the UNRRA found that although "lying and stealing" would exist among any group of two hundred to three hundred children, when one had been compelled "to lie and steal for survival, it was especially difficult to treat this problem."[74] Jews were hungry and desperately poor; most had lost everything. A report on the 17,100 inmates in the Zweiberg facility, many of whom had survived the concentration camps, stated, "The whole of this group are suffering from malnutrition, disease, and filth."[75] Furthermore,

> There was an intense craving for personal possessions—just to have things, whether one needed them or not. There was an even stronger urge to eat and hide food. Bread was always found under the pillow in their beds, no matter how much we assured them there would be a next meal. One of the older boys explained that taking bread from the dining room was almost an unconscious act. Having had so little for so long, never knowing from where and when the next bit of food would come—it was almost impossible to believe that there would always be a next meal and a next one.[76]

Numerous accounts describe aggressiveness and defiance of authority. Because former Nazis who had served as policemen and SS members were among the supposedly reconstituted local governments, few survivors believed that the occupation meant a totally new order in which they would be fairly treated.[77] In his capacity as adviser to Generals Joseph T. McNarney and Lucius D. Clay in Germany and Mark Clark in Austria, Philip Bernstein devoted considerable effort to continuing Judge Simon Rifkind's goal of keeping armed Germans away from Jews. These special advisers had to find a means of balancing the need for overall security and protection of Germans' private property with the need to "prevent friction" between Jewish DPs and American soldiers, and they sought to ensure that Jewish DPs would not encounter armed German policemen.[78]

A CRISIS OF LEADERSHIP? PERSPECTIVES
ON THE BLACK AND GRAY MARKETS

Particularly in the early months of the Allied occupation, Jews sometimes were bestowed with items and even food for which they had no use—and this surplus prompted their activity in the black market. A report from Dachau on May 27, 1945, described "a belated avalanche" of food, "far surpassing the needs of the diminished camp population."[79] A number of Jewish survivors were given precious commodities upon their first encounter with American soldiers; the GIs seemed willing to give away "whatever they had: cigarettes, chocolates, all kinds of canned food—sardines, corn beef, cheeses."[80] Oscar Lichtenstern, a survivor from the Netherlands, found the conditions in Bamberg appalling, but "in contrast, food allowances are good and plentiful and everyone even received cigars or cigarettes." An American working for the UNRRA wrote his parents, "Most DP camps, alas, do constitute a real black market problem. Of course there are reasons: the DPs get only a very limited amount of clothes, for example; no money and probably not the opportunity to work in their trade, etc."[81]

Although the Jewish DP population was not static, the black market was a constant feature of DP and German life between 1945 and 1948 (and much later), and the degree of conflict it caused apparently worsened over time. U.S. Army Chaplain Abraham J. Klausner wrote with great candor about the situation of Jewish DPs in a confidential memo of May 2, 1948 to the American Jewish Conference.[82] He reported that there were "approximately 100,000 Displaced Jews in the American Zone. The official figure varies from 114,000 to 124,000. A camp averages a 20% 'population margin.' The population picture adequately presented would be in terms of 35,000 family units."[83] Most of these DPs had no means of employment; "the great majority of the people are idle," Klausner wrote, despite the implementation of a "rehabilitation program." These circumstances stemmed partly from most Jews' belief, upon entering the American zone, that they would not remain in Germany for long, and from the fact that they renounced every relationship with the German community. At that time the sympathy of the U.S. forces and policy sustained the Jew. As the infiltration of the Polish Jews continued through the year, the policy was maintained but only in word. The people found their way out of the camp into every sordid aspect of German society. In time the Jew was involved in illegal endeavors ranging from prostitution to highly involved black-market transactions. I do not believe it necessary to indicate the degree to which the Jew insinuated himself upon the sordid aspects of German post-war society. Of importance are the results of these activities. In recent months the number of full scale raids upon Jewish camps have increased. The camps of Heidenheim, Eschwege and Zeilsheim were raided. During the Heidenheim raid a Jew was killed.[84]

Each of these raids, to be discussed in detail below, was partly fueled by tension between American servicemen and DPs, which caused Jews to be publicly shamed in "the presence of [their] German neighbors" and caused a tide of "resentment" among the Jews "that will make it practically impossible to extricate [them] from [their] antagonisms."[85]

Without indicating a source, Klausner asserted that "a minimum of 30%" of Jewish DPs were involved in the black market, which excluded "those who traffic in what may be termed the 'gray market' or the basic food market."[86] For better and for worse, Jews were forced to adopt the black market as an "occupation," and "a rigid interpretation of regulations regarded barter" as black-market activity. Thus, "a father who might exchange a package of cigarettes for a bottle of milk for his child would be regarded as a law-breaker."[87] Indeed, the legal-aid division of the Joint struggled over "whether black marketing on a small scale constitutes moral turpitude," but as a group, the members found that German judges had little sympathy for Jewish DPs, despite maintaining that they were "more considerate" in sentencing Jews than Germans.[88] Klausner maintained that "the luxury market, as contrasted to the basic food market, ranges from single dealings in American PX items to carloads of cigarettes. The earnings in this market likewise range from a few American dollars per year to 60 or 70 thousand dollars per year." All of this activity, he reported was "no secret" to relevant officials.

I am told that the State Department has knowledge of the fact that a number of Jews living in the Berlin camp, drawing their food rations regularly, purchased cigarette concessions from the Russians at a reputed $20,000 each. Similarly it may be reported that a large number of Jewish custodians who received Nazi property during the early days when the German authorities were out to appease the Jew as a means to conquer the good will of the Occupation forces, maintain these firms as fronts for illegal traffic which has come to involve government representatives and police officials in a number of German communities.

In his published memoir Klausner writes that the day after he submitted his analysis, American newspapers revealed that "650 American troops raided the Jewish DP camp at Windsheim, and 'The Army said the soldiers confiscated narcotics, foreign money, food and gasoline.' "[89]

In a personal letter to Philip Bernstein on October 10, 1947, Klausner wrote in depth of his anguish about the actions of the "Committee for Liberated Jews," which he believed had exploited German officials. Klausner warned that "we are headed for an era of bitterness" exacerbated by unwise decisions and practices of the Jews themselves:

> The secondary committees [of the DP organization] went into "official" business with the German representatives. As long as these representatives were completely dependent upon the Military authorities they were quite willing to go along with the Jew who at that time represented to them the cause of their defeat. In the City of Munich an intricate pattern of corrupt police practices has been woven out of the persistent briberies on the part of the Jewish leadership. I am certain that every official knows that the Munich Committee has bribed the police officialdom for the purpose of extracting from the claws of justice those of the Jews who persist in nefarious practices and are caught. All this is done at a price. As it is known to the German officials, it surely is known to the top Jewish leadership. Why, would one ask, is nothing done to root out this evil. There are two reasons. On the one hand the Committee consists of individuals who are primarily interested in their party and personal needs. Upon an occasion when the Committee does step forward to root out the evil, it is halted in its tracks with a particular need satisfied by those who are responsible for the current situation. The second reason is a prevailing philosophy. It has been felt that the Jew is entitled to all the help he can possibly receive no matter what his deed. It will avail little to list here the numerous "crimes" committed by Jew against Jew for which he went unpunished because— "After all he is a Jew."[90]

Klausner was aware that this statement was strong stuff, and he provided Bernstein with details. It "has been possible," he wrote, to walk into the Munich synagogue and find upward of 5,000,000 cigarettes stored at a cost of 300RM to the sexton. Likewise, the Munich Committee has supported an "exchange" at which one can purchase practically any item from a live fish to a sparkling diamond as large as the fish. There is no doubt in my mind that this market will yet become the source of tragedy for the Jew in Germany. Here again the question can be raised—Why does the condition persist? Rather than answer that question again, it would be well to indicate that it persists a stone's throw from the combined Jewish leadership of Germany which takes in the Central Committee, the Jewish Agency, the AJDC, etc.[91]

Why, Klausner fumed, should the chief point of intersection between Germans and Jews be the police? Increasingly articles were appearing in the German press putting the Jews in an unsavory light. He continued, "Germans are now asking for the closing of camps as blackmarket centers. The Jew is becoming once again a political weapon." Klausner faulted the Jewish leadership for not taking drastic action, motivated by fears of criticism or of possible loss of their authority.[92]

To a great extent, however, Klausner reveals that the situation had been sown by the deeds of a single individual. "To further aggravate the political scene," Klausner charged, "the office of the pompous, officious [Staatskommissar Dr. Philipp] Auerbach contributes its share."[93] Auerbach, who committed suicide in 1952 upon his conviction for fraud (discussed below), remains a controversial figure despite being officially cleared of the charges posthumously. A press photograph of Klausner and Auerbach at "a public ceremony sponsored by the Central Committee of Liberated Jews in Bavaria" in 1945 or 1946 indicates frosty, if not tense, relations between them.[94] "Upon coming to office," Klausner said, Auerbach styled himself as the preeminent "Leader of the Jews." The Central Committee, however, "thwarted" his aspirations:

On the one hand he set out to fight the Committee, accusing it of misdeeds of one kind or another and on the other hand he sought to placade [sic] the Committee with gifts and promises that seldom materialized. The weakness of the Committee and the Bavarian Government gave him strength. With the Committee he could deal with parties, to the Government he came as the savior of the Vaterland from the nefarious Jew. The Government changed, Auerbach remained. To the new government he was natural. He brought to them the news that there are two kinds of Jews and he would rid the land of one kind. He took upon himself the job of punishing the Jews for blackmarket activities. At once he became policeman and judge of the Jews. Here again, the Jew was brought into the political arena, and again he was brought in the ugly way.[95]

Klausner perceived that as opposed to the "self-delusion" of the Central Committee "its legalization is fraught with meaning and power, . . . the Jews in Germany have delegated the leadership of the group to American and Palestinian Jewry" because this step seemed to be the "safe" course. "The Americans have let the Jews down in that they have tied up the destiny of the Jew in community fund raising while the Palestine community has spent its energies on the attainment of an end, which though of great consequence to the Jew in Germany, is of little consequence to the every day life of the Jew in Germany." Not only the highest levels of officialdom were to blame: "The camp picture is still more discouraging. Here again we have the official denunciation of the German by the leadership and continued business ventures with the men denounced by the camp residents."[96] Historian Zeev Mankowitz's dispassionate and generous assessment of Auerbach, "the State Commissioner for the victims of Nazi persecution," stresses that Auerbach "played an active and formative role" in facilitating compensation claims, welfare provision, and support for "cultural activity."[97] In 1951 Auerbach, who was then head of the "Bavarian Restitution Office," was "suspended" and investigated on charges of embezzlement by the German government.[98] Interestingly, when he was so charged the Central Committee of German Jews did not say that the accusations against Auerbach were unfounded but that they were being used to slander the entire community and to undermine efforts at restitution.[99]

Klausner wrote that much of his own time was taken up at court proceedings, where "each day our people appear charged with one or another criminal act. I continue to act upon the philosophy I note in connection with the Committee, i.e., regardless of the deed, help the Jew." He believed, however, that much activity went unpunished, as "many of the misdeeds of the people do not come before the courts."[100]

The "criminal" behavior of the Jews tormented him. He clearly spent a great deal of time reflecting on it:

I have come to divide the "criminal" acts of the people into two groups, (a) those committed against the Germans, and (b) those committed against Jews. I forgive neither, but I am disturbed by the second grouping. True, there is a blackmarket in every camp. The market that supplies that additional amount of food that keeps the child healthy, is not to be condemned. But there is a market which exchanges huge quantities of foods and valuables which have nothing to do with the camp, other than that the camp is used as a base of operation. Sooner or later, as a result of these transactions, a Jew comes before the court. Prostitution has made strides in the camps. German women are brought into the camps and their services sold by the Jewish vendor. Dealings with American soldiers has [sic] increased. The sale of liquor, severely punishable, has sent a number of our people to jail. Recent cases in this area include the sale of everything from a nine carat stone to a cow. But most tragic of all are the crimes committed by Jew against Jew.[101]

In Ziegenhain, for example, "the poorest of our camps . . . in a series of weeks the following thefts took place: 10,000 cigarettes, 45 sacks of flour, and 100 kg of meat." These injustices by Jew against Jew were "separate cases" implicating leaders of the camp. "At Pocking a case is now being heard which involves the selling of truckloads of food outside the camp. Shall I continue? You are only too familiar with these many incidents." There appeared to be little chance to rectify the situation, in Klausner's view, because of the DPs' unwillingness to work, and the agencies supposedly helping the Jews were hopelessly embroiled in "party politics."[102]

Perhaps we should not be surprised that Klausner, a man with intense convictions, exercised no censorship in revealing the warts of the Jews. He bluntly challenged his friend and superior officer:

With all this in mind, Phil, I ask you—what can be done? I feel that in a measure you are responsible for the present situation. Whether or not you would have been able to change it had you tried, I do not know, but I feel that the effort was not made. Please understand me. In the first place, it is again my feeling, that you, and I may add, most of our Jewish American leadership, permitted themselves to be threatened by the United Jewish Appeal and consequently to tread lightly on vital issues. In this way, the Joint was permitted, as a non-political organization to control the political life of the Jews in Germany by not permitting political activity in the form of political representation. It was felt, and was backed by leadership, that the Joint is America's answer to the Jewish DP problem. Again, it is my feeling that criticisms of Zionist activities which should have been voiced were not because of the fear that the wrath of the Zionist leadership would come tumbling down upon those who dared. There has been criticism, that I know, but it has been a quiet, unobtrusive criticism. I think this has been the point on which we have differed at times and which was demonstrated clearly when I was not permitted to return to Munich after serving in Kassel. I also emphasized the point made with regard to the Joint. My being kept out of Munich was indeed political.[103]

Historian Yehuda Bauer writes that Klausner "was engaged in a running fight against the Joint Distribution [Committee], and in fact against any and all Jewish organizations; no wonder they disliked him so intensely." Klausner fumed that all of these bodies "had come too late to Germany, a good three months after the war had ended; they brought with them nothing of much use to start with." Klausner's requests for assistance were regularly rebuffed, and not surprisingly, we find him "[accusing] them of not doing what they could have done." Bauer, author of three books on the Joint, asserts that the organization "has tremendous achievements to its credit—however, the first year or so of its work in the DP camps is 'problematic,' and I have said so. One need not accept all of Abe Klausner's strictures to arrive at that conclusion, and there is no doubt, as the polite saying goes, that he has a point." As opposed to using innuendo or allusion, Klausner offers solid evidence that fund-raising was the main reason for the hostility of the Joint. On September 28, 1945, the Joint cabled its Paris office that the "critical letters" of Klausner were "doing great damage to fundraising efforts" in the United States.[104]

The spring of 1948 was certainly not the first nor the last time that Zionist politics and fund-raising (distinct from that of the Joint), and the politics of Jewish fund-raising, would became a major bone of contention among committed Zionists and Jews generally. Immediately following the First World War a dispute erupted in the movement, in large part along similar lines, between Louis Brandeis and Chaim Weizmann, with Brandeis (correctly, in my view) chastising Weizmann for making Zionism's goals subservient to the demands of the movement's fund-raising mechanisms. The means, Brandeis argued, had apparently become the ends of the movement, and this mixup of priorities led Zionism into a quagmire. In 1948 (and earlier) Klausner argued that Jewish organizations were failing to serve those who so desperately required their help and best efforts, which was leading to a downward spiral of morale and morality among the DPs. In another diatribe to Bernstein, Klausner wrote that "the [Jewish] Agency is an all out political organization that justifies the corruption in that it continues to back the political parties. [The] Joint continues as a relief organization, thwarting all political activity even on the part of others, thus keeping the main problems from treatment. The Adviser's office," which Bernstein no longer headed, "is again bound by the [United Jewish] Appeal and Zionism, both excuses for a disease that grows more desperate from day to day."[105] Situated as he was in a marginal position in Kassel, Klausner lamented the fact that "I can do little other than scrounge a few items here and there" for Jewish schools "and keep as many Jews out of jail" as possible. He had sought a position in which he could have served the DPs to greater effect: "I failed. . . . [But] I feel that my failure was not of my own making. I have tried my best, done all I could and would do a thousand-fold more if given the opportunity, but to repeat, I will not battle a Jew for the sake of the Jew and likewise will not fight Jewish leadership in order to help the Jew." Before concluding, Klausner seemed to take a step back: "Strange, a year ago I begged you to help me back to Germany, today I excuse myself for wanting to leave."[106]

Sentiments similar to Klausner's were also having an effect on other U.S. observers in Germany—including congressmen who had visited in October 1947 prior to a special session of Congress that aimed to resolve the DP problem—prompting unequivocal endorsement of Jews' entrance to Palestine and further opening the doors of the United States to refugee resettlement. But "a terrible fly in the ointment" emerged: "The Dueppel Camp in Berlin has made a fearful impression on some of the borderline Congressmen who didn't get a chance to see any other camps in Germany. The accusations: filth, dregs, ingratitude, Communists, black market, idleness. It doesn't do much good to tell these Congressmen—after they've returned—that Dueppel is atypical and abnormal. Someone is slipping up in Germany [first], in not cleaning it up, [second] in showing it off, [third] in not explaining the context."[107] When a U.S. Congressional Judiciary Committee delegation inspected the camp at Zeilsheim and had an opportunity to solicit testimony about the situation of DPs, the subject of "black-market operations" came up. Abraham Hyman felt, however, that "the boys did all right."[108]

In the "Second Congress of the 'She'erith Hapleithah' " in the American zone, held in Bad Reichenhall, the U.S. Third Army Liaison Officer, Col. George R. Scithers, addressed directly the problem of those who refused to "comply with military directives." This issue occupied nearly half of his address. "In any group of human beings," Scithers said,

> there are some irresponsible persons, some are ignorant, some are mischievous and some are bad. These individuals are present among the Jewish population as well as any other group. They do not represent the feelings or intentions of the group but by their foolish or wicked deeds they cast a blot on the good reputation of hundreds of respectable, law abiding

people of their community. It is unfortunate that this is so but it is. Therefore it behooves the Committee and all responsible Jewish people to do their utmost to suppress the irresponsible actions of this small minority. By judious [sic] leadership, moral suasion, and education much can be done to enhance the repute of the Jewish DPs. I know that you do not want illegal activity in your midst: by cooperating with authorities in stamping it out we can achieve a high state of law and order and will eliminate most of the silly misunderstandings and mistrusts between the military and yourselves. We all know that most incidents are really trivial in nature but in many cases are disterted [sic] all out of proportion to their true importance. By keeping cool in such instances and avoiding exaggeration and unfounded rumor we can keep these matters in their true status. This will be to the advantage of the authorities and greatly to the advantage of the hundreds of earnest people who are trying to reach a better life.[109]

The speech that followed, by Mr. Leon Retter, the General Secretary of the Central Committee of Liberated Jews, partially answered Scithers's portrait: "What did the six years of persecution under the Nazis signify? . . . These years taught [the Jews] that by respecting law and order you have to die . . . by working—you have to die . . . by telling the truth—you have to die. . . . Our people had lost their honour, they had lost their confidence, they had lost everything" until liberation by the Allied armies.[110]

In the document he prepared for public consumption, however limited and confidential, Klausner did not make explicit his allegations that the Joint and the Zionist Organization had contributed measurably to the Jews' distress. "The rehabilitation of the people, as anticipated," Klausner concluded in his report of 1948, "has not materialized. The demoralization of the people increases rapidly." Almost everything about the Jews' situation made the black market one of their only options for a livelihood.[111]

Predictably, a number of strong reactions emerged to Klausner's analysis.[112] At a "meeting of major Jewish welfare organizations" in response to Klausner's report on conditions facing the stateless, held in New York City on May 4, 1948, his statements about Jews in the black market proved to be especially controversial. Judge Louis Leventhal said, "Klausner did not give a fair picture of the average DP; the bad ones are in the minority." Leventhal faulted Klausner for not consulting with the advisers on Jewish affairs who had preceded him. Philip Bernstein, however, chose not to dispute the details, confirming that "the dark picture drawn by Klausner requires our serious attention," and Herman Gray assented: "Many elements in Klausner's presentation tally with Dr. [William] Haber's findings."[113] Bernstein himself had reported, on May 12, 1947, that "the black market problem [among the Jewish DPs] has become overwhelming. I hasten to add that this reflects the total situation. Most people in Germany, regardless of nationality, seem to get things they want most through the black market. But among Jews, it is a particularly unfortunate problem because they are concentrated in a separate group and their participation brings infamy down on the entire Jewish group."[114]

When Moses Leavitt challenged Klausner's claim that 30 percent of Jews were involved in the black market, suggesting it was overstated by 20 percent, Klausner shot back with an even harsher assessment:

> It must be maintained that the Jewish DP role in the black market is tremendous, scandalous, and dangerous. Incredible rackets of other kinds, like kidnapping, bribery, people making millions by getting operators out of jail, high Jewish officials involved, etc. In any camp, any day, hundreds of Jews can be seen engaged in business, some of them wholesale. Germans are being flooded by offers from Jewish traders, even when they descend from streetcars. On one occasion, four Jewish peddlers were shot by a German policeman, and we had to hush up the matter because we were in the wrong. The problem is there; it must be dealt with.[115]

Indeed, Klausner was not alone among Jews in calling attention to flagrant instances of "'unbecoming behavior' of some survivors."[116] Zeev Mankowitz writes, "M. Gavronsky, the editor of *Das Fraye Vort* took issue with those 'who do "bad things" like pilfering, stealing, making a row, molesting passengers on a train,' and believe that by doing so 'they are taking revenge for our suffering and our dead.' . . . The forms of symbolic revenge," Mankowitz shows, "were many and diverse and there were constant debates in an attempt to stake out the boundaries of the permissible and the unacceptable."[117]

Bernstein provided some perspective on how and why the situation had developed as it did. "At the early stages," he said, "we resisted any attempt at forcing DPs into the German economy because the paramount interest was to get them out to Palestine. Today we face the fact of steady, catastrophic demoralization. Even the so-called 'workers' are mostly idling, and the majority is prey to the inevitable calamity and shame of illicit activities. Of course, we should get them out as soon as possible, even against their will."[118] In a press release of September 7, 1946, Bernstein himself had addressed the problem in the wake of a large wave of refugees, termed "infiltrees," who had entered the American zone through Poland:

These Jewish infiltrees present not only problems of physical care, but, also, difficult problems of understanding and adjustment. The American G.I. finds it hard to understand their language and their psychology. He has always lived in freedom. These people have never enjoyed his advantages. The way they think, their manners and their conduct are strange to him, and he may, consequently, be tempted toward unjustified generalizations. Let us look at some of them.

Black marketeering is one of the gravest problems faced by Mil. Government. Seeing a displaced person exchange some cigarettes for eggs, the soldier may get the impression that these people are responsible for the black market. However, on thinking it over, he will realize that no one group creates the problem. For the black market involves all elements of the population, since it is produced by the general scarcity of commodities. In actual fact, the responsible leadership of the D.P. camps is as rigorously opposed to the black market as is the Theater Commander.

Or he may think these people devious, tricky, compensating for physical weakness by mental unscrupulousness. Even if true of some, his sympathy should inform him that this would be the inevitable product of years of the most frightful persecution. For example, one prominent leader of the D.P.s was forced to chloroform his own child and carry it away in a bag of potatoes in order to save its life. But the generalization is far from true. In every D.P. camp there are former partisans—strong, brave fellows, who are prepared to meet the world on its own terms. In or near most camps are "kibbutzim," settlements of splendid young people training in agriculture and industry for life in Palestine.[119]

In an interesting twist, Nahum Goldmann, who was probably the most illustrious international Jewish figure at the 1948 gathering, was the most disparaging about Palestine's ability to provide a solution to the DP problem. "Let us face the realities," he said,

The Jewish State, in the prevailing terrific situation, will have to care for itself, not for refugees. It can use, under the dictate of *sacro egoismo*, only young people who can shoot. It cannot be interested in this time in youth aliyah, in children, families, and old people.

The DPs, in general, do not represent the human material Eretz Yisroel needs today. In Cyprus, in Eastern Europe, and notably in the Moslem countries we have an infinitely more desirable material available.

Still, he argued, "the DP situation must be solved, independently from Palestine interests. The situation in Germany is explosive. . . . The subterfuge of DP resistance to 'strengthening Germany' cannot be accepted in this scandalous situation any longer."[120] Meir Grossman, a former confidant of Jabotinsky's among the right-wing Zionist Revisionists, was perhaps the most pessimistic of the group, believing that little should even be attempted, save paying off the most outrageous offenders, "to answer the morality question." Stephen S. Wise was most interested to state for the record that Nahum Goldmann's views were not those of the World Zionist Organization. "As for myself," Wise concluded, "I cannot conceive that the DPs could be forced to sink into the life of Germany."[121]

On May 28, 1948, William Haber responded in detail to Klausner's report, ascribing Klausner's views largely to an idiosyncratic variety of "militant Zionism," fueled by his frustration that the DPs were not more animated by Zionism and that the movement was not a more effective force among them. Such a single-minded attitude had distorted his critique and recommendations, causing him to simplify a complex situation. About Klausner's "Black Market Charges," Haber conceded, "it is impossible to exaggerate the sense of frustration and helplessness that is etched on the faces of our people vegetating in the camps." Nevertheless, Klausner offered, according to Haber,

> a description that borders on a vilification and that, in turn, can lead one to question whether the people are worth salvaging for Israel or any other country. The truth, as I see it, is that some people are heavily involved in the black market, some may engage in the sale of false documents, and some may use custodian property as fronts for some illegal enterprise. However, the intimation that this is typical of all the Jewish DPs has nothing to support it but Klausner's eagerness to sustain his theory that the Jewish DP is so sick that nothing short of surgery is necessary to save him from physical and moral destruction. On the basis of my experience, I would categorically deny that many of our DPs use the so-called "luxury" items distributed by the JDC to "set themselves up in business." The fact is that these items are used in trading for the staple necessities of life. As to Klausner's figure that thirty percent of the DPs are involved in the black market, presumably for profit, it is my view that the figure is grossly exaggerated.[122]

An undated report from Chaplain Mayer Abramowitz, probably from early 1948, estimated the percentage of Jewish "large operators of huge proportions" in the black market to be "less than five per cent." He added, however,

"Some American personnel in various Jewish voluntary agencies are not entirely guiltless in black marketeerings." Overall, though, Abramowitz figured that in the DP camps the black market occupied the same position it did "in American Army barracks. A great part of the former black market constitutes minor acts aimed at the acquisition of better food rations, or in view of the uncertainty of the future, DPs are intent upon acquiring a small [amount of] capital to help them start life anew in their future homes." He noted, in tune with Klausner, "a strong psychological desire to 'empty Germany' as a means of revenge."[123]

Haber contended that Klausner's report contradicted the most blatant evidence:

> The overall shabby appearance of our DPs convinces me that the real "operators" constitute a very small fraction of our people. I will concede that most of them are engaged in what Klausner appropriately calls the grey market. In that respect, and even to the extent in which some of them are the big entrepreneurs, they only follow the normal pattern of life in Germany. In this crazy economy, all of us are guilty of participating in the black and grey market in varying degrees, and the exclusive identification of the Jewish DPs with the black market is decidedly unfair and untrue. On the question of the black market, I believe that Klausner can afford to be as charitable as General Clay. In my first conference with the general, he dismissed as sheer nonsense the conclusion that the Jewish DP is the principal black market offender.[124]

As much as Haber found Klausner's assessment of the black market disconcerting, he "was literally shocked" to "read the charge that there is no moral standard to which the Jews will adhere." Here, Haber accuses Klausner of an almost dastardly selectivity:

> What Jewish DPs is Klausner talking about? Is he talking about the men who sit in yeshivas and study all day? Is he referring to the thousands who remarried in the camps and are devoting their lives to the rearing of their children? Does he have in mind the men engaged in the camp administration, in the camp committee, in the JDC work projects, and in the ORT programs? Surely, in a situation as bleak as camp life presents, there are many occasions when the DPs will reflect man at his worst. However, that does not, by the wildest stretch of the truth, indicate that the deterioration has reached a point that the DPs have thrown all moral values to the winds.[125]

Only some fifty years later would scholars follow up Haber's analysis with comprehensive treatments of the lives of DPs that stressed their efforts at self-help and mutual rehabilitation, as is evident in the work of Atina Gross-mann and Zeev Maknowitz.[126] Continuing a tradition to which Haber may himself have been oblivious, he ultimately defended the Jews by means of "criminal statistics": "While it does not bear directly upon Klausner's charge that the Jewish DPs are amoral, it is interesting to note that the Jewish DPs have the best record with respect to crimes of violence, and that for all crimes, their conduct measured by court statistics (inadequate though this test may be), is superior to that of any group in Germany today."[127]

Other sympathetic observers found that the DPs' fervent desire to accumulate money was not evidence of "avarice" as much as it was an indicator of their sense of insecurity. "Through experience," an American Jew who worked with DPs in Austria reported, "they learned that those who had the means could buy their way even with the Gestapo; with money they knew that borders, passports, visas and passage could be negotiated practically anywhere in Europe."[128]

Another perspective on the morality, or lack thereof, of the "surviving remnant" of Jewry in postwar Europe raised the question of the "type" of people who were able to evade death or capture by the Nazis. This argument can be seen as a sort of reverse social Darwinism: that those who were kindly, of gentle spirit, had little chance of survival, whereas those who cared for no one but themselves, or were willing to do anything in order to live another day, had a greater chance of surviving past 1945. This element was now noticeable, if not predominant, among Jews in postwar Germany. On another level, this argument suggested that survivors were callous, hardened by their experience in a way that made them different from any Jews who had existed before. In 1943 a Zionist publication sadly reported:

It has been established that four million Jewish civilians—men, women, and children—have been done to death by the Nazi masters of central and eastern Europe. The programmatic slaughter has taken every conceivable form: starvation, exposure, mass shooting, gas poisoning. It is passed only before consideration of practicality or utility. The difficulty of disposing of so many corpses, the fear of epidemics, and the possibility of extracting slave labor from the able-bodied, have kept the physical destruction from completeness. But the condition of the survivors reflects the second, or limited objective of the Nazis. . . .

The actual effect of these years of horror on the Jews themselves can only be surmised. There are tens of thousands of young people who have never known, or who no longer remember, what it means to be treated like a human being by the non-Jewish world. For them the badge of shame, the state of segregation, the continuous exposure to maltreatment and humiliation, are normal things. Their elders are . . . hardly better. . . . During the period of Nazi domination they have lived in a world whose horizons have never been more than twenty-four hours away. How to find food and shelter for the next day, how to evade, for one day more, the seekers of slave labor, how to prevent, if possible, for one day more, the disruption of the remainder of the family—these have been their preoccupations. It has been one long nightmare of privations, terrors, anxieties, uncertainties, and degradations.[129]

In a "meeting with Jewish leaders" on August 23, 1946, including Philip Bernstein, Abraham Hyman, and Samuel Gringauz, acting president of the Central Committee of Liberated Jews, one of the participants surmised:

The Jews who survived and who constitute the DP population do not represent the best of Jewry. They were those whom the SS selected for survival. The best of European Jewry, the less vigorous, and the cultured were exterminated. A small percentage of the survivors are educated. The spiritual problem of the survivors is complicated by the fact that the DPs consist of divergent groups. The expatriates are demoralized and come with an orientation that is unique to them. Those who hid as Aryans are, necessarily, not of the best of Jewry. The partisans also constitute a special group with a unique type of psychology. It is difficult to reconcile the cultural needs of these groups. The problem of discipline is complicated because of these differences and because of the shattered nervous systems of all DPs.[130]

Though this interpretation was fairly common, it also was frequently challenged: "Were the best of the European Jews destroyed? This is almost true, but not quite. The Nazis deliberately sought out and murdered the leaders, the intellectuals, the scholars and rabbis, but they did not entirely succeed. In these camps are gifted men and women. In one large camp, the chairman is a former Court of Appeals Judge of Lithuania. In another, the doctor was head of a hospital in Poland. Academies of learning have been established by able scholars. Newspapers, concerts and drama flourish. The children show signs of great promise."[131] The social, cultural, and political achievements of the DPs are indeed a matter of record that have not been widely noted and were absent, until quite recently, in general treatments of postwar European history.[132]

Philip Bernstein, in his capacity as adviser on Jewish affairs to the U.S. Army, contended that "the number of incidents in which Jewish DPs have clashed with the German civilian population and, as an outgrowth, with the American military authorities, has been remarkably few," and that this low incidence was equally "true of the number of incidents in which Jewish DPs have participated in crimes of violence or in offenses involving moral turpitude." Nevertheless, he was compelled to respond to a spate of "major incidents" in 1946 between Jewish DPs and the U.S. Army that became pressworthy. Bernstein furthermore sought to revisit these flashpoints to minimize the possibility of their recurrence.[133]

From his perspective, things seem to have been more tranquil in the first year of the occupation:

> In view of the arrival of new infiltrees from Poland who have not had the experience of contact with the American soldier, and, conversely, with the arrival from the States of young occupation troops who have not had the experience of contacts with concentration camps and DPs, everything possible must be done to prevent friction. The DPs and the soldiers do not, as a rule, come directly in conflict with each other but, rather, meet as a result of some incident in which Germans are involved. However, it is my belief that certain measures can be taken that will continue to keep such incidents down to the very minimum.

In his preface to an extensive report covering the period from March to September 1946, he wrote:

> An analysis of the major incidents that have occurred in the past might prove helpful in furnishing suggestions as to what might be done, both by the Army and by the agencies that serve the DPs to maintain the high standards of law and order requisite in a military establishment. . . . I am submitting herewith an analysis of each incident, the conclusions I have drawn from it, and a summary of recommendations for the Army and for the organizations serving and representing the Jewish DPs. I recommend that these be transmitted to the appropriate military authorities and to those organizations.[134]

The first "incident" that merited Bernstein's attention occurred in Oberammingen on the evening of March 28, 1946. The episode was apparently triggered by two Jewish DPs who were on a motorcycle:

[They] became involved in a scuffle with four or five Germans. Later that evening one of these DPs and others entered three German homes in search of the men who had previously participated in the scuffle, and beat up two Germans. When the burgomeister [sic] learned of this, he had a bugle blown, to which alarm signal approximately one hundred of the four hundred Germans in the village responded. Armed with sticks and stones, they descended upon a schoolhouse, occupied by twelve of the forty-four Jewish DPs that live in the village. On the way they attacked several Jewish DPs. When they reached the schoolhouse, they surrounded it, shouted threats, broke some of the windows and the door, and assaulted one of the DPs in the schoolhouse. German police from a neighboring village, called to the scene of the disturbance, dispersed the crowd.[135]

Although Bernstein does not mention this fact, clearly the Germans perceived the Jews' behavior as aggressive, which was compounded by the fact that it so flagrantly violated what most Germans had been taught to believe about weak, cowardly Jews. In the Nazi Weltanschauung, Jews simply did not ride motorcycles, even for quick getaways. The spectacle probably was confusing and sent shivers down the spines of onlookers.

This matter, in the larger context, did not have grave consequences. Nevertheless, Bernstein saw reason to bring to the authorities' attention the fact that "this incident would have been avoided had the DPs who were involved in the earlier phase of the altercation, reported their grievances to the UNRRA or military authorities." If a recurrence was to be prevented, the onus was on the DPs themselves: "The Jewish DP must be taught that one of the primary functions of the Army is to maintain law and order and that, under no circumstances, will the Army tolerate acts of revenge on the part of an injured person. Affirmatively, the DP must be educated to subdue his anger and report any attack upon his person or property to the proper camp authorities." But such educational efforts had to be initiated and supported by a number of sources: "Namely, representatives of the UNRRA, the voluntary Jewish agencies, and the Central Committee of Liberated Jews, as well as the Jewish chaplains, could be used to orient Jewish DPs on the role of the Army as a law enforcing agency."[136]

Compared to the "Oberammingen Incident," the "Stuttgart Incident" constituted a much more significant confrontation, with ominous and far-reaching implications.[137] Two months after the altercation at Oberammingen, on March 29, 1946, in the early morning hours, approximately two hundred German policemen and policewomen staged a black market search of the DP camp at Stuttgart. They acted under the supervision of a small number of [U.S.] soldiers, headed by a non-commissioned officer. Employing loud speakers, the German police shouted for the people to leave their houses at once. To arouse those who were still asleep, they banged on doors. Frightened by this spectacle, the people began to hurl sticks and stones at the police. In the melee that followed, in which the German police are reported to have shot point blank into the walls and into the people on the street, one DP was killed and three were wounded.

Following this incident a directive was issued (SOP 81, 16 Mar 1946) which provided, inter alia, that no German police would be allowed in a Jewish DP camp except to identify a DP who had committed an offense outside of the camp and, then, only when accompanied by American military personnel.[138]

Again, the reaction of the Jews did not reflect the expectations of Germans. Jews physically fighting back had virtually no place in the vast panorama of anti-Semitic images and references. This behavior was attributable only to Jewish thuggery. Bernstein attempted to put the behavior of the Stuttgart Jews into perspective through the explicit "conclusions" he drew from the case: first, that it was "quite natural for the Jewish DP to associate the armed German in uniform with the things he found hateful in the Nazi regime. It follows that contact between the German policeman and the Jewish DP must be kept at the very minimum." If, however, "it is found necessary to conduct a search of a Jewish DP camp, the means used should not be such as will strike terror in the camp."[139]

Not surprisingly, when Bernstein graphically referred to this incident during his work for the United Palestine Appeal, the fund-raising instrument for the American Zionist movement, he emphasized that in the long run, the situation could be alleviated only by mass Jewish emigration under the auspices of Zionism. Taking this step was simply "a matter of life or death. Palestine's doors should be opened," he stated emphatically, "without delay."[140] The fundamental dissonance between the U.S. Army and the DPs could never be totally overcome because of vast "psychological and spiritual" differences between the aims of the Army and the mind-set of most of its personnel and the DPs. This disconnect was the reason why the U.S. military authorities had permitted some two hundred German policemen to make a raid on a DP camp "which manifested all the characteristics of the early Nazi pogrom raids." Clearly, this raid was no genocidal outburst, but nevertheless the Jews were outraged:

> It was conducted at 6:00 in the morning, without warning and began with shreiking [sic] sirens and blaring loud speakers, precisely such as the Nazis had employed. The German police did not knock on the doors but kicked them open and roughly handled the Jews. Is it any wonder that these poor uprooted people, having seen their families murdered under similar circumstances and being without any security in their own lives, became terrified and hysterical. They did not possess arms, but if they had, their use of them in desperation would have been understandable. The women began throwing bottles, cans, utensils at the German police. The latter in turn began shouting. The death of one Jew and the wounding of others followed.[141]

To this Jewish audience he assumed a more critical stance than he had when describing the incident in his official report. But remaining true to the event, Bernstein asserted, "The entire incident was misjudged and mismanaged by the military authorities, as was admitted to me in Germany. But, apart from the specific casualties, this situation shows with painful clarity the danger of leaving the Jewish problem unresolved. Daily the Displaced Persons become more tense, nervous, strained and desperate. I saw one group driven from one crowded camp to another. There was hysterical weeping because already one camp in which these people were living for a period of weeks and months had become home, the only home they knew."[142]

In his recommendations to the Army about the series of incidents, Bernstein also was compelled to report that "there was a major disturbance at Landsberg" on April 28, 1946. This episode had been triggered by a "rumor," proved to be unfounded, "that two Jewish youths in a nearby Kibbutz had been abducted while standing guard."[143] ("Kibbutz" here refers to a training and staging area for those intending to emigrate to Palestine.) A precise cause was never determined. Certainly the general anxiety about relations between the Jews and Germans contributed substantially to the panic that ensued. "When the news reached the Landsberg Camp," the Jews there

> became aroused and assaulted about twenty Germans who were in the vicinity of the camp. Troops were called to the scene of the disturbance and, after the camp appeared to have quieted down, another disturbance broke out in the rear of the camp in which several Germans were attacked.

Troops were dispatched to this scene. When they arrived, they arrested two DPs whom they found in the act of assaulting some Germans. A large group of DPs were attracted to this scene and, when they saw several members of their camp being removed from the field by the MPs, they staged a mass protest in which they were reported as having referred to the American troops as "SS" and "Gestapo."[144]

An unusually large trial followed in which twenty Jewish men were formally charged. "Three of the men," it was determined, had "participated actively in the protest. . . . Fifteen of the men were stopped as a group several hundred yards away from the scene of the disturbance while on their way (according to their version) to petition the MP authorities to release the two men that had been arrested. One man was found hiding in a bunker at the edge of the field where the disturbance took place and one man was arrested for failing to go into his house, located about five hundred yards from the field, when ordered to do so by a Military Government sergeant."[145]

Bernstein came to the following conclusions: first, that "this incident further illustrates the need for orientation among the Jewish DPs to refrain from taking the law into their own hands."[146] Interestingly, in Bernstein's earlier report to General Clay on the clash, he adopted a more rabbinical posture as intercessor. "The obligation to justice," he wrote, "is absolute, but the application is relative." Citing an "ancient Hebraic teaching," Bernstein implored General Clay not to "judge another until thou hast stood in his place." Leaving no room for doubt that this was a Christian and universal principle, he asserted that it was "as valid in the Landsberg case as it was in the time of Christ."[147] Bernstein probably was referring to the well-known story of Jesus and the prostitute, in which Jesus chided only those who were totally free of guilt themselves to throw the first stone. "The guilt or innocence of these men," Bernstein stated unequivocally, "cannot be justly determined apart from the circumstances of their lives and the particular incidents . . . for which they are being held accountable." He sought to remind the general that "these are young men. They were hardly more than boys when the Nazis descended upon them and destroyed all that was precious in their lives. Their parents, brothers and sisters were seized before their eyes and killed. They suffered torture, hunger and debasement in concentration camps for years. That they survived at all is a miracle. That they survived without utter degradation of the soul is an even greater miracle."[148]

Although he was careful not to blame the U.S. Army, or to equate the American soldiers with the Nazis as the DPs had done, Bernstein reminded the general that although a full year had passed since their "liberation . . . these men still found themselves in a camp in Germany. Their lives were abnormal; their basic problems were unsolved. They were in the midst of a growingly assertive German population whom they held guilty of perpetrating, abetting or tolerating the slaughter of their families, and their own tragic plight." The events of April 28, 1946, then, "must be viewed against this background of understandable desperation and resentment." "In the first place, it should be noted that these nineteen men did not participate in the acts of violence that occurred in the early morning incidents. The court found 'In the eight days of this trial there has been no conclusive proof that the defendants tried here were the ones who participated in the beating, stabbing or actual destruction of property.' "[149]

After elaborating on the fact that the men who were tried were not involved in the violence that was at the center of the fracas, Bernstein wrote the general that the men gave themselves up to the U.S. authorities voluntarily when one of them was taken into custody. A man who was carrying a knife was arrested, and the others were told to go back to the camp. "It was at this point," Bernstein reported, "that one member of the group, Rosen, said 'We are all brothers. If you take him, we all want to go.' " The presiding officer "fulfilled their request."[150]

"It seems clear," Bernstein continued, "that these men were expressing a sense of solidarity with a fellow victim of the Nazis and intended no disobedience to the United States Army, to whom they are everlastingly grateful for their liberation. The entire situation was not a challenge to military authority but was the natural reaction to what was considered a new act of aggression on the part of the Germans." The Jewish DPs, Bernstein assured the general, knew that they did not behave correctly and were fully aware that the Military Government of the United States would not tolerate "lawlessness." "These men," Bernstein stated emphatically, "who are not and have never been criminals, but have been the victims of criminals, these men who have intended no rebellion against United States military authority and who were not identified as having committed any acts of violence against Germans, have already served nearly three months of imprisonment. It is enough."[151]

At no moment was the perception of Jews as criminals confronted, and contested as forcefully as in Bernstein's appeal for clemency for the nineteen men: "Not only the larger concept of justice but compassionate understanding should justify their release at this time." He then played his trump card: "On 8 July 1946 you announced 'an amnesty for youthful ex-Nazis (those born after 1 January 1919.)' Do these youthful victims of Nazis deserve less?" As further, if lesser, proof of the Army's hypocrisy or anti-Semitism, Bernstein added, "After the conclusion of the war, American soldiers conducted demonstrations against prolonged service in this theater. Account was taken of the circumstances, and they were not punished. Shall account not be taken, also, of the extenuating circumstances in the Landsberg Case?" In the form of a sermon, showing the consistency of ancient Hebraic wisdom, the Gospels, and the U.S. Supreme Court, Bernstein prefaced his final recommendation, that "the Deputy Military Governor exercise clemency toward the nineteen men found guilty in the Landsberg case and suspend their sentence," by quoting Supreme Court Justice Owen J. Roberts. Roberts had instructed "a special War Department clemency board" that "clemency is and always has been the capstone of the whole system of military justice." Bernstein concluded, "The larger interests of the Occupation, as well as informed public opinion, will support the exercise of clemency in this case." At Landsberg, the Army had actually acted against bystanders on the pretext of their having failed to take "affirmative steps to quell the riot. I am informed that this is not in harmony with the practice under civilian law. Since it is good policy for people to know in advance what rules govern their lives, I recommend that, in the orientation of the DP, he be informed that he must not become part of any uncontrolled mob and that, if he does, he is likely to be tried and convicted for anything the group does."[152]

The next altercation addressed by Bernstein, the so-called Fahrenwald Incident, reveals that such clashes could be fatal. This episode furthermore exhibited Jews' resolve not to accept what they saw as unfair treatment. Such responses, however, seemed to fuel accusations of their lawlessness. On July 24, 1946, a crisis was precipitated when a Jewish DP was shot to death and another was wounded

> by two armed German motorcycle policemen who had stopped to question the German driver of a truck that was discharging three DP passengers on the main highway, directly in front of the entrance to the DP camp at Fahrenwald. In the investigation that followed, the two policemen maintained that they discharged their weapons only after they were attacked by a group of DPs that attempted to disarm them. DP witnesses stated that before the altercation the police held their guns in a threatening manner and used provocative language in addressing the Jews. An official investigation conducted by the Ninth Infantry Division held the shooting to have been accidental.[153]

The Jews had every reason to be incensed by this verdict. Now that they had some control over their lives, they would not stand idly by after a Jew was murdered. Understandably, the funeral for the victim, even before it occurred, was seen as combustible:

> During the afternoon of 25 July, funeral services for the deceased DP were conducted within the camp. It was prearranged that sixteen DPs could accompany the hearse to the burial. However, after consulting the MP in charge of a detail of MPs stationed just outside the camp, an UNRRA member announced to the rest of the crowd that they could, also, leave the camp. When the people started to do so, the camp committee chairman concluded that this step, taken contrary to the arrangements that *he* had made, was fraught with danger. He asked the MPs to help in getting the people back into the camp. As members of the camp committee, UNRRA personnel, the MPs and the personnel of other voluntary agencies formed a cordon and were engaged in shoving the crowd back into the camp, tactical troops under the command of a captain who had formed two road blocks on either side of the camp during the funeral services, and who were mounting their trucks to depart, were ordered by the sergeant to dismount and to fix bayonets. The troops obeyed this order and, while shoving the crowd back, wounded six of the DPs with their bayonets. It was the feeling in the camp that the action of the troops was unnecessary since, when they entered the picture, the people were already retreating into the camp.[154]

Bernstein challenged the story that appeared in the official U.S. Army newspaper, *Stars and Stripes,* which alleged that "Germans" had been "taken into the camp after the shooting and were held as hostages when, in fact, they were removed there to a place of safety by the camp police, where they remained of their free will until the air had been cleared of tension."[155] The notion that Jews were taking "hostages" intimated that now the Jews were the enemy—as opposed to the non-Jewish Germans—or perhaps that the Jews were acting as criminals or terrorists, in threatening the lives of innocent Germans.

In his "conclusions" about this case Bernstein asserted that the "Theater directive" that was supposed to "eliminate the possibility" of German police intimidation instead served to "inflame the Jewish camp population by their very presence among the DPs. It is my opinion that the same policy which excludes German policemen from the camp proper should exclude them from the immediate vicinity of the camp. This must be given a reasonable construction." The display and "use of bayonets at the funeral, where there was no security threat involved," Bernstein asserted, was a failure of judgment on the part of the occupation authorities. "It is my conviction," he asserted, "that the Jewish DP has more respect for the American uniform than he does for the weapons the American soldier carries. The Jewish DP is, essentially, a law-abiding person and, especially in dealing with American troops, will not resort to violence." Yet getting "a group of Jewish DPs to respond to orders" would remain difficult "due to several factors; namely their excitability and the language barriers."[156]

As opposed to the accusation that the DPs had taken hostages, Bernstein stressed that the Jews' own police force had acted commendably in protecting the lives of the Germans. This act was worthy of special recognition; he believed that it "would improve their morale, give them status, and would increase their general efficiency as a partner in the law enforcing scheme."[157]

The "Windsheim Incident" of July 25, 1946, resulted from a scuffle between an American soldier and a DP, leaving another DP injured from a shot in the leg. Despite "considerable tension in the camp as a result of the incident," it did not escalate because the Jews were convinced that the offending soldier would be tried in an impartial manner. Bernstein suggested that if something similar were to happen in the future, a fair amount of "publicity might be given to such a trial, just as publicity is given to breaches of the peace on the part of the DPs. Such publicity would do much to convince the DPs that the Army's law enforcing program is not only rigid but impartial."[158]

An in-depth report on the incident at Windsheim and on the conditions of the camp was submitted on August 27, 1946, by Captain Abraham S. Hyman, who was the "Legal Consultant to the Adviser to the Theater Commander on Jewish Affairs." This analysis is instructive in determining the significance of the problem that triggered the incident. "The Windsheim camp," Hyman stated, "is located approximately thirty miles due west of Nürnberg. Established on 4 June 1946. . . . At the present time it has about 2800 DPs . . . there are already 600 more persons in the camp than it can adequately house." The primary aim of Hyman's investigation "was to determine the general mood of the camp, particularly its reaction to the incident that occurred on 25 July 1946; to ascertain what ground, if any, there was for the charge that there was a lawless element operating within the camp, and what constitutes the camp's major problems." After finding, to his satisfaction, that a number of unsympathetic Army and UNRRA officials had been replaced, which had a positive influence on the atmosphere, Hyman turned to the issue of crime in the camp. Two of the local administrators concurred that there was, in fact, a group among the DPs who regularly flaunted the law. One estimated the number at twelve; the other, twenty. "Although they have no specific evidence against these men, they have the feeling that this group operates as a coordinated unit." The nefarious activities of this group "received special attention" in an Army report of August 5, 1946, and it was "recommended that Jewish civilian investigators . . . be placed in this camp, with the view of clearing up this situation" and "those against whom specific evidence is uncovered should be removed from the camp." Once these steps are accomplished, the report suggests, "this camp has the potential of a smooth functioning community."[159]

Yet Hyman, as perceptive as he was, failed to make the connection explicit between the so-called lawless element in the camp and the problem that he believed "dwarfs all others . . . that of supplies. . . . When the Germans vacated" the premises in order to create the camp, apparently they stripped it bare—leaving no furniture, cooking equipment, or even cleaning supplies. As a result the DPs had to scrounge for all materiel to provide even basic amenities. When the Army had set up the camp, it had assumed that the fixtures and equipment needed for the normal function of the camp were already there. In reality, however, there was "no means of getting sufficient supplies to meet the minimum requirements of the camp."[160] This situation was not easy to rectify, in large part because of the attitude of local Germans. Hyman then quoted—reserving comment—from a report of Lt. Colonel Charles W. Matheny, Executive Officer of the 33rd Field Artillery Battalion, to the Commanding General, 1st U.S. Infantry Division (August 5, 1946): "The Germans (in Windsheim) resent the fact that many of their homes in Windsheim have been requisitioned for the Jewish DP camp. Germans do not miss an opportunity to cause trouble among the Jews or for the Jews."

The onus, however, Matheny assigned to "the Jews," who "are even more antagonistic towards the Germans and seem to go out of their way to cause trouble. The Jews will not compromise on any problem that may arise. The Jews seem to feel that it is alright to steal from the Germans, and so far, none of them have been punished for their crime."[161] Clearly Bernstein had scant regard, if not contempt, for such an evaluation. He wrote elsewhere that all too often American servicemen had tended to give Germans the benefit of the doubt. In a rather sweeping generalization, he lamented that "Despite these bitter fruits of the war . . . the German people are unregenerate. They do not regret having started the war, only having lost it. Unfortunately, they are exercising a greater influence on American GI's through their girls, their hospitality and [ingratiating] habits than the Americans are exercising on them. The too rapid demobilization of American forces in Germany has led to an increasing attitude of defiance and cynicism on the part of the Germans. We stand in serious danger of having our war aims undone in Germany."[162]

Another American Jewish serviceman expressed similar views in a letter to his family:

> There are many things happening here in Germany that make me begin to wonder whether we aren't doing the things that the Germans want us to do. I think that in many instances our treatment of DPs in our town is bad enough, but in many cities and sections I have inspected it is far worst [sic]. At least I fight to have them treated as human beings, not as the dirt of this earth. There are some [men in the Military Government who] believe their job is to assist the Germans in the reconstruction and rehabilitation of their country. These men feel that their job is to make the DP as uncomfortable as possible. And I might say they succeed.[163]

Yet almost at the same moment Bernstein described the scene in somewhat less stark terms. "Considering all that these surviving Jews [had experienced] at the hands of the Germans, there has been surprisingly little friction between the two groups." Only a "small number" of clashes had occurred, and they were "marginal and do not represent fundamental trends." This last statement conflicted with his characterization of the situation to Jewish organizations, as well as with a number of his suggestions to U.S. governmental authorities. Nevertheless, he wanted to acknowledge that "Jews and Germans live side-by-side in many towns and cities without any disturbance of the peace. In many camps Germans are employed for special functions including that of vocational training. This is not to minimize the unforgiving hatred of the Jews for those who murdered their families and despoiled them. Nor is it meant to overlook the unchanged German attitudes reported by Army Intelligence. However, both Jews and Germans have established a temporary though uneasy pattern of living peaceably as neighbors." As for the general U.S. policy toward the DPs, Bernstein stated that "On the whole, the relations between the Jewish displaced persons and the military have been as satisfactory as could be expected under the circumstances. The basic army policies have been good. Such difficulties as have arisen occur out in the field on the local level. Attempts are now being made to strengthen the mutual understanding of G.I. and D.P. in order to reduce such incidents to the minimum."[164]

In his report on Windsheim Hyman reiterated the opinion of one of the camp administrators that adequate supply and maintenance would "minimize the contact between the Jews and Germans," who also clashed over use of the only theater in the town, as well as over the failure of local Germans to deliver a shortwave radio and the necessary material for the DPs to publish their own newspaper.[165] Most likely the Jews' bold-faced "stealing," as Matheny called it, was an attempt to replace the materiel that was supposed to have been available in the camp and to provide the most basic level of sustenance.

The life of the Jews at Windsheim was not that of people living off the fat of the land. "Typical of the rooms that I visited," Hyman wrote,

> is one inhabited by six persons, a husband and wife, another man, two brothers and a sister. The only furniture that I saw in this room or, for that matter, in any of the rooms that I visited, were folding cots. Most of the cooking in the camp is done in tin cans over improvised field stoves (a couple of bricks) in back of the homes. There are not sufficient brooms to keep the already overcrowded rooms clean and there is almost a complete absence of garbage cans. . . . All efforts at camp sanitation are frustrated by the lack of supplies.

Hyman's main recommendation, then, was to undertake a survey of the camp's needs, "and thereafter, to supply it with the minimum that this camp requires to operate."[166]

The "Transport Incident" of August 9, 1946, which again resulted in the gunshot injury of a Jewish DP, occurred during the transport of a group from Salzburg to Hof, when the train stopped at Regensburg: "According to reports, some of these DPs attempted to desert the train. When the soldier's orders to halt were not heeded, the soldier fired one shot and hit one of the DPs in the foot." Bernstein said that this episode pointed to the necessity of "having someone, preferably a Jewish chaplain, accompany the trains conveying the new infiltrees into this Zone. It is doubtful that this incident would have occurred had the soldier been able to make his wishes known to the DP. Following this incident, the practice was adopted to have chaplains serve as escorts for these trains, with obviously good results."[167] A subtext not addressed by Bernstein, however, is that the DPs were still being treated like prisoners.

Despite the efforts to mollify the tension, more violent outbreaks occurred between Jewish DPs and Germans. In a letter of November 10, 1947,

Klausner reported that he had to deal with "a shooting of four DPs by a German policeman at Camp Mochenberg." Klausner felt that the DPs had unwittingly precipitated the tragedy. "A thousand times," he wrote, "we begged the people not to parade up and down the Military Thoroughfare stopping the Germans, peddling their wares." These requests went unheeded, until a day when "a German stopped a Jew with a valise outside the camp. One incident led to another until the policeman was surrounded and threatened—thus the firing." Almost immediately afterward Klausner "had to rush to Fritzlar where 200 troops were ready to march on the camp in search of livestock."[168]

The attitude of the Military Government toward the perceived Jewish role in the black market was particularly evident in the "raid on the Ulanen Kaserne" of November 25, 1946, which followed similar operations in the DP camps of Bamberg and Zeilsheim. According to a detailed report by Abraham Hyman, the U.S. Army used five hundred troops "in conducting the raid." The entire population of the camp was twenty-one hundred, so the manpower devoted to the operation was excessive from the outset. Although Hyman found that the detachment proceeded in "an orderly fashion" and that "the men who participated in the maneuver were well briefed prior to the operation," the majority of the arrests were "either unjust or where warranted were for minor infractions." Some one hundred nineteen persons "were arrested during the course of the raid." Fifteen people in this group were convicted, with twenty-one "awaiting trial" at the time of Hyman's writing. "The most serious offender," Hyman wrote, "is one DP who is charged with the possession of a suitcase containing quantities of penicillin, drugs and hypodermic needles. Except for a five inch knife there were no weapons found in the raid."[169]

Hyman was indignant. He was furious that this and other such operations were precipitated by exaggerated fears of Jewish criminality, and that the raids themselves perpetuated these damaging stereotypes. "While the raid may have netted several major offenders," Hyman pointed out,

the apprehension of these few men can hardly justify the magnitude of the operation and the demoralizing effect of the raid upon the entire camp community. Regardless of how sympathetic the military personnel conducting the raid may have been, the immediate effect of a group of 500 armed men swooping down on a community only four times the size of the raiding party is to strike in the heart of the camp. This is especially true of this raid which was commenced in the dead of the night. The raid could only be reminiscent of experiences that the camp inhabitants are trying to forget. Moreover, while it is recognized that in a DP camp, as in every German and military community, there are people who violate food and other ration regulations, it is patently unjust to subject every person in the community—the innocent as well as the guilty—to the indignities incident in an all inclusive search. Any search, regardless of how conducted, involves an invasion of privacy of the people affected and, when the search, as in this instance, did not produce a single offender whose infraction of the law constitutes a threat to the military mission of the Army or to its personnel, the comprehensive search can hardly be deemed to have been necessary from the standpoint of an occupying force.[170]

The purported aims of the Army did not begin to justify its means. This fact should have been apparent before the raid on the Ulanen Kaserne. "What is gained in these mass operations," Hyman asserted, "is more than cancelled by the harm they produce." Such actions were "indictments of entire camp communities. By their very nature they attach to an entire group the stigma of guilt that should be borne only by the offending parties of the community." Although Hyman would not state that these raids were inspired by and exacerbated anti-Semitism, that idea is his unmistakable subtext. They "exaggerate the criminality of minor offenses that are rather common throughout the world where scarcity in consumer goods exists," and they "create the false and very damaging impression that the offence of black marketing is unique to Jewish DPs as a class. . . . Experience in the Bamberg raid, as in the search conducted recently at Zeilsheim (where about nine arrests were made and only one or two were held for trial) indicates that only a few major offenders are uncovered by these maneuvers. Yet, the mass search and the spectacular publicity which inevitably follows cannot but help create the false impression that the Jewish DP camps, as camps, are the focal points of lawlessness." As a consequence, many Germans found solace, if not delight, in such spectacles: "They present the Jewish DP in a humiliating light in the eyes of the Germans, who are eager to seize upon any argument to justify their former treatment of the Jews. This the Jewish DP deeply resents."[171]

Rather than improving the overall situation in Germany, Hyman said, the raids also inflict harm because "they stimulate the resentment of military personnel against all Jewish DPs which, in turn, results in frictions and tensions between elements that should have respect for each other." But the harm to Jews was not restricted to Germany. "By virtue of the publicity" generated by these raids, the kind of "public sentiment" engendered "is bound to interfere with the efforts being made to resettle the Jewish DPs in other lands. This is preeminently unfair to the vast majority of DPs whose conduct is above reproach and whose chances for resettlement should not be prejudiced by what a few of their numbers do."[172] Hyman was fully aware that impressions fostered by the raid would provide ammunition for those wishing to shoot down Jewish chances for immigration to any of the countries to which they desperately sought admission.

Making clear his revulsion for those who exploited their status as DPs to engage in the black market, as well as his steadfast desire to uphold the law as Legal Consultant to the Judge Advocate General, Hyman did not wish to argue for "special privileges" for Jewish DPs. In his opinion, however, "there are too many disadvantages attending a mass raid that has as its objective the apprehension of black market offenders to warrant their further use as an instrument to deal with the black market problem." Rather than focusing their law enforcement endeavors on locating "specific individuals suspected of law violations," the soldiers who conducted the raids on the Ulanen Kaserne and the DP camps in Bamberg and Zeilsheim essentially treated the Jews as a unified criminal element.[173] The very means that the United States used to combat black marketeering and "lawlessness" in the DP camps indicated an assumption that large numbers of Jews were guilty of such offenses, or were plotting to exploit the chaotic order in which they found themselves.[174] Americans were fully aware that "a thriving black market . . . grew like a healthy weed" during Nazi times when Jews had been eliminated from the German economy[175] but still located the source of the postwar problem largely with non-Germans. William Haber reported at the end of August 1948 that eight of the previous nine U.S. Army raids for the purpose of cracking down on the black market targeted Jewish DP assembly centers. Repeating the steps that Hyman had undertaken, Haber said, "The study I have made of these raids convinced me that they do not promote law and order; that they fail to achieve their objectives and, in general, serve no purpose except to indict an entire camp community for the illegal activities of the few."[176]

There is perhaps no more savage irony than the fact that a relatively genteel version of anti-Semitism in the postwar German order nurtured the "crooked" taint of Jewry.[177] It was, indeed, a topsy-turvy world in which a Jew might be a policeman on the street among Gentiles and in which a previously fatal yellow star could grant one access to chocolate and cigarettes.[178] "The relationship between the Jews and the Germans," Philip

Bernstein wrote at the end of his tenure as adviser to the American occupation forces, "is paradoxical." As one could only expect, the Jews, generally, "regard the Germans who despoiled them and murdered their families with an unforgiving hatred." And they had good reasons to remain on guard: "The studies made of German attitudes indicate no basic changes. I have seen nothing to prove that the Germans regret their anti-Semitism. They may regret the effects of it on world opinion. They may think that the Nazis were too crude in their techniques of persecution and extermination, just as most of them seem to regret only that Hitler lost the war, not that he started it. But they remain anti-Semitic." Although he was right that most Germans were still anti-Semitic, the form of their anti-Semitism, and the ways it was expressed, had changed. It was now less direct, less racialized, and more prone to seemingly rational justifications than it had to be during Nazi times. But how could the presence of Jews on German soil after 1945 result in anything but a tense and tempestuous situation? "One might expect," Bernstein continued, "this combination of unforgiving hatred and unregenerate anti-Semitism to lead to grave friction. Actually it does not. In many camps and centers the Jews live peaceably side by side with the Germans. Outbreaks of antagonism between them are rare, marginal rather than general. They may seem more general because it is the sensational isolated incident which is featured by the press whereas the daily, quiet living together never makes the headlines. However they do live together for most part in an unbroken though uneasy peace."[179]

The fact remained, as it had been since the eighteenth century or earlier, according to Bernstein, that the greatest impetus for Germans and Jews to live together harmoniously was conceived and manifested by Jews, such as demonstrated by a "recent incident in a camp near Munich, [in which] the Jews actually took under their wing the German employees of the camp, not as hostages as was erroneously reported in the newspapers, but for their protection until the excitement was calmed down."[180] Most Jews, whether they were survivors or part of the occupation forces, saw "no indication of a widespread sense of remorse for what [the Germans] did to the Jews."[181] Even in the presence of rabbis from America at a retreat in 1947, German clergy would not acknowledge "the guilt of the Germans," and "each in turn whined about his fate and the unhappy fate of his people and pleaded for special help. Where was this sense of guilt with which some say the Germans are obsessed?" His German colleagues, another disgusted rabbi observed, "were morbidly obsessed with their own misery and begrudged the survivors" anything and everything they asked for "simply in order to accommodate their basic maintenance."[182] Theologian Richard Rubenstein discovered to his great dismay in 1961 that Heinrich Grüber, the Protestant Dean of East Berlin, harbored views that Rubenstein regarded as anti-Semitic. This discovery was shocking, because Grüber had worked to save Jews during Nazism, and after the war he devoted himself to fostering reconciliation "between Germany and Israel on the political level, and between German Christians and Jews at the religious level." Without prompting by a question, the Dean informed Rubenstein that "once again Jews were influential in the banks, the press, and other areas of public interest." Jews themselves, he insisted, had precipitated the recent wave of anti-Semitism, because they were prevalent as owners of "brothels and risqué night clubs." When challenged by Rubenstein that he was exaggerating the problem, the Dean "asserted that the Jews had as much right to produce scoundrels as any other people," but then steered the conversation toward an exploration of God's expectations of the Jews. There was no doubt that Probst Grüber, a good man who had stood up to the Nazis and continued to promote Jews' well-being, persisted in believing that Jewish criminality—in the 1960s—was one of the graver issues facing his nation.[183]

SEVEN

Jewish DPs
Confronting the Law

Prescriptions, Self-Perceptions, and Pride of Self-Control

For me [Mordo Nahum, "The Greek"] was a revelation. I knew that he was nothing but a rogue, a merchant, expert in deceit and lacking in scruples, selfish and cold; yet I could feel blossom out in him, encouraged by the sympathy of the audience, a warmth, an unsuspected humanity, singular but genuine, rich with promise. . . .

I was forced to realize that I had infringed an important moral principle of his, that he was seriously scandalized, that on this point he was not prepared for compromise or discussion. Moral codes, all of them, are rigid by definition; they do not admit blurrings, compromises, or reciprocal contaminations. . . .

The basis of his ethic was work, which to him was a sacred duty, but which he understood in a very wide sense. To him, work included everything, but with the condition that it should bring profit without limiting liberty. The concept of work thus included, as well as certain permissible activities, smuggling, theft and fraud (not robbery; he was not a violent man). On the other hand he considered reprehensible, because humiliating, all activities which did not involve initiative or risk, or which presupposed a discipline and a hierarchy; any relationship of employment, any services, even if they were well paid, he lumped together with "servile work." But it was not servile work to plough your own field, or to sell false antiques to tourists at a port.

PRIMO LEVI
The Reawakening

ALTHOUGH MANY JEWISH DPS, as well as those entrusted with their welfare, sensed that they remained largely victims of circumstance after the Nazi defeat, concerted efforts were undertaken to dislodge the "Jewish criminality" stereotype and the grounds that sustained it in postwar Germany. This chapter first examines the prescriptions of the Jewish Affairs office of the U.S. occupation forces that tackled the problems surrounding "Jewish crime." The office expended a great amount of energy to reduce the friction between Jews and Germans that seemed to emanate mainly from the black market. The chapter then explores the self-perspectives of the DPs in their engagement with the black and gray markets. Finally, I investigate the organizational response of the DPs in assuming responsibility for law and order among themselves in coordination with U.S. and UNRRA authorities.

Various parties, especially the office of the Special Adviser on Jewish Affairs, made an intensive attempt to control both the reality and perception of law and order among the DPs. In late 1946 Philip Bernstein proposed educating the DPs to show clear deference toward military authority as well as to use other means to prevent further friction, which he believed could be attained as long as "armed German police" were "instructed to make no arrests in the immediate vicinity of a Jewish DP camp unless it was necessary to intervene in a serious offense." He was resigned, however, to the fact that any incident that subjected Jews to German discipline would spark distress among the DPs.[1]

In the first instance, Bernstein and others assumed that a change in attitude had to be stimulated among the Jewish DPs for the situation to improve. In September 1946 Bernstein wrote that "the Jewish DP requires a proper 'orientation' to refrain from taking the law in his own hands," and specifically, not "to call the American troops names." He urged the Army, through its own training, to prevent such outbursts as occurred in Landsberg. The "Public Safety Officer," in his view, must

> make a special effort to become acquainted with the DP camps under his jurisdiction. An occasional visit to the camp and assurance from him that the Army is here to protect the lives of all the people in this zone would, in my opinion, prove helpful in establishing cordial relations between the DPs and the Army, and would give the DPs the assurance of security and safety that they need. A friendly remark from the Public Safety Officer, where there is peace in the camp, might do far more good than the greatest tact or the display of force after an incident has developed.[2]

Bernstein thereby attempted to preempt what he saw as a major contributor toward conflict by appointing explicitly commissioned personnel. Furthermore, "Public Safety Officers" ought to be "selected on the basis of their ability to cope with a critical situation with calm and good judgment." Such officials needed to take a proactive role to "establish cordial relations with DP camps under their jurisdiction and utilize appropriate occasions to interpret the Army law enforcement program to the DPs."[3]

Overcoming the language barrier was a high priority, because a number of disputes seemed to have been exacerbated because of poor communication. "The DPs must be cautioned," Bernstein wrote, "not to use any language, in addressing American soldiers, that will lead to misunderstanding." In many situations in which suspicion ran high among the soldiers that the Jews were up to no good, and Jews were wary and angry, the DPs' simple failure to understand orders made them seem to be more "lawless" and petulant than they intended. "Whenever there is likely to be friction between the military authorities and the Jewish DPs," Bernstein cautioned, "the military authorities should be accompanied by someone who is familiar with Yiddish and who will be able to interpret the wishes of the military to the DPs."[4] The goal was to have a Yiddish-speaking Jewish GI or officer available at all times to deal with the DPs upon any hint of trouble.

Bernstein agreed that the Jewish DP police forces (to be discussed below) needed to be armed but thought that they should be encouraged to discharge their weapons only in "extreme situations; namely, when there is an actual threat to security." Good behavior on the part of Jewish police should be publicized and reinforced, and the Army needed to see that "newspaper accounts of incidents involving DPs should be as accurate as conditions permit and, when soldiers and others offend against DPs, these offenses should also receive publicity." Bernstein obviously was perturbed that the press of the U.S. armed forces as well as the local Germans persisted in depicting the DPs as untrustworthy, insolent, and prone to "mob action" and criminality.[5]

But even greater efforts had to be extended for the soldiers and local communities to understand the DPs. In a statement to the press Bernstein attempted to explain why the Jewish DPs acted as they did—in ways that seemed strange, outlandish, and even violent to the GIs and to the outside world. This perception was in no small part a combination of misunderstanding and the continued influence of anti-Semitism. "It was Hitler's trick," Bernstein wrote, "to disseminate lies about the Jews among the democracies in order to disunite them. We must not be suckers for it now." The sole generalization "which can be fairly made" about the Jewish DPs is that all of them show the effects of what they have suffered:

> Considering all that these people have been through and remembering our war and peace aims, the good American will seek to help, not to hurt them. He should try to understand them. He should, where possible, visit the camps and meet these people in the company of Jewish soldiers who speak their language. In their desire for friendly contact with Americans, many of them are studying English and would be glad to converse with their liberators. The soldier might arrange for parties to hear their concerts or watch their dramatic performances. Gifts to the orphaned children establish a link of sympathy and fellowship. Many of our hospitalized soldiers have used the workshops to make toys for these boys and girls.[6]

This suggestion was, evidently, put into practice in the following months, as the DPs were able to demonstrate their engagement with the arts, sports, and culture with the soldiers and other visitors.

Yet allegations of criminal behavior by Jewish DPs were so much a part of the cultural landscape in postwar Germany that the U.S. government commissioned a report "on the maintenance of law and order among Jewish Displaced Persons" late in 1946. The report was to answer several specific questions: "Whether the offenses committed by the Jewish DP assume any fixed pattern; what reasonable grievances, if any, are there against the present law enforcement machinery as it affects the Jewish DP; to what extent the Jewish DP contributes to the preservation of law and order within the assembly centers; and what measures may be taken to improve discipline among Jewish DPs."[7] The very asking of these questions indicated the shape of public opinion and the attitudes the DPs had to confront among the occupation personnel.

Although Abraham Hyman, who was assigned to address these problems, admitted that "no exact figures on the Jewish DP could be secured," he ascertained that "the offenses committed by the Jewish DPs fall principally" in the categories of "black marketing, registration offenses, and violation of regulations governing the possession of and trading in foreign currency and 'border crossing offenses.' " Hyman stated that there existed broad consensus that "only in very rare instances are Jewish DPs charged with offenses of violence, with crimes involving moral turpitude, or with offenses that constitute a threat to military security."[8] Perhaps more than any other survey of its type, this report places the black market in a social and historical context, relatively devoid of stereotypes:

> The offense of black marketing presents a complex and very stubborn law enforcement problem. There is no reason to believe that any single national or racial group is more culpable than any other with respect to this offense. . . . The Jewish DP has, on the whole been a law observing individual. . . . However, like others in Germany, he is not exempt from the temptations for improving his creature comforts. As a result, most of his encounters with the law are directly or indirectly related to some prohibited deal in rationed goods.
>
> Aside from the reasons rooted in the economic atmosphere prevailing in Germany, one of the difficulties presented by the offense of black marketing is that this infraction of the law is not condemned by people generally as a serious breach of law and order. The black market operator presently enjoys a reputation similar to that of the trafficker in liquor during the prohibition days in the United States. His standing in the community suffers—and then only slightly—only if he is caught. Not only is the conscience of the community not shocked by the discovery that one in its midst is a flagrant violator of ration regulations, but the offender frequently becomes the source of supply for the most respectable members of the community.

Hyman then reiterated his contention that "mass raids" are counterproductive. The entire mind-set condoning such activity would have to be fundamentally altered to alleviate the problem. "Registration offenses" and "violation of currency control regulations" were found to be largely products of a system that was impossible to reconcile with the particular circumstances of the DPs.[9]

Hyman's report attempted to give voice to DP "complaints against the manner in which the law is enforced by the Military Government." Some of their criticisms, Hyman found, were worthy of "serious consideration. . . . There is a growing conviction that on the arresting end of the law enforcement program the Jewish DP is the object of considerable discrimination. Jewish DPs who were liberated by the American forces frequently speak of the difference between the American soldier they first met and those that they now encounter as MPs or as members of the constabulary."[10]

Again, the notion was raised that the later detachments of U.S. soldiers were less understanding of the DPs than their liberators had been. Bernstein and Hyman apparently disagreed about the extent of this change in attitude. Those who had "liberated" the Jews were thought to be kind and sympathetic while those they meet today are openly hostile. They [Jewish DPs] complain of repeated instances of unprovoked assault upon them by American soldiers. They allege that in searches made by the MPs, the constabulary, or the German Land Police, Germans and others are passed over while anyone responding to the description of a Jew is detained for search and investigation. I am informed that this selective search had led to the practice of Jewish DPs acquiring German identification cards which they flash before the soldier or German who detains them, in order to insure immunity from search. Several people that I interviewed felt that the MPs and the constabulary were sadly lacking in orientation on the Jewish DP. There is the feeling that the average soldier whose duties bring him in close contact with the Jewish DP believes that all Jewish DPs are black marketeers and that this offense is the monopoly of the Jewish DP. The fact that the Jewish DP lives in Assembly Centers in which the soldier seldom appears, and then only on a law enforcement mission, coupled with the fact that the soldier's social life brings him in intimate contact with people who have not repudiated Hitler's racial theories combine to alienate the soldier against the Jewish DP.[11]

Hyman emphasized that he did not expect the U.S. Army to devote itself to the Jewish DP population at the expense of other significant aspects of its mission in Germany. Certainly he did not anticipate that bonds of true affection or solidarity between the victor and the Nazis' victims would develop. "However," Hyman stated, "so long as the Army has chosen to provide a haven in this Zone for the Jewish DP, it must assume some responsibility for providing the atmosphere in which the Jewish DP can live on friendly terms with the soldiers to whom he basically feels he owes the greatest debt and for whom he has the greatest respect." The Jewish DPs longed for acceptance and humane treatment, and they wished to enjoy a harmonious relationship with the American occupation forces. Yet the bizarre circumstances of their existence, a climate of scarcity in a general atmosphere of fear and mistrust, meant that German perceptions of Jews as irritants or worse could easily be assimilated by the U.S. soldiers. Repeating the advice given on numerous occasions by Rifkind and Bernstein, Hyman urged "a systematic and intelligent indoctrination program for the benefit of the soldier whose duties bring him into frequent and close contact with the Jewish DP."[12]

Other substantial issues raised by camp officials and the DPs suggested to Hyman that the soldiers assumed that Jewish DPs were guilty of criminal offenses or otherwise inclined toward unlawful activity and therefore should be dealt with severely. "For all practical purposes," Hyman found, "the right of bail does not exist for the DP." This practice contravened a specific order of the Theater commander. Another serious complaint was that the soldiers who served as "summary court officers" lacked the qualifications to do their jobs effectively. Although Hyman elaborated on this complaint, he said that he did not have enough information to critically evaluate such allegations. Nevertheless, he presented the opinion of several DPs that many, if not most, of the summary court officers had no legal background and allowed their prejudices to influence their decisions. DPs complained that the men "pre-judged cases" and that some of them clearly "discriminated against the DPs." These officers apparently showed little understanding of the background of German anti-Semitism and had almost no sense of "rules of evidence and established practice." Rather than make grand generalizations, Hyman reported "that in Greater Hesse the quality of the summary court officers is improving," as "all but a few men" had had a formal legal education, and "in Württemberg-Baden all of the 9 summary courts are presided over by men with legal background. On the other hand, by way of contrast, in Bavaria, where there is the greatest concentration of DPs, only about 6 of the 120 summary court officers are men with legal training." This situation constituted a significant failing: "Since the bulk of the offenses in which the Jewish DP becomes involved are tried in summary courts, he is sensitive to any deficiency in the qualifications of judges who preside over the summary court cases."[13]

Another of the DPs' complaints that Hyman believed was deserving of his superiors' consideration was that "sentences were unduly severe" and that the courts rarely took into account "the background of the accused, his age, and whether or not he was a first-time offender." Every legal officer with whom Hyman spoke fervently contested this charge: "In fact, they all felt that the sentences of the Military Government courts are, if anything, too mild and compare favorably with sentences of the military justice courts. I have no opinion as to whether there is any basis for this complaint. One could probably cite instances to support either proposition." In any event, Hyman noted great inconsistency in sentencing. One man, he reported, "received a 60 day sentence for not having a DP card and in another case a man received 6 months for the same offense. Among the prisoners I interviewed at Schwäbisch-Hall, I found a woman who claims that she was sentenced to confinement for one year for the possession of 50 packages of American cigarettes. It is difficult to defend sentences of this nature."

Hyman was able, however, to verify the DPs' charge that "there is little use made of the suspended sentence in the case of first offenders." Although there were differences among jurisdictions, in the important region of Bavaria "the chief legal officer frankly admitted that this form of judicial clemency is not encouraged in cases of DPs." The reason he cited for this policy was "that the DP has no permanent abode and that, therefore, his parole would not be practical." Hyman interjected that in his opinion, "there is no basis for this view. The Jewish DP lives in Assembly Centers where he is serviced by UNRRA representatives and the representatives of responsible voluntary agencies who are well qualified to discharge the duties of probation officers."[14]

Hyman found the issue of excessive sentences for Jewish DPs to be very complicated. The problem was compounded by the fact that DPs were "generally not well defended." For the most part he urged that the occupation authorities follow their own guidelines. He did, however, recommend that the decisions of the courts, regarding the length of confinement for those convicted of crimes and pleas for clemency, needed to be scrutinized: "The sentence of the court, as a general rule, represents a judgment of the maximum penalty the offense deserves."[15] Hyman's analysis reflected the fact that many of the men who now found themselves behind bars were not only victims of Nazi persecution, incarceration, and torture. A disproportionate number of them had existed on a knife edge for months or years in hiding or fighting as partisans, and these experiences had a profound impact on how they saw the world and behaved after their liberation. Hyman's main argument, though, was that many of the Jews now in U.S. custody had been cocombatants with the Americans and should be respected as such. "My personal experience with the few Military Government cases of which I have an intimate knowledge," Hyman detailed,

> leads me to believe that the stress in Military Government sentences is punishment rather than rehabilitation. Especially for minor offenses that do not involve a threat to the security of the armed forces—and it is in this category that most of the Jewish DP offenders fall—I believe that the emphasis should be placed on the rehabilitation of the offender. There are many Jewish DPs who are now in confinement who, as members of partisan groups and guerilla bands, fought the same enemy that our troops opposed. Others suffered at the hands of the Nazis more than any other group in the world. In my judgment these people are entitled to the same quality of justice that the American soldier receives in military justice courts and from the

post-trial reviewing and parole machinery. At the present time there is an inequality between the two systems of justice applied to people who fought on the same side that is difficult to justify. Although denied by the legal officers I interviewed, it is my guess that the reason for the disparity is that the mentality of those dealing with the Military Government Courts is conditioned by the assumption that Military Government Courts are established to deal with enemy nationals.[16]

In other times and places Jews had been unfairly classified as enemy aliens, such as in a variety of settings during the First World War, and even in Britain during the Second World War. In a particularly horrible twist of fate the Jewish DPs were cast in the role of "enemy nationals" well into 1946 while Germans seemed to be treated generously by the occupying power. "I believe that it was never contemplated," Hyman surmised, "that one of the 'major functions' of the Military Government Courts of the United States [would have to be] to mete out justice to the most deserving victims of Nazi brutality."[17]

Hyman's report, in addition to dealing with complaints about and problems with the administration of justice, also sought to illuminate the extent to which the DPs themselves, with the assistance of various organizations, had contributed "toward the preservation of law and order. . . . Following the incident at Stuttgart on March 29, 1946, German Land police were prohibited from entering Jewish DP Assembly Centers except for the purpose of identifying Jewish DPs who committed offenses outside of the Assembly Center, and then only when unarmed and accompanied by U.S. military personnel." Therefore, "for all practical purposes, the Jewish Assembly Centers are policed almost solely by the DP Camp Police whose status is officially recognized as part of the law enforcement scheme within the confines of the assembly centers. Although there is authorization to arm these police in the same manner that the German civil police are armed, there is no camp where the Jewish DP police have been armed, so far as I have been able to determine, there is no necessity for doing so." Hyman may not have been correct about whether the DP police were armed or had access to arms. In any event, given the number and variety of camps, and differences in the quality in their administration, one could not generalize about the "effectiveness" of these forces in 1946.[18]

Hyman accentuated the widely held view that "these police have done a creditable job in maintaining law and order within the camp." But in a few instances of "serious offenses . . . they have fallen down in the detection and apprehension of offenders who would perforce have to be surrendered to military authorities for trial."[19] This problem apparently derived from the "group psychology of the Jewish DPs." His analysis, however, evinces an appreciation of the dissonance between the wartime lives of the Jews and the system of justice to which they were subjected after the war. "These people," Hyman wrote,

> the victims of pressure from without, in which they lost their identity as individuals but shared the common fate as a group, have developed a group resistance and a group loyalty that comes to the surface in any conflict or clash between a member of the group and an outsider. It is quite pointless to debate the logic of the situation and to advance the argument that the American authorities are fair and sympathetic. The feeling of group solidarity and reciprocal loyalty on the part of its members, developed by common suffering, is too deeply ingrained in these people to be dissipated by the cold logic of the situation. It is elementary that no police can be expected to function without the active sanction and social approval of the group that it serves. In the situation that obtains in the Jewish DP Centers, the police could not live among their people if they worked effectively in the area of law enforcement that would result in the surrender of the offender to military authorities for trial. The real disposition to protect the offender has notable exceptions—such as in cases of murder, rape, burglary, etc.—but in each case the police would be acting in harmony with what they believe would receive social approval from the law abiding element in the Assembly Center.

If one accepts this analysis as relevant, "it follows that the more effective use of the camp police can only result from the grant of greater autonomy to the camp community." Such a change would also have a salutary impact on the camp courts.[20]

The camp courts, which had become an important institution among the DPs, also discharged duties for which they had not originally been intended. The courts had been "set up to try Capos who were discovered in the camp communities—in order to prevent lynch law from operating." Gradually their jurisdiction came to "include all minor offenses that occurred within the Assembly Centers. Examples of the offenses tried by these courts are petty larceny, assault, and perjury. The 'courts' were generally selected by the camp director and in numerous instances the director himself sat as a member of the 'court.' The 'courts' meted out punishment in the form of fines and/or confinement."[21] Perhaps in no other venue was the DPs' hunger for, and even fascination with, the proper, impartial dispensation of justice so evident:

In the case of one Capo he was ordered confined in the camp jail so long as the camp existed. In another instance a Capo was sentenced to three years. Most of the sentences of confinement ranged from one to thirty days. On one occasion, in May 1946, I attended the trial of a Capo in Landsberg. He was tried by a three man court, consisting of the camp director, an ex-judge of Lithuania (a DP) and a camp leader. Assuming the jurisdiction of the "court" over the offense and over the accused, the trial was, in my opinion, conducted in harmony with the highest standards of the common law tradition. Both the prosecutor and the defense counsel were competent lawyers enlisted from the DP camp. They discharged their duties in an able manner and the court, in its rulings, showed the finest example of judicial temperament. Although the people of the camp were enraged against the accused when he was discovered in their midst—the charge was that he had denied them the privilege to eat scraps and particularly potato peelings while he was supervising the kitchen in the concentration camp they shared with him—they filled the "court-room" as calm observers and watched the proceedings with amazing detachment. It was this case that introduced me to the potentialities of an institution of this nature and convinced me that such an institution should be incorporated into the military government law enforcement machinery.[22]

To be sure, as a whole the Jewish DPs were neither angels nor noblemen. Many among them would undoubtedly have problems adjusting to the postwar order. As a group, their instinct for protecting their own members seemed frenzied. Yet they also exhibited a passion for the kind of justice that had been withheld from them under the Nazis and their accomplices. Moreover, they were frustrated that more exacting standards of justice, influenced by cognizance of their unprecedented historical circumstances, had not been a greater animating force for the occupation authorities. Nevertheless, through staunch if not brilliant defenders such as Hyman, achieved in part by sanctioning practices that survivors had initiated on their own, the DPs found that some aspects of the type of justice they regarded as a hallmark of civilization could be practiced even on German soil.[23] The development of their own police and courts, and the sense that the U.S. forces could engender fairness, probably played a significant role in the overwhelmingly positive regard that many DPs came to hold for the American government, which of course supplemented the perception that the U.S. armed forces had been the chief agent of their liberation.

When Hyman wrote this report, however, he wished to call attention to the fact that the U.S. occupation forces, since November 20, 1946, "directed that the 'courts' cease to operate until their status was officially determined by the Army." This directive was the consequence, apparently, of a single controversial case, which was instigated by a man who had been "tried at Fahrenwald as a Capo." Moreover some in the Army seemed to be uneasy with what they perceived as the " 'usurpation of the jurisdiction of the Military Government courts' and expressly enjoined the Assembly Centers against the imposition of fines or imprisonment as forms of punishment."[24]

Hyman was deeply disturbed by this turn in policy. Given that he was writing less than two months after this directive had gone into effect, at first he saw wisdom in withholding judgment, as it was "too early" to determine its impact "on camp morale and discipline." But he saw the policy as ominous. He maintained that "responsible leaders among the Jewish DPs fear the consequences of this turn of events. They believe that the suspension of the 'courts' removed from the camp communities a stabilizing force for which there is no substitute. The argument is that under existing conditions there will still be no inclination to report minor offenders to military authorities; that potential offenders know this; and that, consequently, the elimination of the 'courts' amounts to an open invitation and license to violate with impunity some of the basic laws of the community." Hyman therefore dedicated a significant portion of his report to arguing for the reinstatement of the camp courts. In tackling the general problem of discipline, he saw no substitute for substantial, effective work and training programs, increased autonomy for the DPs within the assembly centers,[25] and unequivocal signs that their stay in Germany would conclude with their legal entry into Palestine or the nation of their choosing.

At the end of January 1947 Philip Bernstein wrote a confidential report to major Jewish organizations:

[There] seems to be either some growth of anti-Semitism amongst the Germans or more overt expressions of it at the present time. This does not take on serious forms (as yet), but is to be found in German mail, in more anti-Semitic talk in the street cars, railroad stations, etc., and in the occasional singing of anti-Semitic songs near a Jewish camp and even, in a few instances, in the hurling of rocks in the windows of camps.

I have discussed this matter with General [Lucius] Clay, and a two-fold program was immediately agreed upon:

1. Instructions will be issued for the immediate severe punishment of overt offenders.

2. Information Control Division is being requested to develop a program to counteract anti-Semitism among the German people.[26]

Several months later, on June 2, 1947, realizing that the reputation of the Jewish DPs would continue to arouse interest, Bernstein recorded a conversation with General Clay "on the general behavior of the Jewish Displaced Persons." He quoted this in his "Statement on Jewish Displaced Persons" delivered to the House of Representatives Judiciary Committee Hearings on June 13, 1947, in his article "Displaced Persons" in *The American Jewish Year Book* for 1947–48, and in his "Final Report" upon the completion of his tenure in the European Theater.[27] Earlier in his career, Bernstein had written about Jews and crime, stating that "the Jewish record" in "crime and delinquency" was "relatively good." Jews made up, at that time, 3.4 percent of the U.S. population, but only around 1.7 percent of its prison inmates. He turned the anti-Semitic query "Why are there so many Jewish criminals?" on its head. He asked, "To what extent is Judaism responsible for the prevention of crime and delinquency among the Jews?"[28] He was aware that no reliable, comparative crime statistics were available in late 1947, which is one reason why he asked for the general's view "on the record." General Clay's statement is a succinct, reasonable assessment of criminality among the Jewish DPs:

> The behavior of the Jewish Displaced Persons has not been a major problem at any time since the surrender of Germany. I wish that I could say the same for all other groups. The Jewish Displaced Persons were quickly gathered into communities where their religious and selected community leaders insisted on an orderly pattern of community life. Of course, we have had many minor problems resulting from the assembly of large numbers of Jewish Displaced Persons in the midst of people who had caused their suffering.
>
> Moreover, the unsettled economic conditions in Germany have made barter trading and black market operations a common problem. Even in this field, the Jewish Displaced Persons have not been conspicuous in their activities as compared to other Displaced Persons groups or, in fact, as compared to the German population itself.
>
> The Jewish Displaced Persons have on the whole established an excellent record in so far as crimes of violence are concerned, and in spite of their very natural hatred of the German people have been remarkably restrained in avoiding incidents of a serious nature with the German population.
>
> In view of the conditions under which they have had to live in Germany, with their future unsettled and their past suffering clear at hand, their record for preserving law and order is in my mind one of the remarkable achievements which I have witnessed during my more than two years in Germany.[29]

In his remarks to the House Judiciary Committee, Bernstein added that "the United States Army" deserved "the highest praise" for fostering the "steady progress" of the Jewish DPs' "physical rehabilitation," and the fact that "no epidemics have occurred among them." Returning to the question of their moral state, he said, "They reveal the usual variations of the human soul. There are also occasional manifestations of the abnormalities of camp life," probably an allusion to the outbursts of violence and displays of disrespect toward authority. However, "the average individual human being is an average individual human being."[30] A report to the U.S. Department of State by the chief of the Field Contact Station in Frankfurt concurred that "non-Germans have committed proportionally less" crime than the Germans themselves, whereas there have been repeated "exaggerated reports of DP misbehavior." His source was none other than "the German Bureau of Criminal Identification and Statistics."[31] Citing another indicator of the DPs' moral level, Bernstein noted in his final report that "in lands where venereal disease had become almost ubiquitous among the military and civilian populations, it was negligible among the Jews."[32]

The notion, however, that they were thought of as "criminals" weighed heavily on the DPs themselves. Leon Wells recalls that when he arrived in Munich one Friday in the winter of 1946, he was unaware that it was illegal to ride on the steps of the city's streetcars. A German policeman arrested him but was unable to assess a fine because Wells, as a DP, was not under his jurisdiction and "could be fined only by the American Military courts." The U.S. court, however, was not in session and would not be open until Monday. Therefore, he was taken to an overcrowded city jail, where people convicted of minor offenses were thrown in with hardened criminals. In the end Wells was admonished but not compelled to pay the nominal fine. "And so my stay in Germany began with jail," Wells writes. "I was not surprised."[33]

It is little wonder that crime and punishment were writ large in Wells's thought. He is one of very few "big operators" in the postwar black market to reflect with candor about this experience.[34] Despite the fact that there was little or nothing extraordinary about the Jews' participation in these economic netherworlds, as surveyed by General Clay, their past and current status meant that they would continue to be stigmatized as "criminals." Many survivors ruminated over, and sometimes struggled with, their relationship to the conventions of law and order. "From the outset" of their sojourn in postwar Germany, Zeev Mankowitz writes, "the disparity between the [DPs'] poor living conditions and what they perceived as the relative well-being of the German population was a constant source of tension and anger."[35] The moral complexity of engaging in black-market and other behaviors associated with criminal activity is a common topic in memoirs of the "surviving remnant." A survivor from Warsaw writes of his time at the Landsberg DP camp that "naturally"

> the black market flourished there. When the demand for goods is high and the supply is low, as it was in post-war Europe, the black marketeers surface. There was nothing that a person wanted that couldn't be bought— for a price.
>
> I felt that, for the sake of my family, I needed to earn a lot of money quickly if we were to ever be anything more than "D.P.'s," so I actually attempted to take advantage of the situation. I went out one morning with some yard goods (cloth) that I was going to sell at an exorbitant price. With the money I was "going" to earn, I intended to buy more goods and pyramid my meager possessions into a fortune. After two days of standing around waiting to be approached because I didn't have the courage to make the initial advance, and feeling like I was the worst of criminals, I gave up "my life of crime." I realized I just wasn't cut out for that type of life and went back to the profession that had always kept me alive during the worst of times: tailoring.[36]

Through survivors' reminiscences we can see why and how participation in the black market became commonplace. Occasionally survivors were both given food and paid for work; sometimes these offerings were the incentive for staying on in a particular camp.[37] Exploiting one's trade or expertise with the demands of the black market was common, as in Heidenheim an der Brenz, north of Ulm, where "shoemakers, tailors, [and] butchers worked overtime" while "the Black Market was booming."[38] Such trades or services were considered part of the black market because they operated outside any government regulation and system of taxation.

A survivor from Szurowicz, Poland, traded in dresses and fur hats in Lemberg; the "black market" there was simply a "bazaar." Immediately after the war, the Russian Army had set him up brewing beer in Lopatin. He ventured to the American zone upon hearing from other survivors that they had been treated "wonderfully," given food, drink, and good care. " 'The Americans,' " he was told, " 'gave us [food] to eat and the Americans gave us cigarettes and there's nothing better than the Americans.' So we figured let's go [to] the American [zone]." He was not disappointed; he was resuscitated both psychologically and physically. Whereas he had gotten used to identifying himself as "a Greek," he was now told by a Yiddish-speaking American soldier that there was no need to be afraid or ashamed to call himself a Jew. After enjoying as much food, drink, and coffee as he could consume, he recalls that "we were so happy, you know, happy; we were like doped up in ourselves." When he reached the Fahrenwald DP camp he was given a position as "a kind of Judge," one of three survivors placed in this role—ruling mostly over cases involving stealing. The other two men had legal backgrounds, as opposed to the writer, who saw himself as "the easiest of them all. I always told them, 'Try to look at it through his eyes. Try to see what he did with his thoughts and reasons.' I always wanted to let them go.' "[39] A woman at the Bergen-Belsen DP camp reported that inmates who ventured away from the camp, which was "illegal, . . . would often bring back little trinkets of china or jewelry, some of which had been bartered for, others stolen. 'Why pay?' was the attitude. 'Didn't the Germans take all our possessions, even the gold teeth from both the living and the dead?' " Occasionally altercations arose between displaced persons and German civilians, but the British tried to ignore them.[40]

Other Jews showed similar compassion toward their coreligionists who bent or broke the rules. At the Pocking DP camp, one of the women in charge of "free food coupons" was supposed to dispense them to the camp's one hundred yeshiva students. Other Jews, who were not studying, made themselves look like *yeshiva-bochers* (student-boys) and were not rebuffed. The woman "knew that they were getting more than they were entitled but she closed her eyes for she felt that the young men needed more food."[41] In the Adriatica camp outside Milan, people knew that some Jews obtained two ration cards by dressing in different clothes for photo identification.[42]

In addition to feeling compelled to act as they did, DPs' balanced any sense of "Jewish" guilt for wrongdoing by their awareness that black marketeering was not an exclusively Jewish preserve. Similarly, the American forces knew that non-Jews, whether Eastern European or German, were active in the black market—although accusations of German wrongdoing were greeted more skeptically than charges against Jews and Poles.[43] American soldiers, too, contributed to the atmosphere of lawlessness: Germans complained of theft and lewd behavior, and both German and U.S. officials deduced that the troops' possession of bicycles and motorcycles was indicative of wanton pilfering.[44] "Polish [non-Jewish] tradesmen," one Jewish woman wrote, "used to enter abandoned homes, loot or 'shnorr' whatever they could lay their hands on, anything which would sell, such as clothes, blankets, dishes, furniture and, of course, food if they could find any. After looting these homes, they returned to Poland and transacted business."[45] Not surprisingly her view of marauding Poles bears great similarity to countless accusations against Jews, except that the Jews lacked a home to return to. Some Jews also lamented that, consistent with behavior in the ghettos and camps, Jews continued to "steal food from each other";[46] thus they were victimized by crime, not simply benefiting from it. An American Jewish visitor to Germany in 1947 described the black market as an overwhelmingly "German" problem, which he termed "Germany's cigarette economy. The Germans will do anything for cigarettes. German girls sleep with GI's for cigarettes and a chocolate bar. Any kind of labor can be purchased with cigarettes." Germans who had been household servants to top Nazis and now worked for American officials were reputed to be "sullen, obsequious and will steal anything and everything the moment your back is turned."[47]

Perhaps most significantly, many Jews had no choice but to participate in the black market because they found that Germans would sell them neither the food nor clothing necessary for basic sustenance.[48] One of the workers in the Vilseck camp, of some fourteen hundred DPs, reported that the biggest problem was the shortage of appropriate clothing, especially with the onset of winter. The DPs had to find some means of adapting.[49] Reports also indicated that Germans routinely refused to comply with requests for foodstuffs intended for Jews. "The fact is," a visitor asserted, "that the German farmer has been hoarding. Recently [July 1947] the Army has sent out soldiers to the farms to discover hoarded stocks—and each village and a group of farmers have been given quotas by the Army which they now must fulfill—for shipment into the cities. The fact is that the farmer is the only wealthy man in Germany today. He alone can enjoy the luxury of a smoke."[50] Whether or not this perception was exaggerated, certainly supplies of fresh food were erratic. Obtaining canned and processed food was not necessarily simple. German shopkeepers who turned away Jewish DPs with ration cards frustrated American forces.[51] This withholding of supplies contributed to the kind of barter system that characterized the black market in Feldafing and other DP camps. One observer at Zeilsheim reported that the "barter market was an Army device to legalize, control, and make fair the flourishing black market." "The real currency in occupied Germany," a survivor wrote, "was food, coffee, and cigarettes."[52]

Little if any evidence exists that survivors saw the black market as a permanent solution to their problems or that any of them wished for their children to follow this kind of livelihood. Black marketeering was rationalized as necessary for day-to-day needs and as a transitional means of earning a living—an essential step toward establishing oneself in a legitimate business. The director of the DP camp at Gnadenwald, an inmate reported, was a "large scale black marketeer—and eventually wound up on Wall Street."[53] The vast majority wanted desperately to emigrate to Palestine or the United States in order to re-create their lives.

The only prerequisite for participating in the black market was to have something to sell or trade. One DP, who made some money by taking in clothes to be washed, "bought beef and butchered it and sold it in the DP camp. It was illegal all the way, but people had to eat. We used to get the UNRRA rations, which was *[sic]* oatmeal and canned foods; and you get tired of that stuff. The first two weeks the camp food was a great thing. Then we couldn't eat. So we bought meat. Then, of course, we had access to Americans, more sources; so we found cigarettes; we found coffee. The Germans loved it; so we traded with them." The writer was, in fact, the chief of police in the Hessisch-Lichtenau DP camp near Kassel, a position he deprecates: "Big deal."[54] Although compared to being a police chief in a typical American or German city his status was far from grand, the existence of such an office and force was often prized as a symbol of Jewish dignity and autonomy.

As noted by Hyman, Bernstein, and others, Jews' establishment of their own law enforcement and self-defense became a crucial feature of Jewish life in post–World War II Europe. Like the history of Jewish partisans,[55] the Jewish police and security forces in DP camps have received little scholarly attention. No general history of these police forces exists, and the sole detachment that has received in-depth treatment is that of Feldafing.[56] Although no relationship existed between the generally despised ghetto police forces and those that emerged among the DPs, the strong taint of the Jewish police in wartime ghettos may have made any discussion of the subject taboo or otherwise distasteful.[57] In the postwar situation a large number of photographs, from diverse locales, attest to the significance of Jewish police and European *haganah* (defense) detachments to the Jewish remnant.[58] That Jews were able, even within carefully prescribed limits, to take matters of law and order into their own hands was important to them. The key role of the Jewish police in instilling pride and self-respect in decimated Jewry rarely has been acknowledged. Although their primary function was law enforcement, Jewish police forces nevertheless had to operate in a greater milieu that often perceived Jews as outlaws.

One survivor from Hungary who wound up in the Poppendorf camp wrote that being "a police officer those days had many good side effects. First I never had to stay in line for food or whenever a person had to stay in line. Police had the edge above all the rest and besides my words were the final words and I got paid for it." Police force positions in Poppendorf and most other camps were not simply handed out; six weeks' training at the police academy in Stuttgart was required, including coursework, self-defense, and "riot control," leading to what one memoirist calls "an excellent diploma." Although one might have to work twenty-four-hour shifts, the assignment was valued by many: "I am telling you I had it made."[59] One might even see a Jewish policeman outside the DP camps—on the streets of Berlin, for example, a sight that most Germans believed they would never see again after the removal of Bernhard Weiss, the former Deputy Chief Constable of Berlin, in 1933.[60] At least a few Jewish policemen used their training to enter "regular" police forces in Germany. One survivor appreciated the chance to return to his hometown and join the police, which offered him "a place to stay, barracks like in the Army, a uniform and wages. The reason I was able to get the job, even though I did not have the height for it, was the special treatment that they were to give to people who had come out of the camps." He "worked as a policeman until deciding to come to America" in 1949.[61]

Nearly every Jewish enclave of significance in postwar Germany—including Feldafing, Landsberg, Liepheim, Foehrenwald, Bergen-Belsen, Zeilsheim, Giebelstadt, Bindermichl, Traunstein, Schlachtensee, Stuttgart, Eschwege, Vinnhorst, Wetzlar, Lechfeld, and Kassel—formed a squad of "Jewish police" numbering at least a half-dozen men. Many of these squads were officially sanctioned as "UNRRA teams."[62] The police forces were distinct from the Jewish Brigade, which originated under British auspices but came to expressly serve the Zionist cause of "illegal immigration"[63] and is sometimes portrayed as or assumed to be the chief Jewish paramilitary organization in postwar Europe. At least scores of former partisans were able to constructively channel their skills and energy in the numerous Jewish police forces in occupied Germany, whereas others allied themselves with the Jewish Brigade.[64]

Of course, at the most basic level the Jewish police were entrusted with ensuring order and minimizing conflict among the surviving remnant of the Jews. In large part, they were to see that the people under their control were officially accounted for, ensuring that "allied civilians" and "enemy and ex-enemy civilians" had "proper credentials." In any event, physical violence between Jews, and by Jews toward the greater community, was not pronounced. A search for weapons at the Feldafing camp on September 11, 1945, turned up "four knives, one rifle with ammunition, two pistols, one bayonet, and one set of brass knuckles"[65]—not a significant haul for a camp of five thousand persons. Some sources recall that much of the police forces' energy was devoted to keeping German prostitutes out of the DP camps.[66] Given the history of accusing Jews of being preeminent in pimping and prostitution, the fact that one of their major preoccupations was to keep "Aryan" prostitutes at bay is ironic. Beyond this duty, one way they attempted to deal with the vast injustices that had been visited on Jewry in the Holocaust was to apprehend those who had served as Kapos or otherwise helped the Nazis. The Jewish police often helped serve the "honor courts" that functioned in the DP camps. Concomitant with preserving law and order was the emphasis on demonstrating that Jews were capable of taking on such responsibilities and doing so in a professional manner. Hence groups of Jewish police had frequent demonstrations and drills and were often photographed in uniform and in formation.[67]

Jewish police were prominent in the many anniversaries and memorial ceremonies that punctuated Jewish life. They were visible in honor guards to welcome important dignitaries, such as Eleanor Roosevelt when she visited Zeilsheim and Generals Dwight D. Eisenhower and George S. Patton when they visited Feldafing. After their years of being decimated and ignored, Jews were now accorded a measure of respect by world leaders, and these leaders made known how impressed they were by the Jews' collective rehabilitation and goodwill. In May 1945 Colonel George R. Scithers was sent to evaluate the possibility of officially recognizing the "Central Committee of Liberated Jews," which historian Zeev Mankowitz sees as a major collective achievement of the DPs.[68] Upon arrival at Feldafing he was briefed by Erwin Tichauer, "in uniform," who was said to look "just like an American, but in fact he was one of the very few surviving German Jews. He had worked in the French underground, spent more than a year at Auschwitz, and for the past year had served brilliantly as an UNRRA welfare worker and organizer, and director of the police force at Feldafing for which he was commended by General Eisenhower."[69]

Tichauer, "son of a distinguished law professor in Berlin, spoke English with enviable fluency. He drew a vivid picture of the persecution of both Christians and Jews under the Nazi regime and recounted in detail the routine to which the inmates at Auschwitz were subjected. His simple, factual description of Nazi murder techniques, obviously something of a surprise to the [American GI] new arrivals, made a profound impression on them.

Scithers noted some handkerchiefs dotting the sea of khaki in the hall." This scene is particularly important given the feeling among many U.S. servicemen toward the Jewish DPs was that they were, at best, "unpleasant."[70]

In the visit of Generals Eisenhower and Patton to Feldafing, Patton already knew their main interlocutor, Tichauer, as a bona fide war hero. Before being sent to Auschwitz, Tichauer had fought with the resistance in France. After the liberation of the camp he helped prevent German troops from crossing the Remagen Bridge in the Battle of the Bulge. In this operation he gained the nickname *"Eisenbrecher"* (Iron Breaker). Patton claimed that he wanted to introduce the "Eisenbrecher" to (the) "Eisenhower."[71] The public meeting between Tichauer, as the UNRRA security officer for the region, and General Eisenhower was a poignant show of the continuity between the DP police force and the U.S. military.

A UNRRA report on Feldafing dated November 8, 1945, corroborated earlier reports on the character and influence of the Jewish police. Edward S. Richeson of UNRRA wrote:

> We have our own police department. They operate probably the most efficiently of any department. The chief is very alert and honest. All the people say of him "he is very honest but 'a little crazy.'" He too finds many black market operators but hates to turn over anyone but a major offender to military government officials. He raids suspects daily and always returns with money, meat, ARC [American Red Cross] packages or some articles. The other day he raided a block and found several violators. The next day he returned to the same block to visit a friend and three hundred pounds of meat descended from the second floor. No one claimed ownership of said meat.[72]

"They called him crazy," his wife recalls, "because he was honest."[73] He was incorruptible.

Just as the photographic record of the Jewish partisans has become an important historical resource,[74] the rich archive of images of the Jewish police provides superlative documentation, capturing them as they wished to be seen and preserved. Although many of the pictures are almost indistinguishable from portraits of contemporary police forces almost anywhere in the modern world—with the exception of Hebrew writing on signs and overtly Jewish symbols—they have at least one distinguishing characteristic: in a number of scenes the men are touching each other. In a picture of the Feldafing DP police, reportedly taken in Dachau where they "had gone

The Feldafing DP Police Force. Police chief Erwin Tichauer is in the rear center. In August 1945 the policemen were photographed in Dachau, where they were sent to identify SS members for war-crimes prosecution. Reproduced courtesy of Joseph Kugleman, pictured at the front right. Desig. no. 322.38305, W/S no. 97112, CD no. 0263, USHMM.

to identify SS men for a later war crimes trial," the chief, Tichauer, has his arms around three colleagues, while his hand rests on the shoulder of another. That man has his hand on the shoulder of the man kneeling in front of him. The men include former soldiers in the Greek Army, as well as Jews from Romania and Poland.[75] Similarly, in a group shot of the Jewish police of the Liepheim DP camp, fifteen men, seven of them are placing their hands on each other.[76] These poses may simply be a photographic convention; even amateur photographers will request such poses. Yet the subjects appear happy in these postures and prized such souvenirs and records of their experience.

With rare exceptions, the postwar Jewish police forces were exclusively male.[77] In part, this fact seems to be a reflection of their professionalization. They were able to be discriminating and subscribe to supposedly universal standards of recruitment and training. Although some pictures show Jews with guns and rifles, especially in ceremonial duties, most show the men uniformed but unarmed. They had no reason to appear menacing.

They did not have to be seen brandishing firepower, inspiring fear. The postwar groups were preeminently to be keepers of the peace. But like the partisan portraits the police photos exude a certain confidence and even charm. The men smile; they are calm and good-looking. They take to the motorcycles, in their own uniforms, heads held high.[78] The landscape they traversed, however, was that of an irrevocably decimated European Jewry.

Overall a great deal of unremarkable contact took place between Germans and Jews, and the Jews in Germany had the freedom to express and organize themselves as they desired. They published newspapers, they played chess, they boxed and played football, and they protested both large and small injustices. A great many Jews, however, encountered palpable uneasiness among the Germans. In 1947 one of the leaders among the DPs, Dr. Shmuel Gringauz, described what he termed the post–National Socialist, "neo-anti-Semitism" of Germans. "In their hearts," he asserted, "they knew the truth" about their role in the annihilation of European Jewry "and sought to protect their souls by fabricating an alibi for their people." None was possible, however, "in defense of the murderer"—so they "turned against the victim . . . telling themselves and the occupation forces that [the Jews among them] were crooked, thieves, underhanded, black-marketeers and filthy—in a word, the kind of people they should be rid of."[79] Gringauz probably recognized that Jews were, unfortunately, "particularly vulnerable to the charge of black marketing" because of a long history of the association of Jews with criminality, which was not simply an outgrowth of the fact that there were highly visible "operators" among the Jews.[80] Despite his sardonic portrayal of the postwar German-Jewish situation, Gringauz took for granted that most of the Germans around him indeed possessed hearts and souls.

Epilogue
The Estonia Enigma

Betrayed! Betrayed! A false alarm on the night bell, once answered—it can never be made good.

FRANZ KAFKA

"Ein Landarzt"

THE ANNIHILATION OF ESTONIAN JEWRY in the forefront of the Holocaust is well known, especially because of its mention at the Wannsee Conference (January 1942) as the sole instance in which the Jewish problem had been "solved." No ghettos needed to be created, nor were Estonian Jews transported to concentration and extermination camps. Because the Jews in Estonia were massacred, in total, before the end of 1941, these steps simply were not necessary.

However, survivors of pre–Second World War Estonian Jewry do exist, because in the wake of the Soviet Union's occupation of the Baltic countries in June 1940, and following these countries' annexation in August, about two-thirds of the Estonian Jews fled the country before the Nazis invaded. Not a single Jew who stayed in Estonia, however, is known to have survived the country's absorption into the Reich Commissariat Ostland. Although the forty-five hundred Jews of Estonia formed one of the smallest prewar national Jewish communities in Europe, the genocide of Estonian Jewry is particularly instructive in understanding the perpetration of the Holocaust, as well as postwar manifestations of anti-Semitism, in light of the association of Jews with criminality.

With the benefit of hindsight, Estonia seems to be a nation that might have challenged Nazi Jewish policy, much like Denmark and Bulgaria did. The country had no deep-seated tradition of anti-Semitism; the native church was not particularly anti-Semitic; Jews had not, before the Second World War, been associated with the threat of Bolshevism. Departing from the typical pattern, as well as the stereotype, Jews did not comprise a significant element of the commercial middle class in Estonia; "Baltic Germans" primarily filled that role. Perhaps most tellingly, as has been illuminated by the pioneering scholarship of Anton Weiss-Wendt, Jews were not singled out as the reviled "other" when Estonians delved into their own variety of "race science." The "race" they posed as the antithesis of Estonian was "Russian"—not Jewish. In fact, among the Estonians themselves, the urge was to persecute and deport ethnic Russians—but the Nazis resisted this move. Weiss-Wendt has found little evidence that popular passions were inflamed against Jews, as there were no pogroms, on the part of locals, before the comprehensive murder of the community by Einsatzgruppe A and Estonian collaborators between August and October 1941. But after their own nation's Jews were slaughtered, Estonians helped run the Klooga concentration camp and the Vaivara and Kalevi Liiva forced-labor camps, which were among the final, fatal destinations for Jews rounded up from Kovno, Vilna, and other ghettos.[1]

As a scholar seeking to understand Estonian complicity in the Holocaust, Weiss-Wendt argues that as in other cases in Eastern Europe, the Soviet invasion and occupation proved to be a "traumatic" experience for most Estonians. Certainly the Estonian case bears comparison with the perpetration of the Holocaust in Latvia, where the canard of "Judeo-Bolshevism" proved lethal.[2] Although Jews suffered proportionally, at least, under the Soviets, the Nazis and native collaborators attempted to show that Jews were overwhelmingly sympathetic to, and benefited from, the Soviet occupation. In his research, Weiss-Wendt discovered that for a murdered Jewish population of 963 in Estonia, police dossiers were compiled on at least 400 individuals.[3] In so many other places in the sweeps of the Einsatzgruppen and other phases of the Holocaust, Jews were simply taken out and shot. Why would the Nazis have bothered to expend the time and effort necessary to assemble police-type files on most of Tallinn's Jews?

A possible answer, which comes as little surprise in the context of Nazi anti-Semitism, is that the Nazis invariably sought to establish connections between Jews and Bolsheviks. Yet here the body of concocted documents and proceedings is perhaps even murkier. In a number of cases, rather than simply declaring someone to be a communist or communist sympathizer, the Nazis threw in a variety of "crimes." Why?[4]

I think that the answer lies in the discrepancy between the attitudes of non-Jews toward Jews in Estonia and the lethal stigmatization the Nazis sought to achieve. Estonians, apparently, did not believe Jews to be a threatening element, in either the racial or the religious formulations the Nazis knew and exploited throughout most of the rest of Europe. From their experience, however, the Nazis, and in this case local Estonians, learned that charging Jews with particular crimes was an effective instrument for separating and persecuting them. "Painting Jews as communists" was the most expedient method. This approach made it easier for a local population, in which Jews might have been well ensconced, to accept the stripping of Jewish rights and the confiscation of their property and other assets—and eventually turn a blind eye to murder. The German Security Police in Estonia, according to Weiss-Wendt, was not concerned about how Estonians generally and Estonian policemen in particular went about marking Jews for destruction as long as the Jews were all murdered. For some six months, to take one example, the Estonian Security Police investigated a Jewish woman. They faced a dilemma: they could not release her because she was Jewish, yet they were unable to pin specific charges on her. The woman in question "was pro-Estonian; she spoke Estonian at home; she communicated only with Estonians; her husband was a high-ranking Estonian police official who was deported by the Soviets. The police questioned witness upon witness who could do nothing but testify to the innocence of the Jew. Finally, the head of the (German) Gestapo had had enough and ordered the Estonian branch of the police to immediately execute the woman. She was murdered the next day."[5]

Perhaps, if one is looking for more psychological motivations, such behavior helped the Nazis and their collaborators live with themselves—enabling them to act as if they were punishing people who had done something wrong, who had committed a crime. Of course, the particular Estonian dynamic was likely fueled by the Estonians' belief that they were of a racial stock that was close to the German "Aryans" and their resulting desire to prove their mettle. But the fact remains that the Estonians, at the behest of the Nazis, went to unusual lengths to taint Estonian Jewry with criminality, a strategy similar to the one the Nazis and their accomplices had practiced elsewhere.

As has been shown in other settings, the Nazis were, in a way, playacting a game of crime and punishment, which was actually a perversion of fundamental rights and justice, whether defined by the Ten Commandments, Jesus, or Kant. The fabrication of the edifice of Jewish criminality, followed by the massacre of the community, was probably meant, as well, to be an object lesson to Estonian non-Jews, to show what happens to those who venture beyond the Nazi conception of law and order.

But the Jews of Estonia, like their brethren in Europe, had done nothing to deserve their destruction. A universe of crime, punishment, and retribution was cynically and minutely created to undermine their lives. The genocide of Jewry was propounded and perpetrated because of the Nazis' perception that Jewry as a race had to be exterminated in order for Aryans to survive. Yet the annihilation of Jewry also was precipitated and sustained by the carefully contrived fraud that Jews, individually and collectively, had done something wrong—that they deserved a nasty end because they had been, and acted like, criminals. This accusation that Jews tended toward criminality had been part of the debate about the *Judenfrage* since Jewish emancipation in the German states and elsewhere. It played a substantial role in how Jews were seen and treated, and it influenced how Jews saw and sought to defend themselves. The characterization of Jewish communal and especially Zionist organizations as all-embracing criminal conspiracies was invented by the Nazis in 1944 to rationalize mass murder—literally, to provide a good explanation to give their children, should they ask. Although German anti-Semitism assumed a more genteel guise in postwar Germany, the charge of a "Zionist conspiracy" was perpetuated and intensified by neo-Nazis after the Second World War, as well as by those wishing to demean and delegitimate the State of Israel. Despite the fact that the Nazis found the stereotype of "Jews as criminals" ready-made, they inflated it to gargantuan proportions and allowed for pieces of their twisted vision to have a life beyond the Third Reich, even without the support of an explicit racial ideology. While the Jews of Europe were being slaughtered, Nazi journalists were told to propagate the view that "The destruction of Jewry is not a loss to mankind, but for the peoples of the world just as useful as capital punishment or penitentiaries for criminals. Nor do we make any distinction between the Biblical people of Israel and the Jews of today, for both are criminal."[6] The potency of associating Jewry with criminality was always a trusted part of the Nazi arsenal, and this particular weapon—one of their most effective—far outlived Nazism itself. "In the eyes of the Third Reich," a survivor writes, "we Jews were murderers, thieves, bandits, or—worse yet, Jews."[7]

The dark irony that the Nazis—who were supposedly so indignant about the corruption of Weimar politicians—turned out to be the most duplicitous and thieving regime of all time has not been lost on later generations.[8] Many of the Nazis' victims perceived this fact immediately: that Jews were called criminals so that the Nazis could rob and kill them with impunity. As one survivor wrote in her wartime diary from a hiding place in Poland, "It's convenient to believe that stealing from a Jew isn't a crime of which one should be ashamed. They just walk into a Jewish home and take whatever they like without paying a penny. Why shouldn't they believe Hitler's lies?" Other survivors recalled thinking of the Nazis and their henchmen as "assassins" and "pigs." Germans, Austrians, and their accomplices outside of Central Europe allowed themselves to be transformed, survivors recall, into "gangsters, criminals, and thieves."[9] In many cases Jews managed to preserve their own humanity—and perhaps their own lives—by distinguishing between "resistance" to the Nazi regime and "criminal" misdeeds. "On one occasion in Lieberose," Hugo Gryn wrote,

I was party to the killing of a guard. There were a lot of Ukrainian volunteers in the SS and they were even nastier than the German Nazis. They really enjoyed torturing and beating up prisoners. But there was one who was particularly dangerous, and particularly violent. He could not have been more than eighteen or nineteen. When his superiors were not looking he had the vicious habit of swinging his rifle above his head and bringing its butt down anywhere at random on a head, a shoulder, a leg—and once that happened to you, you were finished. They were lethal blows. He was a terrible menace and the whole camp was in terror of him.

Once on a work detail, we had to go back in the middle of the day to fetch the soup containers. Two people with wooden staves per container, and we were entitled to two such containers, so four people went back with this one guard. We stopped, he came close to see why and I was one of the people who held him while one of the others used that bloody gun of his. He was beaten to death because we did not want to make a noise and we buried him there. Fortunately he was not wearing his steel helmet. It was just a cloth cap. . . . Looking back on it, I think we had both a moral and a physical responsibility to resist, if needs be, with violence. Passive resistance would have been absolutely no use in such a desperate situation. I had heard that if you could get sugar into a combustion engine, it would seize up. So during my Bauhof period, once a week or so we were given some marmalade. I assumed that there had to be some sugar in it, although I suspected it was all synthetic. I did not eat the marmalade. I collected it. I had a funny little tin. I collected portions and portions of marmalade, carried them on my person and when I could, unobserved, I would open the petrol cap of lorries and pour it all in. Or, when working near railway lines, my favourite occupation was to remove bolts and nuts, hoping that one day a train might break down. It was really a pathetic form of sabotage, but it motivated me a lot.[10]

Although all resistance to Nazi authority was deemed "criminal" and used as a justification for torture and murder, Gryn and others—such as the thousands of Jewish partisans—knew that they were in no way "criminals." But Jews' perspectives, sometimes even their acts of resistance, were partly "motivated" and shaped by the "criminality" canard. Marcel Reich-Ranicki proudly refers to the Warsaw ghetto "smuggling racket" as "people who took calculated risks and were not afraid of death." Again inverting the normal discourse of criminal versus society, Reich-Ranicki was honored and flattered when he was approached by Emanuel Ringelblum to assist in compiling the secret ghetto archive. He characterized the endeavor of the historian—whom he admired as "a silent, indefatigable organizer, an open-minded historian, an impassioned archivist, a remarkably self-controlled and determined person"—as his "conspiratorial activities."[11] After the end of the war, Primo Levi was thrilled to encounter a group of young DPs in Munich who "attached their truck" to Levi's train without "asking anybody's permission." They "hooked it on, and that was that. I was amazed, but they laughed at my amazement: 'Hitler's dead, isn't he?' replied their leader, with his intense hawk-like glance. They felt immensely free and strong, lords of the world and of their destinies."[12]

In the immediate wake of the Holocaust, efforts to memorialize some of the destroyed communities corrected the libel against Jewry by joining the terms "Nazi" and "criminal." The survivors of Auschwitz and Theresienstadt living in the Lindenfels DP camp erected historical markers at the sites of destroyed Frankfurt synagogues, reading (in German and English), "Here stood the Hauptsynagogue Börnestrasse" and "here stood the Börneplatz Synagogue which were destroyed by Nazi criminals on the 9th day of November 1938."[13] Although some among the Jewish partisans and other survivors did try to take "revenge" when they could, this was not the spirit that animated most Jews. After 1945, many Jews who had opportunity to exact revenge by killing Nazis—even those they personally knew to be murderers—refrained from doing so. "All during the war," Lucille Eichengreen writes,

I had wished for a gun. I had wanted to kill one German—just one—before I died. Seconds passed; the revolver was heavy and trembled in my hand. The German's eyes avoided mine, but his lips quivered an almost inaudible "please."

I closed my eyes. Almost immediately I heard my father's voice reaching me from Dachau where they had murdered him: "If you let yourself hate too long and too much, it will destroy you in the end."

I put the revolver down, placing it on the table in front of Major Brinton, and walked to the door. Outside the hallway, I sank slowly to the floor and leaned against the cold wall, remembering . . . remembering.

I was confronted with a cruel irony: somehow I still could not justify killing another human being; somehow, I had retained my faith in a just system of courts and juries.[14]

The Nazis' use of the allegation of criminality, of assigning a collective criminal intent to the Jews, has proven to be one of the more resilient but less obvious aspects of their legacy. In the eyes of Victor Klemperer, it was "one of the many paths along which Hitlerism could march."[15] Like many of the Nazis' horrific and bizarre notions, seeing Jews as criminals was unoriginal, even hackneyed. But it probably helped a huge number of Germans and their fellow perpetrators, as well as bystanders, to accept what the Nazis were doing to the Jews.

After completing his postwar service to the U.S. Army and returning home to Rochester, New York, Rabbi Philip Bernstein delivered a sermon entitled "The Truth about Germany" on November 28, 1947. The stigma of Jewish criminality was fresh in his mind. "It is hard," he told his congregation, "to know the truth about individual human beings. It is equally hard or harder to learn about groups. A man may come to Rochester and within a short period read that the police shot the young negro ex-soldier who claimed he had a revolver, and shortly thereafter a negro shopkeeper killed another negro attempting to burglarize his establishment. Having only these facts before him, he could describe Rochester in such a way as to indicate that ours is a city of violence and that negroes as a whole are murderous and law-breaking." To adopt such a view, though, means that one would inadvertently "ignore completely the normal contacts of life in Rochester, and the overwhelming fact that most of our negroes in Rochester are decent, law-abiding men and women. The individual facts in this report would be correct, but the total picture would be incorrect."[16]

Not only race hatred in itself unsettled the rabbi but also the fact that it was often bolstered by what otherwise reasonable people thought to be "facts." With Hitler pointing the way, the grotesque, exaggerated projection of Jews as criminals was pushed to its greatest extreme. The systematic annihilation of European Jewry was later whitewashed as a defense against the Jews' alleged criminal intent. "I was always fair and decent," a former Nazi guard screamed during her interrogation. She ignored the fact that there stood in front of her a woman who had witnessed her merciless beating of hundreds of Jews. "I never did anything unless they deserved it."[17] The institutionalized hypocrisy of calling Jews "criminals" eased the consciences and fostered opportunistic delusions in the shooters, desk-murderers, and various other practitioners of genocide and their wartime and postwar apologists. The insipid cliché "Where there is smoke there is fire" has been used to justify anti-Semitism, to say that "there must be a reason" for the hatred of Jews. The smoke, in this case, was a choking stench, the fires stoked by the Nazi lust for riches, power, and world domination. Yet it was accompanied by a desire to appear guiltless, even heroic, and to be viewed as upholders of law and order as defined by so-called Western culture and civilization. Certainly minority groups who have struggled to gain a foothold, and those in marginal economic spheres, have been (and continue to be) stigmatized because of their supposed propensity to crime.[18] Although genocidal regimes existed before and after Hitler, the Nazi imagination of Jews as criminals is one of the grossest perversions of the respect for law ever to be instituted.

NOTES

ABBREVIATIONS

B-C   Berlin Document Collection, YIVO

BDC, NA   Berlin Documents Collection, United States National
               Archives, College Park, MD

Die Judenfrage   *Mitteilungen über die Judenfrage*

PSB   Papers of Philip S. Bernstein, University of Rochester
               Archives, Rochester, NY

RG   Record Group (in USHMM archives)

USHMM   United States Holocaust Memorial Museum,
               Washington, DC

YIVO   YIVO Institute for Jewish Research, New York, NY

PREFACE

1. Leon Neiberg, "Zikhronos vegn oyfshtand in varshe" (Memories of the Uprising in Warsaw), *Undzer Veg,* no. 28 (April 15, 1946): 7, quoted in Zeev W. Mankowitz, *Life between Memory and Hope: The Survivors of the Holocaust in Occupied Germany* (Cambridge: Cambridge University Press, 2002), p. 225.

2. W/S no. 11189, CD no. 0008, from National Archives, Archives of the United States Holocaust Memorial Museum (hereafter USHMM).

3. In response to the important question raised by Richard Breitman "To whom do I refer throughout this study in discussing Nazis?" generally I wish to include all so-called Aryan Germans who lived under the Nazis. An "Opinion Survey" of "Anti-Semitism in the American Zone," Report Number 49, March 3, 1947, ODIC, Opinion Surveys Headquarters, OMGUS (Rear), APO 757, stated: "It is interesting to note that neither service in the Wehrmacht nor membership in the NSDAP have much bearing on the degree of anti-Semitism held. Nor are the people who grew up under the nazi regime much more prejudiced than are people who were adults when Hitler came into power. . . . The propaganda was so far reaching that it affected all population groups almost equally"; p. 8, item 29, box 2, "Advisor" [on post–World War II Jewish Affairs] section, Papers of Philip S. Bernstein, University of Rochester Archives, Rochester, NY (hereafter PSB).

4. The great exception is the prolific Sander L. Gilman, who approaches the subject in several of his books; see especially *Jewish Self-Hatred: Anti-Semitism and the Hidden Language of the Jews* (Baltimore: Johns Hopkins University Press, 1986).

5. Nikolaus Wachsmann, *Hitler's Prisons: Legal Terror in Nazi Germany* (New Haven: Yale University Press, 2004); Robert Gellately, *Backing Hitler: Consent and Coercion in Nazi Germany* (Oxford: Oxford University Press, 2001); Robert Gellately and Nathan Stoltzfus, eds., *Social Outsiders in Nazi Germany* (Princeton: Princeton University Press, 2001); Harold Marcuse, *Legacies of Dachau: The Uses and Abuses of a Concentration Camp, 1933–2001* (Cambridge: Cambridge University Press, 2001); Richard Bessel, *Nazism and War* (London: Weidenfeld and Nicolson, 2004); David Bankier, *The Germans and the Final Solution: Public Opinion under Nazism* (Oxford: Basil Blackwell, 1992); Claudia Koonz, *The Nazi Conscience* (Cambridge, MA: Harvard University Press, Belknap Press, 2003). On myths versus realities of Nazism's impact on workers, see Shelley Baranowski, *Strength through Joy: Consumerism and Mass Tourism in the Third Reich* (Cambridge: Cambridge University Press, 2004).

6. Peter Duffy, *The Bielski Brothers: The True Story of Three Men Who Defied the Nazis, Saved 1,200 Jews, and Built a Village in the Forest* (New York: HarperCollins, 2003), pp. 43, 67–70, 77–82, 88–105, 124, 129, 133, 137, 152, 183, 221.

7. Elsewhere I deal with how this functioned among Jewish partisans; see Michael Berkowitz, "The Nazi Equation of Jewish Partisans with 'Bandits' and Its Consequences," *European Review of History-Revue européenne d'histoire* 13, no. 2 (June 2006): 311–33.

8. E. J. Hobsbawm, *Primitive Rebels* (Manchester: University of Manchester Press, 1959); Hobsbawm, *Bandits* (Harmondsworth: Penguin, 1985).

9. Victor Klemperer, *I Shall Bear Witness: The Diaries of Victor Klemperer 1933–1941,* trans. Martin Chalmers (London: Weidenfeld and Nicolson, 1998), p. 381.

10. The first use of this term, in English, was probably by Gerhard Jacoby, *Racial State: The German Nationalities Policy in the Protectorate of Bohemia-Moravia* (New York: Institute of Jewish Affairs of the American Jewish Congress and World Jewish Congress, 1944); among scholars from the late twentieth century onward, it is associated mainly with Michael Burleigh and Wolfgang Wippermann, *The Racial State: Germany, 1933–1945* (Cambridge: Cambridge University Press, 1991).

11. See Omer Bartov, *Murder in Our Midst: The Holocaust, Industrial Killing, and Representation* (New York: Oxford University Press, 1996).

12. Robert Gellately, *The Gestapo and German Society: Enforcing Racial Policy, 1933–1945* (Oxford: Clarendon Press, 1990).

13. Robert Lewis Koehl, *The Black Corps: The Structure and Power Struggles of the Nazi SS* (Madison: University of Wisconsin Press, 1983), pp. 117–19.

14. Götz Aly, Peter Chroust, and Christian Pross, eds., *Cleansing the Fatherland: Nazi Medicine and Racial Hygiene,* trans. Belinda Cooper (Baltimore: Johns Hopkins University Press, 1994).

15. This is the clear subtext of the memo from Rudolf Hess, reporting an order from Hitler of April 11, 1935, "Verkehr mit Juden—Anordnung des Stellvertreters des Führers, den 20. Juli 1935, Reichssicherheitshauptamt (RSHA)–SD, Berlin (Osobyi fond 500) (Main State Security of Germany–SD, Berlin [manuscript RG-11.001M.01], reel 4, folder 260, USHMM); see Saul Friedländer, *Nazi Germany and the Jews* (New York: HarperCollins, 1997); Marion Kaplan, *Between Dignity and Despair: Jewish Life in Nazi Germany* (New York: Oxford University Press, 1999).

16. George L. Mosse, ed., *Nazi Culture: Intellectual, Cultural, and Social Life in the Third Reich,* trans. Salvatore Attanasio et al. (New York: Grosset & Dunlap, 1966), p. 322.

17. For a striking illustration, see Nathan Stoltzfuss, *Resistance of the Heart: The Rosenstrasse Protest and Intermarriage in Nazi Germany* (New Brunswick, NJ: Rutgers University Press, 2001).

18. Letter to [Kurt] Daluege, Berlin, October 19, 1935; June 17, 1935; August 19, 1935; August 14, 1935, specifying "non-Aryan" officers in the Prussian security police; memo "Juden im Reichsluftschutzbund," May 16, 1936, July 13, 1935, "Juden—Motorsportgruppen," folder 303, Deutsche Arbeitsfront (DAF), Reichssicherheitshauptamt (RSHA)–SD, Berlin (Osobyi fond 500) (Main State Security of Germany–SD, Berlin [manuscript RG-11.001M.01], reel 4, USHMM).

19. Folder 303, German Labor Front, Reichssicherheitshauptamt (RSHA)–SD, Berlin (Osobyi fond 500) (Main State Security of Germany–SD, Berlin [manuscript RG-11.001M.01], reel 4, USHMM). There are Gestapo and NSDAP reports about the work of Jews in high posts in Germany between 1935 and 1938, and various reports about Jewish employees in important industrial facilities and in public life, such as Jews in the police, Lufthansa, and so on (1935). These include samples of

complaints by SS members and other Germans to newspapers and the authorities about the continued presence of Jews in public life (USHMM).

20. George C. Browder, *Foundations of the Nazi Police State: The Formation of the Sipo and SD* (Lexington: University Press of Kentucky, 1990) and *Hitler's Enforcers: The Gestapo and the SS Security Service in the Nazi Revolution* (New York: Oxford University Press, 1996); Gellately, *Backing Hitler* and *The Gestapo and German Society;* Bankier, *The Germans and the Final Solution;* Eric A. Johnson, *Nazi Terror: The Gestapo, Jews and Ordinary Germans* (New York: Basic, 1999); Friedrich Wilhelm, *Die Polizei im NS-Staat* (Paderborn: Ferdinand Schöningh, 1997).

21. Christopher R. Browning, *Nazi Policy, Jewish Workers, German Killers* (Cambridge: Cambridge University Press, 2000), and *Path to Genocide: Essays on Launching the Final Solution* (New York: Cambridge University Press, 1992); Richard Breitman, *The Architect of Genocide: Himmler and the Final Solution* (New York: Knopf, 1991), and *Official Secrets: What the Nazis Planned, What the British and Americans Knew* (New York: Hill and Wang, 1998).

22. Christoph Dieckmann, "Der Krieg und die Ermordung der litauischen Juden," in Ulrich Herbert, ed., *Nationalsozialistische Vernichtungspolitik 1939–1945: Neue Forschungen und Kontroversen* (Frankfurt a.M.: Fischer Taschenbuch Verlag, 1998), pp. 292–93; here Dieckmann builds on the important work of Helmut Krausnick, "Hitler und die Befehle an die Einsatzgruppen," in *Der Mord an den Juden im Zweiten Weltkrieg. Entschlussbildung und Verwirklichung,* ed. Eberhard Jäckel and Jürgen Rohwer (Stuttgart: Deutsche Verlags-Anstalt, 1987), p. 99; Eberhard Jäckel, "Die Entschlussbildung als historisches Problem," in Jäckel and Rohwer, *Der Mord an den Juden,* pp. 9–17. See also Dieckmann, "Das Ghetto und das Konzentrationslager in Kaunas 1941–1944," in *Die nationalsozialistischen Konzentrationslager 1933–1945,* ed. Ulrich Herbert, Karin Orth, Christoph Dieckmann (Göttingen: Wallstein, 1998), pp. 439–71; Martin Dean, *Collaboration in the Holocaust: Crimes of the Local Police in Belorussia and Ukraine, 1941–1944* (Houndmills, Basingstoke: Macmillan; New York: St. Martin's, 2000); Hsi-Huey Liang, *The Rise of the Modern Police and the European State System from Metternich to the Second World War* (Cambridge: Cambridge University Press, 1992), p. 252; Bob Moore, *Victims and Survivors: The Nazi Persecution of the Jews in the Netherlands, 1940–1945* (London: Arnold, 1997).

23. Robert G. Waite, "Judentum und Kriminalität: Rassistische Deutungen in kriminologischen Publikationen 1933–1945," in *Rassismus, Faschismus, Antifaschismus: Forschungen und Betrachtungen* (Gewidmet Kurt Paetzold zum 70. Geburtstag), ed. Manfred Weissbecker and Reinhard Kühnl (Cologne: PapyRossa, 2000), pp. 46–62; Richard Wetzell, *Inventing the Criminal: A History of German Criminology, 1880–1945* (Chapel Hill: University of North Carolina Press, 2000); Raphael Gross, *Carl Schmitt und die Juden: eine Deutsche Rechtslehre* (Frankfurt a.M.: Suhrkamp, 2000); Patrick Wagner, *Hitlers Kriminalisten: die*

deutsche Kriminalpolizei und der Nationalsozialismus zwischen 1920 und 1960 (Munich: C. H. Beck, 2002); Patrick Wagner, *Volksgemeinschaft ohne Verbrecher: Konzeptionen und Praxis der Kriminalpolizei in der Zeit der Weimarer Republik und des Nationalsozialismus* (Hamburg: Christians, 1996); Bernward Dörner, *"Heimtücke": das Gesetz als Waffe: Kontrolle, Abschreckung und Verfolgung in Deutschland 1933–1945* (Paderborn: Schöningh, 1998); Ingo Müller, *Hitler's Justice: The Courts of the Third Reich,* trans. Deborah Lucas Schneider (Cambridge, MA: Harvard University Press, 1991).

24. Alan E. Steinweis, *Studying the Jew: Scholarly Antisemitism in Nazi Germany* (Cambridge, MA: Harvard University Press, 2006), pp. 137–42.

25. Breitman, *Official Secrets.*

26. Ibid., pp. 27–44; Christopher R. Browning, *Ordinary Men: Reserve Police Battalion 101 and the Final Solution in Poland* (New York: HarperPerennial, 1998), pp. 4–27; Ulrich Herbert, *Best: Biographische Studien über Radikalismus, Weltanschauung und Vernunft, 1903–1989* (Bonn: J. H. W. Dietz, 1996). In the latter the emphasis on "reason" *(Vernunft)* in Best's character is highly significant.

27. Lucille Eichengreen with Harriet Hyman Chamberlain, *From Ashes to Life: My Memories of the Holocaust* (San Francisco: Mercury House, 1994), pp. 25, 18.

28. Victor Gans, "Memoir," RG-02.092, p. 43, USHMM, p. 17; see also Dodo Liebmann, "We Kept Our Heads: Personal Memories of Being Jewish in Nazi Germany and Making a New Home in England," RG-02.201, p. 44, USHMM.

29. Liebmann, "We Kept Our Heads," p. 44.

30. Konrad H. Jarausch, "The Conundrum of Complicity: German Professionals and the Final Solution," Joseph and Rebecca Meyerhoff Annual Lecture, June 11, 2001 (Washington, DC: United States Holocaust Memorial Museum, 2002), pp. 1, 7.

31. Roger Griffin, *The Nature of Fascism* (London: Pinter, 1991), p. 184.

32. See, for example, Alan E. Steinweis, *Art, Ideology and Economics in Nazi Germany: The Reich Chambers of Music, Theater, and the Visual Arts* (Chapel Hill: University of North Carolina Press, 1993).

33. Koonz, *The Nazi Conscience.*

34. Initiation of a new propaganda campaign against Jewry, by Wolf Meyer-Christian, "Die Behandlung der Judenfrage in der deutschen Presse," June 1944, Record group 215, G-117, box 6, Berlin Document Collection, YIVO (hereafter B-C, YIVO); see chapter 5 of this book.

35. I believe, however, that Hilberg overstates his case: "In the German scheme, racism has a reinforcement function only." Raul Hilberg, *Prologue to Annihilation: A Study of the Identification, Impoverishment and Isolation of the Jewish Victims of Nazi Policy* (Ph.D. thesis, New York: Columbia University, 1955), p. 33.

36. Ibid., chart (frontispiece).

37. Ian Kershaw, *Popular Opinion and Political Dissent in the Third Reich: Bavaria 1933–1945* (Oxford: Oxford University Press, 2002). Nazis were

enthusiastic to demonstrate both Protestant and Catholic precedents for their anti-Semitism; see Benedikt Fontana, "Der historische Antisemitismus der katholischen Kirche," in *Mitteilungen über die Judenfrage* (hereafter *Die Judenfrage*), December 20, 1937, pp. 1–4, followed by "Warum denkt die römische Kirche heute anders?" pp. 5–7; Dr. Walter Hafner, "Die Päpste und der Talmud," in *Die Judenfrage*, September 15, 1938. Islam was also cited for support: Prof. Dr. Johann von Leers, "Koran gegen Judentum," in *Die Judenfrage*, December 11, 1938, p. 14.

38. Mosse, *Nazi Culture*, p. 321, and "The Genesis of Fascism," *Journal of Contemporary History* 1, no. 1 (1966): 14–26. See Emilio Gentile's superb evaluation of the development of Mosse's concept of fascism in "A Provisional Dwelling: The Origin and Development of the Concept of Fascism in Mosse's Historiography," in *What History Tells: George L. Mosse and the Culture of Modern Europe*, ed. Stanley G. Payne, David J. Sorkin, and John S. Tortorice (Madison: University of Wisconsin Press, 2004), pp. 73–77.

39. George Mosse, *Confronting History: A Memoir* (Madison: University of Wisconsin Press, 2000), p. 177.

40. Mosse, "The Genesis of Fascism," p. 17; Gentile, "A Provisional Dwelling," pp. 76–77.

41. Mosse, *Nazi Culture*, p. xix.

42. Ibid., p. xxii.

43. See Robert A. Nye, "Mosse, Masculinity, and History of Sexuality," in Payne, Sorkin, and Tortorice, *What History Tells*, pp. 190–95.

44. Koehl, *The Black Corps*, p. xviii.

45. Supreme Party Judge Walther Buch, cited in Mosse, *Nazi Culture*, p. 336.

46. Roger Cohen, "The Lost Soldiers of Stalag IX-B," *New York Times Magazine*, February 27, 2005; this article appeared in advance of the publication of Cohen's book *Slaves and Soldiers* (New York: Alfred A. Knopf, 2005).

47. While this book was in process, important scholarship has appeared on Nazi plans to destroy the Jewish settlement in Palestine. See Klaus-Michael Mallmann and Martin Cüppers. "Beseitigung der jüdisch-nationale Heimstätte in Palästina. Das Einsatzkommando bei der Panzerarmee Afrika 1942," in *Deutsche, Juden, Völkermord. Der Holocaust als Geschichte und Gegenwart*, ed. Jürgen Matthäus and Klaus-Michael Mallman (Darmstadt: Wissenschaftliche Buchgesellschaft, 2006), pp. 153–340; and Mallmann and Cüppers, *Halbmond und Hakenkreuz. Das Dritte Reich, die Araber und Palästina* (Darmstadt: Wissenschaftliche Buchgesellschaft, 2006).

48. Gerhard Fürmetz, Herbert Reinke, Klaus Weinhauer, eds., *Nachkriegspolizei. Sicherheit und Ordnung in Ost- und Westdeutschland 1945–1969* (Hamburg: Ergebnisse, 2001).

49. Hermann Leyes, "Under the Nazi Regime, 1933–1938," RG-02.203, Acc.1994.A351, UHSMM, p. 17. This memoir is dedicated "to the German Jew that I used to be."

ACKNOWLEDGMENTS

1. See Martin Gilbert, *Holocaust Journey: Travelling in Search of the Past* (London: Weidenfeld and Nicolson, 1997).

2. Richard Newman with Karen Kirtley, *Alma Rosé: Vienna to Auschwitz* (Portland: Amadeus Press, 2000), p. 11.

1. ABOVE SUSPICION?

Epigraph: Rosenzweig quoted in Jacob Boas, "Countering Nazi Defamation: German Jews and the Jewish Tradition," in *Year Book XXXIV of the Leo Baeck Institute* (London: Secker & Warburg, 1989), p. 203.

1. Peter Schäfer, *The History of the Jews in the Greco-Roman World* (London: Routledge, 2003).

2. Benzion Netanyahu, *The Origins of the Inquisition in Fifteenth Century Spain* (New York: New York Review Books, 2001).

3. Raul Hilberg, *The Destruction of the European Jews,* 3rd ed., vol. 1 (New Haven: Yale University Press, 2003), cf. pp. 559 n 49, 576 n 210 (in original).

4. Peter Aldag [Fritz Peter Krueger], *Das Judentum in England* (Berlin: Nordland, 1943). Material on the forgery of documents for attribution to Benjamin Franklin in Record Group 22, file 102, Berlin Document Collection, YIVO Institute for Jewish Research (hereafter B-C, YIVO).

5. Letter, August 7, 1935, from the *Polizeipräsident* in Aachen, relates news from the German consulate in New York that Capone is "American-Italian"; letter from Washington, January 4, 1936, Record Group (hereafter RG) 215, G-65, B-C, YIVO, p. 519 n 11.

6. "First Great Seal Committee—July 1776," available at www.greatseal.com/committees/firstcomm.

7. See Eli Faber, *A Time for Planting: The First Migration 1654–1820,* vol. 1 of *The Jewish People in America* (Baltimore: Johns Hopkins University Press, 1992), p. 99.

8. This too was fully exploited by the Nazis; see Franz [Karl Anton] Rose, *Politische Mordschuld Judas bis Grünspan* (Berlin: Verlag Johann Kasper, 1939).

9. "Medieval Sourcebook: Martin Luther (1483–1546): On the Jews and Their Lies, 1543," available at www.fordham.edu/halsall/basis/1543-Luther-JewsandLies-full.html.

10. Eric Rentschler, *The Ministry of Illusion: Nazi Cinema and its Afterlife* (Cambridge, MA: Harvard University Press, 1996), pp. 149–69; Karsten Witte, "Film im Nationalsozialismus," in *Geschichte des deutschen Films,* ed. Wolfgang Jacobsen, Anton Kaes, and Hans Helmut Prinzler (Stuttgart: Metzler, 1993), pp. 152–53.

11. Harold James, *The Deutsche Bank and the Nazi War against the Jews: The Expropriation of Jewish-Owned Property* (Cambridge: Cambridge University Press, 2001).

12. Riccardo Calimani, *The Ghetto of Venice*, trans. Katherine Silberblatt Wolfthal (New York: M. Evans, 1985), pp. 10, 34.

13. Edward J. Bristow, *Prostitution and Prejudice: The Jewish Fight against White Slavery, 1870–1939* (New York: Schocken, 1983); Marion A. Kaplan, *The Jewish Feminist Movement in Germany: The Campaigns of the Jüdischer Frauenbund* (Westport, CT: Greenwood, 1979); Jenna Weissman Joselit, *Our Gang: Jewish Crime and the New York Jewish Community, 1900–1940* (Bloomington: Indiana University Press, 1983); Victor A. Mirelman, "The Jewish Community versus Crime: The Case of White Slavery in Buenos Aires," *Jewish Social Studies* 46, no. 2 (1984): 145–68; Lloyd P. Gartner, "Anglo-Jewry and the Jewish International Traffic in Prostitution, 1885–1914," *Association for Jewish Studies Review* 7–8 (1983): 129–78.

14. Herwig Hartner-Hnizdo, *Das jüdische Gaunertum* (Munich: Hoheneichen-Verlag, 1939), pp. 355–60; Josef Keller and Hanns Andersen, *Der Jude als Verbrecher* (Berlin and Leipzig: Nibelungen-Verlag, 1937), pp. 118–37.

15. See Calimani, *The Ghetto of Venice*, pp. 77, 85, 88; Gershom Scholem, *Und alles ist Kabbala: Gershom Scholem im Gespräch mit Jörg Drews* (Munich: Edition Text + Kritk, 1980), p. 9; Herwig Hartner-Hnizdo, *Volk der Gauner. Eine Untersuchung des jüdischen Gaunertums* (Munich: Hoheneichen-Verlag, 1939), pp. 11–23.

16. Calimani, *The Ghetto of Venice*, pp. 50–52.

17. Alan Block, *East Side, West Side: Organizing Crime in New York, 1930–1950* (Cardiff, Wales: University College Cardiff Press, 1980), pp. 131, 219–35.

18. See Gershom Scholem, *From Berlin to Jerusalem: Memories of My Youth*, trans. Harry Zohn (New York: Schocken, 1988), p. 46.

19. Klaus L. Berghahn, *Grenzen der Toleranz: Juden und Christen im Zeitalter der Aufklärung* (Cologne: Böhlau, 2000); David Sorkin, *The Transformation of German Jewry, 1780–1840* (New York: Oxford University Press, 1987); Mordechai Breuer and Michael Graetz, *German Jewish History in Modern Times*, vol. 1, *Tradition and Enlightenment, 1600–1780*, trans. William Templer, ed. Michael Meyer with Michael Brenner (New York: Columbia University Press, 1996).

20. Christian Wilhelm von Dohm, "Concerning the Amelioration of the Civil Status of the Jews (1781)," in *The Jew in the Modern World*, ed. Jehuda Reinharz and Paul Mendes-Flohr, 2nd ed. (New York: Oxford University Press, 1995), p. 31.

21. Johann David Michaelis, "Arguments against Dohm (1782)," in Reinharz and Mendes-Flohr, *The Jew in the Modern World*, p. 42.

22. Moses Mendelssohn, "Remarks Concerning Michaelis' Response to Dohm (1783)," in Reinharz and Mendes-Flohr, *The Jew in the Modern World*, p. 48.

23. Jason Sanders, "From Burglars to Businessmen: Jewish Bandits in Eighteenth and Nineteenth Century Germany," unpublished paper, Brandeis University, 1993.

24. I. Wolf and Gotthold Salomon, *Der Charakter des Judentums nebst einer Beleuchtung der unlängst gegen die Juden von Prof. Rühs und Fries erschienenen Schriften* (Leipzig: Carl Gottlob Schmidt, 1817), p. 141.

25. Salomon Carlebach, *Geschichte der Juden in Lübeck und Moisling, dargestellt in 9 Vorträgen* (Lübeck: privately published, 1898), pp. 137–39; following pp. 208, I–XVIII. Gabriel Riesser's contribution was initially published as "Einiges zur Entgegnung auf den Aufsatz Juden und Dünste," in No. 44–46 der *N.L.Bl.* vom Jahre 1841," *Neue Lübeckische Blätter,* January 2, 1842.

26. Barnard Van Oven, M.D., *Ought Baron Rothschild to Sit in Parliament? An Imaginary Conversation between Judaeus and Amicus Nobilis,* 2nd ed. (London: Effingham Wilson, 1848), p. 15.

27. Gerson Wolf, *Die Juden in der Leopoldstadt im 17. Jahrhundert in Wien* (Vienna: Herzfeld & Bauer, 1864), pp. 97–99.

28. L. Gordon Rylands, *Crime: Its Causes and Remedy* (London: T. F. Unwin, 1889), p. 76; Michael Berkowitz, "Jews, Crime, and Criminology: From Enrico Ferri to Sir Leon Radzinowicz; from Simone Luzzatto to Cesare Lombroso; from Moses Mendelssohn to Eduard Gans to Karl Marx; or: Was Lombroso Really an Ass?" paper presented at the European Association for Jewish Studies conference, Amsterdam, July 21, 2002; Gerson Wolf, *Geschichte der Israelitischen Cultusgemeinde in Wien 1820–1860* (Vienna: Wilhelm Braumüller, 1861), p. 189.

29. Ruth R. Wisse, "Introduction to Romance of a Horse Thief," in *A Shtetl and Other Yiddish Novellas,* ed. and trans. Ruth R. Wisse (Detroit: Wayne State University Press, 1986), p. 143.

30. Joseph Opatoshu, "Romance of a Horse Thief," pp. 150, 151.

31. Sigmund Freud, quoted in *Forms of Prayer for Jewish Worship, III: Prayers for the High Holidays,* ed. Assembly of Rabbis of the Reform Synagogues of Great Britain, 8th ed. (London: 1985), p. 450.

32. Hartner-Hnizdo, *Volk der Gauner,* pp. 71–72. See Eric A. Johnson, *Urbanization and Crime: Germany 1871–1914* (Cambridge: Cambridge University Press, 1995), pp. 8, 76–95.

33. Yitzhak Melamed, "Leaving the Wound Visible: Hegel and Marx on the Rabble and the Problem of Poverty in Modern Society," *Iyyun* 50, no. 1 (2001): 23–39; Norbert Waszek, "Eduard Gans on Poverty: Between Hegel and Saint-Simon," *Owl of Minerva* 18, no. 2 (1987): 167–78; Shlomo Avineri, "The Hegelian Origins of Marx's Political Thought," *Review of Metaphysics* 21, no. 1 (1967): 33–56; "Feature Book Review: The Discovery of Hegel's Early Lectures on the Philosophy of Right," *Owl of Minerva* 16, no. 2 (1985): 199–208.

34. Heinrich Heine, "Der Apollogott," in *Sämtliche Schriften,* ed. Klaus Briegleb et al. (Munich: Hanser, 1976), vol. VI, part 1, p. 32.

35. Otto Ulbricht, "Criminality and Punishment of the Jews in the Early Modern Period," in *In and Out of the Ghetto: Jewish-Gentile Relations in Late Medieval and Early Modern Germany*, ed. R. Po-chia Hsia and Hartmut Lehmann (Washington and Cambridge: German Historical Institute and Cambridge University Press, 1995, p. 70). See Herbert Reinke, "Kriminalität als 'zweite Wirklichkeit' von Tätigkeitsnachweisen der Justizverwaltung. Bemerkungen zu Kriminalstatistiken des 19. Jahrhunderts als Materialien einer historisch orientierten Kriminologie," in *Unrecht und Rebellion. Zur Sozialgeschichte der Kriminalität und des Strafrechts*, 2. Beiheft der Zeitschrift *Kriminologisches Journal* (1992): 176–84; Reinke, "Die 'Liaison' des Strafrechts mit der Statistik. Zu den Anfängen kriminalistischer Zählungen im 18. und 19. Jahrhundert," in *Zeitschrift für Neuere Rechtsgeschichte/ZNR* 12 (1990): 169–79.

36. See Gareth Stedman Jones, introduction to Karl Marx and Friedrich Engels, *The Communist Manifesto* (London: Penguin, 2002).

37. This appears in the unedited manuscript *Theorien über den Mehrwert*, sometimes referred to as the fourth volume of *Kapital*, which Marx wrote between January 1862 and July 1863. The material was first published by Kautsky in a controversial edition between 1905 and 1910. The most easily accessible edition is *Karl Marx, Friedrich Engels, Werke*, vol. 26, part 1 (Berlin: Dietz, 1956), pp. 363–64. The translation follows *Karl Marx, Friedrich Engels, Collected Works* (Moscow: Progress Publishers, with New York: International International, and London: Lawrence & Wishart, 1975), pp. 306–10. See also Francis Wheen, *Karl Marx* (London: Fourth Estate, 1999), pp. 308–09.

38. Quoted in Francis Wheen, *Karl Marx* (London: Fourth Estate, 1999), pp. 308–9.

39. Karl Marx, "Theses on Feurbach, VIII," in *The Marx-Engels Reader*, ed. Robert C. Tucker (New York: W. W. Norton, 1972), p. 109; Wheen, *Karl Marx*, p. 309.

40. See Sander Gilman, *Jewish Self-Hatred: Anti-Semitism and the Hidden Language of the Jews* (Baltimore: Johns Hopkins University Press, 1986).

41. Friedrich Schiller, "The Robbers," act 1, scene 2, trans. F. J. Lamport, in *The Robbers and Wallenstein* (London: Penguin, 1979), p. 41.

42. Ivan Kalmar, *The Trotskys, Freuds and Woody Allens: Portrait of a Culture* (Toronto: Penguin, 1994), pp. 187–88.

43. For example, in their depiction of leftist extremists, the Nazis identified Leon Franz Czolgosz, the assassin of President William McKinley as Jewish, along with other non-Jewish figures; Keller and Andersen, *Der Jude als Verbrecher*, pp. 158–210.

44. See Michael Berkowitz, *The Jewish Self-Image: American and British Perspectives, 1881–1939* (London: Reaktion, 2000), pp. 94–102.

45. Carl Philipp Theodor Schwencken, *Aktenmässige Nachrichten von dem Gauner-und-Vagabunden = Gesindel sowie von einzelnen professionirten Dieben, in*

den *Ländern zwischen dem Rhein und der Elbe, nebst genauer Beschreibung ihrer Person von einem kurhessischen Criminal-Beamten* [Cassel, 1822] (Leipzig: Zentralantiquariat der DDR, Ausgabe für Kriminalistik Verlag, Heidelberg, 1981), pp. 1–11, 71; Friedrich Christian Benedict Avé-Lallemant, *Das deutsche Gaunerthum in seiner social-politischen, literarischen und linguistischen Ausbildung zu seinem heutigen Bestande* (Leipzig: F. A. Brockhaus, 1858), pp. viii, 14; Avé-Lallemant, *Physiologie der deutschen Polizei* (Leipzig: F. A. Brockhaus, 1882), pp. 4–42, 45, 170–74, 184–202, 258–71; Avé-Lallemant, *Die Mersener Bockreiter des 18. und 19. Jahrhunderts: Ergänzender Beitrag zur Geschichte des Deutschen Gaunerthums* (Leipzig: Brockhaus, 1880), pp. 132–33.

46. Avé-Lallemant, *Physiologie der deutschen Polizei,* p. 46; Hartner-Hnizdo, *Volk der Gauner,* pp. 11ff.

47. Avé-Lallemant, *Das deutsche Gaunerthum,* p. xvi. Sander Gilman, *Jewish Self-hatred: Anti-semitism and the Hidden Language of the Jews* (Baltimore: Johns Hopkins University Press, 1986), pp. 60–72.

48. Anti-Semites were not shy about exposing *Kriminalstatistik* as a euphemism; see Hartner-Hnizdo, *Volk der Gauner,* pp. 15–16; Keller and Andersen, *Der Jude als Verbrecher,* pp. 9–24, 29–36. Scores of books and pamphlets exist focusing on alleged Jewish criminality; see, for example, Theodor Fritsch, ed., *Handbuch der Judenfrage. Eine Zusammenstellung des wichtigsten Materials zur Beurteilung des jüdischen Volkes* (Hamburg: Sleipner-Verlag, 1919); Eugen Dühring, *Der Ersatz der Religion durch Vollkommeneres. Und die Ausscheidung alles Judenthums durch den modernen Völkergeist* (Karlsruhe: H. Reuther, 1883); Heinrich Lux, *Die Juden als Verbrecher. Eine Beleuchtung antisemitischer Beweisführung* (Munich: M. Ernst, 1893).

49. Johnson, *Urbanization and Crime,* p. 201; see Ludwig Fuld, *Das jüdische Verbrecherthum. Eine Studie über den Zusammenhang zwischen Religion und Kriminalität* (Leipzig: T. Huth, 1885). For example, for such a debate in the Netherlands, see Jacob Israël de Haan, "Naar aanleiding van eene crimineele statistiek van de Joden," *Tijdschrift voor Strafrecht,* XXI (1910), offprint in the Universiteit van Amsterdam library archives.

50. See Alan Steinweis on the distortion of the Talmud in Nazi anti-Semitism, *Studying the Jew: Scholarly Antisemitism in Nazi Germany* (Cambridge, MA: Harvard University Press, 2006).

51. Franz von Liszt, *Das Problem der Kriminalität der Juden* (Giessen: Alfred Töpelmann, 1907).

52. Heinrich Lux, *Die Juden als Verbrecher. Eine Beleuchtung antisemitischer Beweisführung* (Munich: M. Ernst, 1893).

53. Franz Lütgenau, *Die Judenfrage ökonomisch und ethisch* (Berlin: Dümmlers Verlagsbuchhandlung, 1893); W. Giese, *Die Juden und die deutsche Kriminalstatistik* (Leipzig: Verlag von F. W. Grunow, 1893).

54. Steinweis, *Studying the Jew,* pp. 308–18.

55. Samuel Löwenfeld, *Die Wahrheit über der Juden Antheil am Verbrechen. Auf Grund amtlicher Statistik* (Berlin: Verlage der Stuhr'schen Buchhandlung, 1881).

56. Karpel Lippe, *Die Gesetzsammlung des Judenspiegels zusammengestellt und gefälscht von Aron Briman Pseudodoctor Justus. Beleuchtet und Berichtight von K. Lippe* (Jassy: H. Goldner, 1885); Gottlieb Klein, *Zur "Judenfrage": Unsere Anforderungen an das Christenthum des Herrn Stöcker* (Zurich: Verlags-Magazin, 1880); *Antisemiten-Spiegel: Die Antisemiten im Lichte des Christenthums, des Rechtes und der Wissenschaft* (Danzig: A. W. Kafemann, 1900); Paul Nathans, *Die Kriminalität der Juden in Deutschland* (Berlin: Verlag Siegfried Cronbach, 1896); Paul Fiebig, *Juden und Nichtjuden: Erläuterungen zu Th. Fritschs Handbuch der Judenfrage* (28. Aufl.) (Leipzig: Dörffling & Franke, 1921); Ludwig Jacobowski, *Der Juden Anteil am Verbrechen: nach amtlichen Quellen dargestellt* (Berlin: Max Hoffschläger, 1892), Vorbemerkung. Jacobowski was also a Yiddish novelist.

57. *Antisemiten-Spiegel*; J. S. Bloch, *Gegen die Anti-Semiten* (Vienna: D. Löwy, 1882).

58. Rudolf Wassermann, *Beruf, Konfession und Verbrechen. Eine Studie über die Kriminalität der Juden in Vergangenheit und Gegenwart* (Munich: E. Reinhardt, 1907). The author, although dismissive of the charge of disproportionate Jewish criminality, strongly dissents from the views of Zionist Arthur Ruppin (p. 6). At the beginning of his article he lists his selection of the major works in the field, covering dozens of articles and pamphlets (pp. 5–8). There appears to be another "Rudolf Wassermann" who wrote on similar subjects at a slightly later date.

59. See Michael Berkowitz, "Herzl and the Stock Exchange," in *Theodor Herzl: Visionary of the Jewish State*, ed. Gideon Shimoni and Robert Wistrich (Jerusalem: Hebrew University Magnes Press and New York: Herzl Press, 1999), pp. 99–111.

60. Hugo Hoppe, *Alkohol und Kriminalität in allen ihren Beziehungen* (Wiesbaden: J. F. Bergmann, 1906). I thank John Efron for this reference.

61. John M. Efron, *Medicine and the German Jews: A History* (New Haven: Yale University Press, 2001).

62. Leon Radzinowicz, *Adventures in Criminology* (New York: Routledge, 1999), p. 76.

63. Derek J. Penslar, *Shylock's Children: Economics and Jewish Identity in Modern Europe* (Berkeley: University of California Press, 2001), pp. 19–36.

64. Joseph Roth, *The Wandering Jews,* trans. Michael Hofmann (New York: W. W. Norton, 2001), p. 2, originally published in German in 1937; Walter Lohmann, "Das Berliner Ghetto 1918," *Mitteilungen über die Judenfrage,* published by the Institut zum Studium der Judenfrage (originally in Berlin), June 16, 1938, pp. 1–2, followed by an unattributed article, "Wie sie Berlin eroberten," pp. 2–3. This journal (hereafter *Die Judenfrage)* was the Nazi publication exclusively focused on the Jews, from which hundreds, perhaps thousands, of articles in the Nazi press were derived.

65. Penslar, *Shylock's Children*, p. 21; Johnson, *Urbanization and Crime*, p. 82n.

66. Gerald D. Feldman, *The Great Disorder: Politics, Economics, and Society in the German Inflation, 1914–1924* (New York: Oxford University Press, 1994), pp. 61–62. On how this played out in two German cities see Anthony Kauders, *German Politics and the Jews: Düsseldorf and Nuremberg, 1910–1933* (Oxford: Clarendon Press, 1996), pp. 126–27, 130–36, 144–51, 160.

67. Feldman, *The Great Disorder*, pp. 201–2; David G. Roskies, *Against the Apocalypse: Responses to Catastrophe in Modern Jewish Culture* (Cambridge, MA: Harvard University Press, 1984), pp. 110, 116–26.

68. Feldman, *The Great Disorder*, p. 202.

69. Ibid., p. 843.

70. See Karl Radek, *Die Barmat-Sozialdemokratie* (Hamburg: C. Hoym Nachf., 1925). This pamphlet is cited in Ernst Nolte's controversial book *Der europäische Bürgerkrieg 1917–1945* (Munich: Herbig, 2000), p. 185.

71. Erich Eyck, *A History of the Weimar Republic*, trans. Harlan Hanson and Robert Waite (Cambridge, MA: Harvard University Press, 1967), pp. 326–28.

72. For a totally "[anti-]Jewish interpretation," including the Zionist artist Hermann Struck as a leading culprit, see Ludwig F. Gengler, "Die deutschen Juden und das Versailler Diktat. Stimmungsmache und Umfall auf jüdischen Befehl," *Die Judenfrage*, June 8, 1939, pp. 8–10.

73. Koppel Pinson, *Modern Germany: Its History and Civilization*, 2nd ed. (New York: Macmillan, 1966), pp. 344–45; Hartner-Hnizdo, *Volk der Gauner*, pp. 71–72. Important scholarly treatments include Martin Geyer, "Die Sprache des Rechts, die Sprache des Antisemitismus. 'Wucher' und soziale Ordnungsvorstellungen im Kaiserreich und der Weimarer Republik," in *Europäische Sozialgeschichte: Festschrift für Wolfgang Schieder*, ed. Christof Dipper, Luz Klinkhammer, and Alexander Nützenadel (Berlin: Duncker & Humblot, 2000), pp. 413–30; Feldman, *The Great Disorder*, pp. 61–62; 201–2.

74. Harold James, *The Nazi Dictatorship and the Deutsche Bank* (Cambridge: Cambridge University Press, 2004), pp. 6–7.

75. Eyck, *History of the Weimar Republic*, p. 328.

76. Ibid., pp. 328–29.

77. Hans Mommsen, *The Rise and Fall of Weimar Democracy*, trans. Elborg Foster and Larry Jones (Chapel Hill: University of North Carolina Press, 1996), p. 235. Nowhere is this more apparent than in the copious files of Walter Lütgebrune, which comprise over ten rolls of microfilm in the Berlin Documents Collection; see T-253, Berlin Documents Collection, United States National Archives, College Park, MD (hereafter BDC, NA).

78. Hartner-Hnizdo, *Volk der Gauner*, p. 71; a similar list with slight modifications can be found in Institut zum Studium der Judenfrage, *Die Juden in Deutschland* (Munich: Verlag Franz-Eher, 1936), pp. 57ff. This list is cannibalized on a number of twenty-first century anti-Semitic web sites; see, for example,

www.ety.com/berlin/korrupt1.htm, www.louisbeam.com/heinz2.htm, abbc .com/berlin/rosenb08.htm (accessed September 1998), www.vho.org/D/pj/7.html.

79. Kurt Vogtherr, "Das Judenporträt. Michael Holzmann. Internationale Geschäfte mit Waffen und Geld," *Die Judenfrage,* April 6, 1939, pp. 4–5; "Gift für die Völker: Der Rauschgiftschmuggel—eine jüdische Domäne," *Die Judenfrage,* August 4, 1938, p. 1–5 (the famous French case of "Stavitski" is added here); G. E. Daun, "Jüdische Falschspieler. Der Schuldschein des Staatssekretärs—Es geht die Polizei nichts an . . . ," *Die Judenfrage,* December 1, 1938, p. 5.

80. "Das Judenporträt. Isaak Liefer. Oberrabbiner und Rauschgiftschmuggler," *Die Judenfrage,* September 1, 1938, p. 5. Liefer identified himself as "a grand rabbi of Brooklyn." He was, in fact, convicted of smuggling narcotics to the United States; see "Ex-rabbi Loses Appeal: Isaac Liefer must serve French Sentence as a Smuggler," *New York Times,* January 31, 1940, p. 7.

81. Pinson, *Modern Germany,* p. 415.

82. See the description in Ben Barkow, *Testaments to the Holocaust: Series One: Archives of the Wiener Library, London,* www.osa.ceu.hu/library/special_ collections/Holocaust/testament.pdf + Semi-K%C3%BCrschner&hl = en&ie = UTF-8, p. 12; Friedrich Grimm, M.d.R., "Prozesse als Mittel der Propaganda," *Die Judenfrage,* February 1, 1937, p. 2.

83. "Jüdischer Märtyrer-Schwindel. Einen Staat für einen Kopf—Mischung von Verbrechen und politischer Berechnung," *Die Judenfrage,* August 18, 1938, pp. 1–2.

84. Donald Niewyk, *The Jews in Weimar Germany* (Baton Rouge: Louisiana State University Press, 1980), p. 77; for such pictures and thumbnail sketches, see, for example, the year-by-year chronology in Johann von Leers, *14 Jahre Judenrepublik. Die Geschichte eines Rassenkampfes* (Berlin: NG, 1933); Alfred Rosenberg, *Novemberköpfe* (Munich: Zentralverlag der NSDAP, 1939).

85. L. F. Gengler, "Jüdische Räteregierung 1919 in München. Tatsachen und Kundgebungen vor 20 Jahren," *Die Judenfrage,* May 11, 1939, pp. 5–6.

86. Johann von Leers, *Juden sehen Dich an* (Berlin-Schöneberg: NS.-Druck und Verlag, 1933).

87. W/S no. 30642, CD no. 0238, from Deutsches Historisches Museum, United States Holocaust Memorial Museum (hereafter USHMM). Fritz Redlin, "Das Judenporträt: Bernard M. Baruch," *Die Judenfrage,* November 1, 1938, p. 9.

88. K. V., "Das Judenporträt: Dr. Fritz Mannheimer. Börsenjobber und Baissespeculant," *Die Judenfrage,* April 19, 1939, pp. 5–6.

89. See www.dhm.de/lemo/objekte/pict/ba108964: "Einlieferung von Regimegegnern in das KZ Oranienburg"; see also Gerhart Seger, *A Nation Terrorized* (Chicago: Reilly & Lee, 1935), pp. 105–7.

90. Ibid., pp. 77–78, 107.

91. Cited in Z. A. B. Zeman, *Nazi Propaganda* (London: Oxford University Press, 1966), p. 23, from the *Sammlung F. J. Rehse Archiv fur Zeitgeschichte und Publizistik* (now the NSDAP-Parteiarchiv in Munich), p. 221.

92. G. E. Daun, "Jüdische Falschpieler," p. 5.

93. Helmut von Wilucki, "Tested Methods of Modern Proganda," from Gustav Straebe, "Bewährte moderne Propagandamethoden," *Unser Wille und Weg* 2 (1932): 230–33, available at www.calvin.edu/academic/cas/gpa/wilweg02.htm.

94. Entry for "Sklarek" in *Grosse Jüdische National Biographie,* ed. S. Wininger (Czernowitz: Orient, 1931), p. 548.

95. Vogtherr, "Das Judenporträt. Michael Holzmann," pp. 4–5.

96. Ibid., p. 5, cf. n 97 (earlier edition). Among the charges against Holzmann was that he had deceitfully sold a large number of gas masks to the Dutch, claiming that the masks were necessary for their civil defense.

97. Entry for "Ivan Kutisker" in *Semi-Kürschner,* vol. III, pp. 838–39. *Sigilla Veri (Philip Stauf's Semi-Kürschner.) Lexikon der Juden, -Genossen und Gegner aller Zeiten und Zonen, insbesondere Deutschlands, der Lehren, Gebräuche, Kunstgriffe und Statistiken der Juden sowie ihrer Gaunersprache, Trugnamen, Geheimbünde usw.* 2nd edition, ed. E. Ekkehard (Erfurt: Bodung Verlag, 1929–31). *Semi-Kürschner oder literarisches Lexikon der Schriftseller, Dichter, Bankiers, Geldleute, Ärzte, Schauspieler, Künstler, Musiker, Offiziere, Rechtsanwälte, Revolutionäre, Frauenrechtlerinnen, Sozialdemokraten usw. jüdischer Rasse und Versippung* (Berlin: self-published, 1913).

98. Keller and Andersen, *Der Jude als Verbrecher,* unpaginated section.

99. Entry for "Camillo Castiglioni" in *Semi-Kürschner,* vol. I, pp. 975–79.

100. Hannah Arendt, *Antisemitism* (New York: Harcourt, Brace & World, 1968), pp. 90–95.

101. Entry for "Jakob Michael" in *Semi-Kürschner,* vol. IV, p. 551; Sincton Upclair (pseud.), *Der Rattenkönig. Revolutions-Schieber und ihre Helfer . . . Die Wahrheit über den Fall Sklarz* (Berlin: F. Warthemann, 1920).

102. Leers, *14 Jahre Judenrepublik,* p. 57.

103. V. I. Lenin described Helphand as "the gifted German journalist who writes under the pseudonym of Parvus": review of Parvus, *The World Market and the Agricultural Crisis: Economic Essays,* trans. from German into Russian by "L. Y." (St. Petersburg: Educational Library, 1898), available in the online site of Lenin's *Collected Works:* www.marxists.org/archive/lenin/works/1899/feb/parvus .htm.

104. Z. A. B. Zeman and W. B. Scharlau, *The Merchant of Revolution: The Life of Alexander Israel Helphand (Parvus), 1867–1924* (New York: Oxford University Press, 1965).

105. Assessment of Lars Fischer, unpublished seminar presentation "(Chronology), Alexander Israel Helphand (Parvus), The Russian Revolution and Civil War, 1917–1921," Queen Mary and Westfield College, University of London, December 3, 1998; cf. the much more rosy picture in Kalmar, *The Trotskys, Freuds, and Woody Allens,* p. 210. My colleague John Klier enlightened me about Parvus in the Soviet and post-Soviet contexts.

106. Leers, *14 Jahre Judenrepublik*, pp. 50–53.

107. Siegmund Kaznelson, ed., *Juden im Deutschen Kulturbereich. Ein Sammelwerk* (Berlin: Jüdischer Verlag, 1959), p. 782; entry for "Duriex, Tilla," in *International Biographical Dictionary of Central European Émigrés 1933–1945*, vol. II/part 1: *A–K: The Arts, Sciences, and Literature*, ed. Herbert A. Strauss and Werner Röder et al. (Munich: K. G. Saur, 1983), pp. 230–31.

108. Niewyk, *Jews in Weimar Germany*, p. 77; see Alfred Wiener, "Müssen wir 'abrücken'?" *Central-Verein Zeitung*, February 7, 1925; Otto Nuschke, "Das Untersuchungsergebnis des Barmat-Ausschusses," *Central-Verein Zeitung*, October 23, 1925; Werner Rosenberg, "Der Schutzherr der Sklareks," *Central-Verein Zeitung*, November 15, 1929.

109. Paul Ufermann, *Könige der Inflation* (Berlin: Verlag für Sozialwissenschaft, 1924).

110. Pinson, *Modern Germany*, p. 415.

111. Feldman, *The Great Disorder*, p. 203.

112. Upclair, *Der Rattenkönig*, p. 4.

113. Hartner-Hnizdo, *Volk der Gauner*.

114. The literature on the ingrained anti-Semitism in German society is immense. Among the most insightful analyses are Shulamit Volkov, "Antisemitism as a Cultural Code: Reflections on the History and Historiography of Antisemitism in Imperial Germany," *Year Book of the Leo Baeck Institute*, 23 (1978): 25–46; George L. Mosse, *The Crisis of German Ideology: Intellectual Origins of the Third Reich* (New York: Grosset and Dunlap, 1964). For Nazi rationalizations to the German public, see Slavoj Žižek, *The Sublime Object of Ideology* (London: Verso, 1999) p. 49. On the realities of Jews and their purported financial crimes, see Feldman, *The Great Disorder*, pp. 61–62, 200–203, 314–15, 844.

115. Kauders, *German Politics and the Jews*, p. 19.

116. Johann von Leers, "Die hebräische Sprache als Grundlage der Gaunersprache der europäischen Völker," *Die Judenfrage*, June 2, 1937, pp. 2–6; filmstrip image, "Verbrecher-Jude d. 18. Jhrhrt.," from "Judentum, Freimaurerei und Bolschewismus" (reproductions of frames), W/S no. 7612, CD no. 0153, USHMM.

2. THE CONSTRUCTION OF "JEWISH CRIMINALITY" IN NAZI GERMANY

1. Slavoj Žižek, *The Sublime Object of Ideology* (London: Verso, 1999), pp. 48, 49.

2. Ibid., p. 125.

3. Wolf Meyer-Christian, "Die Behandlung der Judenfrage in der deutschen Presse," June 1944, Record Group (hereafter RG) 215, G-117, box 6, Berlin Document Collection, YIVO Institute for Jewish Research; (hereafter B-C, YIVO); see ch. 5 of this book.

4. Speech by Hitler, German press, November 10/11, 1940, quoted in Raul Hilberg, *Prologue to Annihilation: A Study of the Identification, Impoverishment and Isolation of the Jewish Victims of Nazi Policy* (Ph.D. thesis, New York: Columbia University, 1955), p. 29.

5. Johann von Leers, "Die hebräische Sprache als Grundlage der Gaunersprache der europäischen Völker," *Mitteilungen Über die Judenfrage* (hereafter *Die Judenfrage*), June 2, 1937, pp. 2–6.

6. Hilberg, *Prologue to Annihilation,* p. 30.

7. Ibid., pp. 340–41.

8. W/S no. 32662, CD no. 0248, from the Deutsches historisches Museum, United States Holocaust Memorial Museum (hereafter USHMM).

9. See Alan E. Steinweis, *Studying the Jew: Scholarly Antisemitism in Nazi Germany* (Cambridge, MA: Harvard University Press, 2006).

10. Letter from Ludwig Schupp to Daluege, Berlin, July 22, 1935; letter, August 7, 1935, from the Polizeipräsident in Aachen—not able to confirm that Diamond is Jewish, but he is a member of a Freemason lodge; last correspondence relates news from German consulate in New York that Capone is "American-Italian"; letter from Washington, January 4, 1936, RG 215, G-65, B-C, YIVO.

11. J. Keller and Hanns Andersen, *Der Jude als Verbrecher* (Berlin and Leipzig: Nibelungen-Verlag, 1937), pp. 160–65; Johann von Leers, *Die Verbrechernatur der Juden* (Berlin: Hochmuth, 1944), pp. 142–48; Michael Berkowitz, "Crime and Redemption? American Jewish Gangsters, Violence, and the Fight Against Nazism," in *Studies in Contemporary Jewry* 18, ed. Peter Medding (New York: Oxford University Press, 2002), pp. 95–108. One of the most explicit Nazi discussions of American Jewish criminals—including the claim that Al Capone was a Jew—is in Johann von Leers, *Kräfte hinter Roosevelt* (Berlin-Steglitz: Theodor Fritsch Verlag, 1941), pp. 59–75. Leers's interpretation that these crooks comprised part of the "power behind Roosevelt," as well as served the interests of communism, required the full power of his active imagination.

12. Richard Wetzell, *Inventing the Criminal: A History of German Criminology, 1880–1945* (Chapel Hill: University of North Carolina Press, 2000).

13. Steinweis, *Studying the Jew,* pp. 308–18.

14. Victor Klemperer, *I Shall Bear Witness: The Diaries of Victor Klemperer 1933–1941,* trans. Martin Chalmers (London: Weidenfeld and Nicolson, 1998), p. 381.

15. Folder 63, B-C, YIVO; see Hilberg, *Prologue to Annihilation,* pp. 273–74.

16. Harry Richard Loewenberg, "Homeless in Exile: Days of Persecution in Fall and Winter, 1938–1939," RG-02.061*01, p. 11, USHMM.

17. Hermann Leyes, "Under the Nazi Regime, 1933–1938," RG-02.203, Acc. 1994.A351, UHSMM, p. 29.

18. Anna and Leo Bluethe, "Letters concerning *Kristallnacht* in Kaiserslautern, Germany, 1939," Survivor testimonies, RG-02.099, USHMM.

19. Klemperer, *I Shall Bear Witness,* p. 380.

20. Anna and Leo Bluethe, "Letters," pp. 2, 5.

21. Nikolaus Wachsmann, *Hitler's Prisons: Legal Terror in Nazi Germany* (New Haven: Yale University Press, 2004), p. 188.

22. Lucille Eichengreen, *From Ashes to Life: My Memories of the Holocaust* (San Francisco: Mercury House, 1994), p. 26; Charlotte Kahane, "In the Safety of the Third Reich," RG-02.181, USHMM, pp. 70–73. This book's title is a quotation from Kahane, p. 71.

23. Kahane, "In the Safety of the Third Reich," pp. 70–71.

24. Victor Gans, "Memoir," RG-02.092; Acc. 1994.A.064, p. 43, USHMM.

25. Hsi-Huey Liang, *The Rise of the Modern Police and the European State System from Metternich to the Second World War* (Cambridge: Cambridge University Press, 1992), p. 252.

26. Hilberg, *Prologue to Annihilation,* pp. 203–11, 228–30.

27. Leyes, "Under the Nazi Regime, 1933–1938," pp. 26–27.

28. Kahane, "In the Safety of the Third Reich," p. 24; see also Mojsze Kisielnicki, "Mojsze Kisielnicki memoir relating to the Judenrat in Kaluszyn," Poland, RG-02.067*01, pp. 3–4, 6–8, USHMM.

29. Loewenberg, "Homeless in Exile," pp. 21–22.

30. Hilberg, *Prologue to Annihilation,* p. 208.

31. E. S. [?], "Kennzeichen für jüdische Geschäfte. Die dritte Verordnung zum Reichsbürgergesetz schafft eine öffentliche Liste aller jüdischen Gewerbebetriebe," *Die Judenfrage,* June 23, 1938, p. 5; Klaus Szameitat, "Das Ende des jüdischen Advokaten. Zahlen über die Verjudung des Rechtsanwaltsstandes 1933–1938," *Die Judenfrage,* December 22, 1938; Klaus Szameitat, "Verbrechen gegen das Volk," *Die Judenfrage,* February 2, 1939, pp. 5–6; Martin Dean, "The Development and Implementation of Nazi Denaturalization and Confiscation Policy up to the Eleventh Decree to the Reich Citizenship Law," *Holocaust and Genocide Studies* 16, no. 2 (fall 2002): 217–42.

32. Gans, "Memoir," p. 15.

33. Hilberg, *Prologue to Annihilation,* pp. 214, 221.

34. Fred Angress, "Survival in the Lion's Den," as told to Ursula Angress (1989), RG-02.019, p. 7, USHMM.

35. Hilberg, *Prologue to Annihilation,* p. 178; Keller and Andersen, *Der Jude als Verbrecher,* pp. 25–37.

36. "Devisenschieber. Leo Israel Fabian aus Königsberg," *Preussische Zeitung,* Königsberg, January 31, 1939, RG 222, folder 64, B-C, YIVO.

37. Unattributed article, "Getreidespekulation als jüdisches Druckmittel. Jugoslawien wehrt einen Anschlag auf seine Wirtschaftspolitik ab," *Die Judenfrage,* June 30, 1938, p. 3; Gustav Erich Daun, "Geschäfte mit dem Hunger der Völker.

Die Verjudung des internationalen Getreidehandels," *Die Judenfrage,* March 30, 1939, pp. 1–2.

38. E. Stein, "Jüdische Sabotage in Ungarn," *Die Judenfrage,* October 13, 1938, p. 10.

39. Kurt Vogtherr, "Hollands Abwehrkraft. Im Kampf gegen Verleumdung, Terror und Brotraub," *Die Judenfrage,* March 21, 1939, pp. 5–6.

40. Nathan Stoltzfus, *Resistance of the Heart: Intermarriage and the Rosenstrasse Protest in Nazi Germany* (New York: Norton, 1986), pp. vii, xv. Hilberg, *Prologue to Annihilation,* pp. 247, 248.

41. "Talmudgesichter blicken Dich an," RG 222, folder 64, B-C, YIVO. See Russell Lemmons, *Goebbels and Der Angriff* (Lexington: University of Kentucky Press, 1994); Oron Hale, *The Captive Press in the Third Reich* (Princeton, NJ: Princeton University Press, 1964); Lucjan Dobroszycki, *Reptile Journalism: The Official Polish-Language Press under the Nazis, 1939–1945,* trans. Barbara Harshav (New Haven: Yale University Press, 1994); "Das ist er! Der Schmugglerkönig Jud Leuchttag (Zu unserem Artikel in der Ausgabe 20 d.J)," RG 222, folder 64, B-C, YIVO.

42. Article about Louis "Israel" Lübeck, RG 222, folder 64, B-C, YIVO; cf. Hsi-Huey Liang, *The Rise of the Modern Police,* pp. 252–76; Robert G. Waite, "Judentum und Kriminalitaet: Rassistische Deutungen in kriminologischen Publikationen 1933–1945," in *Rassismus, Faschismus, Antifaschismus: Forschungen und Betrachtungen* (Gewidmet Kurt Paetzold zum 70. Geburtstag), ed. Manfred Weissbecker und Reinhard Kühnl (Cologne: PapyRossa, 2000), pp. 46–62. See also James Harris, *The People Speak! Anti-Semitism and Emancipation in Nineteenth-Century Bavaria* (Ann Arbor: University of Michigan Press, 1994), who argues that racism did not play much of a role in midcentury Bavaria, where more traditional forms of hatred were nevertheless in force.

43. "Jüdische Kriminelle—Berlin 1938," (attributed to "Zinn"), *Die Judenfrage,* November 1, 1938, pp. 11–12.

44. Leyes, "Under the Nazi Regime, 1933–1938," pp. 26–27.

45. In the case of Weimar, Düsseldorf, and Nuremberg, in comparison, Anthony Kauders argues that "anti-Semitism was seldom linked to individual Jews"; see his *German Politics and the Jews: Düsseldorf and Nuremberg, 1910–1933* (Oxford: Clarendon Press, 1996), p. 12.

46. Keller and Andersen, *Der Jude als Verbrecher,* pp. 25–37; Eric A. Johnson, *Urbanization and Crime: Germany 1871–1914* (Cambridge: Cambridge University Press, 1995), pp. 3–4; Raphael Gross, *Carl Schmitt und die Juden: eine Deutsche Rechtslehre* (Frankfurt a.M.: Suhrkamp, 2000); Patrick Wagner, *Hitlers Kriminalisten: die deutsche Kriminalpolizei und der Nationalsozialismus zwischen 1920 und 1960* (Munich: C. H. Beck, 2002).

47. Szameitat, "Das Ende des jüdischen Advokaten," and Willy Zimmermann, "Der jüdische Verbrecherkult. Auflösung der völkischen Ordnung durch Zersetzung des Strafrechts," *Die Judenfrage,* December 22, 1938, pp. 10–12; Klee,

"Das Judentum im Strafrecht," p. 12; see book review, "Jüdisches im Recht," a review of a journal, *Judentum und Recht*, ed. Hermann Schroer, and pamphlet by Hans Seidel, "Unter jüdischer Pfandknechtschaft" (Munich: Eher, 1938), *Die Judenfrage*, January 19, 1939, p. 11.

48. Seidel, "Unter jüdischer Pfandknechtschaft"; Szameitat, "Das Ende des jüdischen Advokaten"; and Willy Zimmermann, "Der jüdische Verbrecherkult," pp. 10–12. Among those denounced are Max Alsberg, Magnus Hirschfeld, Arnold Freymuth, Emil Julius Gumbel, Alfred Kantorowicz, Moritz Liepmann, and Johannes Werthauer. As one of his authorities Zimmermann holds up "Dr. Klee," author of an article "Das Judentum im Strafrecht," p. 12 of this issue; see book review, "Jüdisches im Recht."

49. Herwig Hartner-Hnizdo, *Volk der Gauner: eine Untersuchung des jüdischen Gaunertums* (Munich: Hoheneichen-Verlag, 1939), pp. 41–43, 49, 51.

50. Gans, "Memoir," pp. 10, 15; Memoir of Cilia Borenstein, RG-02.002*15, p. 2, USHMM. These are two of over one hundred examples.

51. Article with picture of Alfred "Israel" Reichmann from Berlin-Charlottenburg: he had attempted to help other Jews escape across the border, RG 22, folder 64, B-C, YIVO.

52. Anita Boyko Fox testimony, Survivor testimonies, RG-02.090, p. 5, USHMM.

53. Hilberg, *Prologue to Annihilation*, p. 69.

54. Quoted in Helmut Eschwege, ed., *Kennzeichen J: Bilder, Dokumente, Berichte zur Geschichte der Verbrechen des Hitlerfaschismus an den deutschen Juden 1933–1945* (Berlin: Deutscher Verlag der Wissenschaften, 1981), p. 159.

55. W/S no. 32663, CD no. 0248, from Deutsches Historisches Museum, USHMM.

56. RG 222, folders 53, 59, 60, B-C, YIVO: correspondence from Magdeburg, June 12, 1939, Staatliche Kriminalpolizei to *Der Stürmer* in Nuremberg-A.

57. Memo dated May 8, 1936, concerning "Ermittlung von Aktenmaterial, das Beweise für eine landesverräterische Betätigung von Juden erbringt"; letter from NSDAP Reichsleitung, Reichsrechtsamt, April 24, 1936; request from Hauptarchiv, NSDAP, Munich, April 8, 1936. The most "substantial" proof, apparently, was well-known instances of Jewish communists; see report from Unterabteilung II 1, Berlin, May 6, 1936; Reichssicherheitshauptamt (RSHA)–SD, Berlin (Osobyi fond 500) (Main State Security of Germany–SD, Berlin [manuscript RG-11.001M.01], reel 4, USHMM.

58. Copy of unsigned memo specifying that there were examples only of financial-related crime in East Prussia; letter from April 11, 1936, finding no evidence of crimes of "Jewish organizations as such"; memo from May 26, 1936, saying no such material is in their department, "Abteilung III"; similar note from May 6, stamp-dated April 28, 1936; another letter stating that "this department does not handle such matters," Berlin, April 18, 1936; Reichssicherheitshauptamt

(RSHA)–SD, Berlin (Osobyi fond 500) (Main State Security of Germany–SD, Berlin [manuscript RG-11.001M.01], reel 4, USHMM.

59. Folder 240, Reichssicherheitshauptamt (RSHA)–SD, Berlin (Osobyi fond 500) (Main State Security of Germany–SD, Berlin [manuscript RG-11.001M.01], reel 4, USHMM.

60. RG 215, G-65: Jews among the criminals: correspondence dated August 31, 1935, Ludwig Schmidt to Daluege; October 24, 1935, memo from Koschorke; July 26, 1935, B-C, YIVO.

61. RG 215, G-65, memo from Koschorke; July 26, 1935, B-C, YIVO.

62. RG 215, G-65, July 26, 1935; letters of August 1, 1935, August 8, 1935, December 14, 1935, B-C, YIVO; "Discussions by the Authorities following Kristallnacht: Stenographic Report of the Meeting on the Jewish Question held under the Chairmanship of Field Marshal Göring in the Reich Air Ministry at 11 A.M. on November 12, 1938," in *Documents on the Holocaust: Selected Sources on the Destruction of the Jews of Germany and Austria, Poland, and the Soviet Union,* ed. Yitzhak Arad, Yisrael Gutman, and Abraham Margaliot, trans. Lea Ben Dor (Lincoln: University of Nebraska Press and Jerusalem: Yad Vashem, 1999), p. 111.

63. Memo from Müller to police officials and institutions, April 24, 1937; Reichssicherheitshauptampt (RSHA)–SD, Berlin (Osobyi fond 500) (Main State Security of Germany–SD, Berlin) [manuscript RG-11.001M.01], reel 4, folder 500–1, USHMM.

64. From the Zeitschriftendienst (Periodical Service), January 9, 1942, 140./9. Edition no. 5989–6018, under "Topics of the Times" [no.] 5990, quoted in Alexander G. Hardy, *Hitler's Secret Weapon: The "Managed" Press and Propaganda Machine of Nazi Germany* (New York: Vantage, 1967), p. 197.

65. "Die Devisenschieberin," article pasted from *Saarbrücker Zeitung,* June 4, 1939, including picture; RG 222, folder 64, B-C, YIVO.

66. Correspondence between Staatliche Kriminalpolizei, Kriminalpolizei, and editors of *Der Stürmer,* June 12, 1939, RG 22, folder 59, B-C, YIVO.

67. RG 222, folder 59: material about the trial of Giza Lucacs, February 28, 1939, to Kriminalpolizei Transtein from *Der Stürmer;* request by G. A. Engelharz for photos of "these Jews"; folder 60: correspondence concerning photographs of "Jewish criminals": June 12, 1939, between Staatlich Kriminalpolizei, Kriminalpolizei, and editors of *Der Stürmer,* B-C, YIVO.

68. RG 215, G-83, box 4, report of May 26, 1944, on "Entwicklung der Kriminalität," B-C, YIVO.

69. Entry for June 4, 1944, *Die Tagebücher von Joseph Goebbels,* Teil II, Diktate 1941–1945, Band 12, April–Juni 1944, ed. Elke Fröhlich (Munich: K. G. Saur, 1995), p. 397.

70. Circular from Berlin, dated October 25, 1944, from Ernst Kaltenbrunner, Der Reichsführer-SS and Chef der Deutschen Polizei, labeled "Streng vertraulich!" (strictly confidential). Sent under the jurisdiction of three departments

to another nine, so there was a substantial body of well-informed officials; T178, roll 11, Berlin Document Collection, United States National Archives, College Park, MD.

71. Leers, *Kräfte hinter Roosevelt.*

72. Manuscript RG-15.055M, Records of the Feldkommandantur Radom, 1944–1945; manuscript RG-15.062M, Kommandeur der Sicherheitspolizei und des SD Radom, Aussenstelle Petrikau records, 1940–1944; manuscript RG-11.001M.24, Dokumente von besonderer Bedeutung (Sammlung) (Osobyi Fond no.1525); manuscript RG-15.063M, Kommandeur der Sicherheitspolizei und des Sicherheitsdiensts im Distrikt Radom, Aussenstelle Kielce records, 1940–1944; manuscript RG-15.064M, Kommandeur der Schutzpolizei im Distrikt Radom records, June 15, 1944–December 12, 1944; manuscript RG-15.069M; Teka Lwowska = Lwów files, 1898–1979 (bulk 1941–1945); manuscript RG-18.002M, Latvian Central State Historical Archive (Riga) records, 1941–1945; manuscript RG-11.001M.05, Befehlshaber der Sicherheitspolizei und des SD in Riga (Osobyi Fond no. 504) (Commander of the German SIPO and SD in the Occupied Territories of the Soviet Baltic States, Riga), USHMM.

73. This is discussed extensively in ch. 5.

74. Wolf Meyer-Christian, "Judenfrage-Weltproblem. Rechtfertigung statt Verurteilung Deutschlands in Evian," *Die Judenfrage,* July 21, 1938, pp. 1–2; Meyer-Christian, "Worte und Taten. Kein Staat aufnahmebereit. Bermerkenswerte Aussprüche auf der Internationalen Flüchtlingskonferenz in Evian," *Die Judenfrage,* July 14, 1938, pp. 1–2; Kurt Vogtherr, "Wohin mit den Emigranten? Die Weltmeinung über das Judentum im Spiegel der Aufnahmebereitschaft," *Die Judenfrage,* November 1, 1939, pp. 3–7; Fritz Redlin, "Englands versteckte Judengegnerschaft. Geheime Massnahme gegen jüdische Einwanderer—Zollbeamte sollen Jagd auf Juden machen," *Die Judenfrage,* December 22, 1938.

75. Alphonse Bertillon, *Die gerichtliche Photographie. Mit einem Anhange über die anthropometrische Classification and Identificirung* (Halle, 1895) (originally appeared in French in 1890). The Nazis were more consistent about taking photographs of Jews and using them in publications than they were about photographing other ethnic groups; for example, the case files of the Gestapo in Düsseldorf reveal only a few such pictures of non-Jews among Poles; see RG-14.001M, Germany, Geheime Staatspolizei, case files from the Gestapo in Düsseldorf, 1937–1944, USHMM.

76. Eschwege, *Kennzeichen J,* p. 91.

77. "Jüdische Devisenschieber!" folder 64, RG 222, B-C, YIVO.

78. Gans, "Memoir," p. 26.

79. RG 222, folder 63, picture labeled PH 82, B-C, YIVO.

80. "Ist das eine Fischerfamilie von der Ostsee?" and "Saul," RG 222, PH 82, folder 63, B-C, YIVO.

81. Gans, "Memoir," p. 33.

82. W/S no. 58829, CD no. 0375, from *Der Stürmer* Archive, USHMM.

83. Desig. no. 485.15, W/S no. 58812, CD no. 0375, from *Der Stürmer* Archive, USHMM.

84. W/S no. 58826, CD no. 0375, from *Der Stürmer* Archive, USHMM.

85. W/S no. 58825, CD no. 0375, from *Der Stürmer* Archive, USHMM.

86. Keller and Andersen, *Der Jude als Verbrecher,* pp. 158–60; Leers, *Die Verbrechernatur der Juden,* p. 41; W/S no. 40197, "*Der Stürmer* advertisement depicting Jewish types. The German text of the poster reads: When Jews laugh. Jews are born criminals. They cannot be free and open when they laugh lest they betray themselves with a devilish grin. Read the latest issue 11 of the *Stürmer*"; USHMM.

87. "5000 Mark ins Ausland verschoben," article from *Württembergische Landeszeitung,* Nr. 112, May 15, 1939, RG 222, folder 64, B-C, YIVO.

88. "Eine jüdische Tarnung. Das Kunstgewerbehaus Kaiserdamm gehört der Jüdin Seligmann," RG 222, folder 64, B-C, YIVO.

89. "Ein jüdisches Ehepaar als Devisenschieber," article from *Der Oberschlesische Wanderer,* Gleiwitz, April 18, 1939, RG 222, folder 64, B-C, YIVO.

90. "Wieder ein 'anständiger' Jude. Er erteilte 'Ratschläge,' die ihm die Taschen füllten," RG 222, folder 64, B-C, YIVO.

91. See especially George Mosse, *Masses and Man: Nationalist and Fascist Perceptions of Reality* (New York: Howard Fertig, 1980); Saul Friedländer, *Reflections on Nazism: An Essay on Kitsch and Death* (New York: Harper and Row, 1984).

92. See ch. 4 of this book.

93. See Gertrude "Sarah" Solomon, Mainz, RG 222, folder 64, B-C, YIVO.

94. Especially utilized by Herwig Hartner-Hnizdo, *Das jüdische Gaunertum* (Munich: Hoheneichen-Verlag, 1939) and *Volk der Gauner.*

95. RG 222, folder 63, PH 82, B-C, YIVO.

96. See, for example, Keller and Andersen, *Der Jude als Verbrecher,* for the amalgam of politicians, business and cultural figures, and criminals.

97. Hartner-Hnizdo, *Volk der Gauner,* p. 71.

98. Although Arno Mayer's analysis of the Holocaust is problematic from a number of perspectives, his discussion of the connection between anti-Semitism and anti-Bolshevism is compelling; see Arno Mayer, *Why Did the Heavens Not Darken? The "Final Solution" in History* (New York: Pantheon, 1990). See also Keller and Andersen, *Der Jude als Verbrecher.*

99. See Dietz Bering, *The Stigma of Names: Antisemitism in German Daily Life, 1812–1933,* trans. Neville Plaice (Ann Arbor: University of Michigan Press, 1992), pp. 3–5ff.; Dietz Bering, *Kampf um Namen: Bernhard Weiss gegen Joseph Goebbels* (Stuttgart: Klett-Cotta, 1991); Werner Angress, "Bernhard Weiss: A Jewish Public Servant in the Last Years of the Weimar Republic," in *Jüdisches Leben in der Weimarer Republik—Jews in the Weimar Republic,* ed. Wolfgang Benz, Arnold Paucker, and Peter Pulzer (Tübingen: Mohr Siebeck, 1998), pp. 49–64. An entire

volume was produced to demonize Weiss: Joseph Goebbels, *Das Buch Isidor* (Munich: F. Eher, 1931); Keller and Andersen, *Der Jude als Verbrecher,* photo section.

100. Meyer-Christian, "Die Behandlung der Judenfrage in der deutschen Presse," p. 2.

101. Christian Gerlach, *Krieg. Ernährung. Völkermord. Forschungen zur deutschen Vernichtungspolitik im Zweiten Weltkrieg* (Hamburg: Hamburger Edition, 1998); Peter Longerich, *Politik der Vernichtung. Eine Gesamtdarstellung der nationalsozialistischen Judenverfolgung* (Munich: Peter, 1998); Ulrich Herbert, ed., *National Socialist Extermination Policies* (Oxford: Berghahn, 1999); Christopher Browning, *Nazi Policy, Jewish Workers, German Killers* (Cambridge: Cambridge University Press, 2000).

102. Quoted in Hardy, *Hitler's Secret Weapon,* p. 202.

103. Ibid., p. 203.

104. Photos from *Der Stürmer:* the entrance to the Dohany St. synagogue in Budapest is described as "Entry into the criminal cave. Portal of the large synagogue on Dohany St.," in *Der Stürmer* 23, August 6, 1944, Desig. no. 625.52, W/S no. 59052, CD no. 0376, USHMM; from *Der Stürmer:* the caption to an undated photo of the Luxembourg synagogue reads: "The temple of Jewish criminals in Luxembourg." Desig. no. 504.0, W/S no. 58999, CD no. 0376, USHMM.

105. Keller and Andersen, *Der Jude als Verbrecher,* pp. 162–63.

106. Gregory Paul Wegner, *Anti-Semitism and Schooling in the Third Reich* (New York: Routledge-Falmer, 2002), pp. 23–24.

107. Rose Van Tyne, "Never Again (Auschwitz)," RG-02.002*13, USHMM, unpaginated.

3. THE SELF-FULFILLING PROPHECY OF THE GHETTOS

Epigraphs: *Notes from the Warsaw Ghetto: The Journal of Emmanuel Ringelblum,* ed. and trans. Jacob Sloan (New York: Schocken, 1974), pp. 27 (March 31, 1940), 39 (May 9, 1940).

1. Joseph Roth, *Confession of a Murderer: Told in One Night,* trans. Desmond I. Vesey (London: Pan Books, 1988), p. 5.

2. Victor Klemperer, *The Language of the Third Reich. LTI, Lingua Tertii Imperii: A Philologist's Notebook,* trans. Martin Brady (London: Athlone, 2000). Klemperer also made numerous references to this project in his diaries; see *I Shall Bear Witness: The Diaries of Victor Klemperer 1933–1941,* trans. Martin Chalmers (London: Weidenfeld and Nicolson, 1998). Translator Philip Boehm notes that the accounts of survivors also adopted such terms: "The Nazis also invaded with words: an entirely new vocabulary of persecution, terror and genocide camouflaged in colorless bureaucratic German euphemisms. These words infiltrated the local languages—in the case of the Warsaw Ghetto, Yiddish and Polish—and gradually became declined, conjugated, and abbreviated into a horribly quotidian grammar";

Boehm, introduction to *Words to Outlive Us: Eyewitness Accounts from the Warsaw Ghetto,* ed. Michal Grynberg, trans. Philip Boehm (New York: Picador, 2002), p. 12. Calel Perechodnik, *Am I a Murderer? Testament of a Jewish Ghetto Policeman,* ed. and trans. Frank Fox (Boulder: Westview Press, 1996), p. 31.

3. Sloan, *Notes from the Warsaw Ghetto,* entry for December 14, 1942: "Until now, the Polish Christian spiritual leaders have done very little to save Jews from massacre and 'resettlement,' to use Their euphemism" (p. 336).

4. Martin Broszat, in Helmut Krausnick and Martin Broszat, *Anatomy of the SS State,* trans. Dorothy Long and Marian Jackson (Frogmore, St. Albans, United Kingdom: Palladin, 1968), p. 146; *Colonel Neave Report: Final Report on the Evidence of Witnesses for the Defense of Organizations Alleged to be Criminal, Heard before a Commission Appointed by the Tribunal Pursuant to Paragraph 4 of the Order of the 13th of March, 1946,* in Nuremberg Trial Proceedings, vol. 42, Avalon Project at Yale Law School, www.yale.edu/lawweb/avalon/imt/proc/naeve.htm, p. 40.

5. The terms "Jews," "prisoner" *(Häftling),* and "deportee," are mixed in the explanatory plaques in the Natzweiler-Struthof concentration camp memorial site.

6. Johannes Tuchel, "Planung und Realität des Systems der Konzentrationslager 1934–1938," in *Die nationalsozialistischen Konzenstrationslager,* Band 1, ed. Ulrich Herbert, Karin Orth, and Christoph Dieckmann (Frankfurt a.M: Fischer, 2003), pp. 43–59.

7. Ulrich Herbert, "Von der Gegnerbekämpfung zur 'rassischen Generalprävention.' 'Schutzhaft' und Konzentrationslager in der Konzeption der Gestapo-Führung 1933–1939," in Herbert, Orth, and Dieckmann, *Die nationalsozialistischen Konzenstrationslager,* pp. 60–81. There is a great deal of scholarly comment on the term "born criminal," particularly as it applies to the seminal figure of Cesare Lombroso. For the most illuminating recent studies see Dan Vyleta, "Jewish Crimes and Misdemeanors: In Search of Jewish Criminality in Germany and Austria, 1890–1914," *European History Quarterly* 35 (2005): 299–325; Oliver Liang, *Criminal-Biological Theory, Discourse, and Practice in Germany, 1918–1945* (Ph.D. diss., Johns Hopkins University, 1999). For the arguments about the Jews as criminals not deserving rights, see Herbert, "Von der Gegnerbekämpfung zur 'rassischen Generalprävention,' " p. 65.

8. See article by "Dr [?] Zirpins," identified as SS Sturmbannführer Kriminaldirektor, in *Die Deutsche Polizei,* Nr. 21, 1.11.41, pp. 379–80; continued: "Das Getto in Litzmannstadt, kriminalpolizeilich gesehen," Nr. 22, 15.11.41, pp. 394–95; continued: (same title as previously), Nr. 23, 1.12.41, pp. 409–10.

9. "Judentum und Kriminalität," *Mitteilungsblätter für die weltanschauliche Schulung der Ordnungspolizei.* Herausgegeben vom Chef der Ordnungspolizei. Gruppe "Weltanschauliche Erziehung." Gruppe A. June 10, 1941. Folge 16, United States Holocaust Memorial Museum (hereafter USHMM).

10. Isaiah Trunk, *L'odzsh'er geto: a historishe un sotsyologishe shtudye me doku-mentn, taveles un mape* (New York: YIVO, 1962); draft of translation by Robert Moses Shapiro, ch. 7, p. 109. This work has recently appeared as Isaiah Trunk, *Lodz Ghetto: A History*, trans. and ed., Robert Moses Shapiro; introduced by Yis-rael Gutman (Bloomington: Indiana University Press, 2006). The section of the draft from which most citations are taken are in pages 349–78 of the published edition. I wish to thank Robert Moses Shapiro for his graciousness in sharing the working draft.

11. A facsimile of the report, the "complete list of executions carried out in the EK 3 area up to 1 December 1941," is available at www.holocaust-history.org/works/jaeger-report/htm/intro000.htm (hereafter *Jaeger Report*). The translations here are guided by those appearing on that site, from *The Good Old Days,* ed. E. Klee, W. Dressen, V. Riess (New York: Free Press, 1988); web site pre-pared by Daniel Keren, with an introduction by Yale Edeiken, transcription by Albrecht Kolthoff, and translation by Gord McFee.

12. *Jaeger Report,* p. 6.

13. Ibid., p. 9.

14. Reuben Kronik, "The Story of the Jews of Vilkomir by Reuben Kronik," Record Group (hereafter RG) 02*170, pp. 5, 11, USHMM. This testimony, ver-ified by two other family members, was given at Camp Hasenleke, Kassel, No-vember 24, 1948. Christoph Dieckmann, "Der Krieg und die Ermordung der litauischen Juden," in *Nationalsozialistische Vernichtungspolitik 1939–1945: Neue Forschungen und Kontroversen,* ed. Ulrich Herbert (Frankfurt a.M.: Fischer Taschenbuch Verlag, 1998), pp. 292–93; here Dieckmann builds on the impor-tant work of Helmut Krausnick, "Hitler und die Behehle an die Einsatzgrup-pen," in *Der Mord an den Juden im Zweiten Weltkrieg. Entschlussbildung und Verwirklichung,* ed. Eberhard Jäckel and Jürgen Rohwer (Stuttgart: Deutsche Verlags-Anstalt, 1987), p. 99; Eberhard Jäckel, "Die Entschlussbildung als hi-storisches Problem," in Jäckel and Rohwer, *Der Mord an den Juden,* pp. 9–17. See also Christoph Dieckmann, "Das Ghetto und das Konzentrationslager in Kau-nas 1941–1944," in *Die nationalsozialistischen Konzentrationslager,* ed. Ulrich Herbert, Karin Orth, Christoph Dieckmann (Göttingen: Wallstein, 1998), pp. 439–71.

15. *Jaeger Report,* pp. 3, 7.

16. Ibid., p. 4.

17. Interview with the author, with Chaim Bargman as guide and translator, November 23, 2001; the woman being interviewed did not give us her name. The author had gone to the village not for the sake of research about the Holocaust, but simply to see the shtetl, *Shakot,* where my grandfather, Moses Berkowitz, was born. My grandmother, Edith Berkowitz (née Berk), came from Pašušys. The in-terviewee reported that she testified in the mid-1960s in a trial against the Lithuanian policeman, and he received a sentence of twenty to twenty-five years.

18. Kronik, "The Story of the Jews of Vilkomir," pp. 2, 5.

19. Sonja Haid Greene, "Between Life and Death (My Memoirs)," RG-02.112, p. 8, USHMM.

20. Interview, November 23, 2001.

21. See Dieckmann, "Der Krieg und die Ermordung der litauischen Juden," pp. 292–329. Dieckmann's important work deserves to be followed up by more detailed studies, possibly incorporating testimony of Lithuanian bystanders and the postwar trials under the Soviets.

22. *Jaeger Report,* pp. 8–9, 3.

23. Chaim Hasenfus, in Grynberg, *Words to Outlive Us,* p. 36.

24. Samuel Puterman, in Grynberg, *Words to Outlive Us,* p. 49.

25. Sloan, *Notes from the Warsaw Ghetto,* pp. 276–77.

26. H. G. Adler, *Theresienstadt: das Antlitz einer Zwangsgemeinschaft: Geschichte, Soziologie, Psychologie* (Tübingen: Mohr, 1960), pp. 138ff., 153ff., 453ff.

27. Ibid., pp. 141, 249ff., 353ff., 367ff., 468ff., 481ff., 487ff., 489ff., 673.

28. Anonymous informant, former lawyer and policeman, in Grynberg, *Words to Outlive Us,* pp. 73–75.

29. Trunk, *L'odzsh'er geto,* p. 101.

30. Lucille Eichengreen with Rebecca Camhi Fromer, *Rumkowski and the Orphans of Lodz* (San Francisco: Mercury House, 2000), p. 3.

31. Trunk, *L'odzsh'er geto,* p. 101; Eichengreen, *Rumkowski and the Orphans,* p. 11.

32. Avraham Tory, *Surviving the Holocaust: The Kovno Ghetto Diary,* ed. and introduced by Martin Gilbert, textual and historical notes by Dina Porat, trans. Jerzy Michalowicz (Cambridge, MA: Harvard University Press, 1990), entry for January 9, 1944: "The Ninth Fort, a military fortress near Kovno, for a long time served as part of the Kovno prison for dangerous criminals. During the Nazi occupation it became a place of torture and mass executions. In secret the Nazis called it Vernichtungsstelle nr. 2: Extermination place no. 2. Here were murdered some 25,000 of Kovno's Jews, as well as 10,000 Jews deported from Germany, Austria and Czechoslovakia, thousands of Jewish prisoners-of-war who had served in the Red Army, and many other Jews" (p. 508). See also Christoph Dieckmann, "Das Ghetto und das Konzentrationslager in Kaunas 1941–1944," pp. 439–71.

33. Christopher Browning, *Nazi Policy, Jewish Workers, German Killers* (Cambridge: Cambridge University Press, 2000); Dalija Epsteinaite et al., eds., *The H.K.P. Jewish Labor Camp, 1943–1944: Documents* (Vilnius: Valstybinis Vilniaus Gaono zydu muziejuus, 2002) (volume in Lithuanian, Russian, and English).

34. Perechodnik, *Am I a Murderer?* p. 11.

35. Brief biographical sketch and Natan Zelichower, in Grynberg, *Words to Outlive Us,* pp. 474, 46, respectively.

36. Boehm, introduction to Grynberg, *Words to Outlive Us,* p. 11; see also Stefan Ernst, in *Words to Outlive Us,* p. 43.

37. Hasenfus, in Grynberg, *Words to Outlive Us,* p. 33.

38. Stanislaw Sznapman, in Grynberg, *Words to Outlive Us,* p. 19.

39. See the photos of Arthur Grimm in the *Berliner Illustrierte Zeitung;* from the Bildarchiv Preussischer Kulturbesitz (WWII 23); Desig. no. 481.053, W/S no. 26613, CD no. 0243, USHMM.

40. Raul Hilberg, *Prologue to Annihilation: A Study of the Identification, Impoverishment and Isolation of the Jewish Victims of Nazi Policy* (Ph.D. thesis, New York: Columbia University, 1955), pp. 341, 342.

41. See, for example, Tory, *Surviving the Holocaust,* pp. 18, 22, 33.

42. Ibid., pp. 34–35, 131.

43. Hilberg, *Prologue to Annihilation,* pp. 367, 368, 372–73.

44. The most comprehensive treatment of the Jewish police is in Isaiah Trunk, *Judenrat: The Jewish Councils in Eastern Europe under Nazi Occupation* (New York: Macmillan; London: Collier-Macmillan, 1972), pp. 475–569. See also Sloan, *Notes from the Warsaw Ghetto,* pp. 139, 142,146–47, 226, 233; Perechodnik, *Am I a Murderer?*

45. Sloan, *Notes from the Warsaw Ghetto,* pp. 214, 87.

46. Michal Grynberg, in Grynberg, *Words to Outlive Us,* p. 53.

47. Sloan, *Notes from the Warsaw Ghetto,* pp. 330–31. Even more graphic depictions of "incomprehensible brutality" follow.

48. Ibid., pp. 158–60, 277.

49. Jan Mawult, in Grynberg, *Words to Outlive Us,* p. 64.

50. Trunk, *L'odzsh'er geto,* pp. 107, 110–11.

51. Sloan, *Notes from the Warsaw Ghetto,* p. 271; from "Anonymous Man," in Grynberg, *Words to Outlive Us,* p. 76, which provides a very detailed description of the structure and function of the Warsaw Jewish prisons, pp. 73–78.

52. Trunk, *L'odzsh'er geto,* pp. 111–12.

53. Tadeusz Pankiewicz, *The Cracow Ghetto Pharmacy,* trans. Henry Tilles (Washington, DC: United States Holocaust Memorial Museum, 2000), pp. 5–6, 31, 34; originally published in 1947.

54. Mawult, in Grynberg, *Words to Outlive Us,* pp. 64–65; the editor corrects his account: "The information is imprecise. Fels died as the result of wounds inflicted during a shootout between the resistance fighters and the Nazis. Before he died he supposedly said, 'I'm happy to have fallen from the bullets of our brothers' " (p. 65).

55. Sloan, *Notes from the Warsaw Ghetto,* pp. 231–32.

56. Tory, *Surviving the Holocaust,* pp. 54–55, 58–59; Stefan Ernst details how the Jewish police helped control the typhus epidemic in the Warsaw ghetto; in Grynberg, *Words to Outlive Us,* pp. 44–45; Sloan, *Notes from the Warsaw Ghetto,* pp. 231–33.

57. Tory, *Surviving the Holocaust,* passim; Yudel Beiles, *Yudke,* trans. Vida Urbonavičius-Watkins (Vilnius: Baltos lankos, 2002), pp. 61–77.

58. Solon Beinfeld, "Life and Survival," in *Hidden History of the Kovno Ghetto* [exhibition catalogue of the United States Holocaust Memorial Museum] (Boston: Little, Brown, 1997), p. 34. Cf. Dmitri Gelpernus, *Kovno Ghetto Diary,* trans. Robin O'Neil and Chaim Bargman (Moscow: State Publishing House, "Der Emes," originally published 1948), online at www.jewishgen.org/yizkor/kaunas/Kaunas.html, pp. 7, 34.

59. Beinfeld, "Life and Survival," p. 34.

60. Glepernus, *Kovno Ghetto Diary,* p. 7; Joel Elkes, *Values, Belief and Suvival: Dr Elkanan Elkes and the Kovno Ghetto. A Memoir* (London: Vale, 1997), p. 22.

61. Beinfeld, "Life and Survival," pp. 34–35. For a glowing view of Kovno's Jewish police, see Elkes, *Values, Belief and Survival,* pp. 24–25.

62. Hilberg, *Prologue to Annihilation,* p. 283.

63. Zelichower, in Grynberg, *Words to Outlive Us,* p. 47.

64. Perechodnik, *Am I a Murderer?* p. 95.

65. Mawult, in Grynberg, *Words to Outlive Us,* p. 71.

66. Ernst, in Grynberg, *Words to Outlive Us,* p. 24.

67. Interview with Chaim Bargman, June 22, 2004.

68. Perechodnik, *Am I a Murderer?* p. 108.

69. Marek Stok, in Grynberg, *Words to Outlive Us,* p. 51.

70. Perechodnik, *Am I a Murderer?* pp. 124, 88.

71. Mawult, in Grynberg, *Words to Outlive Us,* p. 71, n. 4, pp. 442–43.

72. "Mojsze Kisielnicki memoir relating to the Judenrat in Kaluszyn, Poland," RG-02.067, pp. 3–4, 6–7, 11, USHMM.

73. Aryeh Shamri, Shalom Soroka et al., eds., *Seyfer Kalushin: geheylikt der horev gevorener kehile* (Tel Aviv: Irgun Yots'e Kalushin be-Yisr'el, 1961).

74. Trunk, *L'odzsh'er geto,* pp. 100, 105–8, 137–38. The inhabitants' reference to "organizing" is taken from an interview with Chaim Bargman about his mother's work in the potato stores at the First Fort, Kovno, November 9, 2003.

75. Trunk, *L'odzsh'er geto,* p. 105.

76. Perechodnik, *Am I a Murderer?* p. 31.

77. Tory, *Surviving the Holocaust,* pp. 21, 32.

78. Trunk, *L'odzsh'er geto,* p. 109.

79. Tory, *Surviving the Holocaust;* Sloan, *Notes from the Warsaw Ghetto;* Primo Levi, *Survival in Auschwitz: The Nazi Assault on Humanity,* trans. Stuart Woolf (New York: Collier, 1961).

80. Perechodnik, *Am I a Murderer?* p. 29.

81. Sloan, *Notes from the Warsaw Ghetto,* p. 12.

82. Ibid., p. 168.

83. Ibid., p. 239. Ringelblum had earlier believed that the Jewish police were responsible for this abomination, which he termed "the deepest pit of degradation"; see p. 211.

84. Sloan, *Notes from the Warsaw Ghetto*, pp. 265–66.

85. Ibid., pp. 268–69.

86. Pankiewicz, *Cracow Ghetto Pharmacy*, pp. 41, 45, 87.

87. Ibid., p. 78.

88. Gelpernus, *Kovno Ghetto Diary*, p. 3.

89. This office was directed by a notorious collaborator, Abraham Gancwajch. The leader of the *Judenrat*, Adam Czerniaków "struggled against their attempts to infiltrate the Council. Moryc Kon and Zelig Heller used their connections with the Gestapo to obtain various concessions, notably to develop their transportation business"; note by Philip Boehm, in Grynberg, *Words to Outlive Us*, p. 55; see also Sloan, *Notes from the Warsaw Ghetto*, pp. 149, 158, 185, 188–89.

90. Sloan, *Notes from the Warsaw Ghetto*, pp. 110, 171, 178, 192.

91. The character tries to marry off his daughter to a respectable suitor by commissioning a torah scroll; ibid., p. 192.

92. Ibid., p. 278.

93. Hilberg, *Prologue to Annihilation*, p. 328. In 1939, with the imposition of both armbands and yellow stars, Hilberg writes that in Warsaw, "for example, the sale of armbands became a regular business. There were ordinary armbands of cloth, and there [were] fancy plastic armbands which were washable."

94. Perechodnik, *Am I a Murderer?* pp. 86, 118, 122,169, 170, 195; Sloan, *Notes from the Warsaw Ghetto*, p. 273; Helena Midler, in Grynberg, *Words to Outlive Us*, p. 380; Pola Glezer, in Grynberg, *Words to Outlive Us*, p.354; Gunnar S. Paulsson, *Secret City: The Hidden Jews of Warsaw, 1940–1945* (New Haven, CT: Yale University Press, 2002).

95. Hilberg, *Prologue to Annihilation*, p. 274. The request was made August 20, 1941, but Hitler's consent was not recorded until September 19, 1941 (p. 275).

96. Ibid., pp. 288, 274–77.

97. Ibid., pp. 277, 308.

98. Stok, in Grynberg, *Words to Outlive Us*, pp. 49–50.

99. Ibid., p. 50.

100. Ibid., p. 51; for a similar description see Sloan, *Notes from the Warsaw Ghetto*, p. 272.

101. Trunk, *L'odzsh'er geto*, p. 101.

102. Ibid.

103. Lucille Eichengreen, e-mail correspondence with the author, July 28, 2003: "As far as I know, and have been told, the Germans entered a room at the Jewish Community House and among the 20 to 30 odd men there picked one at random. It is assumed that they saw his white hair, and thought he might be

a good choice. At that point in time they had no idea of who or what Rumkowski was. I was told this by Neftalin, Spiegel and others."

104. Lucille Eichengreen with Harriet Hyman Chamberlain, *From Ashes to Life: My Memories of the Holocaust* (San Francisco: Mercury House, 1994), p. 71.

105. Ibid., p. 83.

106. Eichengreen, *Rumkowski and the Orphans,* p. 46.

107. Ibid., pp. 88–90.

108. Sznapman, in Grynberg, *Words to Outlive Us,* p. 319.

109. Michael Temchin, *The Witch Doctor: Memoirs of a Partisan* (New York: Holocaust Library, 1983), p. 124.

110. Ibid., pp. 165–67. Along with the possibility that he died in the ghetto resistance, some surmise that Baumsecer was murdered in Treblinka.

111. Pankiewicz, *Cracow Ghetto Pharmacy,* pp. 64–65.

4. INVERTING THE INNOCENT AND THE CRIMINAL IN CONCENTRATION CAMPS

Epigraph: Hugo Gryn with Naomi Gryn, *Chasing Shadows* (London: Viking, 2000), p. 185.

1. Ulrich Herbert, "Von der Gegnerbekämpfung zur 'rassischen Generalprävention.' 'Schutzhaft' und Konzentrationslager in der Konzeption der Gestapo-Führung 1933–1939," in *Die nationalsozialistischen Konzenstrationslager,* Band 1, ed. Ulrich Herbert, Karin Orth, and Christoph Dieckmann (Frankfurt a.M: Fischer, 2003), pp. 60–81.

2. See Leon Weliczker Wells, *The Janowska Road* (Washington: Holocaust Library, 1999).

3. There is, ironically, no mention of the photographic process actually used at Auschwitz in Yasmin Doosry, ed., *Auschwitz: 50 Years of Photographs, Paintings, and Graphics* (Auschwitz: Auschwitz-Birkenau State Museum, 1995).

4. Janina Struk, *Photographing the Holocaust: Interpretations of the Evidence* (London and New York: I. P. Tauris with the European Jewish Publication Society, 2004), pp. 99–119.

5. *KL Auschwitz Documentary Photographs* (Warsaw: Krajowa Agencja Wydawnicza, 1980), caption on p. 86, photos on pp. 83–86. None of those pictured in this limited section are Jews. Another publication, less useful for research, also has mug shots but there seem to be no Jews among them; see *Auschwitz-Birkenau* (Auschwitz: Panstowowe Muzeum, 1982), pp. 69–70. For the number that remain, see Danuta Czech, *Auschwitz Chronicle, 1939–1945* (New York: Henry Holt, 1997), p. xi. Of these 405,000, estimates indicate that only one-sixth, fewer than 60,000 survived; see International Auschwitz Committee, ed., *Nazi Medicine: Doctors, Victims and Medicine in Auschwitz,* part II (New York: Howard Fertig, 1986), p. 1.

6. Tadeusz Iwaszko, "Deportation to the Camp and Registration of Prisoners," in *Auschwitz: Nazi Death Camp,* ed. Franciszek Piper and Teresa Swiebocka, trans. Douglas Selvage (Auschwitz: Auschwitz-Birkenau State Museum, 1996), p. 61. See also Gideon Greif, "The 'Auschwitz Album': The Story of Lili Jacob," in *The Auschwitz Album: The Story of a Transport,* ed. Yisrael Gutman and Bella Gutterman, trans. Naftali Greenwood and Jerzy Michalovic (Jerusalem: Yad Vashem; Auschwitz: Auschwitz-Birkenau State Museum, 2002), pp. 81–82.

7. For background consult Record Group (hereafter RG) 50.030*0446; Acc. 1996.A.0523, "Oral History interview with Helen Tichauer and Anna Palarczyk, 1996, August 16–August 17, 1996 [sound recording]," United States Holocaust Memorial Museum (hereafter USHMM); and RG-50.030*0462, "Oral History interview with Helen Spitzer Tichauer, September 7, 2000 [sound recording]," USHMM. See also Lore Shelley, ed., *Secretaries of Death: Accounts by Former Prisoners Who Worked in the Gestapo of Auschwitz* (New York: Shengold, 1986).

8. One of a series of situation reports, focusing primarily on economic matters but including other concerns, "Die wirtschaftliche Lage in den besetzen Ostgebieten, 31" December 1941, from Wirtschaftsstab Ost, T-178, roll 19, Berlin Documents Collection, United States National Arhives, College Park, MD (hereafter BDC, NA). Whether these photos were used for this purpose never will be known for certain, given that the material was intentionally destroyed.

9. Helen (Zippy) Tichauer is mentioned in the account of Dr. Susan E. Cernyak-Spatz, in Shelley, *Secretaries of Death,* pp. 111–12.

10. Robert Jan van Pelt and Deborah Dwork, *Auschwitz: 1270 to the Present* (New Haven, CT: Yale University Press, 1996), pp. 300–1.

11. An interview is available online, conducted while she was in a DP camp, with David Boder; see http://voices.iit.edu/interviews/tisch_t.html. A slightly different version appears in *Fresh Wounds: Early Narratives of Holocaust Survival,* ed. Donald L. Niewyk (Chapel Hill: University of North Carolina Press, 1998), pp. 354–69; see also Deborah Dwork, "Agents, Contexts, Responsibilities: The Massacre at Budy," in *Catastrophe and Meaning: The Holocaust and the Twentieth Century,* ed. Moishe Postone and Eric Santner (Chicago: University of Chicago Press, 2003), pp. 154–69.

12. Karin Orth, *Die Konzentrationslager-SS. Sozialstrukturelle Alalysen und biographischen Studien* (Göttingen: Wallstein Verlag, 2000), pp. 23–31; Orth, *Das System der nationalsozialistischen Konzentrationslager. Eine politische organisationsgeschichte* (Hamburg: Hamburger Edition, 1991), pp. 34ff., 54ff.

13. Van Pelt and Dwork, *Auschwitz: 1270 to the Present,* pp. 174–76; Wolfgang Sofsky, *The Order of Terror: The Concentration Camp,* trans. William Templer (Princeton, NJ: Princeton University Press, 1997), pp. 226–32. See Gordon J. Horwitz, *In the Shadow of Death: Outside the Gates of Mauthausen* (New York: Free Press, 1990), pp. 8, 12.

14. See *Le camp de concentration du Struthof. Konzentrationslager Natzweiler. Collection documents-tome III* (Schirmeck: Essor, 1998), map opposite p. 336; Klaus F. Schmidt-Macon, *Aschenspur. Gedichte. Trace de Cendres. Poems* (Wörthsee bei Munich: Groh, 1988), p. v.

15. Site visit, July 3, 2004.

16. Van Pelt and Dwork, *Auschwitz: 1270 to the Present*, p. 172; Gordon J. Horwitz, *In the Shadow of Death: Living Outside the Gates of Mauthausen* (New York: Free Press, 1990), pp. 16–17.

17. On the legality of genocide per se, see Henry Friedlander, "Concerning the Extra-legal Decisions of the German State in the Nazi Era," in *Jüdische Welten: Juden in Deutschland vom 18. Jahrhundert bis in die Gegenwart*, eds Marion Kaplan and Beate Meyer (Göttingen: Wallstein Verlag, 2005), pp. 304–16.

18. Discussion follows Raul Hilberg, *Prologue to Annihilation: A Study of the Identification, Impoverishment and Isolation of the Jewish Victims of Nazi Policy* (Ph.D. thesis, New York: Columbia University, 1955), pp. 50–51.

19. Iwaszko, "Deportation to the Camp," p. 61. One of the descriptions of the Erkennungsdienst repeats this in even stronger terms: Bernhard Walter and Ernst Hoffmann "were responsible for taking the portrait photos of each prisoner (except Jews and Gypsies)." Does this mean that other people took photos of the Jews and "Gypsies," or that none were taken? Or that they were not part of this process? Certainly there are numerous photos of Jews and "Gypsies." See Greif, "The 'Auschwitz Album,'" pp. 81–82; this work makes no reference to the memoir of Hugo Gryn (*Chasing Shadows),* who refers explicitly to the album.

20. Danuta Czech, "Origins of the Camp, Its Construction and Expansion," in Piper and Swiebocka, *Auschwitz: Nazi Death Camp,* pp. 21–23.

21. Ibid., p. 23.

22. Pery Broad, *KZ Auschwitz: Reminiscences of Pery Broad, SS-Man in the Auschwitz Concentration Camp,* trans. Krystyna Michalik (Auschwitz: Panstwowe Museum, 1965), p. 24.

23. "The Autobiography of Rudolf Höss," in *KL Auschwitz as Seen by the SS: Rudolf Höss, Pery Broad, Johann Paul Kremer,* ed. Kazimierz Smolen, Danuta Czech, Tadeusz Iwaszko, Barbara Jarosz, Franciszek Piper, Irena Polska, and Teresa Swiebocka, trans. from the German by Constantine FizGibbon (Höss) and Kystyna Michalik (Broad and Kremer) (Warsaw: Interpress, 1991), p. 44.

24. William Eisen, "William Eisen Testimony," RG-02.136; Acc. 1994.A055, USHMM, p. 33.

25. "Interview with Helen Spitzer Tichauer (New York, New York), 23 March 2000," Georgetown University, Washington, DC, Seminar no. 433, The Holocaust in Historical Perspective, instructor: Dr. Wendy Lower, p. 15.

26. Eugon Kogon, *The Theory and Practice of Hell,* trans. Heinz Norden (New York: Berkley, 1998), p. 19. Much of this does not apply to camps dedicated exclusively to plunder and the assembly-line extermination of Jews; see Yitzhak

Arad, *Belzec, Sobibor, Treblinka: The Operation Reinhard Death Camps* (Bloomington: Indiana University Press, 1987).

27. Lucille Eichengreen with Rebecca Camhi Fromer, *Rumkowski and the Orphans of Lodz* (San Francisco: Mercury House, 2000), pp. 94–95.

28. Ibid.

29. Orth, *Das System der nationalsozialistischen Konzentrationslager*, pp. 35–38, 57–61, 76–80, 95–97.

30. See "Tattoos and Numbers: The System of Identifying Prisoners at Auschwitz," www.ushmm.org/wlc/en/index.php?ModuleId=10007056&Type=normal+article; Leon Glogowski, "From 'Guinea Pig' in Auschwitz to the Post of Head of the Hospital in Birkenau," in International Auschwitz Committee, *Nazi Medicine*, p. 173.

31. Konrad Kwiet and Helmut Eschwege, *Selbstbehauptung und Widerstand: deutsche Juden im Kampf um Existenz und Menschenwürde, 1933–1945* (Hamburg: Christians, 1984), p. 272.

32. According to Patricia Heberer, "There was no color assigned specifically to Gypsies as a Winkel. Gypsies wore black and more rarely brown, as 'asocials,' which was their usual designation as pertained to badges"; note to the author, September 3, 2004.

33. See Kogon, *The Theory and Practice of Hell*, pp. 30–31, 35–36; interview with Helen Spitzer Tichauer, March 23, 2000, pp. 10–11.

34. Interview with Helen Spitzer Tichauer, March 23, 2000, pp. 4–6.

35. Kwiet and Eschwege, *Selbstbehauptung und Widerstand*, p. 273; Orth, *Die Konzentrationslager-SS*.

36. Jerzy Rawicz, "Foreword," in Smolen et al., *KL Auschwitz as Seen by the SS*, p. 18.

37. "Autobiography of Rudolf Höss," in Smolen et al., *KL Auschwitz Seen by the SS*, pp. 39–40; see Raul Hilberg, *The Destruction of the European Jews*, 3rd ed., vol. 1 (New Haven: Yale University Press, 2003), pp. 912–13.

38. Compare this case with the similar one in Buchenwald; Kogon, *The Theory and Practice of Hell*, p. 57.

39. Wladyslaw Fejkiel, "Health Service in Auschwitz I Concentration Camp/Main Camp," in International Auschwitz Committee, *Nazi Medicine*, pp. 19–20.

40. Leon Glogowski, "From 'Guinea Pig' in Auschwitz," pp. 166–68.

41. Rawicz, "Foreword," p. 20.

42. Glogowski, "From 'Guinea Pig' in Auschwitz," pp. 166–68.

43. Stanislawa Leszczynska, "Report of a Midwife from Auschwitz," in International Auschwitz Committee, *Nazi Medicine*, p. 181.

44. Ibid., pp. 188–89. She estimated that 1,500 newborns were drowned, and with "ruthless severity" Jewish women's children were always murdered in this way (pp. 190–92). A different report states, "In 1944 Jewish children were no

longer murdered directly after births, but one day the news was spread that mothers with small children would be sent to the gas. The children were killed and the mothers were immediately crossed off the list of the 'Revier' and sent to the camp. In the blankets Katarzyna L., a fellow prisoner, found two babies that were still alive. And it was possible to save these two." Janina Kosciuszkowa, "Children in the Auschwitz Concentration Camp," in International Auschwitz Committee, *Nazi Medicine,* p. 220.

45. Elise Kramer, "Hell and Rebirth: My Experiences during the Time of Persecution," RG-02.037, p. 7, USHMM.

46. Kwiet and Eschwege, *Selbstbehauptung und Widerstand,* p. 273.

47. Walter Stras, "Walter Stras memoir" in "Strangers in the Heartland," Survivor Testimonies compiled by Donald M. Douglas, RG-02*142, p. 142, USHMM.

48. Ibid.

49. Ibid., pp. 138–39.

50. Erwin Foley, "Oral history interview with Erwin Foley, September 19, 1995 [sound recording]," RG-50.106*0018; Acc. 1995.A.1200, USHMM.

51. Joseph Berger, "My Life Story," RG-02*123, USHMM.

52. Benno Fischer, "Death March: April 14, 1945–April 24, 1945," RG-02.039, June 1945, RG-02.039, p. 4, USHMM.

53. Bernard Nissenbaum, "My Deportation," RG-02.005*01, p. 28, USHMM.

54. Broad, *KZ Auschwitz,* pp. 18–19.

55. Ibid., pp. 19–20; Dr. Stanislaw Klodzinsi, "Phenol in the Auschwitz-Birkenau Concentration Camp," in International Auschwitz Committee, *Nazi Medicine,* pp. 101–3.

56. Broad, *KZ Auschwitz,* pp. 36–23.

57. Henry Friedlander, *The Origins of the Nazi Genocide: From Euthanasia to the Final Solution* (Chapel Hill: University of North Carolina Press, 1995).

58. Broad, *KZ Auschwitz,* p. 26; Iwaszko, "Deportation to the Camp," p. 66.

59. Wells, *The Janowska Road,* pp. 218ff., 231ff.; Helen Tichauer, interview with the author, July 1, 2003.

60. Iwaszko, "Deportation to the Camp," p. 66; Helen Tichauer, interview with the author, July 1, 2003.

61. Iwaszko, "Deportation to the Camp," p. 66.

62. Broad, *KZ Auschwitz,* pp. 84–85.

63. Shelley, *Secretaries of Death,* p. 10, note; Helen Tichauer, interview with the author, July 1, 2003.

64. Explanation provided by Patricia Heberer, personal communication with the author, September 3, 2004.

65. Testimony of Sophia Litwinska, the Belsen Trial, Trial of Josef Kramer and 44 Others, British Military Court, Luneburg, September 17–November 17, 1945, in Judge Advocate General's Office: War Crimes Case files, Second World

War, 1945–1953, RG-59.016M, numbered p. 5 on the document, also labeled p. 169, USHMM. I am grateful to my colleague Balázs Szelényi at the Center for Advanced Holocaust Studies (USHMM) for locating and sharing this document. This testimony has been used by Holocaust deniers to try to prove that the gas chambers are a myth. They point to a mistaken date given by Litwinksa, but that error was recognized immediately as a simple misstatement and clarified—and accepted by the court; see Litwinksa testimony, pp. 4, 168.

66. Ibid., pp. 5, 169. Helen Tichauer, interview with the author, July 1, 2003.

67. [Item] "(131) Deposition of Sophia Litwinska (Pole, aged 28)," in Raymond Phillips, ed., *Trial of Joseph Kramer and Forty-four Others (The Belsen Trial)* (London: William Hodge, 1949), p. 745.

68. It is also reported that, if killed, they were the only Jews for whom death certificates were to be made out, and that "the majority of Jews who fell into this category were Mischehen [persons in mixed marriages], whose 'Aryan' partners were informed of their spouses' decease and allowed to purchase an urn full of ashes for a certain sum of money"; Irene Frenkel (wid. Loewinger, née Gruenwald), in Shelley, *Secretaries of Death,* p. 216; another qualifies that this was the practice, but that it was soon discontinued; Jenny Schaner (wid. Spritzer), in Shelley, *Secretaries of Death,* p. 251.

69. Hermine Markovits disputes this: "I doubt it was possible, as some claim, to have transformed the RSHA inmates into Gestapo or Kripo arrivals and so to have saved them from being gassed. There was no waiting period during which the files could have been altered. In the Politische Abteilung one could help only in the way I did, by making intentional typographical errors or interpretations in favor of the accused"; in Shelley, *Secretaries of Death,* p. 125. On this matter the author clearly sides with Shelley and Tichauer.

70. Helen Tichauer interview with the author, New York City, August 28, 2003; Markovits, in Shelley, *Secretaries of Death,* p. 125.

71. Shelley, *Secretaries of Death,* p. 10, note; Lily Hoenig (née Reiner) in Shelley, *Secretaries of Death,* p. 89.

72. Gryn, *Chasing Shadows,* pp. 193–94.

73. Struk, *Photographing the Holocaust;* van Pelt and Dwork, *Auschwitz: 1270 to the Present;* Sofsky, *The Order of Terror;* Yisrael Gutman and Michael Berenbaum, eds., *Anatomy of the Auschwitz Death Camp* (Bloomington: Indiana University Press, 1994).

74. Jewish prison workers were not assigned to the Erkennungsdienst; Shelley, *Secretaries of Death,* p. 3. Although she also states that "none of the members of our [Jewish women's] Kommando worked in the Erkennungsdienst or the Aufnahmeabteilung," Helen Tichauer affirms that they were often given different tasks that overlapped with other departments; interview with the author, July 1, 2003.

75. Nissenbaum, "My Deportation," p. 18.

76. Eichengreen, *Rumkowski and the Orphans,* p. 20; Tikva Fatal-Knaani, *Zo lo lotah Grodnoh: Kehilat Grodnoh u-sevivatah ba-milhamah uva-Sho'ah, 1939–1943* (Grodno Is Not the Same: The Jewish Community of Grodno and Its Environs during the Second World War and the Holocaust, 1939–1943, in Hebrew) (Jerusalem: Yad Vashem, 2001), p. 45; interview with Helen Tichauer, July 1, 2003.

77. Kramer, "Hell and Rebirth" p. 14.

78. Ibid., p. 15.

79. Kogon, *The Theory and Practice of Hell,* pp. 63–71.

80. Iwaszko, "Deportation to the Camp," pp. 61, 54–69.

81. One of the most recent discussions of photography by the Nazis does not raise the issue of "criminal" photographs; see Nina Springer-Aharoni, "Photographs as Historical Documents," in Gutman and Gutterman, *The Auschwitz Album,* pp. 87–97.

82. Hermann Langbein, *Menschen in Auschwitz* (Vienna: Europaverlag, 1987), p. 560; Struk, *Photographing the Holocaust,* p. 103.

83. Bernd Sösemann and Michael Schulz, "Nationalsozialismus und Propaganda. Das Konzentrationslager Oranienburg in der Anfangsphase totalitärer Herrschaft," in *Konzentrationslager Oranienburg,* ed. Günter Miorsch and Corinna Cossmann (Oranienburg: Hentrich, 1994), pp. 78–94, esp. p. 88, and p. 181; see the elaborately staged photographs in the catalog, pp. 181–84.

84. W/S no. 08459, CD no. 0327, from Panstowowe Muzeum w Oświęcim-Brzezinka, USHMM; Czech, *Auschwitz Chronicle,* p. 133.

85. W/S no. 13061, CD no. 0327, from Panstowowe Muzeum w Ośięcim-Brzezinka, USHMM; Czech, *Auschwitz Chronicle,* p. 117.

86. W/S no. 12936, CD no. 0327, from Panstowowe Muzeum w Oświęcim-Brzezinka, USHMM; Czech, *Auschwitz Chronicle,* p. 106.

87. W/S no. 08471, CD no. 0327, from Panstowowe Muzeum w Oświęcim-Brzezinka, USHMM; Czech, *Auschwitz Chronicle,* p. 98.

88. Czech, *Auschwitz Chronicle,* p. ix.

89. Friedlander, "Concerning the Extra-legal Decisions"; Czech, *Auschwitz Chronicle,* pp. 71, 69, 81.

90. Hermann Langbein, *People in Auschwitz,* trans. Harry Zohn; foreword by Henry Friedlander (Chapel Hill: University of North Carolina Press, 2004), photo opposite p. 3.

91. Friedlander, "Foreword," *People in Auschwitz,* p. xiii. See also Langbein, *People in Auschwitz,* pp. 4–5.

92. Aleksander Lasik, "Organizational Structure of Auschwitz Concentration Camp. 5.7. The Identification Service and the Interrogation and Investigation Office," in *Auschwitz 1940–1945: Central Issues in the History of the Camp,* Volume I: *The Establishment and Organization of the Camp,* ed. Aleksander Lasik, Franciszek Piper, Piotr Setkiewicz, and Irena Strzelecka (Auschwitz: Auschwitz-Birkenau State Museum, 2000), pp. 184–86.

93. Ibid., pp. 185–86. See also Renata Boguslawska-Swiebocka and Teresa Ceglowska, in *KL Auschwitz Documentary Photographs* (Warsaw: Krajowa Agencja Wydawnicza, 1980), pp. 11–12.

94. Hermann Langbein, *Menschen in Auschwitz* (Vienna: Europaverlag, 1987), pp. 137ff. The most comprehensive treatment of the event, stressing the significance of gender, is Dwork, "Agents, Contexts, Responsibilities." Dwork raises the possibility that there may indeed have been some kind of attempted rebellion or possibly an outbreak by the Jewish women prisoners (pp. 164–67).

95. The account of the massacre and its aftermath largely follows the description of Broad, *KZ Auschwitz*, pp. 39–45. Although we cannot determine the date precisely, it was prior to October 24, 1942; "Eine Seite aus dem Tagebuch von SS-Obersturmführer Dr. Johann Kremer," in *Hefte von Auschwitz* 3 (1960): 125. For other scholarly treatments of this subject see Adam Rutkowski, "Uprising in the Budy Camp?" *Yad Vashem Studies* 18 (Jerusalem, 1987): 259–74, and Anna Zieba, "Wirtschaftshof Budy," *Hefte von Auschwitz* 10 (1967): 67–86. Rutkowski succeeds in proving that there was nothing resembling a "revolt" in Budy, and Zieba primarily discusses the relationship between the camp and the surrounding non-Jewish Polish population.

96. Broad, *KZ Auschwitz*, p. 40; Czech, "The Origins of the Camp," p. 27.

97. Rutkowski, "Uprising in the Budy Camp?" p. 260; Franciszek Piper, *Auschwitz Prison Labor: The Organization and Exploitation of Auschwitz Concentration Camp Prisoners as Laborers,* trans. William Brand (Auschwitz: Auschwitz-Birkenau State Museum, 2002), p. 187; Erwin Foley, "Oral history interview with Erwin Foley, September 19, 1995 [sound recording]," RG-50.106*0018; Acc. 1995.A.1200, USHMM. The last roll call *(Appell)* at Budy, January 17, 1945, counted 313 prisoners; Halina Wrobel, "Die Liquidation des Konzentrationslagers," *Hefte von Auschwitz* 6 (1962): 16; Piper, *Auschwitz Prison Labor,* p. 195.

98. Broad, *KZ Auschwitz,* pp. 40–41. For a Jewish prisoner's view of Grabner, see Irene Weiss (née Berger, wid. Maityn), in Shelley, *Secretaries of Death,* p. 60.

99. As late as April 28, 1944, an inquiry was made into his origins; response on May 20, 1944; Pery Broad file, RuSHA, A 3343, RS-A5201, BDC, NA.

100. Rawicz, "Foreword," p. 9; Susan E. Cernyk-Spatz (née Eckstein), in Shelley, *Secretaries of Death,* p. 109; "R.u.S.-Fragebogen," April 22, 1944, Pery Broad file, NA, BDC; Shelley, "Foreword," *Secretaries of Death,* p. xv.

101. Broad, *KZ Auschwitz,* p. 40; Rutkowski, "Uprising in the Budy Camp?" pp. 261–62.

102. Broad, *KZ Auschwitz,* p. 41.

103. Ibid. p. 42. Grabner's assistant is called "Georg," in Shelley, *Secretaries of Death,* p. 368, but identified as "Erich" in several publications of the Auschwitz State Museum. The recollection in Shelley, however, seems to be correct, because a health form *(Sanitäts-Inspektion der Waffen SS, Gesundheits- und Verwendungsprüfstelle beim SS-Lazarett Dachau)* exists for "Georg Wisnitzka," born in Kat-

towitz, August 30, 1911, who had served in the Dachau concentration camp sometime between January 12, 1941, and November 28, 1941. A 3343-RS-G5398–0542, BDC, NA.

104. Langbein, *Menschen in Auschwitz*, p. 137; Rutkowski, "Uprising in the Budy Camp?" p. 260; Broad, *KZ Auschwitz*, p. 40.

105. Shelley, *Secretaries of Death*, p. 368; SS-Untersturmführer u. Gerichtsoffizier an den Chef der 2. Schwadron/SSKRgt.1, Kielce, Betrifft: Briefverkehr des SS-Stm.Lang, January 31, 1941; this is the case of a *Volksdeutsche* soldier, Josef Lang (born November 18, 1918), who was disciplined for using the Polish language in his private correspondence. T-354, roll 797, frame 000020, BDC, NA; using Polish and Czechoslovakian was expressly prohibited for higher SS and police leaders in a directive of July 17, 1940, Lublin, T-354, frame 516, BDC, NA.

106. Iwaszko, "Deportation to the Camp," pp. 64–68; Czech, "Origins of the Camp," p. 28.

107. Broad, *KZ Auschwitz*, p. 42.

108. Dwork, "Agents, Contexts, Responsibilities," p. 164.

109. Broad, *KZ Auschwitz*, pp. 40, 42. The two women were not arrested as prostitutes, per se, but probably for failing to appear to labor assignments and other such infractions; author's interview with Helen Tichauer, New York City, August 28, 2003.

110. Broad, *KZ Auschwitz*, pp. 42–43.

111. Ibid., pp. 43–44.

112. *Commandant of Auschwitz: The Autobiography of Rudolf Höss* (Cleveland and New York: World, 1959), p. 149.

113. Broad, *KZ Auschwitz*, p. 43.

114. Struk, *Photographing the Holocaust*, pp. 103, 105, 109, 111, 119.

115. Broad, *KZ Auschwitz*, p. 44.

116. Rutkowski adds this in his translation, which is not in the English-language version, "Uprising in the Budy Camp?" p. 267, Broad, *KZ Auschwitz*, pp. 43–44.

117. Dwork, "Agents, Contexts, Responsibilities," pp. 163–67; Broad, *KZ Auschwitz*, pp. 44–45.

118. Langbein, *Menschen in Auschwitz*, p. 138.

119. Broad, *KZ Auschwitz*, p. 45.

120. Gary A. Keins, "Journey through the Valley of Perdition Traveled by Gary A. Keins," RG-02.183, p. 64, USHMM.

121. Geoffrey Giles, "The Institutionalization of Homosexual Panic in the Third Reich," in *Social Outsiders in Nazi Germany*, ed. Robert Gellately and Nathan Stoltzfus (Princeton, NJ: Princeton University Press, 2001), pp. 233–55, esp. pp. 238–40.

122. My survey includes over 150 memoirs in RG.02, USHMM, and reports of rape by Germans and collaborators, often SS, and explicit sexual assault are

present in more than two dozen accounts. See, for example, Kramer, "Hell and Rebirth," p. 10; in published sources, see Wells, *The Janowska Road,* pp. 104ff., 209ff., and Michael Temchin, *The Witch Doctor: Memoirs of a Partisan* (New York: Holocaust Library, 1983), pp. 36ff.

123. George L. Mosse, *Nationalism and Sexuality: Respectability and Abnormal Sexuality in Modern Europe* (New York: Howard Fertig, 1985).

124. Revealed in the individual records and monthly (sometimes irregular) compilations of disciplinary matters of SS men in the Ostgebiet; several such reports are mentioned in "finding aid" number 95, which accompanies the Berlin Document Collection in the U.S. National Archives, T-354, BDC, NA.

125. For example, SS Unterscharführer Karl Anton was disciplined for "plundering 100 Zloty from a Jew" on May 21, 1940, in Garwolin, as Jews were being systematically plundered; Der Kommandeur des 2.SS-Totenkopf-Reiterregiments m.d.F. b., memo from Lublin, October 17, 1940, "Gerichtliche Strafen im Monat September 1940," T354, roll 713, frame 387, BDC, NA.

126. Van Pelt and Dwork, *Auschwitz: 1270 to the Present,* p. 196.

127. One of a series of situation reports, focusing primarily on economic matters but including other concerns, "Die wirtschaftliche Lage in den besetzten Ostgebieten," 31 December 1941, from Wirtschaftsstab Ost, T-178, roll 19, BDC, NA.

128. Rutkowski writes that it was a "double" fence; "Uprising in the Budy Camp?" p. 260.

129. This emerges clearly in the early history of the camp; see van Pelt and Dwork, *Auschwitz: 1270 to the Present,* p. 169. Given that Höss's construction budget was "rather generous," and the Erkennungsdienst also documented the Auschwitz building projects, Höss might have diverted the Erkennungsdienst expenses by including them with building costs. "This facility was set up at the end of 1941 by an SS man named Dietrich Kamann to supply more effectively building works photographs to accompany reports"; see Frank Dabba Smith, *Photography and the Holocaust,* Rabbinic diss. (London: Leo Baeck College, 1994), p. 38.

130. Helen Freinbun, "Helen Freinbun testimony," RG-02.068*01, p. 4, USHMM; Gordon Horwitz, *In the Shadow of Death,* p. 17.

131. Broad, *KZ Auschwitz,* p. 14.

132. Ibid.

133. W/S no. 37178, CD no. 0015, 130.120, showing a dead prisoner on the ground, from the Main Commission for the Prosecution of the Crimes against the Polish Nation, USHMM; W/S no. 37175, CD no. 0015, from the Bildarchiv Preussischer Kulturbesitz, USHMM.

134. Helena Rothstein, in *Auschwitz—The Nazi Civilization: Twenty-three Women Prisoners' Accounts: Auschwitz Camp Administration and SS Enterprises and Workshops,* ed. Lore Shelley (Lanham, MD: University Press of America, 1992), p. 15.

135. Broad, *KZ Auschwitz*, pp. 14–15, n. 21.

136. One of the more authoritative works about Auschwitz perpetuates the Höss line, stating that ninety "French Jews" were murdered "for allegedly planning a revolt." See Franciszek Piper, "Living Conditions as Methods of Exterminating," in Piper and Swiebocka, *Auschwitz: Nazi Death Camp*, p. 150. His comment is based on a Polish translation of Höss's autobiography. See van Pelt and Dwork, *Auschwitz: 1270 to the Present*, pp. 195–96: "Himmler's agricultural estate project was carried on with the naked strength of the (mostly women) slave laborers. . . . It was too great an assault for anyone to sustain, and it is possible that one day early in October 1942, women slave laborers at the agricultural farm in the Auschwitz subcamp of Budy tried to break out."

137. See Joanna Bourke, "The Body in Modern Warfare, Myth and Meaning, 1914–1945," in *What History Tells: George L. Mosse and the Culture of Modern Europe*, ed. Stanley G. Payne, David J. Sorkin, and John S. Tortorice (Madison: University of Wisconsin Press, 2004), p. 214; Bourke cites Mikhail Bakhtin from *Rabelais and His World*, trans. Helene Iswolsky (Cambridge, MA: MIT Press, 1985).

138. Höss, *Commandant of Auschwitz*, p. 149.

139. Hilberg, *Prologue to Annihilation*, pp. 50–51.

140. Czech, "The Origins of the Camp," p. 36.

141. An article, which is more in the form of a reminiscence, contradicts Helen Tichauer's statement about Budy being immune from "selections." Zofia Pomysz has written the story of a Polish woman inmate who is saved in Budy because of her beautiful voice; a Jewish woman prisoner with "a Polish number" secretly teaches her the German songs that please the SS. In the story there is a "selection"—but it is among prisoners who are sick; see Zofia Posmysz, "Die 'Sängerin,' " *Hefte von Auschwitz* 8 (1964): 15–32.

142. Richard Newman with Karen Kirtley, *Alma Rosé: Vienna to Auschwitz* (Portland, OR: Amadeus Press, 2000), pp. 255, 266–67.

143. Broad, *KZ Auschwitz*, p. 40.

144. Van Pelt and Dwork, *Auschwitz 1270 to the Present*, p. 359.

145. "The Beginnings of Sam Stammer's Life as written by him in German," RG-O2.178, pp. 10–11, USHMM.

146. "Interview with Helen Spitzer Tichauer, New York, March 23, 2000," p. 11.

147. Entry of Helena Rothstein (alias Ilonka Gutman) in Shelley, *Auschwitz*, pp. 15–16. See also the following in Shelley, *Secretaries of Death*: Hermine (Herma) Markovits (née Hirschler), pp. 120–30; (Janka) (née Berger), p. 31; Irene Weiss, p. 63; Shelley, "Foreword," pp. XV– XVI. Helen Tichauer, interview with the author, New York City, July 1, 2003.

148. Erwin Foley, "Oral history interview with Erwin Foley, September 19, 1995 [sound recording]," tape 1, side 2, RG-50, 106*0018, USHMM.

149. Rutkowski, pp. 272–73; Zieba, "Wirtschaftshof Budy," p. 74; "Oral history interview with Erwin Foley," tape 1, side 2. The women's penal company

(Strafkompanie) was brought to Birkenau when the women's camp was created there on August 16, 1942; another women's camp was established, however, on April 5, 1943; Zieba, "Wirtschaftshof Budy," p. 75.

150. Zieba, "Wirtschaftshof Budy," p. 70; "Oral history interview with Erwin Foley," tape 1, side 2.

151. See Raul Hilberg, *The Destruction of the European Jews* (New York: Holmes & Meier, 1985): "In the death camps the dehumanization of the victims in the eyes of their captors became manifest in a variety of ways. In essence the SS thought of the arriving Jews as having forfeited their lives from the moment they stepped off the train. They staged mock marriages and other amusements with the expectation that in a very short time these objects of their play would be gassed. . . . first in Sobibor and then in Treblinka [a very large Saint Bernard named Barry] had been trained to maul inmates upon the command, 'Man, grab that dog! [Mensch, fass den Hund!]' " (p. 898).

152. Richard Rubenstein, *After Auschwitz: Radical Theology and Contemporary Judaism* (Indianapolis: Bobbs-Merrill, 1966), pp. 33–34.

153. Yitzhak Arad, *Belzec, Sobibor, Treblinka: The Operation Reinhard Death Camps* (Bloomington: Indiana University Press, 1999).

154. Maria Davidson, "Remembrances," RG-02.081*01, p. 5, USHMM; Irene Strzelecka, "Women," in Gutman and Berenbaum, *Anatomy of the Auschwitz Death Camp,* p. 410; see also Hermann Langbein, "The Auschwitz Underground," in *Anatomy,* pp. 500–502.

155. Elie Wiesel, *Night,* trans. Stella Rodway (New York: Avon, 1969), pp. 72–76.

156. W/S no. 94675, photo of "Jewish figures suspended from an anti-Semitic float at a Fasching parade in Nuremberg," USHMM; W/S no. 41979, "Cartoon depicting Jews, communists and other enemies of the Nazis hanging on a gallows," USHMM.

157. Liza Ettinger, "From the Lida Ghetto to the Bielski Partisans," RG-02.*133, translated by B. Caspi, written December 1984, p. 6, USHMM.

158. Samuel Pruchno, "Samuel Pruchno memoir," RG-02.002*12, p. 2, USHMM.

159. Isaiah Trunk, *L'odzsh'er geto: a historishe un sotsyologishe shtudye me dokumentn, taveles un mape* (New York: YIVO, 1962), pp. 107–8; Wells, *The Janowska Road,* pp. 145, 50.

160. Kramer, "Hell and Rebirth," p. 12.

161. Ibid., p. 33.

162. William Eisen, "William Eisen Testimony," p. 63.

163. Sonja Haid Greene, "Between Life and Death (My Memoirs)," RG-02.112, p. 79, USHMM.

164. Yudel Beiles, *Yudke,* trans. Vida Urbonavičius-Watkins (Vilnius: Baltos lankos, 2002), pp. 89–90.

165. Höss,"The Autobiography of Rudolf Höss," p. 42.

166. Regina Steinberg (née Hofstaedter wid. Lebsfeld), in Shelley, *Secretaries of Death,* p. 137.

167. Rubenstein, *After Auschwitz,* p. 7.

168. Dr. Tuli, "Letse teg in nirenberg" (Last Day in Nuremberg), *Undzer Velt,* no. 17, no. 25 (September 29, 1946): 7, quoted in Zeev W. Mankowitz, *Life between Memory and Hope: The Survivors of the Holocaust in Occupied Germany* (Cambridge: Cambridge University Press, 2002), p. 233.

169. Gryn, *Chasing Shadows,* p. 194.

170. Ibid., p. 225.

5. RE-PRESENTING ZIONISM AS THE APEX OF GLOBAL CONSPIRACY

1. See especially the work of Francis R. Nicosia, *The Third Reich and the Palestine Question* (New Brunswick, NJ: Transaction, 2000); "Ein nützlicher Feind; Zionismus im nationalsozialistischen Deutschland, 1933–1939," *Vierteljahrshefte für Zeitgeschichte* 37, no. 3 (1989): 367–400; "The End of Emancipation and the Illusion of Preferential Treatment: German Zionism, 1933–1938," *Leo Baeck Institute Year Book* 36 (1991): 243–65; "Der Zionismus in Leipzig im Dritten Reich," in *Judaica Lipsiensia: zur Geschichte der Juden in Leipzig,* ed. Manfred Unger (Leipzig: Edition Leipzig, 1994), pp. 60–76; "Zionismus und Antisemitismus im Dritten Reich; Folgen für die Zeit nach dem Holocaust," in *Der Umgang mit dem Holocaust: Europa-USA-Israel,* ed. Rolf Steininger (Vienna: Böhlau, 1994), pp. 60–76. Carsten Teichert, *Chasak! Zionismus im nationalsozialistischen Deutschland 1933–1938* (Cologne: Elen-Verlag, 2000).

2. Yfaat Weiss, "The Transfer Agreement and the Boycott Movement: A Jewish Dilemma on the Eve of the Holocaust," *Yad Vashem Studies* 26 (1998): 129–71.

3. Sonja Haid Greene, "Between Life and Death (My Memoirs)," Record Group (hereafter RG) 02.112, p. 8, United States Holocaust Memorial Museum (hereafter USHMM); Danuta Czech, *Auschwitz Chronicle, 1939–1945* (New York: Henry Holt, 1997).

4. Norman Cohn, *Warrant for Genocide: The Myth of the Jewish World Conspiracy and the Protocols of the Elders of Zion* (London: Serif, 1996); George L. Mosse, *Toward the Final Solution: A History of European Racism* (Madison: University of Wisconsin Press, 1985).

5. Compare this to an article appearing in the summer of 1939: Heinz Ballensiefen, "Weltjudentum—Wesen und Gefahr," *Mitteilungen über die Judenfrage* (hereafter *Die Judenfrage*), June 8, 1939, pp. 1–3. Zionists are referred to as one of several significant "groups" (p. 2). Interestingly, this piece was followed by two articles on Zionism.

6. Max Weinreich, *Hitler's Professors: The Part of Scholarship in Germany's Crimes against the Jewish People* (New Haven, CT: Yale University Press, 1999; first publ. 1946); Joseph [Josef] Wulf, ed., *Presse und Funk im Dritten Reich: Eine Dokumentation* (Gütersloh: Sigbert Mohn Verlag, 1964); Richard J. Evans, *In Hitler's Shadow: West German Historians and the Attempt to Escape from the Nazi Past* (New York: Pantheon, 1989); Roni Stauber, "From Revisionism to Holocaust Denial—David Irving as a Case Study," H-Antisemitism Occasional Papers, posted July 25, 2000, at http://www2.h-net.msu.edu/~antis/papers/stauber/stauber.006.html; Robert Wistrich, *Hitler's Apocalypse: Jews and the Nazi Legacy* (New York: St. Martin's Press, 1985); O. John Rogge, *The Official German Report: Nazi Penetration 1924–1942, Pan-Arabism 1939–Today* (New York: Thomas Yoseloff, 1961).

7. For another attempt "to interpret the persecution of the Jews as a justified . . . defensive measure," see Patricia von Papen, *"Scholarly" Antisemitism during the Third Reich: The Reichsinstitut's Research on the "Jewish Question" 1935–1945* (Ph.D. diss., Columbia University, 1999), pp. 247–49.

8. Lucille Eichengreen, *Rumkowski and the Orphans of Lodz* (San Francisco: Mercury House, 2000), p. 75.

9. See Yehuda Bauer, *Jews for Sale? Nazi-Jewish Negotiations, 1933–1945* (New Haven, CT: Yale University Press, 1994).

10. Abraham Barkai, *German Jewish History in Modern Times,* ed. Michael Meyer (New York: Columbia University Press, 1997), pp. 320, 322–23; Shlomo Aronson and Richard Breitman, "The End of the 'Final Solution'? Nazi Plans to Ransom Jews in 1944," *Central European History* 25, no. 2 (1993): 177–203.

11. See Brian Amkraut, *Between Home and Homeland: Youth Aliyah in Nazi Germany* (Tuscaloosa: University of Alabama Press, 2006).

12. There is no mention of Zionism in the first programmatic statement of the journal *Mitteilungen über die Judenfrage;* see "Zur Einführung," issue of February 1, 1937. In an article summarizing the history of the movement, the writer stresses that Zionism came on the scene "too late" to make much of a difference in solving the Jewish question, and the same conflicts as in Europe were emerging between the Jews, the British, and the Arabs in Palestine; see Wilhelm Ziegler, "40 Jahre Zionismus," *Die Judenfrage,* February 1, 1937, pp. 3–4.

13. Hans Hummel, "Finden die Juden ihren Staat?" *Die Judenfrage,* March 25, 1938, pp. 11–14; Christopher R. Browning, *The Final Solution and the German Foreign Office: A Study of Referat D III of Abteilung Deutschland, 1940–1943* (New York: Holmes & Meier, 1978).

14. W/S no. 94208, CD no. 0325, from Stadtarchiv Fürth, USHMM; W/S no. 98544, CD no. 0294, from Bundesarchiv, USHMM.

15. Raul Hilbert, *Prologue to Annihilation: A Study of the Identification, Impoverishment and Isolation of the Jewish Victims of Nazi Policy* (Ph.D. thesis, New York: Columbia University, 1955), p. 273.

16. See Wistrich, *Hitler's Apocalypse,* pp. 155–58.

17. Adolf Hitler, *Mein Kampf,* trans. Ralph Manheim (Boston: Houghton Mifflin, 1999), pp. 56–57.

18. Ibid., pp. 324–35, italics added.

19. See Gerhard L. Weinberg, "World War II Leaders and Their Visions for the Future of Palestine," J. B. and Maurice C. Shapiro Annual Lecture, January 31, 2002 (Washington, DC: United States Holocaust Memorial Museum, 2002).

20. Entry for October 26–27, 1941, evening, in *Hitler's Table Talk 1941–1944: His Private Conversations,* trans. Norman Cameron and R. H. Stevens (New York: Enigma, 2000), pp. 92–93.

21. Entries for November 11, evening, and for night of January 4–5, 1942, ibid., pp. 125, 179.

22. Henry Friedlander, *Origins of the Nazi Genocide: From Euthanasia to the Final Solution* (Chapel Hill: University of North Carolina Press, 1995).

23. Entry for night of January 4–5, 1942, *Hitler's Table Talk,* p. 179.

24. Entry for July 1, 1942, midday, ibid., p. 545.

25. Entries for February 9, 1942, midday, and for July 5, 1942, evening, ibid., pp. 306, 561.

26. Entry for April 10, 1942, evening, ibid., pp. 421–22.

27. Entry for July 5, 1942, evening, ibid., p. 563.

28. Entry for July 1, 1942, midday, ibid., p. 547. See also a review of a book on the Mufti: "Der Grossmufti über die Palästinafrage," *Die Judenfrage,* May 26, 1938, p. 5.

29. Dennis E. Showalter, *Little Man, What Now? Der Stürmer in the Weimar Republic* (Hamden, CT: Archon Books, 1982), pp. 158–59.

30. See cover article, *Der Stürmer,* October 1939: "Judenstaat Palästina: Die Judenfrage ist die Schicksalsfrage des englischen Volkes."

31. It was reissued in a slightly different form in 1937.

32. Alfred Rosenberg, *Die Spur des Juden im Wandel der Zeiten* (Munich: Deutscher Volksverlag, 1920), p. 111.

33. Ibid., pp. 112–13.

34. Whenever possible, Rosenberg, who fancied himself a scholar, liked to support himself with footnotes; he especially relished culling citations from the enemy.

35. Rosenberg, *Die Spur des Juden,* pp. 114–15.

36. Entry for "Melchior, Carl," in *Encyclopedia Judaica,* vol. 11 (Jerusalem, 1974), cols. 1286–87.

37. Rosenberg, *Die Spur des Juden,* p. 114; see also ch. 2 of this book.

38. Rosenberg, *Die Spur des Juden,* p. 114.

39. This quote was used in Zionist polemics; see Boris Shusteff, "For Truth and Zionism," available at http://www.gamla.org.il/english/article/1999/june/b1.htm.

40. Alfred Rosenberg, *Novemberköpfe* (Munich: Zentralverlag der NSDAP, Franz Eher Nachf., 1939), pp. 258, 325–27.

41. Ibid., pp. 31, 50ff.

42. Ibid., pp. 68, 73.

43. Ibid., p. 88.

44. Alfred Rosenberg, *The Myth of the Twentieth Century: An Evaluation of the Spiritual-Intellectual Confrontations of Our Age* (Newport, CA: Noontide, 1993), pp. 300–302. This reliable translation was produced by an anti-Semitic press.

45. See Wistrich, *Hitler's Acopalypse;* Evans, *In Hitler's Shadow;* Deborah E. Lipstadt, *Denying the Holocaust: The Growing Assault on Truth and Memory* (New York: Free Press, 1993). Nazi attempts at rationalization are closer to the efforts of scholars seeking to minimize Nazi Germany's culpability for the Holocaust in the controversy known as the *Historikersteit;* see Evans, *In Hitler's Shadow;* Charles S. Maier, *The Unmasterable Past: History, Holocaust, and German National Identity* (Cambridge, MA: Harvard University Press, 1988); Peter Baldwin, ed., *Reworking the Past: Hitler, the Holocaust, and the Historians' Debate* (Boston: Beacon, 1990).

46. See the testimony of Adolf Eichmann, in "The Trial of Adolf Eichmann," Session 96 (part 2 of 4), available at http://www.nizkor.org/hweb/people/e/eichmann-adolf/transcripts/Sessions/Sesion-096–02.html (accessed September 2001); and "The Testimony of Theodore Horst Grell" (part 2 of 2), available at http://www.nizkor.org/hweb/people/e/eichmann-adolf/transcrip . . . /Theodor_Horst_Grell-02.htm (accessed September 2001). For examples of how this has been appropriated by anti-Semites see "The Jewish Declaration of War on Nazi Germany: The Economic Boycott of 1933," *Barnes Review* (January/February 2001): 41–45; Franz J. Scheidl, "Deutschland und die Juden in Vergangenheit und Gegenwart," available at http://www.vho.org/D/dudj/10.htm; David Irving, "Extracts from confidential Manuscript by Karl Wolff, May 11, 1952," available at http://www.fpp.co.uk/Hitler/docs/adjutants/WolffMS1.html.

47. Maier, *The Unmasterable Past;* Baldwin, *Reworking the Past.*

48. Alexander G. Hardy, *Hitler's Secret Weapon: The "Managed" Press and Propaganda Machine of Nazi Germany* (New York: Vantage, 1967), p. 188.

49. Derrick Sington and Arthur Weidenfeld, *The Goebbels Experiment: A Study of the Nazi Propaganda Machine* (New Haven, CT: Yale University Press, 1943), pp. 61–62.

50. Gregory Paul Wegner, *Anti-Semitism and Schooling in the Third Reich* (New York: Routledge-Falmer, 2002).

51. Helmut Sündermann, *Die Grenzen fallen: von der Ostmark zum Sudetenland* (Munich: Zentralverlag der NSDAP, F. Eher Nachf., 1939).

52. Sington and Weidenfeld, *The Goebbels Experiment,* p. 65.

53. Helmut Sündermann, *Der Weg zum deutschen Journalismus: Hinweise für die Berufswahl junger Nationalsozialisten* (Munich: Zentralverlag der NSDAP, Franz Eher, 1938).

54. Sington and Weidenfeld, *The Goebbels Experiment*, p. 65.

55. Quoted in Hardy, *Hitler's Secret Weapon*, pp. 190–91.

56. See ch. 2.

57. Quoted in Hardy, *Hitler's Secret Weapon*, pp. 191–92.

58. February 5, 1943, Periodical Service, 196.65/Edition, no. 8312–8351, "Deutscher Wochendienst," (nos.) 8314 and 8315, quoted in Hardy, *Hitler's Secret Weapon*, pp. 198–99; see also the "Tagesparole of the Reich Press Chief, Secret, April 27, 1944," ibid., pp. 218–19.

59. February 5, 1943, Periodical Service, 196.65/Edition, no. 8312–8351, "Deutscher Wochendienst," (no.) 8314, quoted ibid., pp. 199–200.

60. April 2, 1943, Periodical Service, 204./73 Edition, no. 8613–8647, (no.) 9613, quoted ibid., p. 201.

61. April 2, 1943, Topical Subjects, 204./73 Edition, no. 8613–8647, (no.) 8615, quoted ibid., p. 202; Dietrich's directive of February 15, 1944, ibid., p. 224.

62. Quoted ibid., pp. 214–15.

63. Quoted ibid., p. 217.

64. Wolf Meyer-Christian, "Die jüdischen Absichten auf Süd-Amerika," *Die Judenfrage*, March 16, 1937, pp. 1–2; Meyer-Christian, "37,5 Prozent Juden oder 75 mal mehr Juden in der französischen Regierung als im Volk," *Die Judenfrage*, May 15, 1937, pp. 1–4; Meyer-Christian, "Palästina auf der langen Bank," *Die Judenfrage*, September 29, 1937, pp. 1–2.

65. Wolf Meyer-Christian, "Postscheck-Konto 27016 Paris. An der Quelle der Anti-Deutschland-Hetze," *Die Judenfrage*, July 19, 1937, pp. 3–5.

66. Wolf Meyer-Christian, "Vom Peelbericht zum Weissbuch," *Die Judenfrage*, August 5, 1937, pp. 5–6.

67. Von Papen, *"Scholarly" Antisemitism during the Third Reich*, pp. 8–9, note 24; Hilberg, *Prologue to Annihilation*, p. 403. In addition to Meyer-Christian and Riecke, other writers claimed expertise in this field, such as Karl Friedrich Franck: "Mandate—auf ewig unabänderlich? Völkerrechtliche Kunststückchen um das Palästina-Problem," *Die Judenfrage*, May 12, 1938, pp. 1–2; Hans Hummel, "Palästina noch ohne Ausweg," *Die Judenfrage*, May 26, 1938, pp. 3–4; Hansgeorg Trurnit, "England vor der Entscheidung? Umschau auf die Brennpunkte der Judenfrage," *Die Judenfrage*, November 1, 1938, pp. 1–3; Franz Rose, "Jüdische Drohungen. Die Erpressermethode im Kampf um Palästina," *Die Judenfrage*, November 18, 1938, p. 3–5; Hermann Erich Seifert, "Der Kampf um die Scholle Palästinas. Das Geld des Weltjudentums kauft den besten Boden auf," *Die Judenfrage*, February 16, 1939, pp. 1–2.

68. See, for example, Paul Krellmann, "Woher kommen die Juden? Die Entstehung der jüdischen Rasse," *Die Judenfrage*, February 23, 1939, pp. 3–4. "Aryan" does not often appear in article titles; cf. F. Redlin, "Trennung von arischem u. jüdischem Wohnraum!" *Die Judenfrage*, May 26, 1939, p. 6. The term was apparently propelled to the forefront, however, as a means of inspiring Italy

to comply with "racial laws"; Werner E. Eicke, "Faschismus und Rassenfrage," *Die Judenfrage*, June 23, 1939, pp. 1–4, and the next issue, July 7, 1939, pp. 6–9.

69. Hilberg, *Prologue to Annihilation*, p. 403.

70. See "Bücher zur Judenfrage. Entlarvte Weltpresse. Eine neue Schrift des Reichspressechefs der NSDAP," *Die Judenfrage*, January 17, 1938, p. 10; "Origen der Lüge. Aus 'Weltpresse ohne Maske' von Reichspressechef Dr. Dietrich," *Die Judenfrage*, March 16, 1938, p. 6.

71. Quoted in Hardy, *Hitler's Secret Weapon*, p. 217.

72. Ibid.

73. Weinreich, *Hitler's Professors*, p. 235.

74. On this journal, see von Papen, *"Scholarly" Antisemitism during the Third Reich*, pp. 149, 245–46; Weinreich, *Hitler's Professors*, note 470, p. 235.

75. Goetz Nordbruch, *The Socio-Historical Background of Holocaust Denial in Arab Countries: Reactions to Roger Garaudy's "The Founding Myths of Israeli Politics"* (Jerusalem: Vidal Sassoon International Center for the Study of Antisemitism, 2001).

76. Robert Herzstein, *The War That Hitler Won: The Most Infamous Propaganda Campaign in History* (New York: G. P. Putnam's Sons, 1978), p. 173. See also Jay Baird, *The Mythical World of Nazi Propaganda, 1939–1945* (Minneapolis: University of Minnesota Press, 1974), pp. 28–29; Hardy, *Hitler's Secret Weapon*, pp. 64–70.

77. Herzstein, *The War That Hitler Won*, p. 97.

78. Entry for July 18, 1942, in *Die Tagebücher von Joseph Goebbels*, Teil II, Diktate 1941–1945, Band 5, July–September 1942, ed. Elke Fröhlich (Munich: K. G. Saur, 1995), p. 145; on July 24, Goebbels again noted problems with "the Sündermann case," p. 179; see also the entry for February 11, 1942, Teil I, Band 9, p. 136.

79. Date on the document, "Die Behandlung der Judenfrage," after the first section, p. 11.

80. This is a major argument of von Papen's regarding the Reichsinstitut; see *"Scholarly" Antisemitism during the Third Reich*, pp. 186ff.

81. Baird, *The Mythical World of Nazi Propaganda*, p. 29.

82. Entry for December 5, 1942, in *Die Tagebücher von Joseph Goebbels*, Teil II, Diktate 1941–1945, Band 6, October–December 1942, p. 394; entry for May 28, 1942, Teil II, Diktate 1941–1945, Band 4, April–June 1942, p. 45.

83. Entry for July 1, 1942, in *The Secret Conferences of Dr. Goebbels: The Nazi Propaganda War, 1939–1943*, ed. Willi A. Boelcke (New York: E. P. Dutton, 1970), p. 251; entry for May 28, 1942, in *Die Tagebücher von Joseph Goebbels*, Teil II, Diktate 1941–1945, Band 4, April–June 1942, p. 384.

84. Ludwig F. Gengler, "Die deutschen Juden und das Versailler Diktat. Stimmungsmache und Umfall auf jüdischen Befehl," *Die Judenfrage*, June 8, 1939, pp. 8–10; "Anlage. Einzelheiten für die Sprachregelung bei der Behandlung des Zionismus durch die Presse" (middle document), YIVO; Herzstein, *The War That Hitler Won*, p. 96.

85. The directive was also signed off by, and therefore supported by, Oberregierungsrat (senior government official) Karl August Stuckenberg and Dr. L. Franz Gengler on the front of the document. Gengler was a contributor to *Die Judenfrage;* see Dr. L. F. Gengler, "Jüdische Räteregierung 1919 in München. Tatsachen und Kundgebungen vor 20 Jahren," *Die Judenfrage,* May 11, 1939, pp. 5–6.

86. Weinreich, *Hitler's Professors,* and Wulf, *Presse und Funk im Dritten Reich,* pp. 120–21. On Wulf see Nicolas Berg, *Der Holocaust und die westdeutschen Historiker: Erforschung und Erinnerung* (Göttingen: Wallstein, 2003).

87. One of the early instances, outside of books dealing with Zionism, in which the "Jewish Agency" is mentioned as a threatening institution is by Hansgeorg Turnit, "Das Ende der Kompromisse," *Die Judenfrage,* November 18, 1938, p. 18.

88. Weinreich, *Hitler's Professors,* p. 235.

89. Chb [?], "Das Judenporträt: Louis Dembitz Brandeis. Zionistenführer—'Weltfriedensvermittler'—höchster amerikanischer Richter," *Die Judenfrage,* May 11, 1939, p. 4; and Dr. W [?], "Das Judenporträt: Stephan *[sic]* S. Wise. Weltjudenführer und Amerikas Rabbi Nr. 1," *Die Judenfrage,* April 13, 1939, pp. 3–4.

90. Hitler, *Mein Kampf,* pp. 324–25.

91. Ballensiefen, "Weltjudentum—Wesen und Gefahr," pp. 1–3.

92. "Palästinaplan und Rassenhygiene," *Die Judenfrage,* July 19, 1937, pp. 7–8.

93. Letter from Koerber to Sündermann, June 13, 1944, p. 2, YIVO.

94. Wolf Meyer-Christian, "Die Behandlung der Judenfrage," p. 2. Part of the translation follows Weinreich, *Hitler's Professors,* p. 236.

95. Chb [?], "Das Judenporträt: Louis Dembitz Brandeis." A small item in June 1939 did not notice the Jewish Agency as a threatening entity: "England. Eine Million für den jüdischen Kampffonds," *Die Judenfrage,* June 23, 1939, p. 10.

96. Meyer-Christian, "Die Behandlung der Judenfrage," pp. 2–3.

97. Ibid., p. 3.

98. Walther Lohmann, "Die Juden in den Vereinigten Staaten," *Die Judenfrage,* March 16, 1937, pp. 3–5, and Lohmann, "Die Juden im öffentlichen Leben der Vereinigten Staaten," *Die Judenfrage,* April 3, 1937, pp. 3–6; Hans Hummel, "New York—die jüdische Machtzentrale," *Die Judenfrage,* February 16, 1938, pp. 1–4; Schach al Roy, "Ihre Hauspolitik. Die jüdischen Führerfamilien. Montefiore, Rothschild, Goldsmid—Beherrscher des Weltkahal," *Die Judenfrage,* September 15, 1938, pp. 9–10.

99. The Nazi knowledge of the sharp divisions among Zionists, at the very moment they claimed to have coalesced, is revealed in Hermann Erich Seifert, " 'Sechs Wochen mit der Waffe in der Hand.' Ein neuer Bericht des 'Irgun' über den jüdischen Terror in Palästina," *Die Judenfrage,* July 22, 1939, pp. 1–3.

100. Quoted in Hilberg, *Prologue to Annihilation,* p. 75.

101. Theodor Herzl, *Der Judenstaat. Versuch einer modernen Lösung der Judenfrage* (Vienna: M. Breitenstein, 1896).

102. Derek J. Penslar, *Shylock's Children: Economics and Jewish Identity in Modern Europe* (Berkeley: University of California Press, 2001), pp. 237–48.

103. Ibid., pp. 248, 237.

104. Ibid., p. 248.

105. (Unattributed, possibly by Walter Hafner), "Lord contra Lord. Das Kulissenspiel um Palästina," *Die Judenfrage*, August 5, 1937, pp. 1–3. A follow-up article was even more dismissive, questioning the possibility that Jews could make a go of it under the partition; (unattributed article), "Geteiltes Palästina— lebensfähig? Bemerkenswerte englische Feststellungen zur Wirtschaftsfrage," *Die Judenfrage*, June 2, 1938, p. 3.

106. Entries for August 19 and 20, 1937, *Die Tagebücher von Joseph Goebbels*, Teil I, Band 4, March–November 1937, pp. 271, and 273. Ormsby-Gore was Colonial Secretary. See also Wolf Meyer-Christian's book to be discussed below, *Die englisch-jüdische Allianz: Werden und Wirken der kapitalistischen Weltherrschaft* (Berlin-Leipzig: Nibelungen Verlag, 1940), pp. 163–67.

107. W/S no. 59105, CD no. 0376, from *Der Stürmer* Archive, E39 Nr. 1240/14, USHMM.

108. Georg Haller, "Palästina vor der Entscheidung," *Die Judenfrage*, June 19, 1937, p. 2. Here the point appears to be first raised about Jewish world solidarity within the scope of Zionism, but its materialization is described as "hopeful" by Jewry (p. 3). A later article specifically said that the Jews in the diaspora (Galuth-Judentum) would prevent the fulfillment of Herzl's plan; Walter Hafner, "Herzl und der Judenstaat," *Die Judenfrage*, August 5, 1937, pp. 4–5.

109. Gerhart Rentner, "Professor Selig Brodetsky. Ein Führer des Weltzionismus in Prag," *Die Judenfrage*, October 13, 1938, pp. 9–10; Gerhart Rentner, "Wladimir Jabotinsky. Vorkämpfer der Gewaltpolitik und des 'Selbstschutzes,'" *Die Judenfrage*, December 1, 1938, pp. 6–7; Gerhart Rentner, "Das Judenporträt: Chaim Weizmann," *Die Judenfrage*, November 18, 1938, pp. 8–9. There is no hint here of the aggressive stance toward Germany with which he was later charged. See Hermann Erich Siefert, "Der 'Irgun' ruft zum Kampf. Englands 'neue' Vorschläge' für eine Palästina-Lösung," *Die Judenfrage*, April 19, 1939, pp. 1–2.

110. Chb. [?], "Judenparteien in Palästina," *Die Judenfrage*, May 26, 1939, p. 3.

111. See Rosenberg, *Myth of the Twentieth Century*.

112. Meyer-Christian, "Die Behandlung der Judenfrage," p. 3.

113. *Die Tagebücher von Joseph Goebbels*, Teil II, Diktate 1941–1945, Band 3, January–March 1942.

114. Letter from Chaim Weizmann to Neville Chamberlain, London, August 29, 1939, item 123 in *The Letters and Papers of Chaim Weizmann*, general ed. Barnet Litvinoff, vol. XIX, series A, January 1939–June 1940, ed. Norman Rose (New Brunswick, NJ: Transaction; Jerusalem: Israel Universities Press, 1979), p. 145.

115. Chaim Weizmann letter to Neville Chamberlain, March 24, 1939, item no. 37, *The Letters and Papers of Chaim Weizmann*, vol. XIX, series A, pp. 32–34.

116. Evans, *In Hitler's Shadow*, pp. 39, 82, 84.

117. *Book of Remembrance: The German, Austrian and Czechoslovakian Jews Deported to the Baltic States*, vol. 1, compiled by Wolfgang Scheffler and Diana Schulloe, ed. Volksbund Deutsche Kriegsgräberfürsorge e.V. and the Riga-Komitee der deutschen Städte, in cooperation with the Stiftung Neue Synagoge Berlin-Centrum Judaicum and the Memorial House of the Wannsee Conference (Munich: K. G. Saur Verlag, 2003), pp. 252–75.

118. Meyer-Christian, "Die Behandlung der Judenfrage," p. 3. Part of the translation here follows Weinreich, *Hitler's Professors*, p. 236.

119. The Nazis announced the problem of German Jewry "solved" on a number of occasions, including some five months before *Kristallnacht*, when it was proclaimed that the situation had changed "fundamentally": E. S. [?], "Kennzeichnen für jüdische Geschäfte. Die dritte Verordnung zum Reichsbürgergesetz schafft eine öffentliche Liste aller jüdischen Gewerbetriebe," *Die Judenfrage*, June 23, 1938.

120. Meyer-Christian, "Die Behandlung der Judenfrage," p. 4.

121. Letter from SS-Standartenführer und Kommandeur der 1. SS-Totenkopf Reiterstandarte Hermann Fegelein, "An sämtliche Einheitsführer der 1. SS-Totenkopf Reiterstandarte," Warsaw, February 15, 1940, T-354, roll no. 666, frame 000373, Berlin Documents Collection, United States National Archives, College Park, MD (hereafter BDC, NA).

122. Meyer-Christian, "Die Behandlung der Judenfrage," p. 5. Part of the translation follows Weinreich, *Hitler's Professors*, p. 237.

123. Ibid.

124. Ibid., p. 5.

125. Ibid., p. 6. Part of the translation follows *Hitler's Professors*, p. 238.

126. Ibid., pp. 6–7.

127. See Dr. W [?], "Das Judenporträt: Stephan *[sic]* S. Wise. Weltjudenführer und Amerikas Rabbi Nr. 1," *Die Judenfrage*, April 13, 1939, pp. 3–4; this is one of the first indications of a change in Nazi thinking (p. 4).

128. Meyer-Christian, "Die Behandlung der Judenfrage," pp. 8–9.

129. Rogge, *The Official German Report*, p. 380.

130. Meyer-Christian, "Die Behandlung der Judenfrage," pp. 10–11. Part of the translation follows Weinreich, *Hitler's Professors*, p. 238.

131. "Anlage. Einzelheiten für die Sprachregelung bei der Behandlung des Zionismus durch die Presse," pp. 1, 2.

132. Heinz Riecke, *Der Zionismus: Lösung der Judenfrage oder eine Weltgefahr?* (Berlin: Theodor Fritsch Verlag, 1939). Riecke's articles in *Die Judenfrage* seem to have influenced Meyer-Christian; see Heinz Riecke, "Politische Soziologie des geplanten Judenstaates," *Die Judenfrage*, pp. 1–3. On Wirsing, see von Papen, *"Scholarly" Antisemitism during the Third Reich*, pp. 243–44.

133. Giselher Wirsing, *Engländer, Juden, Araber in Palästina* (Jena: E. Diederichs, 1939), pp. 7, 117.

134. Ibid., pp. 7–9, 10ff., 17ff., 54.

135. For instance, he makes the common error of elevating Weizmann to a professorship in biochemistry at the University of Manchester; Wirsing, *Engländer, Juden, Araber*, p. 61.

136. Ibid., pp. 93, 106, 120, 79–93.

137. Ibid., pp. 256–65.

138. Ibid., p. 286.

139. "Orden Annahme" [Ordensannahme] decoration awarded to Giselher Wirsing: "Im namen des deutschen Volkes erteile ich dem Hauptschriftleiter Dr. Giselher Wirsing die Genehmigung zur Annahme des Komturkreuzes des Königlich Bulgarischen Zivilverdienstordens. Berlin. Den 19.November 1943 (signed, Adolf Hitler) der Führer." T-70, RDP 45, roll no. 131, frame no. 954, BDC, NA. Also included in the file is a note suggesting that Wirsing refrain from wearing the medal and further referring to this honor in light of the fact that Bulgaria had now set itself against Germany. The note appears to have been sent by Otto Dietrich; from Reichsverband der deutschen Presse, Körperschaft des öffentlichen Rechts, Hauptgeschäftsstelle, September 25, 1944, T-70, RDP 45, roll no. 131, frame no. 955, BDC, NA.

140. Entry for "Giselher Wirsing" in "Lexikon" of the IDGR-Informationsdienst gegen Rechtsextremismus, www.idgr.de/lexikon/bio/w/wirsing-giselher/wirsing.html (accessed September 2001).

141. Entry for April 4, 1945, *Die Tagebücher von Joseph Goebbels*, Teil II, Diktate 1941–1945, Band 15, January–April 1945, pp. 674–76.

142. Ba. [?], "Bücherspiegel. Der Zionismus—Weltgefahr [review of Riecke's *Der Zionismus*]," *Die Judenfrage*, April 27, 1939, p. 4.

143. Riecke, *Der Zionismus*, pp. 32–33.

144. Ibid., pp. 30–31, 53.

145. Ibid., pp. 43, 61.

146. Dr. L. F. Gengler, "Jüdische Räteregierung 1919 in München. Tatsachen und Kundgebungen vor 20 Jahren," *Die Judenfrage*, May 11, 1939, pp. 5–6.

147. Riecke, *Der Zionismus*, p. 33.

148. Ibid., pp. 34–39, 55–57, 62.

149. Meyer-Christian, *Die englisch-jüdische Allianz*.

150. Ibid., p. 207.

151. Ibid., pp. 23–31. See also Benedikt Fontana, "Was sagen Engländer zu dieser Ehre? Die Briten als 'Haus Israel'. Jehova, 'Gott der britischen Waffen'—König Georg auf dem 'Thron Davids,'" *Die Judenfrage*, April 7, 1938, pp. 3–4. For related efforts see von Papen, *"Scholarly" Antisemitism during the Third Reich*, pp. 158–59.

152. Meyer-Christian, *Die englisch-jüdische Allianz*, p. 11.

153. Ibid., pp. 22–78.

154. Ibid., pp. 81–86, pictures opposite pp. 128, 132.

155. Josiah Wedgwood (1872–1943).

156. Meyer-Christian, *Die englisch-jüdische Allianz,* pp. 176–78.

157. Ibid., pp. 178–80.

158. Ibid., pp. 139, 143, 150, 161, 175, 139–43, 147.

159. Ibid., pp. 186–87.

160. Hermann Erich Siefert, "Der 'Irgun' ruft zum Kampf. Englands 'neue Vorschläge' für eine Palästina-Lösung," *Die Judenfrage,* April 19, 1939, pp. 1–2.

161. Meyer-Christian, "Die Behandlung der Judenfrage," p. 3.

162. See Hardy, *Hitler's Secret Weapon,* p. 194; Helmut Sündermann, "Europäische Judendämmerung" (November 1940), in Sündermann, *Die Entscheidungen reifen* (Munich: Franz Eher, 1943), pp. 57–60, quoted in Baird, *The Mythical World of Nazi Propaganda,* p. 7.

163. Sündermann, *Die Grenzen fallen,* pp. 68–71.

164. Geoffrey Giles, "The Institutionalization of Homosexual Panic in the Third Reich," in *Social Outsiders in Nazi Germany,* ed. Robert Gellately and Nathan Stoltzfus (Princeton, NJ: Princeton University Press, 2001), p. 235.

165. *Deutscher Wochendienst,* May 21, 1943, no. 8839, quoted in Ernest K. Bramsted, *Goebbels and National Socialist Propaganda, 1925–1945* (East Lansing: Michigan State University Press, 1965), p. 401.

166. E. I. Thoors, "Jüdische Umsturzorganisationen in Polen. Über das Weltproletariat zur Weltherrschaft," *Die Judenfrage,* October 13, 1938, pp. 11–14; Fritz Redlin, "Der 'Minister König Israels.' Bernard Lecache und seine LICA—Mordhetze mit allen Mitteln," *Die Judenfrage,* November 18, 1938, pp. 1–2, and see also Heinz Ballensiefen, "Jüdische Weltorganisationen," *Die Judenfrage,* August 5, 1939, p. 105; Wolff Heinrichsdorff, "Der XXI. Zionistenkongress in Genf," *Die Judenfrage,* August 19, 1939, pp. 1–2.

167. Tadeusz Pankiewicz, *The Cracow Ghetto Pharmacy,* trans. Henry Tilles (Washington, DC: United States Holocaust Memorial Museum, 2000), p. 126.

6. LINGERING STEREOTYPES AND JEWISH DISPLACED PERSONS

Epigraph: Address by Philip S. Bernstein at a reception at Hotel Biltmore, October 1, 1946, p. 7, papers of Philip S. Bernstein, University of Rochester Archives, Rochester, NY (hereafter PSB).

1. In Bernstein's own words, "In May, 1946, at the invitation of the Secretary of War, I flew to Germany to serve as Adviser on Jewish Affairs to General Joseph T. McNarney, Commanding General of the U.S. Forces European Theater. Shortly thereafter, I was requested to serve in a similar capacity to General Mark Clark, Commanding General of the U.S. Forces Austria. The original commitment was for four months. When in August, 1946, it became clear not only that the problems had not been solved but had vastly increased, General McNarney

urged me to remain on. With the generous consent of my congregation, Temple B'rith Kodesh, Rochester, New York, I agreed to do so and stayed another year, returning to the United States on August 11, 1947." Philip S. Bernstein, "Final Report to Honorable Kenneth C. Royall, Secretary for the Army, from Rabbi Philip B. Bernstein, Adviser on Jewish Affairs to Commander in Chief, EUCOM and Commanding General, USFA, May 1946 to August 1947, item 78, box 2, PSB.

2. See Mary Fulbrook, *German National Identity after the Holocaust* (Cambridge, U.K.: Polity Press, 1999); Jeffrey Herf, *Divided Memory: The Nazi Past in the Two Germanys* (Cambridge, MA: Harvard University Press, 1997); Jay Geller, *Jews in Post-Holocaust Germany, 1945–1953* (Cambridge: Cambridge University Press, 2005); Anthony Kauders, *Democratization and the Jews: Munich, 1945–1965* (Lincoln: University of Nebraska Press for the Vidal Sassoon International Center for the Study of Antisemitism (SICSA), Hebrew University of Jerusalem, 2004).

3. Frederick Morgan, *Peace and War: A Soldier's Life* (London: Hoder and Stoughton, 1961), pp. 218ff.

4. A number of scholars have produced important studies of the DPs; Zeev Mankowitz, in particular, has explored the perceived problem of criminality related to the DPs in a book that deals primarily with the Jews' attempt to rebuild their lives, from the perspective of social and political history. See Zeev W. Mankowitz, *Life between Memory and Hope: The Survivors of the Holocaust in Occupied Germany* (Cambridge: Cambridge University Press, 2002); Yehuda Bauer, *Out of the Ashes: The Impact of American Jews on Post-Holocaust European Jewry* (Oxford: Pergamon Press, 1988); Michael Marrus, *The Unwanted: European Refugees in the Twentieth Century* (New York: Oxford University Press, 1985); Leonard Dinnerstein, *America and the Survivors of the Holocaust* (New York: Columbia University Press, 1982); Mark Wyman, *DPs: Europe's Displaced Persons, 1945–1951* (Ithaca, NY: Cornell University Press, 1998); Angelika Eder, *Flüchtige Heimat: Jüdische Displaced Persons in Landsberg am Lech 1945 bis 1950* (Munich: Kommissionsverlag UNI-Druck, 1998); Jael Geis, *Übrig sein—Leben danach* (Berlin: Philo Verlagsgesellschaft, 2000); Angelika Königseder and Juliane Wetzel, *Waiting for Hope: Jewish Displaced Persons in Post–World War II Germany* (Evanston, IL: Northwestern University Press, 2001); Idith Zertal, *From Catastrophe to Power: Holocaust Survivors and the Emergence of Israel* (Berkeley: University of California Press, 1998).

5. A report of May 12, 1947, stated there were "153,000 Jewish Displaced Persons in the U.S. Zone, Germany. There are believed to be about 22,000 in the U.S. Zone, Austria. The British Zones in Austria and Germany contain about 16,000. The French Zones possibly 2,000. There are reported to be about 25,000 Jewish DPs in Italy. To these should be added a total of about 15,000 in countries like France, Belgium, Holland, Sweden, etc. Thus it is to be seen that

the Jewish D.P. problem in Europe today must be conceived in terms of one quarter of a million Jews. . . . The Jews tend to constitute about one quarter of the D.P. problem [overall]. . . . In the U.S. Zone, Germany and Austria, about 80% of the Jews continue to live in camps." Philip S. Bernstein, "Report on the Jewish Displaced Persons in the U.S. Zones, Germany and Austria," presented to THE FIVE ORGANIZATIONS meeting in the Hotel Biltmore, Monday, May 12, 1947, p. 4, file 44, box 2, PSB. This chapter concludes roughly in the spring of 1947, because at that time there was apparent "a changed attitude at [U.S.] government levels [indicating] that the D.P. problem is no longer in the front of people's minds." From the perspective of nutrition, Jewish DPs were no longer being treated as a special case, and there was an official decision "to deny D.P. care to any new infiltrees" (ibid., p. 6). See "Proposed Agreement between IRO [International Refugee Organization] and the Commander-in-Chief, European Command, May 31, 1947," third revised draft, item 49, box 2, PSB. In September 1946 "the Central Committee of Liberated Jews" received official recognition by the U.S. occupation forces; Philip S. Bernstein, "Final Report to Honorable Kenneth C. Royall, Secretary for the Army, from Rabbi Philip B. Bernstein, Adviser on Jewish Affairs to Commander in Chief, EUCOM and Commanding General, USFA, May 1946 to August 1947," p. 9, item 78, box 2, PSB. In contemporary documents the spelling of his title is inconsistent; both "adviser" and "advisor" are used.

6. Eva Kolinsky, *After the Holocaust: Jewish Survivors in Germany after 1945* (London: Pimlico, 2004); Suzanne Brown-Fleming, *The Holocaust and Catholic Conscience: Cardinal Aloisius Muench and the Guilt Question in Germany, 1946–1959* (South Bend, IN: Notre Dame University Press, 2005); Mankowitz, *Life between Memory and Hope;* see also Michael Brenner, trans. Barbara Harshav, *After the Holocaust: Rebuilding Jewish Lives in Postwar Germany* (Princeton, NJ: Princeton University Press, 1997).

7. Steven E. Aschheim, *Brothers and Strangers: The East European Jew in German and German Jewish Consciousness, 1800–1923* (Madison: University of Wisconsin Press, 1999); Jack Wertheimer, *Unwelcome Strangers: East European Jews in Imperial Germany* (New York: Oxford University Press, 1987); Trude Maurer, *Ostjuden in Deutschland, 1918–1933* (Hamburg: H. Christians, 1986). On how this influenced the postwar period see Kauders, *Democratization and the Jews.* For charges that the Jews were exploiting the Germans, see "UNRRA Aide Scents Jews' Exodus Plot; Morgan Charges Maneuver to Quit Europe, Doubts Pogroms; Statements; Protests," *New York Times,* January 3, 1946, pp. 1, 2; apparently the same reports that Morgan used were also the background for "The Modern Wandering Jew," typescript copy of "excerpt" from Weekly Intelligence Report no. 35, p. 2, which is from "the Vincent La Vista Report on illegal immigration in and through Italy" (hereafter *La Vista Report*), Record Group (hereafter RG) 19.003*01, May 15, 1947, USHMM.

8. For a recent comprehensive analysis, see Kolinsky, *After the Holocaust,* pp. 198–210.

9. Bernstein, address at reception at Hotel Biltmore, p. 7; Atina Grossmann, "Victims, Villains, and Survivors: Gendered Perceptions and Self-Perceptions of Jewish Displaced Persons in Occupied Postwar Germany," *Journal of the History of Sexuality* 11, nos. 1–2 (January/April 2002): 291–318.

10. Jonas Landau, "Jonas Landau: Memoirs, 1993," RG-02.214, Acc. 1996.A.0574, p. 46, USHMM.

11. Greta Fischer, "Greta Fischer papers related to Kloster-Indersdorf displaced children's center and to the UNRRA's postwar work in Europe," RG-19.034*01, p. 27, USHMM. On Kloster Indersdorf see Eva Kolinsky, *After the Holocaust,* pp. 78–92.

12. Helen Waren, "Helen Waren letter concerning displaced persons," RG-19.002*01, p. 9, USHMM, pp. 1–2; Fischer, "Greta Fischer papers," p. 27.

13. Harry and Clare Lerner, "Harry and Clare Lerner correspondence relating to their work with displaced persons and the UNRRA," RG-19.029*01, undated letter, USHMM.

14. Joseph W. Bendersky, *The "Jewish Threat": Anti-Semitic Policies of the U.S. Army* (New York: Basic, 2000), pp. 349–88; Alex Grobman, *Rekindling the Flame: American Jewish Chaplains and the Survivors of European Jewry, 1944–1948* (Detroit: Wayne State University Press, 1993); Abraham Klausner, *A Letter to My Children from the Edge of the Holocaust* (San Francisco: Holocaust Center of Northern California, 2002), pp. 57–58, 74–76, 106–7, 149. I am grateful to Severin Hochberg for enlightening me about Klausner's role and suggesting his memoir as a critical source.

15. "UNRRA Aide Scents Jews' Exodus Plot," pp. 1, 2.

16. "Excerpt from Chaplain Poliakoff's Report," August 1, 1945, from Rabbi Levinger to Philip Bernstein, item 8, box 1, PSB; Herman Dicker, "Report on Activities on Behalf of Displaced Jewish Persons," September 14, 1945, pamphlet in the form of a letter; item 9, box 1, PSB.

17. Earl G. Harrison, *A Report to President Truman: The Plight of the Displaced Jews in Europe* (released by the White House on September 29, 1945; New York: Reprinted by United Jewish Appeal for Refugees, Overseas Needs and Palestine on behalf of Joint Distribution Committee, United Palestine Appeal, [and] National Refugee Service, 1945), USHMM.

18. Klausner, *Letter to My Children,* pp. 23–24; "Jews in U.S. Camps Held Ill-Treated: Military Government Men in Germany are 'Incompetent,' Chaplain Declares," *New York Times,* November 22, 1945; clipping in item 2, box 1, PSB; "Remove Patton from Germany," *New Republic* 113, no. 14, October 1, 1945, p. 420.

19. See ch. 7.

20. Sara Getzler (donor and author), "The Story of Two Sisters," RG-02*168, pp. 35–6, USHMM.

21. Memorandum, "A Program to Deal with Anti-Semitism in Germany," from Rabbi Philip S. Bernstein to General Joseph McNarney, Commander in Chief, USFET, July 16, 1947, pp. 1–2, partially quoted in Brown-Fleming, *The Holocaust and Catholic Conscience,* p. 198; item 65, box 2, PSB. Interestingly, Philip Bernstein's first direct contact with A. H. Sulzberger of the *New York Times* was after he submitted his final report on his tenure as special adviser; October–November 1947, item 80, box 2, PSB. Although Bernstein was uniquely placed to influence events on the ground, his contacts with Jewish organizational grandees such as Stephen S. Wise and Henry Morgenthau were few and formal.

22. See ch. 5.

23. "A Program to Deal with Anti-Semitism in Germany," pp. 1–2.

24. Ibid.

25. "German Attitudes toward the Expulsion of German Nationals from Neighboring Countries," Surveys Branch, Information Control Division, July 8, 1946, box 1, no. 43, PSB; Report of May 26, 1944, "Entwicklung der Kriminalität," RG 215, G-83, box 4, Berlin Document Collection, YIVO Institute for Jewish Research (hereafter B-C, YIVO). Oscar Lichtenstein, "My Struggle for Survival 1940/45," RG-02*118, p. 23, USHMM; see Götz Aly, *The Nazi Census: Identification and Control in the Third Reich,* trans. Edwin Black with Assenka Oksiloff (Philadelphia: Temple University Press, 2004).

26. Paul Erker, *Ernährungskrise und Nachkriegsgesellschaft: Bauern und Arbeiterschaft in Bayern 1943–1953* (Stuttgart: Klett-Cotta, 1990), pp. 25–28. A broader study also did not find Jewish activity significant; see Willi A. Boelcke, *Der Schwarzmarkt 1945–1948: Vom Überleben nach dem Kriege* (Braunschweig: Westermann, 1986).

27. Primo Levi, *The Truce: A Survivor's Journey Home from Auschwitz,* trans. Stuart Woolf (London: Folio Society, 2002); Levi's work exists in several editions with different titles. Hagit Lavsky, *New Beginnings: Holocaust Survivors in Bergen-Belsen and the British Zone in Germany, 1945–1950* (Detroit: Wayne State University Press, 2002).

28. Fischer, "Greta Fischer papers," pp. 31–32.

29. "Review of United States Immigration Activity under the Truman Project—April through December 1946," from Irwin Rosen–European Director of Emigration, American Joint Distribution Committee to Philip Bernstein, December 30, 1946, p. 3, item 98, box 1, PSB.

30. Ibid., pp. 4, 3.

31. Photograph by George Kadish/Zvi Kadshin of document forging, location given as Lodz, W/S no. 11335, CD no. 0071, USHMM.

32. "Review of United States Immigration Activity under the Truman Project—April through December 1946," p. 4.

33. Ibid., pp. 5, 4.

34. *La Vista Report,* pp. 5–6.

35. Bernstein, "Final Report to Honorable Kenneth C. Royall," pp. 2–3.

36. "Postwar Poland and the Jews," by Philip S. Bernstein, research material, 1946, p. 6, item 80, box 1, PSB.

37. Ibid., pp. 6–7; "Conference with President Truman, 11 October 1946," memorandum to General Joseph T. McNarney, October 18, 1946, from Philip S. Bernstein, item 83, box 1, PSB. Toward the end of his tenure as adviser, Bernstein was apparently frustrated that he was characterized as mainly continuing the efforts of Judge Simon Rifkind. Bernstein wished to make it clear, however, that the conditions had changed, and one of the most crucial differences was the massive "infiltration" from Poland—which Bernstein himself had had a role in facilitating; letter from Philip S. Bernstein to Mr. David Niles, Carlton Hotel, Washington, DC, August 29, 1946, item 17, box 1, PSB; Bernstein, address at reception at Hotel Biltmore; "Jewish Displaced Persons," press release by Philip S. Bernstein, September 7, 1946, pp. 4–7, item 66, box 1, PSB; "Report on Poland," by Philip S. Bernstein to General Joseph T. McNarney, August 2, 1946, item 47, box 1, PSB; quotation from "Statement by Philip S. Bernstein on infiltrees into the American Zone," press statement, June 26, 1946, p. 1, item 40, box 1, PSB. Bernstein also helped arrange refuge for limited numbers of Jews in Norway and Italy, under the auspices of the UNRRA; "Report on the Activities of the Jewish Adviser in the United States," memorandum to General Joseph T. McNarney from Philip S. Bernstein, October 18, 1946, pp. 1–2, item 85, box 1, PSB. The most explicit statement that Bernstein was chiefly responsible for the entrance of tens of thousands of Jews from Poland is in a personal communication to Philip and Soph [Bernstein], apparently a circular letter to friends, from "Dotty and Carl," July 8, 1947, reporting on an extended visit to DP camps: The "infiltrees" "owe their lives in great part to Rabbi Bernstein who negotiated with the Army to allow 100,000 of these Polish Jews to come into the American Zone," p. 4, file 8, box 2, PSB. See also Philip Bernstein to Judge Louis Levinthal, July 10, 1947, pp. 1–2, file 8, box 2, PSB, about "recent Roumanian infiltrees in Vienna to U.S. Zone, Austria."

38. Address by Philip S. Bernstein at the "McNarney Luncheon by 5 Organizations," Waldorf [Hotel], N.Y., 1947, item 84, box 2, PSB.

39. Philip Bernstein to David Bernstein (apparently no relation) of the American Jewish Committee, August 8, 1947, file 9, box 2, PSB.

40. "Press statement by Philip S. Bernstein, 26 November 1946 to the Theater Commander on Jewish Affairs, on the need for a decision on Palestine," item 92, box 1, PSB.

41. Bernstein, "Postwar Poland and the Jews," p. 5.

42. Bernstein, "Conference with President Truman, 11 October 1946," pp. 1–2.

43. "Statement by Philip S. Bernstein on infiltrees into the American Zone," press statement, June 26, 1946, item 40, box 1, PSB.

44. Philip Bernstein to Judge Louis Levinthal, July 10, 1947, p. 2.

45. "The Modern Wandering Jew," from the *La Vista Report*.

46. Frederick Morgan, *Peace and War: A Soldier's Life* (London: Hodder and Stoughton, 1961), pp. 235, 246, 237, 230.

47. Dan Vittorio Segre, *Memoirs of a Failed Diplomat* (London: Halban, 2005), p. 32.

48. *La Vista Report*, pp. 9–10.

49. "Report for June 1947," from Abraham Cohen, Regional Director, AJDC Regensburg to AJDC Zone Headquarters, June 30, 1947, p. 1, in American Joint Distribution Committee Reports for the U.S. Zone of Occupation, Germany, June 1947, file 64, box 2, PSB.

50. *La Vista Report*, p. 2

51. Ibid., Appendix, p. 3.

52. Ibid., Appendix, p. 5.

53. "Bundists State Solution of Problem Must Be Found in France," in J.T.A. (Jewish Telegraphic Agency) News, February 8, 1946, p. 7, item 12, box 1, PSB; "Zionism Restated," manuscript by Philip S. Bernstein, [1946?], p. 9, item 102, box 1, PSB.

54. *La Vista Report*, Appendix. p. 4.

55. Ibid.

56. See ch. 5; *La Vista Report*, Appendix, p. 4.

57. Hugo Gryn with Naomi Gryn, *Chasing Shadows* (London: Viking, 2000), p. 238.

58. Randolph L. Braham, "The Nazi Collaborator with a Jewish Heart: The Strange Saga of Jaac Van Harten," *East European Quarterly* 35, no. 4 (January 2002): 411–12; see 411–34.

59. Ibid., pp. 414–15.

60. Samuel Stammer, "The Beginnings of Sam Stammer's Life as written by him in German, 1983–1984," RG-O2.178, pp. 10–11, USHMM.

61. Ibid.

62. Ibid.

63. Ibid., p. 12.

64. Albert Hutler, "Albert Hutler letters relating to displaced persons in the American Zone of occupied Germany," RG-19.028*01, letter of September 16, 1945, p. 1, USHMM.

65. "THE TREND OF CARES AND WORRIES IN GERMANY," November 21, 1946, Surveys Branch Information Control Division, OMGUS (Office of Military Government, United States; Rear), APO 757, item 91, box 1.

66. WAR DIARY, 6 May 1945, RG-09 Liberation .014*02, Malcolm A. Vendig papers relating to post-liberation Dachau, USHMM (hereafter *Vendig Papers*).

67. Ibid.

68. Daily Report, Group V, April 23, 1945, Military Government Report, RG-09 Liberation .014*08, *Vendig Papers;* Morgan, *Peace and War,* p. 238; Waren,

"Helen Waren letter concerning displaced persons," pp. 1–2; Vendig, WAR DIARY, June 8, 1945, *Vendig Papers.*

69. Vendig, WAR DIARY, May 17, 1945 (no pagination), and Vendig, Daily Report, April 4, 1945, *Vendig Papers;* "UNRRA records relating to a riot in a displaced persons center in West Stuttgart," RG-19.030*01, report of incident at UNRRA DP center 502, March 29, 1946, by David Clearfield, USHMM; Joseph Levine, "My Work in Germany with Jewish Survivors of World War II," RG-19.020*01, p. 45, USHMM.

70. Report on Concentration Camp-Zweiberg, April 15, 1945, Calbe, Germany, p. 2, RG-09.014*08, *Vendig Papers.*

71. Lucille Eichengreen, *Rumkowski and the Orphans of Lodz* (San Francisco: Mercury House, 2000), p. 101.

72. Morgan, *Peace and War,* pp. 221–22.

73. Landau, "Jonas Landau: Memoirs," pp. 40–41, 45.

74. Fischer, "Greta Fischer papers," p. 26.

75. Report of April 18, 1945, RG-09 Liberation .014*08, *Vendig Papers.*

76. Fischer, "Greta Fischer papers," p. 26.

77. Report of March 5, 1945, by Lt. Morse, RG-09.-14*06, rough notes and rough transcript of April 1945 war diary, and Daily Report (0001–2400, April 2, 1945), RG-09.14*08, *Vendig Papers.* In a few cases, however, such as in Hederleben, even Jewish survivors conceded that an ex-Nazi might be the best choice for Bürgermeister. Report of April 24, 1945, *Vendig Papers,* April 1945 war diary.

78. Philip S. Bernstein, "Recommendation Relative to Problem of Law and Order among Jewish Displaced Persons," from Philip S. Bernstein to Chief of Staff, September 14, 1946, no. 71, box 1, PSB.

79. WAR DIARY, May 27, 1945, RG-09 Liberation .014*02, *Vendig Papers.*

80. Sonja Haid Greene, "Between Life and Death (My Memoirs)," RG-02.112, p. 8, USHMM, p. 96.

81. Oscar Lichtenstern, "My Struggle for Survival," p. 25; "Harry and Clare Lerner correspondence," letter of July 21, 1946.

82. This document is analyzed in Peter Novick, *The Holocaust in American Life* (Boston: Houghton Mifflin, 1999), pp. 79–80.

83. Appendix A, memo sent from Chicago, reproduced in Klausner, *Letter to My Children,* p. 159.

84. Klausner, *Letter to My Children,* pp. 160–61.

85. Ibid., p. 161.

86. Ibid.

87. Philip S. Bernstein, "Displaced Persons," reprint from *The American Jewish Year Book,* vol. 49, 1947–1948 (New York: American Jewish Committee, 1947), p. 7.

88. "Report for Month of June 1947 of Military Court Branch Legal Division-AJDC," from Mrs. Silvia Fuerst, Legal Aid Division, to Dr. Werner

Peiser and Mr. Jeremiah N. Silverman, [stamp dated] July 13, 1947, p. 3, in American Joint Distribution Committee reports for the U.S. Zone of Occupation, Germany June 1947, file 64, box 2, PSB.

89. Klausner, *Letter to My Children,* pp. 161–62.

90. Abraham Klausner to Philip Bernstein, October 10, 1947, p. 2, file 9, box 2, PSB.

91. Ibid., pp. 2–3.

92. Ibid.

93. Auerbach was a "State Commisar" for "political, racial, and religious affairs" for Bavaria; Kurt Epstein held the position for Hesse; "Od lo awda tikwatenu," *Jüdische Rundschau* 12/13 (Schewat-Adar 5707–March 1947): 11.

94. Kauders, *Democratization and the Jews,* pp. 140–42; photograph, USHMM Photo Archives, W/S no. 80993, CD no. 0144, USHMM.

95. Klausner to Bernstein, October 10, 1947, p. 3.

96. Ibid., p. 4.

97. Mankowitz, *Life between Memory and Hope,* p. 243.

98. For extensive discussion of the Auerbach case, see Wolfgang Kraushaar, "Die Affäre Auerbach; zur Virulenz des Antisemitismus in den Gründerjahren der Bundesrepublik," in *Die Gegenwart der Schoah,* ed. Helmut Schreier and Matthias Heyl (Hamburg: Krämer, 1994), pp. 195–217; Constantin Goschler, "Die Bedeutung der Entschädigungs- und Rückerstattungsfrage für das Verhältnis von Juden und deutscher Nachkriegsgesellschaft," in *Leben im Land der Täter: Juden in Nachkriegsdeutschland (1945–1952),* ed. Julius H. Schoeps (Berlin: Jüdische Verlagsanstalt, 2001), pp. 219–35; Werner Bergmann, "Philipp Auerbach—Wiedergutmachung war 'nicht mit normalen Mitteln' durchzusetzen," in *Engagierte Demokraten: Vergangenheitspolitik in kritischer Absicht,* ed. Claudia Fröhlich and Michael Kohlstruck (Munich: Westfälisches Dampfboot, 1999), pp. 57–70.

99. "German Campaign of Slander Against Jewish Community Irks Jewish Leaders; Protest Voiced," J.T.A. [Jewish Telegraphic Agency] News, March 2, 1951, in "Research material on DPs, Germany and other issues" [1947–51], file 93, box 2, PSB: "The executive of the Central council of German Jews today issued a statement protesting against the campaign of slander and incitement being carried on against the Jews in connection with the recent suspension of Dr. Philip Auerbach, Jewish head of the Bavarian Restitution Office. . . . The announcement of Dr. Auerbach's suspension and the investigation into charges of embezzlement made against him were announced last week-end. Dr. Auerbach, meanwhile, has brought libel suits against Heinrich Junker, Christian Democratic member of the Bavarian Parliament who has charged him with embezzlement, and against Fritz Hollstein, editor of "Die Tat" who charged that the Jewish leader had secured preferential treatment for himself from the Nazis when he was in a concentration camp and that he beat fellow prisoners. So far none of the

charges against Dr. Auerbach has been proved, Bavarian Finance Minister Zorn announced last week-end. . . . The Central Council's statement declared:

1. We condemn attempts made by individuals through public statements to identify Jews as a whole with matters that are of no concern to the Jewish community. A thorough and objective investigation of all events is urgently needed to establish responsibility for any irregularities irrespective of personal considerations. We demand, however, that this inquiry not be made a pretext for paralyzing of the work of the restitution authority, and we insist in particular on all restitution claims pending with the Bavarian Restitution Office being dealt with immediately in accordance with normal procedure. 2. We protest most strongly against the inciting attacks being made in this connection against the Jewish community as a whole. Nothing can be gained by such attacks but to let the flame of hatred flare up anew and to poison public opinion once more. (The New York Times reported today from Frankfurt that the Bavarian Government suspended payments through the restitution office to all victims of Nazism, when it established that many documents on which the claims were based had been obtained improperly. Although the documents were usually obtained from corrupt local officials, the Bavarian Government's campaign was aimed primarily at Dr. Philip Auerbach, head of the restitution office, whose success in establishing restitution in the hurly-burly of post-war Bavarian politics has made him many enemies, the correspondent emphasized.)"

100. Klausner to Bernstein, October 10, 1947, p. 4.

101. Ibid.

102. Ibid.

103. Ibid., p. 5.

104. Yehuda Bauer, Introduction to Klausner, *Letter to My Children,* p. x; ibid., p. 38.

105. Abraham Klausner to Philip Bernstein, November 10, 1947, p. 3, file 10, box 2, PSB.

106. Klausner to Bernstein, October 10, 1947.

107. Herbert A. Fierst, Washington, DC, to Philip Bernstein, October 28, 1947, file 10, box 2, PSB.

108. Abraham Hyman to Philip Bernstein, quoted in a letter to Herbert A. Fierst, Washington, DC, November 10, 1947, file 10, box 2, PSB.

109. "Speech of U.S. Third Army Liason Officer Col. George R. Scithers, in 2nd Congress of the 'Shereit-Hapleita' in the American Zone of Germany," Bad Reichenhall, February 1947, p. 4. This pamphlet was published in English and Yiddish; the address of Mr. David Treger, Chairman of the Central Committee of Liberated Jews, was in Yiddish.

110. Speech of Mr. Leon Retter, the General Secretary of the Central Committee of Liberated Jews, ibid., p. 6.

111. Klausner, *Letter to My Children,* pp. 162, 164–66.

112. In his introduction to Klausner's autobiography, *Letter to My Children,* historian Yehuda Bauer ironically describes Klausner's work after the Holocaust as "illegal": "He stole and he cheated and he lied, because his aim was to enable 'the people,' his favorite term for the survivors, to rebuild their shattered Jewish humanity" (p. x).

113. Appendix B, minutes of the meeting, Klausner, *Letter to My Children,* p. 167. On November 26, 1946, Bernstein wrote, "Although their physical needs are being met, I found the Jews [on his tour of all the DP camps] depressingly low in spirit and their outlook very bleak." Bernstein, November 26, 1946, press statement; Dr. William Haber, Advisor on Jewish Affairs to the European Command.

114. Bernstein, Report to THE FIVE ORGANIZATIONS meeting, pp. 10–11.

115. Klausner, *Letter to My Children,* pp. 168–69.

116. Yitzchak Nementsik, "A shlekht farshtonene nekome" (A wrongly understood revenge), *A Haym,* no. 4 (March 14, 1946): 7, quoted in Mankowitz, *Life between Memory and Hope,* pp. 240–41.

117. M. Gavronsky, "Mir darfn vert zayn di frayhayt" (We must be worthy of freedom), *Dos Fraye Vort,* no. 2 (October 14, 1945): 2, quoted in Mankowitz, *Life between Memory and Hope,* p. 240.

118. Quoted in Klausner, *Letter to My Children,* p. 169.

119. Bernstein, September 7, 1946, press release, pp. 4–5.

120. Klausner, *Letter to My Children,* p. 170.

121. Ibid., p. 171.

122. Quoted in ibid., p. 173.

123. "The Present State of the DPs" by Mayer Abramowitz to the 5 Agencies, [March 1948], item 96, box 2, PSB.

124. Klausner, *Letter to My Children,* pp. 175–76.

125. Ibid., p. 176. ORT, from the Russian for the Society for Trades and Agricultural Labor, is a Jewish charitable organization, established in 1880 and still operating today, that is dedicated to education and vocational training.

126. Mankowitz, *Life between Memory and Hope;* Atina Grossmann, *Victims, Victors, and Survivors: Germans, Allies, and Jews in Occupied Germany, 1945–1949* (Princeton, NJ: Princeton University Press, 2007).

127. Klausner, *Letter to My Children,* p. 176.

128. "Records relating to the work of William Ramkey with displaced persons in Allied-occupied Austria," RG-19.009, Rescue, refugees and displaced persons, document from 19 November 1945, [illegible] DISPLACED PERSONS AND THEIR REHABILITATION, p. 4, USHMM.

129. *After the Victory: A Blueprint for the Rehabilitation of European Jewry* (New York: American Zionist Emergency Council, 1943), pp. 1, 5; item 3, box 1, PSB. The author is unknown.

130. Item no. 5, "Minutes of Philip S. Bernstein's meeting with Jewish leaders, by Abraham S. Hyman, 23 August 1946," item 56, box 1, PSB.

131. Bernstein, September 7, 1946, press release, p. 5.

132. See Mankowitz, *Life between Memory and Hope;* Geller, *Jews in Post-Holocaust Germany;* Kauders, *Democratization and the Jews.*

133. Bernstein, "Recommendation."

134. Ibid., p. 2.

135. Ibid.

136. Ibid.

137. The greater significance of "Stuttgart" to many Jews and non-Jews was the address of U.S. Secretary of State James Byrnes, on September 6, 1946, about Germany's reentry into the comity of nations; I thank Laura Hilton for this insight.

138. Bernstein, "Recommendation," p. 3.

139. Ibid.

140. "RABBI BERNSTEIN SAYS IMMIGRATION TO PALESTINE IS MATTER OF LIFE OR DEATH FOR DISPLACED JEWS," press release from United Palestine Appeal on Philip S. Bernstein's arrival in the United States [September 1946], p. 3, PSB.

141. Ibid., p. 1.

142. Ibid., p. 2.

143. Bernstein, "Recommendation," p. 4.

144. Ibid., p. 4.

145. Ibid.

146. Ibid., p. 5.

147. "Recommendations on the Landsberg Case," memo to General Clay from PSB [July?] 1946. Cover letter memo to General White from PSB, June 17, 1946, on the Central Committee of Liberated Jews in the U.S. Occupation Zone (memo missing), box 1, item 45, PSB.

148. Ibid., p. 1.

149. Ibid., pp. 1–2.

150. Ibid., p. 2.

151. Ibid., pp. 2–3.

152. Ibid., pp. 3–5.

153. Ibid., p. 6.

154. Ibid.

155. Ibid.

156. Ibid., pp. 6–7.

157. Ibid.

158. Ibid., p. 8.

159. "Report on the Inspection of Displaced Persons Camp at Windsheim," to Philip S. Bernstein from Captain Abraham S. Hyman, August 27, 1946, item 60, box 1, PSB.

160. Ibid.

161. Ibid.

162. "RABBI BERNSTEIN SAYS IMMIGRATION TO PALESTINE IS MATTER OF LIFE OR DEATH FOR DISPLACED JEWS," p. 3.

163. Albert Hutler letters, May 7, 1945, p. 1, USHMM.

164. "Press statement by Philip S. Bernstein on the DPs and the U.S. government," [September? 1946], p. 3, item 79, box 1, PSB.

165. "Report on the Inspection of Displaced Persons Camp at Windsheim," item 8.

166. Ibid., items 7 and 9.

167. Bernstein, "Recommendation," p. 9.

168. Klausner to Bernstein, November 10, 1947, p. 2.

169. "Report on the Raid on the Ulanen Kaserne," Abraham S. Hyman to Philip S. Bernstein, December 5, 1946, pp. 1–2, item 94, box 1, PSB.

170. Ibid., p. 2.

171. Ibid., pp. 2–3.

172. Ibid.

173. Ibid.

174. "Final Memorandum" from Simon Rifkind, Advisor to the Theater Commander on Jewish Affairs, to Chief of Staff, Headquarters, U.S. Forces, European Theater, March 7, 1946, pp. 8–9, item 27, box 1, PSB.

175. Delbert Clark, "German Black Market Expected to Survive. Coffee and Other Goods Are Likely to Replace Banned Cigarettes," *New York Times,* undated clipping, probably late 1946, file 111 "On United States immigration policy and DPs [1946–47]," box 1, PSB.

176. William Haber, report to Headquarters, European Command, Office of the Commander in Chief, Civil Affairs Division, document sent to Mr. Abram Rothfeld, Acting Executive Secretary, American Jewish Conference, for transmission to American Jewish Committee [and four other major Jewish organizations], August 31, 1948, p. 6, item 99, box 2, PSB.

177. WAR DIARY, June 2, 1945, *Vendig Papers.*

178. Michael Bernath, "Christians Revenge on the Jews," RG-02.096, p. 122, USHMM; Pauline Buchenholz, "The Postwar Years; a Sequel to As I Remember," RG-02*143, p. 8, USHMM; Lichtenstein, "My Struggle for Survival," p. 23.

179. "Address by Philip S. Bernstein at reception at Hotel Biltmore, October 1, 1946," p. 7.

180. Ibid.

181. Bernstein, "A Program to Deal with Anti-Semitism in Germany," p. 4.

182. "The Truth About Germany," sermon by Philip S. Bernstein, Friday, November 28, 1947, item 82, box 2, PSB; Abraham Hyman, manuscript of "After the Holocaust," folder 2, p. 98, file 43, box 3, PSB.

183. Richard L. Rubenstein, *After Auschwitz: History, Theology, and Contemporary Judaism,* 2nd ed. (Baltimore: Johns Hopkins University Press, 1992), pp. 5–8.

Epigraph: Primo Levi, *The Reawakening,* trans. Stuart Woolf (Boston: Little, Brown, 1965), pp. 44–46.

1. "Recommendations on the Landsberg Case," memo to General Clay from Philip S. Bernstein [July?] 1946. Cover letter memo to General White from Bernstein, June 17, 1946, on the Central Committee of Liberated Jews in the U.S. Occupation Zone (memo missing), box 1, item 45, p. 9, Papers of Philip S. Bernstein, University of Rochester Archives, Rochester, NY (hereafter PSB).

2. Ibid., p. 5.

3. Ibid.

4. Ibid, pp. 5, 10.

5. Ibid.

6. "Jewish Displaced Persons," press release by Philip S. Bernstein, September 7, 1946, pp. 6–7, PSB.

7. "Study on Maintenance of Law and Order among Jewish DPs," memo by Abraham S. Hyman to Philip S. Bernstein, January 13, 1947, p. 1, file 11, box 2, PSB.

8. Ibid., p. 2.

9. Ibid., pp. 3–4, 6–7.

10. Ibid., pp. 8–9.

11. Ibid.

12. Ibid., p. 9.

13. Ibid., p. 10.

14. Ibid., pp. 10–11.

15. Ibid., pp. 12–13.

16. Ibid.

17. Ibid.

18. Ibid., p. 13.

19. Ibid., p. 14.

20. Ibid.

21. Ibid., p. 15.

22. Ibid.

23. Ibid., p. 16.

24. Ibid.

25. Ibid., pp. 16–18.

26. Rabbi Philip S. Bernstein, Adviser to the Theater Commander on Jewish Affairs, to Mr. I. L. Kenen, American Jewish Conference, January 31, 1947, file 3, box 2, "Advisor" section, PSB. Kenen "acts as liaison for the five major Jewish agencies concerned with the DP problem" in Germany; Philip Bernstein to Frank N. Trager, Anti-Defamation League of B'nai B'rith, March 17, 1947, p. 1, file 5, box 2, PSB. Even in this private communication, Bernstein stressed that the main reason for increased hostility toward the DPs stemmed from personal

contacts with Germans, not U.S. policy, and that the Army and the DPs were both in untenable situations: "The unresolved DP program is the cause of growing irritation and tension. The Jewish DPs simply do not belong in Germany and life here is artificial and strained. They have no place in the German economy, etc., etc. We have done various things to further better understanding of the DP problem among the military. I think we have accomplished something. But the basic situation is against us. As long as the DPs remain there, they mean burdens, tension, irritations to the military, who must handle their problems with decreased personnel and funds. I do not want you to misunderstand this. USFET policy on the DPs has been excellent. The problems arise in the field, where direct contacts occur" (p. 2).

27. "Statement on Jewish Displaced Persons" by Philip S. Bernstein "to be presented to House of Representatives Judiciary Committee Hearings," on H.R. [House Resolution] 2910 (the "Stratton bill," emergency legislation for immigration), June 13, 1947, item 56, box 2, PSB; Philip S. Bernstein, "Displaced Persons," reprint from *The American Jewish Year Book,* vol. 49, 1947–48 (New York: American Jewish Committee, 1947), pp. 10–11; Bernstein, "Final Report to Honorable Kenneth C. Royall, Secretary for the Army," pp. 13–14.

28. Draft of an article on Jews and crime, with an attached note that a copy was sent to Miss Mildred McLean, State Probation Commission, Albany, NY, Department of Correction, Division of Probation, box 1, [Publications section], PSB.

29. General Lucius Clay, "Conversation between General Clay and Rabbi Bernstein," June 2, 1947, file 11, box 2, PSB.

30. Bernstein, "Statement on Jewish Displaced Persons," p. 4.

31. "Statement by Lieutenant Colonel Jerry M. Sage . . . before the House and [sic] Subcommittee on Immigration and Naturalization," press release, July 2, 1947, item 63, box 2, PSB.

32. Bernstein, "Final Report to Honorable Kenneth C. Royall," p. 4.

33. Leon Weliczker Wells, *The Janowska Road* (Washington, DC: Holocaust Library, 1999), p. 314.

34. Ibid., pp. 283–314.

35. Zeev W. Mankowitz, *Life between Memory and Hope: The Survivors of the Holocaust in Occupied Germany* (Cambridge: Cambridge University Press, 2002), p. 226.

36. William Eisen, "William Eisen Testimony," Record Group (hereafter RG) 02.136, Acc. 1994.A055, United States Holocaust Memorial Museum (hereafter USHMM), p. 121.

37. Fannie Stern Selig, "Diary: Fannie Stern Selig," RG-19.012*01, p. 30, USHMM; Sara Getzler (donor and author), "The Story of Two Sisters," RG-02*168, p. 43, USHMM.

38. Jonas Landau, "Jonas Landau: Memoirs, 1993," RG-02–214, Acc. 1996.A.0574, p. 46, USHMM.

39. Simon Sterling, "A Survivor's Story: Simon Sterling," RG-02*156, pp. 107–8, 98, 112, 114, 128, USHMM.

40. Lucille Eichengreen with Harriet Hyman Chamberlain, *From Ashes to Life: My Memories of the Holocaust* (San Francisco: Mercury House, 1994), p. 132.

41. Getzler, "The Story of Two Sisters," p. 44.

42. Selig, "Diary: Fannie Stern Selig," p. 27.

43. WAR DIARY, May 23, 1945; DETACHMENT DIARY, June 14, 1945, DETACHMENT DIARY, June 20, 1945; report of January 15, 1945, by Lt. Morse, RG-09.-14*06, Malcolm A. Vendig papers relating to post-liberation Dachau (hereafter *Vendig Papers*), USHMM, rough notes and rough transcript of April 1945 war diary.

44. WAR DIARY, May 31, 1945, RG-09 Liberation .014*02, *Vendig Papers*.

45. Getzler, "The Story of Two Sisters," p. 36.

46. Selig, "Diary: Fannie Stern Selig," p. 27.

47. Personal communication to Philip and Soph [Bernstein], July 8, 1948, p. 5, file 8, box 2, PSB.

48. Helen Waren, "Helen Waren letter concerning displaced persons," RG-19.002*01, p. 9, USHMM; Daily Report, from 0001–2400, March 8, 1945, Oberkassel, Germany, *Vendig Papers*.

49. Harry and Clare Lerner, "Harry and Clare Lerner correspondence relating to their work with displaced persons and the UNRRA," RG-19.029*01, October 30, 1946, USHMM.

50. Personal communication to Philip and Soph [Bernstein], p. 5.

51. WAR DIARY, May 18, 1945, *Vendig Papers*.

52. Helen Tichauer interview, July 2, 2003; "Records relating to Joseph Levine and his work at the Regensburg displaced persons camp," RG-19.020*01, "Life in Regensburg," p. 1, USHMM; personal communication to Philip and Soph [Bernstein], p. 5; Lucille Eichengreen, *From Ashes to Life,* p. 135.

53. Landau, "Jonas Landau: Memoirs," p. 45.

54. Bernard Novick, memoir in "Strangers in the Heartland," Survivor Testimonies compiled by Donald M. Douglas, RG-02*142, p. 56, USHMM.

55. Yehuda Bauer, *Jewish Reactions to the Holocaust,* trans. John Glucker (Tel Aviv: MOD Books, 1989), pp. 119–63, 217–26.

56. Haia Karni, "Life at the Feldafing Displaced Persons Camp 1945–1952" (Rockville, MD: M.A. thesis, Baltimore Hebrew University, 1997).

57. Account of Abba Kovner in film *Partisans of Vilna* (director Josh Waletzky, 1986).

58. Feldafing photo album, no. 9, private collection, Helen Tichauer, New York City. See also the photograph album of Cecilia (Zippy) Orlin, which "contains 1117 thematically arranged images depicting everyday life, including political, cultural and educational activities, in the Bergen-Belsen DP camp and the Blankenese children's home near Hamburg," UHMMM, Desig no. 322.38105, W/S no. 97880, CD no. 0290.

59. Michael Bernath, "Christians' Revenge on the Jews," RG-02.096, p. 122, USHMM.

60. See ch. 3.

61. Martin Alexander, "Survivor Oral History, 1933–1945," RG-02.017, p. 10, USHMM.

62. W/S 29270, USHMM.

63. See Morris Beckman, *The Jewish Brigade: An Army with Two Masters 1944–1945* (Staplehurst, U.K.: Spellmount, 1998); Howard Blum, *The Brigade: An Epic Story of Vengeance, Salvation and World War II* (New York: Simon & Schuster, 2001).

64. Bernard M. Casper, *With the Jewish Brigade* (London: Edward Goldston, 1947), pp. 71–72.

65. "Operation Recovery," memo labeled "Secret" from Headquarters, Third Calvary Group, September 15, 1945, MECZ APO403 U.S. Army, in private collection of Helen Tichauer, New York City.

66. Helen Tichauer interview, August 2003.

67. Photographs nos. 97105, 38311, 97094, USHMM.

68. Mankowitz, *Life between Memory and Hope,* pp. 52–68.

69. Leo W. Schwartz, *The Redeemers: A Saga of the Years 1945–1952* (New York: Farrar, Straus and Young, 1953), p. 182.

70. Ibid.

71. Helen Tichauer interview, August 2003.

72. Edward S. Richeson, Report on Feldafing DP Center, November 8, 1945, private collection, Helen Tichauer, New York City.

73. Helen Tichauer interview, August 2003.

74. See Michael Berkowitz, "The Nazi Equation of Jewish Partisans with 'Bandits' and Its Consequences," *European Review of History—Revue européene d'Histoire* 13, no. 2 (June 2006): 311–33.

75. W/S 97112, USHMM; Helen Tichauer interview, August 2003.

76. W/S 32031, USHMM.

77. W/S 29270, USHMM; Helen Tichauer interview, August 2003.

78. W/S 21028, USHMM.

79. Shmuel Gringauz, "Di psikhologishe wurtslen fun neo-antisemitizm: naye vintn alte mitln" (The psychological roots of neo-antisemitism: new winds old means), *Yiddishe Tsaytung,* no. 38 (106) (May 23, 1947): 5, quoted in Mankowitz, *Life between Memory and Hope,* p. 184.

80. Bernstein, "Displaced Persons," p. 7.

EPILOGUE

Epigraph: Franz Kafka, "Ein Landarzt," *Erzahlungen* (Frankfurt a.M.: Fischer, 1993), p. 117.

1. Anton Weiss-Wendt, "The Soviet Occupation of Estonia in 1940–41 and the Jews," *Holocaust and Genocide Studies* 12, no. 2 (1998): 308–25. A presentation of his research at the United States Holocaust Memorial Museum (hereafter USHMM) led me to use the Estonian case for this epilogue.

2. See Andrew Ezergailis, *The Holocaust in Latvia, 1941–1944: The Missing Center* (Riga and Washington: Historical Institute of Latvia and USHMM, 1996).

3. According to Weiss-Wendt, "The Soviet Occupation of Estonia," approximately 90 percent are from Tallinn.

4. Probing this question also might illuminate why, among the 149,734 Jews who were "registered" in Vichy France, there were between 60,000 and 70,000 "police files," which concerned both families and individuals; see René Rémond, *Le "Fichier juif": rapport de la commission présenté par René Rémond au Premier Ministre* (Paris: Plon, 1996), p. 16. I am grateful to Diane Afoumado for this reference.

5. Anton Weiss-Wendt, personal communication, January 15, 2006.

6. *Zeitschriften-Dienst*, April 2, 1943, no. 8615, quoted in Ernest K. Bransted, *Goebbels and National Socialist Propaganda, 1925–1945* (East Lansing: Michigan State University, 1965), p. 401.

7. Victor Gans, "Victor Gans Memoir," Record Group (hereafter RG) 02.092, p. 16, USHMM.

8. Susanne Meinl, "Bereicherungswettlauf und Verteilungskämpfe—Zwei Neuerscheinungen zu 'Arisierung' und Korruption im 'Dritten Reich,'" *Newsletter—Informationen des Fritz Bauer Instituts* 21 (fall 2001), p. 1; Frank Bajohr, *Parvenüs und Profiteure: Korruption in der NS-Zeit* (Frankfurt a.M.: S. Fischer, 2001).

9. Mina Perlberger, "Mina Perlberger Papers, 1984," RG-02.054, p. 224, Acc. 1990.329, USHMM; Cilia Borenstein, "Memoir of Cilia Borenstein," [in American Gathering of Jewish Holocaust Survivors Collection], RG-02.002*15, p. 2, USHMM; Victor Gans, "Victor Gans Memoir," pp. 10, 15.

10. Hugo Gryn with Naomi Gryn, *Chasing Shadows* (London: Viking, 2000), pp. 235–36.

11. Marcel Reich-Ranicki, *The Author of Himself: The Life of Marcel Reich-Ranicki*, trans. Ewald Osers (London: Weidenfeld & Nicolson, 2001), pp. 145–46, 149.

12. Primo Levi, *The Reawakening*, trans. Stuart Woolf (Boston: Little, Brown, 1965), p. 281.

13. File 2, box 2, Papers of Philip S. Bernstein, University of Rochester Archives, Rochester, NY (hereafter PSB). "Frankfurter Impressionen," in *Jüdische Rundschau*, vols. 12/13 (Schewat-Adar 5707–März 1947): 17.

14. See Lucille Eichengreen with Harriet Hyman Chamberlain, *From Ashes to Life: My Memories of the Holocaust* (San Francisco: Mercury House, 1994), p. 149–50.

15. Victor Klemperer, *To the Bitter End: The Diaries of Victor Klemperer 1942–45,* ed. and trans. Martin Chalmers (London: Phoenix, 1999), p. 616.

16. "The Truth About Germany," sermon by Philip S. Bernstein, Friday, November 28, 1947, p. 1, item 82, box 2, PSB.

17. Eichengreen, *From Ashes to Life,* p. 152.

18. See Paul Gilroy, *There Ain't No Black in the Union Jack: The Cultural Politics of Race and Nation* (London and New York: Routledge, 2002), pp. 84–94, 140.

INDEX

Abramowitz, Mayer, 176–77
Abschnittslager, 105. *See also* Auschwitz-
   Birkenau
"Abschweifung über produktive Arbeit"
   (Karl Marx), 9–10
"abusing the German greeting," 26–27
Abwehr, 159
actors and film stars, 136
Adenauer, Konrad, 18
"administrative detention," 74–75
adultery, 5
"Agro-Joint," 130. *See also* American Jewish
   Joint Distribution Committee ("the
   Joint," JDC)
Ahlbeck, 114
Aktionen (sweeps of killing and roundups
   for deportation), 64. *See also specific
   locations and ghettos*
Alexanderplatz (prison), 94
Allied armies, 173
Allied Powers (post–World War II), xvi, xx,
   145, 162. *See also* Allied armies
Allied occupation (postwar Germany), 151.
   See also specific countries
Alsace (region and people), 78

Ältestenrat (Council of Elders in the Kovno
   ghetto), 61
Aly, Götz, 44
American Consuls (postwar Germany), 151,
   152, 153
American Jewish Conference, 165
American Jewish Joint Distribution Committee ("the Joint," JDC), 130, 151, 153,
   167, 170, 171, 177; legal-aid division, 166
American Jewish Year Book, The, 209
American Red Cross, 217
Americans, xix, xx, 3; Jewish, 3, 4, 5, 18, 26,
   143; leadership of, 170; troops, in
   postwar Germany, 150, 211. *See also*
   American troops (soldiers); Jews: in
   the United States; United States; U.S.
   Army
American troops (soldiers), 148, 149–50,
   175–76, 186, 198, 199, 204–5, 216; perceived differences between "liberators" and replacement troops, 201–2;
   perceptions of Jewish DPs, 201–8. *See
   also* U.S. Army
Am I a Murderer? (Calel Perechodnik), 62
Amsterdam, 31

anarchism (and anarchists), 10, 139

Andersen, Hanns, 45

Anschluss, 30, 121

anti-Bolshevism, 43, 120, 123; equated with Zionism, 120, 139. *See also* "Jewish Bolshevism"

Anti-braunbuch (Anti–Brown Book), 95. *See also* Nazi propaganda

Antisemiten-Katechismus (Theodor Fritsch), 11

anti-Semitic songs, 208

anti-Semitism, xiii, xv, xvii, xviii, 1, 7, 12, 14, 15, 19, 23, 24, 32, 34, 37, 43, 45, 64; deliberate attempt to intensify, 124, 125–26, 127–28, 135, 138–39, 223; in Estonia, 220–22; in postwar Germany, 146–47, 150, 182, 192–93, 194–95, 196, 199, 203, 208–9, 219; refashioned as anti-Zionism, 112–13, 135, 141, 223

anti-Zionism (as an ideological construct), 125–26, 135, 136, 139, 141

Antoniek Camp, 94

Antwerp, 40

Appellplatz, 108–9

Arabs and the Arab world, 113, 126, 131, 136, 137, 138, 141, 174; interests in Palestine, 141, 142

Arad, Yitzhak, 107

Arbeitslager, 105

Argentina, 38

"arms-running," 159

Army Intelligence, U.S., 190

Arrestanstalt, 59. *See also* Pawiak Street (prison)

Arrow Cross, 159

arson, 5, 139

artist(s), xvi, 4, 76, 100, 136, 159

"Aryanization," 3, 31, 32; accusation of Jewish resistance to, 33

"Aryan" looks, 67, 68, 133–34, 179, 223; "Aryan womanhood," alleged Jewish affronts to, 33–34; as division between non-Jews and Jews in Poland, 52, 67, 69, 91, 93; people, xv, 2, 3, 24, 27, 28, 33, 42, 47, 64, 117, 222. *See also* Nazi Germany (National Socialism); Nazi ideology

Asch, Sholem, 8, 67

Aschaffenburg, 78

assault, 206

Assembly Centers, 202, 205, 206, 208. *See also* DP camps

"asylum seekers," 74

"atonement tax," 29

Auerbach, Philipp, 168, 289–90n99

Aumeier, Hans, 87

Auschwitz-Birkenau, xix, 42, 53, 60, 74, 75, 76, 79, 80, 83, 85, 86, 88, 92, 216, 225; attempted revolt and executions, 107; Block 2 at, 89; Block 11 at, 87, 89, 97; card file, 89–90; clothing, 82; destruction of documentation, 95; exceptions to selections for gassing, 89–93; experience of Polish inmates, 89; forensic photography in, 75, 93–107; hangings at, 107; hospital, 83, 91; identification badges, 81–82, 95 (*see also* "blacks"; "greens"); prisoner inductions, 76, 80, 106; scale-model of, 76; statistical survey of, 76; treatment of "criminal" prisoners in, 77, 80, 89–90, 95–97; women's camp, 84. *See also specific subcamps*

Ausgleichsverfahren ("partial satifaction of creditors"), 34

Aussig, 31

Austria and Austrians, 35, 39, 154, 155, 158, 161, 164, 224

Avé-Lallemant, Friedrich Christian Benedict, 7, 11

Babel, Isaac, 8

Bad Gastein, 154

Bad Reichenhall, 172

bail (right of), 203

bail-bonds, 34

Balfour Declaration, 116, 119

"Baltic Germans," 221

Baltic States, xvi, xx. *See also* Estonia; Latvia (and Latvians); Lithuania

Bamberg, 192, 194

Banco Commerciale, 158

bandits (and banditry), 38, 63, 162, 223

bankruptcy laws, alleged abuse of, 34

"baptized Jews," 57

German press, xix, 27, 32, 36, 37, 38, 41, 42, 44, 139. *See also specific journals, newspapers, press agencies*
German radio broadcast service, 19
"German Zionists," attack on, 120
Geschichte der Juden in Lübeck und Moisling, 7
Gesia Street (prison), 52, 60
Gestapo, 28, 47, 54, 55, 63, 64, 67, 69, 72, 92, 93, 94, 97, 102, 159, 178, 222; in postwar Germany, 147
Geyer, Martin, 20
ghettos (under Nazi control), xviii, 28, 61, 74. *See also specific towns and cities*
Ghettoverwaltung (Lodz), 56–57
Giebelstadt, 215
Giesecke, Heinrich, 19
Giles, Geoffrey, 143
G.I.s. *See* American troops (servicemen); U.S. Army
Gnadenwald, 214
"Goddard case," 141
God of Vengeance (Sholem Asch), 67
Goebbels, Joseph, 37, 44, 121, 124, 125, 130–31, 139
Goldmann, Nahum, 175, 176
Goldschmidt, Jakob, 16
Gordon, Harry, 61
Göring, Hermann, 35, 36, 67
Götterdämmerung, 113
Grabner, Maximillian (SS), 87, 98, 99, 101, 103
"grain speculation," accusation of Jewish control, 31
Grand Mufti of Jersualem, 117–18. *See also* Husseini, Amin al-
"grand theft," 5
graphic arts (and artists), 159–60. *See also* artists; Tichauer, Helen
Gray, Herman, 173–74
"gray" market, 150, 165–94, 198–217
"gray zone," 150
Great Jewish-National Biography, 20
Great War, 137. *See also* World War I
Greece and Greek people, 197, 212, 218
Greek Army, 218
"greens" (Auschwitz-Birkenau designation for criminals), 83, 99, 105

(Die) Grenzen fallen: von der Ostmark zum Sudetenland (Helmut Sündermann), 121
Greuelpropaganda ("atrocity propaganda"), 95, 105. *See also* Nazi propaganda
Grimm, Arthur, 55
Gringrauz, Samuel (Shmuel), 179, 219
Grinkisis, 50
Grossman, Meir, 176
Grossmann, Atina, 146, 178
"Group Wendig," 158
Grüber, Heinrich, 196
Gryn, Géza, 92–93, 110
Gryn, Hugo, xiv, 74, 92–93, 110–11, 159, 224–25
Grzesinski, Albert, 18
guerrilla bands, 204. *See also* partisans (anti-Nazi)
"Guidance for Anti-Jewish Journalism" ("Hinweise für antijüdische Pressearbeit"), 125
Gypsies (Roma and Sinti), xiv, 11, 52, 87, 97, 98

Ha'avarah (Transfer) Agreement, 114
Haber, William, 174, 176, 177, 194
Häftling (prisoner and "detainee"). *See* prison and prisons
haganah (Jewish police and security forces in postwar Europe), 214
hair (human), 81, 82
Handbuch der Judenfrage (Theodor Fritsch), 11
handicapped persons, 88, 96–97
hanging, xix, 33, 49, 66, 77, 107. *See also* gallows
Hannover, 40
Hardy, Alexander, 121
Harmense (Auschwitz subcamp), 105–6
Harrison Report, 161–62
Harten, Jaac van, 158, 159
Hartner-Hnizdo, Herwig, 45
Hasenfus, Chaim, 51, 54
"Hauptdaten der zionistischen Politik" ("Major Dates in Zionist Politics"), 124, 125
Hebrew (language), 44, 59, 217
Heidenheim, 166, 211

Petschek (mining enterprises), 31
petty larceny, 206
pharmacists, 30, 59
phenol injections, 102
photographers, 159. *See also* Budy; *Erken-nungsdienst;* forensic photography
pickpockets (and pickpocketing), 13, 53, 72, 86
pillaging, 162
Piscator, Erwin, 18, 21
Pithiviers, 106
Pocking, 170, 212
pogrom of November 9–10, 1938, 28. See also *Kristallnacht*
Poland and Poles, xiii, 13, 14, 31, 38, 48, 53, 54, 59, 62–63, 68, 80, 83, 89, 91, 92, 98, 99, 100, 106, 143, 145, 146, 153, 179, 180, 211, 218, 224; Polish Army, 155; in postwar Germany, 147, 164, 212, 213. *See also specific towns and cities*
police: Austrian, xvi; Estonian, 221; German, xv, xvi, 7, 11, 21, 28, 48, 65, 68, 72, 73, 78, 79; Jewish, in postwar Germany, 187, 194, 199, 205, 214–19; Jews and Jewish, under the Nazis, xv, 57–58, 59, 60–61, 72, 107, 214; Lithuanian, 50; Polish, 62, 72; postwar, xx, 163, 165, 174, 181, 183, 192. See also *Ordnungsdienst* (Jewish police); *specific locations*
police office, 89
police summary court (*Polizeistandgericht*), 79, 89
Polish (language), 62
Political Department (Auschwitz-Birkenau). See *Politische Abteilung* (Auschwitz-Birkenau)
political prisoners, 87, 92–93, 110–11. *See also* reds (Auschwitz-Birkenau designation)
Politische Abteilung (Auschwitz-Birkenau), 87, 91, 92, 98
Polizeistandgericht, 79, 89
Poppendorf, 214, 215
pornography, accusations of Jewish responsibility for, 21
Posen, 68, 84, 93–94, 108
posters, xiii, 36, 70–71
post-traumatic stress syndrome, 221

"power struggle" (within the Nazi press), 125–26
Prague, 95
printers, 159
prison and prisons, xix, 26, 28, 29, 37, 39, 40, 42, 46, 47, 51, 53, 58–59, 77, 79, 85, 88; Polish, 89, 91; in postwar Germany, 172, 203, 210; workers in counterfeiting operations, 159–61. *See also specific prisons, concentration camps*
"prisoner-functionaries," 79
prisoners of war (POWs), xix, 47, 82, 94
"prisoner transports," 96
prison sentences (and suspended sentences), 42, 203–4, 206
"productivity": in debates on Jewish emancipation, 5–7; and treatment of Jews by the Nazis, 53
Prohibition (of alcohol in the United States), 201
Propaganda Ministry (Berlin), 124
Propagandatafeln, 103. *See also* Nazi propaganda
prostitution and prostitutes, 3, 5, 58, 67, 72, 98, 102, 163, 166, 170, 174, 184, 196, 216; at Budy, 100. *See also* "white slavery"
"protective custody," 74–75, 79. See also *Schutzhaft* (protective custody) and *Schutzhäftlinge* (protective custody prisoners)
"Protocols of the Elders of Zion," xix, 112, 142
Provisioning Department (Lodz ghetto), 69
Prussian *Landtag* (Diet), 15, 19
Prussian Postal Service, 14
Prussian State Bank, 14, 20
public entertainment, 4
"publicity work," 94–95
public opinion: in Germany during World War I, 13–14; in Nazi Germany, xvii, 23, 24–25, 133–34; in postwar Germany, 146–47, 149–50, 163, 188–89, 194–95, 208–9, 230n3
Public Safety Officers, 198, 199
Puritanism, 140
Puterman, Samuel, 51
PX (post exchange, U.S. Army bases), 166

Rabbinic law, 12
racial anti-Semitism, xiv, xvii, xviii, xxi, 1,
    3, 25, 32, 44, 77, 102, 115–16, 143, 223;
    shift in emphasis from, 124, 127, 143,
    146
"racial hygiene," 78, 102
"racial pollution," 3, 32, 33, 102
"racial science," 1, 44, 77, 221; departure
    from, 124
raids (on DP camps), 166, 180–96, 201. See
    also specific camps
railways, 66. See also sabotage; "transports"
"raising hell," 163–65
Rajsko (Auschwitz subcamp), 105–6
Ranizow, 95
ransom (extortion), 29
rape, 102, 206
Rassenschande, 3, 32, 33
Rath, Ernst vom. See Kristallnacht
Rathenau, Walter, 18, 19
Räuber, Die (Schiller), 4, 10
Rawicz, Jerzy, 83
Reawakening, The (Primo Levi), 197
receivership (Konkurs), alleged misuse of,
    34
Redelsipp, 161
"reds" (Auschwitz-Birkenau designation),
    83
Reformation, 1. See also Luther, Martin
refugees, 151. See also displaced persons
    (DPs); survivors
Regensburg, 191
rehabilitation (of survivors of the Holo-
    caust), 147, 157, 165, 173, 204, 210
Reich, Moritz, 26–27
Reich Commissariat Ostland, 220
Reich (Party) Press Office
    (Reichspressestelle), xix, 122
Reich Propaganda Ministry, 124, 125
Reich-Ranicki, Marcel, xiv, 225
Reich Security Main Office (Reichssicher-
    heitshauptamt, RSHA), 76, 92, 94
Reichshof (Rzeszow), 95
Reichstag, 19, 25
Reichsvereinigung, 61
Reinke, Herbert, 9
relations, between Jews and Germans in
    postwar Germany, 190, 194–95, 209

relief operations, postwar, 156. See also
    American Jewish Joint Distribution
    Committee ("the Joint," JDC);
    UNRRA (United Nations Relief and
    Rehabilitation Agency)
Remagen Bridge, 217
"resettlement" (Nazi euphemism), 46, 65
"resident aliens," 74
resistance (anti-Nazi), 66, 78, 79, 206, 224;
    French resistance, 78, 216, 217. See also
    partisans (anti-Nazi); sabotage
respectability (of Jews), attempt to under-
    mine, 42, 55, 58, 59, 64, 65, 67
retailers, 136
Retter, Leon, 173
revenge, 64, 224–26
Revisionist Zionism, 129, 176
"Revolt at Budy," 102, 103. See also Budy
    (subcamp of Auschwitz-Birkenau)
Revolution of 1848, 4, 247n42
Revolution of 1918, 4
Ribbentrop, Joachim von, 31
Richeson, Edward S., 217
Riecke, Heinz, 137, 139–40
Riesser, Gabriel, 7
"riff-raff," 5
Rifkind, Judge Simon, 164, 202
right-wing extremism, 18. See also anti-
    Semitism; Nazi ideology
Ringelblum, Emmanuel, xiv, 46, 57–58, 60,
    65, 225. See also Warsaw: ghetto
Ringelheim, Joan, 76
rituals, Nazi-imposed, 76. See also compul-
    sory assemblies, at concentration
    camps
"robber bands," 4, 9, 10, 22, 44
robbery, allegations of, 18, 35, 79
Roberts, Justice Owen J., 186
Robota, Rosa, 107
Rochester, 226
Rohling, August, 11, 12
Röhm, Ernst, 79
"Romance of a Horse Thief" (Joseph
    Opatoshu), 8
Romania (and Romanian people), 157,
    218
Rome, 157, 158
Roosevelt, Eleanor, 117, 216

Text:	11.25/13.5 Adobe Garamond
Display:	Perpetua, Adobe Garamond
Compositor:	Binghamton Valley Composition, LLC
Printer and binder:	Maple-Vail Manufacturing Group